I0887714

MEXICO IN VERSE

Mexico in Verse

A History of Music, Rhyme, and Power

Edited by

STEPHEN NEUFELD AND
MICHAEL MATTHEWS

Foreword by

WILLIAM H. BEEZLEY

THE UNIVERSITY OF
ARIZONA PRESS

TUCSON

The University of Arizona Press
www.uapress.arizona.edu

© 2015 The Arizona Board of Regents
All rights reserved. Published 2015

Printed in the United States of America
20 19 18 17 16 15 6 5 4 3 2 1

ISBN-13: 978-0-8165-3132-5 (cloth)

Cover designed by Leigh McDonald
Cover image: "Gran Fandango y francachela de todas las Calaveras" by José Guadalupe Posada © 1903, hoja suelta publicada por A. Vanegas Arroyo.

Library of Congress Cataloging-in-Publication Data
Mexico in verse : a history of music, rhyme, and power / edited by Stephen Neufeld and Michael Matthews ; foreword by William H. Beezley.
pages cm
Includes bibliographical references and index.
ISBN 978-0-8165-3132-5 (pbk. : alk. paper)
1. Literature and history—Mexico. 2. Music and history—Mexico. 3. Mexican literature—19th century—History and criticism. 4. Mexican literature—20th century—History and criticism. I. Neufeld, Stephen, editor. II. Matthews, Michael, 1978–, editor.
PQ7118.M49 2015
861.009'972—dc23
2014037401

∞ This paper meets the requirements of ANSI/NISO Z39.48–1992 (Permanence of Paper).

Contents

Foreword by William H. Beezley vii

Acknowledgments ix

Introduction: Mexico in Verse 3

1. Sister at War: Mexican Women's Poetry and the U.S.-Mexican War 33
Christopher Conway

2. The Sly Mockeries of Military Men: Corridos and Poetry as Critical Voice for the Porfirian Army 58
Stephen Neufeld

3. The Track from Beyond the Grave: Challenges to Porfirian Policymaking in Popular Verse 109
Michael Matthews

4. "I'm Going to Write You a Letter": Coplas, Love Letters, and Courtship Literacy 145
William French

5. Singing for Cristo Rey: Masculinity, Piety, and Dissent in Mexico's Cristero Rebellion 181
Stephen J. C. Andes

6. El Niño Proletario: Jesús Sansón Flores and the New Revolutionary Redeemer, 1935–1938 218
Elena Jackson Albarrán

7. "That Mariachi Band and That Tequila": Modernity, Identity, and Cultural Politics in Alcohol Songs of the Mexican Golden Age Cinema 257
Áurea Toxqui

8. Let Us Weep Among the Dust: Recycled Poems of 1968 and Operas of Earthquake 298
Amanda Ledwon

Conclusion 337

Contributors 347

Index 351

Foreword

Blaring sounds have accompanied life in Mexico since the Spanish arrived in 1521. The clamor of church bells, merchant squares, military drums, and encouraging shouts of mule drivers and coachmen have become increasingly shrill in later centuries with political and advertising loudspeakers mounted on VWs, screaming radios, and deafening traffic jams, with drivers who understand the green light as "Honk your horn!" This teeth-clenching stridency has captured the attention of residents and visitors, and been described by authors, journalists, and foreign travelers who emphasize dissonance as symptomatic of the multiethnic society and crushing traffic.

Yet imbricated in the panorama of these noisy soundscapes are the subtle, soft, and passionate sounds of verse—songs, poetry, romantic letters, and mirthful conversation. These sounds, spoken or read, capture the textures of the Spanish language that hums with rhythms and tunes. Lives are lived with the heart on the sleeve, and expressed in poems, songs, letters, and perorations repeatedly in verse. This Spanish language in Mexico echoes with the tones and rhythms of Miguel de Cervantes in *Don Quijote*. This language carried through colonial and nineteenth-century poets, anonymous songwriters, and public scribes with books of poems and songs to copy into letters. In the twentieth century, singers of corridos and *sones* that glorify linguistic and instrumental improvisations gave an edge to their verses. Later lyricists and composers such as Agustín Lara and Pedro Infante, to mention only two of at least a dozen, mastered the demands of radio and recording to give their rhymes to the public. There were also poets after World War II, such as Nobel Prize Laureate Octavio Paz and

José Emilio Pacheco (in his verses and his novella *Las batallas en el desierto*), whose language had both timbre and tone that caught the spirit of the community. The language is more than a way to communicate; it belongs to the national patrimony, a heritage to be persevered, valued, and used.

Verses, tunes, and conversations offer a specter, a ghostly shadow in the language of everyday life, and form an overlapping soundscape with the cacophony. The authors of the chapters in this volume examine groups and individuals that form everyday communities and their expressions, often invisible or overshadowed at first glance by the noise of the society. The significance of these communities received a proper valuation from José Emilio Pacheco: when described as Mexico's greatest poet, he responded he was not even the best poet in his neighborhood. Consider the poetry of women during the U.S.-Mexican War, the songs and poetry of late nineteenth-century soldiers, the doggerel and popular rhythms responding to the technology, accidents, and changes accompanying the railroad, the swearing or soliciting of love through artful letters replete with *coplas* and other poetic references, popular corridos during the Cristero Rebellion, the poetry claiming attention for the working-class child, cantina songs of ordinary people who often were recent migrants to the city, and the desperate voices with no other outlet than scribbled verse following the 1985 earthquake.

Each author of these fascinating essays brings experience in the archives, literature, popular publications, and ephemeral visual sources for the periods of his or her analysis. Only with this wealth of contextual information could they write with such commanding voices about topics so subtle and so easily and often overlooked. This represents a major change in the ways historians write about Mexico's past and culture that has been largely described through such major institutions as the government, church, and military, and national biographies of Miguel Hidalgo, Antonio López de Santa Anna, Benito Juárez, Pancho Villa, Emiliano Zapata and Frida Kahlo. These essays change the scale to the ordinary individual, family, and community, that is to say, to lives as lived, crises suffered, technology encountered, professions shared, experiences recalled, and loves and hopes declared, endured, lost, and remembered. Each of these experiences at the individual and local level has a side that is poetic, which can be sung or written in verse and, as these authors show, has been. The authors, inspired by their subjects, write in a lyric way. This is a volume to be read and read again, to savor the richness of these manifold and often unusual verses.

William H. Beezley
University of Arizona

Acknowledgments

Two translations are taken from Gustavo Pellón in Christopher Conway ed., *The U.S.-Mexican War: A Binational Reader* (Cambridge: Hackett Publishing Company, Inc., 2010) and reprinted by permission of Hackett Publishing Company, Inc. Thanks also to *Latin American Research Review* for permission to reprint "Sister at War" from their Spring 2012 volume 47.

MEXICO IN VERSE

Introduction

Mexico in Verse

Songs and wordplay represent an everyday part of the Mexican experience. Innumerable soundscapes fill the street. The chimes of vendors, the cacophony of traffic, the susurration of conversations, they surround you. Most striking, music of all kinds let you know precisely where you stand. The whistling codes of *chilangos* turn slang phrases into tune, the brass trios mark the end of the day with clarion calls, the wandering singers haunt every cantina, and the matched mariachis serenade tourists. All of these present a profound facet of how we remember, experience, and know Mexico.[1] This quintessential element of identity, *mexicanidad* (Mexican-ness), cannot be divorced from our understandings of historical change. Yet so often, researchers willfully ignore the sounds all around as they meander to archives, or relax in the evenings. Musical notes and penned lyrics, of course, represent two different levels of meaning making. Leaving aside the melody, the verses express and preserve the reflective preoccupations and wry humor of ordinary people. In their poetry and lyrics Mexicans expressed their human condition.

This work specifically examines the role of poetry and music from the outbreak of the U.S.-Mexican War in 1846 on through Restoration, Porfirian, Revolutionary, and twentieth-century Mexico. Ultimately, we find that the meanings of modernity, of identity, and of social relations were exhibited by ordinary people in the framework of intimate expressions such as love letters, patriotic poetry, sardonic sonnets, revolutionary folksongs, and children's couplets. The essays reveal the important role that verse and lyrics played in shaping and articulating ideas about the social, cultural, and political transformations during years of tremendous change.

In the lines of song and poem, writers and audiences answered historical questions of identity, of power, and of nation. This volume analyzes how the common vision of collective memory and historical change developed in engaging and intriguing ways. Together, the essays here add to the evocative unveiling of history within better-known narratives of official power, by retelling them from the margins, an angle made possible through our use and analysis of uncommon sources. It has been suggested to us that this is an exploration through "bottom-feeding"—taking seriously the myriad self-expressions that represent people not otherwise historically included, and often omitted as the purveyors of low or amateur cultural expressions. For example, much of the poetry we analyze barely rises to doggerel, yet that is both its charm and its value as an authentic communication. As such, we seek to demonstrate an inversion, through verse, of how we find meaning in the story of Mexico becoming a modern nation by privileging the lyrical expressions that have not captured the attention of literary specialists and, to a lesser degree, historians.[2] We believe this offers understandings of Mexico that go beyond standard narratives, a twist on sources but also in the ways we look for significance in those who produced music, prose, and poetry.

Verse communicates a central facet of the intimate politics of everyday life. Far beyond a mere soundtrack to events, normal people used verse to genuinely connect to the events around them, and thus constituted meanings in a format that made sense to them.[3] Where the official narratives and rhetoric of elite society spoke to one version of events, this was often inverted in the intensely personal reflections of the lower classes who gave verse its power, its resonance. Indeed this re-sounding, the repetitive reiterations of ideas, represents the heart of why lyrical play worked so well to portray and preserve senses of collective experience. The great events and intellectual movements that shaped the trajectory of the nation inspired the voices of both elite and common artists, and in turn their writings altered how people of all classes reacted to change.

Lyrical verse powerfully resonated with audiences who appreciated its potential to challenge power in emotive ways, particularly with its entertainment value, and especially when complemented by drinking alcohol. The twists and humor inherent to many of the genres made light of painful injustices and darker events. Dark humor marks the lyrical sensibility that appealed to many listeners, a sense of shared and wry sorrow that reflects what E. P. Thompson called "rough music." As in popular music, or

Sigüenza y Góngora's contemporary, Sor Juana Inés de la Cruz, lent her own distinctive tone to this national idea in her verses. Her poetry challenged the Church, and patriarchal and colonial authority more generally, but ultimately this led to her relegation into religious seclusion where she succumbed to disease. Despite the limitations imposed by her gender and vows, and in a more direct fashion than the legendary poet-king, her voice gave rise to nationalist ideas still quietly simmering under the surface of the colony. Beyond the famed works of Sor Juana, numerous poets of the colonial period produced works influenced by Mannerist-Baroque writers in the seventeenth century and by the Neoclassicism of the eighteenth century.

To dwell merely on a few well-known poets nonetheless does disservice to the innumerable and anonymous writer-lyricists whose verses received less scholarly attention or whose amateur nature did not lend to wide publication. As noted by Lee Dowling, from the outset of conquest the conquistadors both parodied and composed poems and songs around campfires that, while framed within the Spanish tradition of the *romance* (ballad), nevertheless introduced new local innovations that provided the fecund seeds from which the Mexican corrido developed. The poetic ballad thus flourished in the sixteenth century, with this foundation, despite several royal edicts that sought to ban the importation of Spanish literature to the New World, as royal officials feared they could confuse recent Indian converts. Nevertheless, dozens of Spanish *cancioneros* (collections of song and poetry) would reach the colony where they were consumed and refashioned by criollos, mestizos, and indigenous peoples.[18]

Poetry, as the distinguished cultural scholar Carlos Monsiváis has noted, represented a barometer for Mexico's nineteenth and early twentieth centuries.[19] In its lines one can detect the pressures, the fissures, and the changes that mattered to people at the time. These lines, written for themselves, for their families, or perhaps for a locally public audience, rarely made it into newspapers or collections. Nonetheless, the ones that did survive may lead historians into a better understanding of contemporary and marginalized narratives of the national past. As the nation struggled toward its independence, verse continuously redefined its contours. In their own words people expressed their visions of the political and cultural changes that occurred all around them. Writers of all stripes gave voice to the independence wars, foreign invasions, economic calamities, and social transformations, and ordinary folk read, sang, or heard these tales as participants seeking their fit in the grand scheme of things. The media permitted the configuring of the vague and rumored into more memorable eloquence. Made redolent with classic references and poignantly worded to evoke emotions, verse expressed uncertain events as familiar tales.

It struck a chord with ordinary Mexicans precisely because of its power to capture imaginations and chain impressions to memory and experiences. Poems in broadsheets and papers reaffirmed or subtly challenged worldviews that arose spontaneously out of the satires and songs favored in smaller communities and barrios. No less than with puppet shows discussed by historian William Beezley, popular expressions in lyrics and poems became basic components to the formations of national imagining.[20] Verse afforded the writers an opportunity to display their education and erudition, and for the audience likewise to share in this, or at least pretend they understood the esoteric references. A great advantage in connecting to the audiences was undoubtedly found by writers quite aware of the deep Mexican love of the *albur* and the *doble sentido*—clever wordplay that elevated and made personal the deep critiques of authorities, politics, and disruptions they described. As Sor Juana had elicited identity in the colonial past, new voices continued to speak to the Mexican soul. Other writers, like Octavio Paz in the twentieth century, therefore merely continued a long tradition of critique originally started by ordinary amateurs who slyly shook the foundations of power.

At the outset of independence (1810–1821), popular groups still sang romances and coplas imported from Spain. Elites, in addition to opera, listened to piano music in the salon setting, reflecting their European predilections.[21] Yet, in the early decades of the national period, a distinctly unique and Mexican musical tradition continued to develop in the form of sones and corridos. The son represented a music and dance style from Moorish Andalusian origin, undertaken for courtship and performed with skilled footwork.[22] The corrido, as defined by renowned musicologist Vicente Mendoza, differs from other popular music styles such as the *jarabe* and *canción*,[23] with its defining qualities denoted by lyrical fluidity and an epic narrative style. In a highly illiterate society, corridos' social functions went beyond mere entertainment. Their epic narrative style provided people with gossip, news, and history of places outside their immediate region.[24] These new forms of popular music represented a blending of Spanish musical traditions with mestizo and creole influences.[25] Moreover, the nation's tumultuous nineteenth century, marked by foreign invasions and civil wars, introduced new themes, genres, and instruments. These worked to shape a new musical style that was intimately linked with a new sense of nationalism.[26]

Military brass and wind bands became staples of the various national leaders in their attempts to forge patriotic unity in times of war. Formal and improvised bands held a central place in nineteenth-century communities as Guy Thompson argues.[27] Politically, bands performed as part of state theater and instilled patriotic fervor. They ensured morale among the military, added ambiance to ceremonies, and played for every occasion from inaugurations to marriages to festivals. Indeed, it was the bands' role as wedding singers during the French Intervention (1862–1867) that twisted the French word for marriage into "mariachi."[28] Both Antonio López de Santa Anna—who first introduced the military band to the nation—and Benito Juárez used brass bands as integral parts of their war efforts, and as noted by Thompson, these became as important as rifles and bullets in their war efforts.[29] The Cuban composer Jaime Nunó, hired by Santa Anna to form the country's first military band, would win the 1853 competition that gave Mexico its national anthem. In the nineteenth century, the military bands appeared as common sights in rural and provincial town squares (*zócalos*) as well as large urban centers such as Guadalajara and Mexico City. Brass bands of the era played more than cosmopolitan works imported from Europe. They also reintroduced a local range of musical styles that included sones and jarabes, repertoires that stemmed back to the colonial period but that found wide dissemination in the eighteenth and nineteenth centuries.[30]

The opening of the National Conservatory in 1866 provided liberal leaders of the Restored Republic (1867–1876) with an important vehicle to promote musical education, instruction highly influenced by European traditions.[31] Another example of the emerging stability of the period, the National Philharmonic Society (established in the 1850s) also created the Orfeón Popular (Popular Orpheum), a musical group comprised of artists who sought to popularize high culture among common folk.[32] It was during the years of the Restored Republic, according to Moreno Rivas, that popular music began to fuse with so-called high culture composers. Aniceto Ortega's opera *Guatimozín* reflected this development, incorporating the jarabe as well as adorning one of the violas with the colors of the Mexican flag.[33] The opera also reflected an "Indianist" aesthetic that combined indigenous legend with nineteenth-century musical traditions such as the Italian del canto.[34] In more popular venues, individuals sang corridos and recited décimas, although as Merle Simmons notes, scholars have found few examples of these corridos, suggesting that the genre had not yet reached the popularity that it would during the Porfiriato.[35] Instead the copla, both political and religious in its content, represented the most common form of popular lyrical expression in the middle decades of the nineteenth century.[36] Nevertheless, arrays of literary accounts describing the popular fandangos across the nation serve as testament to the centrality of music in ordinary people's lives. In 1855, for example, José María

Rivera reported in copious detail the merriment, drinking, dancing, and singing that took place at these popular celebrations, describing the fandango as a unique aspect of Mexican identity.[37]

While the copla emerged as the preferred method of lyrical expression among common people, nineteenth-century elite poetic writing remained overwhelmingly of the Romantic tradition. The founding of the Academia de Letrán in 1836 provided an opportunity for Mexican writers to share their works, discuss literature, and study foreign authors. Indeed the Academia would produce generations of the country's romantic poets, from Andrés Quintana Roo (1787–1851) to Ignacio Manuel Altamirano (1834–1893). Margarita Vargas maintains that Mexico's romantic poetry, more than other genres of literature, insisted on repeating European concepts and themes.[38] Moreover, as has recently been shown, the composition of romantic poetry, while definitely an elite genre, was also taken up by women in the mid-nineteenth century. Women's magazines, for example, published works by female poets that exalted the nation's resistance to the foreign invaders of the U.S.-Mexican War (1846–1848). They participated in national discussions regarding politics and war and, in so doing, used the era's gendered assumptions to fashion a discourse that blurred the separation between the domestic and public realms.[39]

During the dictatorship of Porfirio Díaz (1876–1910), new national musical traditions emerged and took shape. While elite institutions such as the National Conservatory continued to cater to the tastes of the well-to-do,[40] popular corridos gained prominence as a musical genre representing a style most distinctly Mexican. Yet, as Mary Kay Vaughn posits, it is easy to overstate the divide between so-called high and low culture and to overly emphasize the "Frenchification" of elite Porfirian musical tastes. As she notes, elite composers produced operas that incorporated national symbols and history such as Gustavo Campo's *El rey poeta* that celebrated Texcoco's Mexica ruler Nezahualcoyotl. While works such as Campo's opera show a shift toward the incorporation of Mexican themes within European musical traditions, the broadsheets and songbooks produced by renowned publisher Antonio Vanegas Arroyo indicate a shift in style. Often in collaboration with the artist José Guadalupe Posada, these materials offered consumers art that focused solely on national images, events, and personages. The works produced by the collaboration between both men served to provide later artists, especially after the 1910 Revolution, with corridos (published by Vanegas Arroyo) and images (produced by Posada) that did not imitate French and Spanish artistic trends but instead celebrated their own national culture.[41] Perhaps more than any other individual, Vanegas Arroyo diffused popular songs to a mass audience and played a crucial role in recording—through the publication of lyrics—popular music that dealt with the topics and themes important to the lower classes. [42]

The corrido lyrics demonstrated central preoccupations with violence, catastrophe, and banditry that normal people found compelling. The dark subject matter perhaps reflects the conditions and realities of everyday life for the poor in the same manner that medieval children's tales in Europe make known the short, precarious lives of the peasantry.[43] Moreover, as both Simmons and Mendoza have argued, corridos provide some of the best sources for understanding the tastes and views of the popular classes—especially considering the nation's high illiteracy rates. Despite the limitations such sources offer in their historical accuracy of the events discussed, and despite a modern-day reader's incapacity to know how people interpreted the verses, they remain invaluable.[44] The corrido also served as an important genre that challenged the regime at least insofar as songs often praised the actions of political opponents (including bandits) and emphasized the seemingly little value that government officials placed on human life and people's struggles.[45]

Chris Frazer uses corridos as historical documents of the *vox populi* to investigate the ways that lower-class groups understood bandits and banditry. He also recognizes that the corridos' fragmentary and incomplete character, as well as contemporary people's distance from their original composition, do not provide a complete estimation of worldviews of popular groups who sang or read these songs. Nevertheless, as he notes, they offer scholars an important source for accessing and interpreting the issues that mattered to marginalized groups, sources of significant value, considering the few documents available to examine lower-class outlooks and expressions.[46] Aside from the corrido, the Porfirian era produced a number of popular songs that are considered as exemplars of *canciones mexicanas* that continue to be sung to the present day. Songs such as "Sobre las olas," "Las mañanitas," "La golondrina," and "La paloma" were either produced or gained popularity during the Díaz dictatorship. These songs, originating from the countryside and from the provinces, also make known the vibrant and dynamic musical traditions from outside the capital that gained popular appeal among city dwellers.[47]

The relative peace and stability of the Porfiriato likewise helped to foster a boom in the production of poetry, both high and low. Poetry, by the end of the nineteenth century, "became the most important form to be cultivated."[48] Among elite circles, Romanticism and Neoclassicism gave way to modernist poetry. The dissemination of modernist poems among the middle and upper classes was largely attributed to the magazines *La Revista Azul* and *La Revista Moderna*, the latter founded by Amado Nervo and Jesús Valenzuela.[49] But it was not only the elite that participated in cultural production. Middle-class magazines such as *Gil Blas Cómico* and women's periodicals such as *Las Violetas de Anáhuac* called on their readers to submit poems for publication. Likewise, penny presses targeting the lower and working classes produced poetry that used sarcasm and sardonic irony to make their grievances known. They challenged elite assumptions and articulated their worldviews and the events of their daily lives. Similar to their middle-class counterparts, penny presses also published poems submitted by their readers. From across the country, scores of amateur writers tendered their verses to journal editors, confirming the centrality of poetry as *the* form of lyrical expression across class and gender lines.[50]

After emerging as the ubiquitous musical genre in the Porfiriato, the corrido became closely associated with national identity during the violence and tumult of the Mexican Revolution (1910–1920), where it also served as a narrative to those dark years. In the many armies that roamed the countryside, the singing of corridos around campfires became an integral aspect of people's military experience.[51] Writers produced a plethora of Revolutionary songs that recounted important battles and the exploits of famed leaders such as Francisco "Pancho" Villa and Emiliano Zapata. Some corridos, for instance, blended the traditional jarabe with the new fox-trot in music and dance.[52] As the devastated nation finally embraced its Revolutionary future, survivors preserved and re-created their music while setting aside their arms. Indeed, in the 1920s and 1930s, the Revolution remained the most common subject matter in popular verse.[53]

The new cadre of Revolutionary leaders made the creation of a national music part of their official policymaking after 1920. Under the direction of José Vasconcelos, for example, the jarabe (erroneously referred to as the Mexican Hat Dance) was promoted in popular venues such as school classrooms and civic events as a distinctly Mexican form of artistic expression.[54] The Indianist movement likewise played a central role in using music to forge a new national cultural identity. Chief among those individuals that promoted the incorporation and celebration of the country's pre-Columbian past was Carlos Chávez. Putting Revolutionary corridos to music and composing an Aztec-themed ballet, among other projects, he promoted the mixing of Indian music, mestizo folk traditions, and urban popular music. In so doing, he created works that were characterized as "profoundly non-European."[55] Revolutionary policymakers and cultural producers built on the Indian themes that emerged during the Porfiriato to celebrate the

importance of indigenous cultures in their attempts to forge a national identity. Composers attempted to create a hybrid musical style that blended "authentic" indigenous musical practices with modernist musical sensibilities. This development was most clearly demonstrated in the 1928 revival of the Porfirian-era opera *Atzimba*, which recounted the tale of a Tarascan princess who falls in love with a Spanish captain and that was set to Italian-styled music.[56] Innovations aside, in the 1940s the corrido remained the most popular form of musical expression, tackling topics ranging from the 1938 oil expropriation to the country's involvement in World War II.[57]

The advent of radio, and later television and film, played a central role in the diffusion of a national music culture in the 1930s, 1940s, and 1950s. Two popular musical forms that gained popularity as a result of radio's capacity to reach mass audiences were the mariachi and the bolero. Mariachi, a collection of sones most often associated with central Jalisco, has become so ubiquitous that it is often a stereotypic sign of Mexican identity, both inside and outside of the country. In the 1930s mariachi became a common staple of the airwaves. It gained such prominence as the national genre of music that President Lázaro Cárdenas had mariachis accompany his political campaign and play his inauguration. The 1930s boom in Mexican cinema—known as the Golden Age—greatly contributed to the popularity of mariachi, branding the brass bands and charro-clad musicians into iconic symbols. This image flourished abroad, especially as a result of the success of the film *Allá en el Rancho Grande*, which introduced the charro to the rest of the world.[58]

Boleros, as noted by Marco Velázquez and Mary Kay Vaughn, "brought the poetry of the Porfirian salon to the twentieth-century brothel, nightclub, movie theater, restaurant, bedroom, kitchen, and patio" in neighborhoods across the country.[59] Agustín Lara, Mexico's most famous composer of boleros, claimed to be liberating Mexicans from Catholic moral standards. Not surprisingly, he received tremendous criticism of his lifestyle, which included considerable alcohol and marijuana use as well as a sexual and marital life that defied the conservative social conventions of the era. Indeed, radio producers often attempted to present Lara's music as foreign-tainted and overly urban, and so played ranchero and mariachi music—seen as rural and more authentically Mexican—as a means to challenge the bolero's widespread popularity. Lara's music, in the 1940s and 1950s, promoted an alternative modern national identity through his music's celebration of city life and a new sexual aesthetic.[60]

While Lara's music was bringing the poetry of a bygone era into the cantina and brothel, Mexican poetry continued to evolve during and after the

Revolution, albeit perhaps losing its position as *the* genre of lyrical expression. Among the host of modernist, postmodernist, and surrealist poets of the twentieth century, Octavio Paz emerged not only as a literary giant of Mexico but of the world. Paz and his generation of poets, publishing in important literary journals such as *Taller* and *Barandal*, modified the modernist tradition they inherited, especially through their interest in leftist political ideologies. Adriana García characterizes twentieth-century Mexican poetry as continuing to adapt its own autochthonous traditions to European themes and issues as well as literary techniques and forms of experimentation.[61] In this regard, we find a continued tradition of poetic syncretism stemming back to the arrival of the conquistadors.

The history of Mexican music after World War II and during the long one-party rule of the Partido Revolucionario Institucional or PRI (1946–2000) has received less attention than the preceding periods.[62] Eric Zolov's *Refried Elvis* represents an exception to this. Examining the rise of the counterculture in the 1950s and 1960s, Zolov makes known the limits of the PRI's cultural nationalism, especially in the wake of the government-orchestrated massacre of students in 1968. Originally representing the rise of a middle class in the 1950s, rock and roll youth culture spurred fears among traditionally minded parents and government officials. Yet, as he also shows, after 1968, the government attempted to label rock music as a foreign influence undermining the social good. Critics from both the left and right portrayed rock music as a form of U.S. imperialism. Government officials seeking to cement a populist following lessened censorship on foreign music at the same time that they promoted folkloric music styles viewed as more organic and truly Mexican.[63]

To some degree the censorship had worked to limit the ways that rock and roll developed in the 1970s and 1980s, demonstrated by the emulative and watered-down versions of the punk movement. Bands such as Chak Mul or SIZE never attained great critical success, or a wide following, and catered primarily to the rebellious children of the better classes in Mexico City who sought merely to imitate U.S. and European fashions.[64] Later groups, such as Massacre 68, formed in the late 1980s and protested what they deemed increasingly incompetent and corrupt governance, especially in the aftermath of the 1985 earthquake. More popular groups began to follow suit, such as the Maldita Vecindad and Los Hijos del Quito Patio, who mixed ska and danzón with punk, or Las Insolitas Imágenes de Aurora, who went on to considerable success as the Caifanes, albeit with a much less edgy sound. In all of these cases, the music and lyrics continued to propose at least a different sense of the nation through their critiques of the government, alternative notions of masculinity, and the questioning of Church values, and, in so doing, built on long traditions of identity formation.

Numerous genres of music continued to gain popularity and influence the national scene, including Colombian *cumbia*, and from the U.S., blues, country, and hip-hop. Especially in the northern border regions, these shaped the larger generic pop-country styling termed "ranchero," with combinations like the *cumbia norteña* and other fusions. As the polka and accordions of Central European immigrants added a particular sound, the context of the borderlands added new thematic elements. For example, the 1920s *tequileros* celebrated Prohibition-era alcohol smugglers who battled U.S. law enforcement and their perfidious ambushes.[65] This potent combination reached a new apogee in 1988 when Los Tigres del Norte began singing of the narcotics trafficking lifestyle as antiheroic narrative.

The corrido had not vanished. In a new iteration, *narcocorridos* both mourn and celebrate the dramatically horrific conflicts of the past two decades of cartel and antidrug violence. [66] The new genre spread swiftly across northern Mexico and over the border into the United States, following both traffickers and migrants to the *otro lado* (other side). Seen by some purists as a degradation of a once noble type of music, others embraced it as a "musical newspaper" that chronicled the times when often journalists could not. As Elijah Wald notes, they provide a soundtrack to the public violence and a popular voice to make sense of the chaos.[67] Their lyrics teem with antiauthority sentiments aimed at governments (both Mexican and U.S.) or against the cartels, sometimes even as commissioned works at the drug lords' behest. They also proved popular among immigrants to the United States who sought an authentic taste of home, many of whom identified with the borderland stories of violence and betrayals.[68] Most of all, the narcocorridos challenge power as corridos have always done. Many radio stations in conflict-torn Sinaloa and Baja California voluntarily imposed their own bans on the music despite numerous phone requests from listeners. President Vicente Fox (2000–2006) proposed his own ban on the genre nationwide. Yet the harshest critical censorship came from the cartels themselves, in the form of dozens of kidnapped and murdered singers in the past decades. [69] These dead attest to the enduring power and importance of the verse in Mexican life.

Theoretical Considerations

Power and identity and memory run fluidly through the line and lyric that Mexicans used to describe their world. Oral and written lore maintained popular themes of loss and desire. Collective memories shaped verse, which in turn built on memory to create community and senses of shared identity. Common frames of reference, assumptions about social hierarchy, and interpretations of novel events all rose from within this discussion between artist and audience.[70] Verses contributed to fields of evolving discourses, in what Michel Foucault described as power unattached to persons, and what James Scott claimed were manifestations of resistance and domination.[71] The limits to what people could say, how they said it, to whom, and where, lay within parameters measured by the verses.[72] Discourse imposed constraints and with repetitions made normal the new limits set on the next lyricist. Some topics became off-limits. Others became regular grist for humor, or for tragedy, but in most cases a regularization of the narratives reflected the societal norms built in historical experience. For example, when presidents proved regularly corrupt and oppressive, it became normal for their iniquities to appear only in satire or oblique reference. This was the power of a dominant discourse, but also reflected the weakness in hegemony that many (such as Chris Frazer) have noted as a persistent characterization of political cultures well past the Mexican Revolution.[73] Vernacular expressions framed both acceptance of, and resistance to, official narratives of power.[74]

Verse actually proves an apt format in which to discuss hegemony. As various essays in this volume assert, ordinary songs and poetry challenged dominant or elite worldviews. The ideas of the philosopher Antonio Gramsci provide a particularly useful framework for undertaking an investigation of these processes. In a Gramscian description, power systems formulate within two overlapping sets of relations: consensus and coercion. [75] To this dynamic we attach corruption. In terms of verse since 1845 we see considerable consensus building in areas of antiforeign attitudes and gender expectations. We also see areas of deep social conflict, particularly along lines of class divisions and religious ideology. Not even children were exempt from this, as when adults used them to represent the socialist agendas of the 1930s. Perhaps most interestingly, verses from all levels of society also illuminated how corruption maintained relationships of power. Whether maligned or mourned in the corrido, alluded to in satirical poems, or purposefully obscured within the commemorations of 1985, the element of corruption infiltrated and pervaded the common sense of mexicanidad. Fundamental injustice and impunity made worse by profound class or gender iniquity marks all of these essays. Corruption thus falls between consensus and coercion; it is largely agreed upon as customary and expected practice, while also a violating force that one cannot avoid without cost. Hegemonic relations normally play along a continuum between the purely coercive and

purely consensual or co-opted, and the subversive element of art can reflect a particular place in between the extremes where corruption is both a topic and a description of power relations. Moreover, the verses examined in this volume demonstrate that ordinary people used poetry and song to discuss, understand, challenge, and situate themselves to the processes that construct unequal relationships of power. In so doing, they employed words, images, and symbols—parts of a shared framework of cultural meaning making—to discuss, and at times act upon, an existing social order characterized by domination.[76]

In verse, corruption takes on other forms. Poems and songs rephrased complaints and buried critiques, using wordplay to fall somewhere between playing along with authority and vociferously resisting it. The message, when repeated, ascribed normality to falling between agreement and opposition, and the corrupt becomes the modus vivendi. Where participants and writers made a prescribed version of events into an everyday sense of the experience, they became accomplices. In truths occluded, in lies retold, the verses' audiences and writers became the agents of their own subjugation, but at least kept some semblance of people owning their own side of the story. A corrupted version of events and sentiments neither fully honest nor totally repressed became a standard condition constituting some part of social stability. Truly hegemonic regimes do not thrive through simply mediating the open conflicts between dissidents and fanatics, but find stability when the co-opted tacitly internalize limits to what they can express or think. This condition repeatedly emerges in our analyses.

Questions of audience and reception always frame a cultural perspective on history. In an odd way the limited reproductions available to researchers have strengthened the point we intend to make. Songs and verse must stand at least some test of time to have been conserved for the modern researcher. Did we miss some integral or significant tunes or poems? Absolutely. Yet, on the whole we see this collection as a beginning point that scans through verses whose currency and circulation have persisted. Each essay deals with the notoriously tricky issues of reception in its own way. In general though, this volume works outward from the assumption that these verses represented narratives known and enjoyed by significant numbers of the people we seek to understand. That these tales had this attention and resonance must, perforce, remain something of a speculation, but it is an informed interpretation. We urge scholars to build on this sampling. Nonetheless, within limits, each paper here gives us a fresh view of events that have largely been addressed in sources heavily biased in favor of the elite paper-creators—invaders, bureaucrats, and investors.

Constructing an intimate lens of the daily and personal perspective of historical events requires this unconventional approach. The conventional has not, perhaps, so far yielded us the results that we might desire. Verse and doggerel have accompanied the regular folks on their path through history. Where nationalist literatures served a relatively narrow few among the elite, the corrido and other lower-class verses could appeal to any who listened to, or sang along with, stories that appealed to their own experiences.

Our essays bring out the voices of the marginal, while not forgetting in the meantime that it was the element of entertainment in the delivery that made verse popular. At levels intimate or public, the words that spoke to Mexicans iterated and reiterated their experiences and gave collective memory its shape. They provide a rare glimpse into how regular people dealt with the events of over a century of change in a psychological and personal way. Shared historical experience represents a sine qua non for the building of an imagining for something called "nation." In the chapters that follow, a number of themes central to this sharing emerge, including gender, family, and nationalism.

Gender as a relational set of behavioral and emotional activities features as a central focus recurrent in poems and lyrics. Verse allowed the expression of sentimental masculinity: it provided means for courtships, but it also took on darker aspects of the patriarchal assumptions. Harsh limitations to gendered behaviors could be prescribed by the lyricist, where women were made into objects, mute of agency, and where poets codified and normalized abhorrent misogyny. The valorization of hyper-masculinity or machismo continued apace in even the most romantic of tropes. The corrido, for example, represented a genre typically given voice by men, and often drunken men at that, and this effectively ensured that their performed masculine traits appeared as both normal and idealized. Where lyrics became political weapons, writers used gendered ascriptions to attack the masculinity or femininity of opponents, pinning negative traits on the "Other" while reinforcing stereotypes of the normal.

Family builds from gender norms and played a central role in lyrics and poetry. Children, spouses, lovers, siblings—all quite naturally appeared in the emotional verses of all genres. Whether in socialist indoctrinations, or betrayal tales, or as love objects, the expectations and aspirations of the ideal family in an ideal space provide a baseline for narrative verse. Wars such as the Cristiada of the 1920s and 1930s saw families sundered by differences of faith, which they expressed in lyrical antagonism. At the same time, and in a much broader sense, Mexican families stood firm in rejecting their

northern neighbors, demonstrating moments of solidarity that could help bridge the rifts caused by periodic instances of national infighting.

Popular notions of what mexicanidad comprised spilled free in verses and satires, particularly including an ever-building sentiment of anti-U.S. suspicions. It should not surprise that common understandings within verses revealed a nationalist preoccupation with the Colossus of the North who had invaded the country in 1846, 1914, and 1917. Particular frictions, imaginary and real, led writers to highlight perceived injuries wrought by the United States that made good Mexicans out of imperialism's victims. The humiliations and resentments from unwarranted invasions, the perception of the gringo as buying the soul of the country, the interference of northern diplomats in Revolution or Cristiada, and the ongoing investment in post–World War II industry, all offended a proud audience primed to seek an external cause for their longstanding hardships. In a context where national hegemonic consensus did not take form until the late nineteenth century at best, and that was interrupted by the ruptures of Revolution, creating this common enemy mattered. Nothing functions better than an enemy to bring together a fractured polity, the shared historical experience of a truly foreign foe. Dread of French, Spanish, or American assault drove the sharpening commitment to a centralized unity. In nearly all instances, this sentiment appeared most clearly and originally in verse that spoke to the threat to Mexico's dignity and sovereignty. Understandings of some essential identity thus formed on the basis of a politics of difference that, at least in part, made Mexico the binary counterpart to the United States. They could feel Mexican, could sing it and put it to poetic meter, because many deeply felt their difference from intruding neighbors and the values they represented. At the very least, nationalism rises from knowing who you are not.

Initial Forays

The stories and perspectives of ordinary people are all too often silent in the historical record, yet their experiences offer historians one of the finest ways to access and make sense of the tangled weave of events in a distant past. Our imagination is fettered by this lack. By bringing new sources and approaches to such a study, scholars can uncover private thoughts and get into the heads of historical actors often rendered unreachable by their limited literacy or public exposure.

Considerable turmoil and conflict marked the early history of Mexico, including, among other things, no less than four invasions by foreigners and average presidential terms of less than seven months. With reason then, scholars have tended to focus on issues of wide political changes, of military successes or failures, or of the economics of a nation halted in its trajectory of development. In contrast, or better, as a complement to this, Christopher Conway offers a unique examination of women's perceptions of the United States' invasion and occupation of Mexico (1846–1848). His study highlights how women used poetry focusing on the U.S.-Mexican War to push the boundaries of domesticity and what defined female subjectivity.

Despite the manifold problems that afflicted early republican Mexico—economic decline, political turmoil, regional divisions, and class hatreds—poetry flourished in the aftermath of independence from Spain as a medium that people used to express the problems and possibilities that they understood faced the new nation. Particularly noteworthy was the work of female poets who used their works to put forward a collective women's voice that placed individual poetic expression within the broader context of the country's tumultuous historical development. In discussing the war, female poets made known their authority to discuss matters typically relegated to the male-dominated public realm. They exalted Mexican heroism, denounced political and military failures, and depicted the horrors of the war. In so doing, women used gender to cloud the division between public and private spheres through their forays into political discussions, an arena where elite men traditionally excluded women.

Moving twenty years ahead into a period where the Mexican elite found themselves better able to consolidate power and centralize politics, Stephen Neufeld's chapter challenges the perceived successes and failures of the turn-of-the-century Porfirian regime. He looks into military poems and corridos that engaged with the official narratives, and breaks the image of a monolithic military apparatus. The growing divide between parts of the military elite and common soldiers is demonstrated through a comparison between forms of nationalist expression where officers' patriotic verses clash with the sardonic cynicism of barrack songs.

In an uncertain era, the men of the Porfirian military (1876–1911) gave voice to their lived experiences in many ways: some officers wrote martial poetry while in the ranks men sang the more common corrido. The lyrics and verses that filled barracks and institutional periodicals offer us a rich glimpse into what it meant to be servants of Porfirio Díaz and his nation. Officers strived to portray themselves as both *hombres de espada* and *hombres de pluma*, men of sword and of quill, offering their verses as homage (*obsequios*) to their superiors and even, at times, to the wife of the president. As literary amateurs they tried to straddle the modern and traditional while invoking a particular martial worldview that encompassed their idea of Mexico. Likewise, soldiers in the ranks took to early corrido ballads to speak of their own army life and in lyrical play mocked the pretensions of the army in some not-so-hidden transcripts. They reimagined their comrades and deeds in ways that defied the regimes' carefully ordered narratives—reinserting rough masculinity, antiforeign sentiments, and racial identity where they had been previously stripped away. By comparing the expressions of these vastly different echelons, an intriguing picture emerges that helps explain the often-unstable position of the army in everyday society during the first decades of the Porfiriato.

Michael Matthews demonstrates how, near the end of the same era, modernity in its most iconic form, the locomotive, inspired concerned classes to give voice in song and poetry to a sense of national change and anxiety—often in ways that again fly in the face of historical convention. Far from being recalcitrant toward modernization, he shows that working-class periodicals celebrated the utopian potential of technology and criticized the *manner* in which the government undertook development, not development itself. Understanding the accelerated rates of change and the devolution of time and space that rails made reality, he argues that the real possibilities and fears of being modern emerge in corridos that attended the expansion of the railways in the early twentieth century.

During the years of the Porfiriato, publishers printed a plethora of songs and poetry focused on the nation's burgeoning railway development. Looking at the later years of the regime (roughly 1895–1910), Matthews's chapter explores how the railway, as discussed in popular venues, represented contradictory impulses of fear and allure about the prospects offered by modernization. While popular groups celebrated the locomotive's capacity to compress time and space, they, at the same time, condemned the increased presence of foreigners in Mexico and the dangers of railway travel such as the train wreck. These sources reveal a rich cultural milieu that at times hailed and at times questioned the benefits of Porfirian progress. He argues that popular groups used ballads and poetry to articulate their ideas regarding economic and political development, national discourses from which the elite often excluded them. Popular ballads and poems published in broadsheets, newspapers, and inexpensive songbooks framed these issues through a discussion of common people's experiences of railway travel. These verses linked quotidian occurrences to broad critiques of how the government promoted railway development, especially its reliance on foreign capital, American workers, and a network operated in the English language.

The critiques and challenges to Porfirian rule outlined in these chapters expressed themselves most radically in the outbreak of the Mexican Revolution (1910), which unleashed a wave of social, political, economic, and cultural forces that reshaped society and the twentieth-century landscape more generally. This considered, it is no surprise that the Revolution continues to be a ubiquitous symbol of both social turmoil and the search for social justice. William French examines intimate life among the poor, amid this tumultuous event, in his analysis of the folkloric poetry of the copla. In the early twentieth century, the violence of the larger nation scarcely appears in the mundane concerns that consumed frustrated or aspiring lovers in small towns around Mexico. Their vision of power and nation reflect the importance of community and family in a time so often characterized as bound up in elite political maneuvering and the violent confrontations that resulted.

The copla's stanzas stand on their own in distinction to the corrido. Looking at this popular form of poetry from the 1890s through armed Revolution and into the 1920s, French's study does not seek to exhaust the possible themes covered by such an extensive collection of verse, but rather explores the relationship between the poetics of the coplas and the poetics of love letters. He examines the blurry line between oral and written literacy, suggesting that in intimate poetry one finds communications that transcend assumed boundaries set on marginal classes. He uses coplas to reflect upon and address additional interpretive possibilities for the romantic and other sentiments expressed in formal letters and poetic outbursts. Largely written during years of incredible violence and tumult, these verses treated everything from passion to honor, understandings of masculinities, *raptos* (kidnappings), proofs of love, written promises of marriage, tensions between the generations, and the alchemy through which the body and the letter became one. These themes echo between the genres of the copla and the love letter, confirming the centrality of themes common to both, including a relatively minor awareness or concern over broader politics of the day. At best, through a kind of sympathetic resonance, the poems add additional and differently nuanced readings of statements and sentiments not immediately apparent within the specific setting or generic conventions of the love-letter form. His work reminds us that poetic expressions of troubled love lives could exist even in the most difficult of historical times.

Moving beyond the ruptures of the 1910s and early 1920s, the nation entered an era of defining itself against an increasingly global and secular standard, and measuring its successes against the backdrop of the violent Mexican Revolution. Not officially modern, nor properly Revolutionary, the

Cristero rebels of the 1920s expressed their own understandings of what it meant to be a modern man in Mexico through songs. Their evocative perspective on Christian masculinity is examined in the chapter by Stephen Andes, who uses their music to restore the voices of a still little understood rebellion. His work stresses how, for many, the unfinished business of the Revolution would extend for decades and pose a direct challenge to fundamental identities, such as their sense of manhood. His examination of masculinity provides a new, cutting-edge approach to questions of religion and rebellion in the changing Revolutionary nation.

Andes questions whether corridos written and sung during and after the Cristero Rebellion (1926–1929) expressed changing notions of Catholic belief and practice in Mexico. Recent research by scholars such as Matthew Butler suggests that alternative Catholic religiosities emerged in the midst of the religious conflict, affected by absentee priests, religious persecution, battles with ecclesiastical authorities, and the schismatic movement.[77] Thus, Andes argues that cultural productions such as corridos are an important source from which to describe these developing Catholic identities. He asks, to what degree did songs written during the period become vehicles for popular discontent with the 1929 modus vivendi signed between Church officialdom and the Revolutionary state? Incorporating material from the Vatican and from Mexican archives, along with ballads written by Catholics, he explores how the Cristero Rebellion helped shape Catholicism and masculinity during the twentieth century.

The national project extended into the 1930s as the regime sought to define Revolutionary Mexico as socialist and populist. Children also had a perspective on the new nation and its leadership, and Elena Albarrán works with the poetry written for and by children, and directed to the Revolutionary government under Lázaro Cárdenas in the 1930s and on into the 1940s. Her analysis of the "Proletarian Child" ("Niño Proletario") offers unique insights into the changing meanings of Revolution, into politicized childhood, and into the subsequent decline of the socialist movements.

The Revolution erupted with promise, but simmered to a standstill by the mid-1930s as reforms remained unimplemented for many. The urgency for change, in a political climate that suggested the resurgence of a politically hierarchical structure, provided the impulse for a radical strand in the formation of the short-lived socialist education experiment during the government of Lázaro Cárdenas. The "Niño Proletario" emerged as a reified image in the public sphere, a reminder of the continued injustices that had gone unaddressed by Revolutionary reform, and a justification for the urgency of political radicalization. In 1935, government educational officials hosted The First Congress of the Proletarian Child, a highly publicized affair boasting participation from school-aged delegates representing schools deemed to be particularly "representative" of the proletarian condition. In this context, the revolutionary poet Jesús Sansón Flores of Michoacán, with the support of the Cárdenas government, penned several collections both for and about children and youth. His verses described the abysmal conditions in which "el Niño Proletario" continued to wallow, the colonial abuses of power that still persisted in the countryside, and the specific activities through which this child could take the mantle of the Revolution upon himself and redeem the failures of previous generations to rectify social wrongs. Albarrán therefore analyzes the verses contained in Sansón Flores's collection of poems in the context of the increasing public visibility of this new social type and metaphor for national redemption: the proletarian child.

The political consolidation among Revolutionary leaders in the 1940s and 1950s—manifesting itself in the 1946 formation of the Partido Revolucionario Institucional (PRI)—represented a shift away from a focus on social justice to a developmentalist economic program based on industrialization. In the aftermath of World War II, Mexicans witnessed an explosion in the production of film and music, a period known as the Golden Age of Cinema. Mass media reflected the often contradictory responses to the Mexican Miracle (1940s–1970s)—a period of sustained economic development, industrialization, and urbanization—highlighting both its agonizing and alluring impact on the nation. New media technologies allowed Mexican cultural producers to produce and consume international culture, a phenomenon that drew Mexico into the wider arena of globalization and global mass media. As such, national identity continued to reshape itself as a multitude of forces intersected at the lives of ordinary people. International consumer culture, Catholicism, commoditized folkloric traditions, and mass media coalesced in the social imaginary as government officials, corporate leaders, traditional authority figures, and media moguls vied for at least some say in how citizens would define themselves and their consumer choices.

It is within this context that Maria Áurea Toxqui explores how the music employed in Golden Age cinema portrayed people's alcoholic consumption, a social practice sometimes stereotyped as characteristic of the national identity. She shows that film producers came to praise the consumption of tequila and other distilled beverages as a suitable social practice for modern citizens while disparaging those individuals that continued to imbibe more traditional drinks such as *pulque*. Her work also discloses how musical works emphasized patriarchal values as they sought to construct a modern mestizo national identity promoted by the post-Revolutionary government, an identity based on the provincial characteristics associated with the state of Jalisco. Hard-drinking cowboy men, unafraid of sentimental tears, became the standard masculine ideal set in contrast to urban and urbane viewers of the cinema.

Transitioning to the years when government violence, as well as ineptness, severely undermined PRI rule, Amanda Ledwon examines various ways that the government commemorated the 1985 earthquake. She shows that poetry published to honor the victims represented reformulations of well-regarded works published about the 1968 student massacre (for example, Octavio Paz's poetry about 1968 was recast to lament the victims of the earthquake). By exploring the connection between these events through the government's attempt to use poetry to co-opt the memory of 1968, her study thus links two important moments when PRI rule came under heavy public scrutiny and explores how officials attempted to mitigate growing opposition to their authority. And, in so doing, her work examines popular responses to official narratives at a time when the ruling party's hold on power became increasingly tenuous.

On the one-year anniversary of the 1985 Mexico City earthquake, commemorative events shaped the healing process of a grieving community. While the infrastructure remained in stagnant disrepair, government agencies planned historic events as a response to the grieving masses. Recently released archival material presents the narrative of a government that ignored the more affected lower class while catering to the lettered community. For instance, a commissioned *loa*-style opera performed at Palacio de Bellas Artes reenacted the events of September 19, 1985, an event targeted toward the well-to-do. Ledwon focuses on selected government-sponsored commemorative events that purported to heal society at large, while, in fact, they only catered to a limited number of people affected by the earthquake. The lower classes pleaded for government action through petitions to Congress and demanded rebuilding efforts in those areas most affected. The government, nevertheless, responded instead by dedicating green space and parks in honor of the victims as well as offering verses from poets of the 1968 student movement to attempt to commemorate the pain of the quake. In this way, Ledwon also draws connections between the 1968 student massacre and the 1985 earthquake as interconnected moments. These revealed popular understandings of government wrongdoing, as well as how officials sought to co-opt the bitter memories of the massacre into a celebration of their response to earthquake victims, a scheme that further highlighted government inequities among the people. The verses of poems and opera clashed with popular demands and emphasized the distance between government efforts and the needs of the barrio.

This volume also invites readers to undertake the work of historians through the incorporation of primary document exercises based on the songs and poems examined by each contributor. Each chapter provides one full-length example of an appropriate verse or song, with translation into English. The intention is for readers to consider the interpretive nature of historical research as an opening to consider how historians ask questions about the primary sources they investigate. Moreover, by providing these document exercises we invite individual interpretations regarding what these sources mean, and what they tell us of the era in which they were produced.

To make sense of turmoil and chaos and war—not to mention times of peace and stability—in the ways that those who experienced them did, requires us to take seriously these unusual expressions that rise from alternative forms of communicating where people made sense of the disquiet. The story told here, in lyric and verse, is the tale of the crucial century and a half for mexicanidad. The nation, in its modern form, came into being out of the aspirations and nightmares of ordinary men and women, children and adults, officials and rebels. And while the victors may write the history, they do so while the majority quipped and hummed along to their own memories of what happened.

Amigos, vamos a contarles,
lo que pasó con la patria,
les diremos muchos verdades,
de gloriosa historia.[78]

Notes

1. On soundscapes and identity, see Anahid Kassabian, *Ubiquitous Listening: Affect, Attention, and Distributed Subjectivity* (Berkeley: University of California Press, 2013), xi–xxx, 18–19, 92–99, 109–117.

2. By contrast, studies on nation formation and music in Europe are better covered; see Jan Passler, *Composing the Citizen: Music as Public Utility in Third Republic France* (Berkeley: University of California Press, 2009); Martha Ward and Anne Leonard, eds., *Looking and Listening in Nineteenth-Century France* (Chicago: University of Chicago Press, 2008).

3. Even without lyrics, music of all sorts can build affect regardless of attention with implications for subjectivities and identities; see Kassabian, *Ubiquitous Listening*, xviii–xxiv, 18–19, 31–32, 92–108.

4. E. P. Thompson, *Customs in Common: Studies in Traditional Popular Culture* (New York: New Press, 1993), 485.

5. Vicente Mendoza, *El corrido mexicano: Antología, introducción y notas* (México: Fondo de Cultura Economíca, 1954) and *Lírica narrativa de México: El corrido* (México: Instituto de Investigaciones Estéticas Universidad Nacional Autónoma de México, 1964); Higinio Vázquez Santa Ana, *Canciones, cantares y corridos mexicanos* (México: Imprenta León Sánchez, n.d.); Merle E. Simmons, *The Mexican Corrido as a Source for Interpretive Study of Modern Mexico (1870–1950)* (Bloomington: Indiana University Press, 1957); Rubén M. Campos, *El folklore y la música mexicana; investigación acerca de la cultura musical en México (1525–1925). Obra integrada con 100 sones, jarabes y canciones del folklore musical mexicano, cuyas melodías están intactas: ilustraciones de tipos, escenas y paisajes pintorescos de antaño y retratos de músicos mexicanos* (Mexico City: Talleres Gráficos de la Nación, 1928) and *El folklore literario de México; investigación acerca de la producción literaria popular (1525–1925) copiosa recolección de adivinanzas, anécdotas, canciones, coloquios, corridos, cuentos, epigramas, fábulas, glosas, juegos infantiles, leyendas, loas, mitotes, narraciones, ocurrencias, pasquines, pastorelas, preces, proclamas, sátiras, sucedidos, tradiciones, versos callejeros, villancicos* (Mexico City: Talleres Gráficos de la Nación, 1929).

6. See, for example, Leslie Bethell, ed., *A Cultural History of Latin America* (Cambridge: Cambridge University Press, 1998); John King, ed., *The Cambridge Companion to Modern Latin American Culture* (Cambridge: Cambridge University Press, 2004).

7. One exception that does make good use of verse is a quite recent work, Mauricio Tenorio-Trillo, *I Speak of the City: Mexico City at the Turn of the Twentieth Century* (Chicago: University of Chicago Press, 2012); a good overview is Mark Pedelty, *Musical Ritual in Mexico City: From Aztec to NAFTA* (Austin: University of Texas Press, 2004).

8. For reasons of brevity, we have omitted from our overview some important genres, including the history of salon music in the nineteenth century, early twentieth-century *indigenista* and revolutionary music, and the music of the twentieth-century Golden Age. On these, among others, see especially Mark Pedelty, *Musical Ritual*; Dan Malmström, *Introducción a la música mexicana de siglo* XX (México: Fonda de Cultura Económica, 1977); Alba Herrera y Ogazon, *El arte musical en México* (México: Dir. Gen. de Bellas Artes, 1917).

9. Claudio Lomnitz, *Death and The Idea of Mexico* (New York: Zone Books, 2005), 139; Pedelty, *Musical Ritual*, 71–76.

10. Yolanda Moreno Rivas, *Historia de la música popular Mexicana* (México: Editorial Oceano, 1979), 32.

11. Catherine Den Tandt and Richard Young, "Tradition and transformation in Latin American music," in *The Cambridge Companion to Modern Latin American Culture*, 240–41.

12. *Sones* refer to a rural musical style popular in Spanish-speaking countries that include the playing of stringed instruments and percussion, the singing of rhyming stanzas, and the dancing of couples. *Coplas* refer to a brand of music based on poetic couplets.

13. Moreno Rivas, *Historia de la música popular*, 16–17; Pedelty, *Musical Ritual*, 59–66.

14. Sergio Rivera Ayala, "Dance of the People: The Chuchumbé," in *Colonial Lives: Documents on Latin American History, 1550–1850*, ed. Richard Boyer and Geoffrey Spurling (Oxford: Oxford University Press, 2000), 178–84.

15. Enrique Florescano, *Memoria Mexicana* (México: Fondo de Cultura Económica, 1994); Pedelty, *Musical Ritual*, 3–82.

16. David Brading, *The First America: The Spanish Monarchy, Creole Patriots and the Liberal State 1492–1867* (Cambridge: Cambridge University Press, 1993), 602, 673–74.

17. Brading, *First America*, 343–61; Pedelty, *Musical Ritual*, 65–67.

18. Lee H. Dowling, "The Colonial Period," in *Mexican Literature: A History*, ed. David William Foster (Austin: University of Texas Press, 1994), 42–43.

19. Carlos Monsiváis, *Escenas de poder y liviandad*, 7th ed. (México: Editorial Grijalbo, 1988), 176.

20. William Beezley, *Mexican National Identity: Memory, Innuendo, and Popular Culture* (Tucson: University of Arizona Press, 2008), vii–xii, 147–49.

21. Den Tandt and Young, "Tradition and transformation," 245–46.

22. Marco Velázquez and Mark Kay Vaughn, "*Mestizaje* and Musical Nationalism in Mexico," in *The Eagle and the Virgin: Nation and Cultural Revolution in Mexico, 1920–1940*, ed. Mary Kay Vaughn and Stephen E. Lewis (Durham, NC: Duke University Press, 2006), 96–97; Pedelty, *Musical Ritual*, 85–106.

23. *Jarabe* refers to a music form derived from the mariachi. *Canción* refers to a stylized music, usually romantic in nature, accompanied by a piano or guitar.

24. Mendoza, *Lírica narrativa de México*, 7; Chris Frazer, *Bandit Nation: A History of Outlaws and Cultural Struggle in Mexico, 1810–1920* (Lincoln: University of Nebraska Press, 2006), 136.

25. Juan Garrido, *Historia de la música popular en México* (México: Editorial Extemporáneos, S.A., 1974), 15.

26. Velázquez and Vaughn, "*Mestizaje* and Musical Nationalism," 95.

27. Guy P. C. Thompson, "The Ceremonial and Political Roles of Village Bands, 1846–1974," in *Rituals of Rule, Rites of Resistance: Public Celebrations and Popular Culture in Mexico*, ed. William H. Beezley, Cheryl English Martin, and William E. French (Wilmington, DE: Scholarly Resources, 1994), 315–17.

28. Velázquez and Vaughn, "*Mestizaje* and Musical Nationalism," 97.

29. Thompson, "Ceremonial and Political Roles," 315–17; Velázquez and Vaughn, "*Mestizaje* and Musical Nationalism," 95.

30. Thompson, "Ceremonial and Political Roles," 314–15.

31. Malmström, *Introducción a la música mexicana*, 27–37; Herrera y Ogazon, *El arte musical en México*, 47–102; Moreno Rivas, *Historia de la música popular*, 76–89.

32. Luis González y González, "La Música," in *Historia moderna de México República Restorada: Vida social*, ed. Daniel Cosió Villegas (México: 1956), 884–90.

33. Moreno Rivas, *Historia de la música popular*, 19.

34. Alejandro Madrid, *Sounds of the Modern Nation: Music, Culture, and Ideas in Post-Revolutionary Mexico* (Philadelphia: Temple University Press, 2009), 143–45.

35. Simmons, *Mexican Corrido*, 12–14.

36. Mendoza, *Lírica narrativa de México*, 13.

37. Ricardo Pérez Montfort, *Estampas de nacionalismo popular mexicano* (México: Centro de Investigaciones y Estudios, 1994), 54–55.

38. Margarita Vargas, "Romanticism," in *Mexican Literature: A History*, ed. David William Foster (Austin: University of Texas Press, 1994), 102–3.

39. See Christopher Conway's chapter in this volume.

40. Pérez Montfort, *Estampas de nacionalismo*, 91.

41. Edward Laroque Tinker, *Corridos and Calaveras* (Austin: University of Texas Press, 1961), 29.

42. Ibid., 31.

43. Robert Darnton, *The Great Cat Massacre and Other Episodes in French Cultural History* (New York: Vintage Books, 1985), ch. 1.

44. Simmons, *Mexican Corrido*, ix–x, 31–35; Mendoza, *El corrido mexicano*, viii–ix.

45. Simmons, *Mexican Corrido*, xv.

46. Frazer, *Bandit Nation*, 131–39.

47. Pérez Montfort, *Estampas de nacionalismo*, 97; Garrido, *Historia de la música popular*, 16–17. For a discussion of Mexico's regional musical traditions, see Román García Arreola, *La música y el baile de "La Chilena" en la costa Oaxaqueña* (Oaxaca: Proveedor Escolar, n/d); Juan Jesús Aguilar León, *Los trovadores huastecos en Tamaulipas* (Ciudad Victoria: Instituto Tamaulipeco para la Cultura y las Artes, 2000); Miguel Civeira Taboada, *Sensibilidad yucateca en la canción romántica* (Toluca: Colección de Arte Popular y Folklore, 1979); Gerónimo Baquero Foster, *La canción popular de Yucatán (1850–1950)* (México: Editorial del Magisterio, 1970).

48. Adriana García, "Twentieth-Century Poetry," in *Mexican Literature: A History*, ed. David William Foster (Austin: University of Texas Press, 1994), 172.

49. Bart L. Lewis, "Modernism," in *Mexican Literature: A History*, ed. David William Foster (Austin: University of Texas Press, 1994), 158; Michael Matthews, "De Viaje: Elite Views of Modernity and the Porfirian Railway Boom," *Mexican Studies/Estudios Mexicanos* 26, no. 2 (2010): 255.

50. Michael Matthews, *The Civilizing Machine: A Cultural History of Mexican Railroads, 1876–1910* (Lincoln: University of Nebraska Press, 2013).

51. Tinker, *Corridos and Calaveras*, 7.

52. Velázquez and Vaughn, "*Mestizaje* and Musical Nationalism," 99–100.

53. Pérez Montfort, *Estampas de nacionalismo*, 146.

54. Velázquez and Vaughn, "*Mestizaje* and Musical Nationalism," 100.

55. Gerard H. Béhague, "Music, c. 1920–1980," in Bethell, *A Cultural History of Latin America*, 315–17; see also Moreno Rivas, *Historia de la música popular*, 128–82.

56. Madrid, *Sounds of the Modern Nation*, 142–52.

57. On oil expropriation, see Velázquez and Vaughn, "*Mestizaje* and Musical Nationalism," 194–95. On corridos about Mexico's involvement in World War II, see Tinker, *Corridos and Calaveras*, 37–38.

58. Velázquez and Vaughn, "*Mestizaje* and Musical Nationalism," 111; Rivas, 182–83.

59. Velázquez and Vaughn, "*Mestizaje* and Musical Nationalism," 108.

60. Pedelty, *Musical Ritual*, 142–205.

61. García, "Twentieth-Century Poetry," 192–99, 207.

62. For an overview, see Pedelty, *Musical Ritual*, 249–75.

63. Eric Zolov, *Refried Elvis* (Berkeley: University of California Press, 1999).

64. Merced Belén Valdés Cruz, *Rock Mexicano, Ahí la llevamos cantinfleando . . .* (México City: Merced B313n, 2002), 238; Merced Belén Valdés Cruz, *¡Qué Onda Ése . . . ! De contracultura y otros rollos* (México City: Merced B313n, 2008); José Agustín, *La Contracultura en México, La Historia y el significado de los rebeldes sin causa, los jipitecas, los punks y las bandas* (México City: Grijalbo, 1996).

65. Elijah Wald, *Narcocorrido: A Journey into the Music of Drugs, Guns and Guerrillas* (New York: Harper Collins, 2001), 3–4.

66. José Pablo Villalobos and Juan Carlos Ramírez-Pimenta, "'Corridos' and 'la Pura Verdad': Myths and Realities of the Mexican Ballad," *South Center Review* 21, no. 3 (Fall 2004), 129–49.

67. Wald, *Narcocorrido*, 4.

68. Ibid., 3.

69. Luis Astorga, "Los corridos de traficantes de drogas en México y Colombia," *Revista Mexicana de Sociología* 59, no. 4 (October 1997), 245–61.

70. For a non-lyrical musical study that examines "cultural production and consumption as a dynamic interplay of power in particular historical contexts," see Madrid, *Sounds of the Modern Nation*.

71. For an overview, see Michel Foucault and Paul Rabinow, *The Foucault Reader* (New York: Pantheon, 1984); James C. Scott, *Weapons of the Weak: Everyday Forms of Peasant Resistance* (New Haven, CT: Yale University Press, 1985).

72. See William Roseberry, "Hegemony and the Language of Contention," in *Everyday Forms of State Formation: Revolution and Negotiation of Rule in Modern Mexico*, ed. G. Joseph and D. Nugent (Durham, NC: Duke University Press, 1994), 357, 360–65.

73. Frazer, *Bandit Nation*, 14–15, 133–39.

74. For an excellent analysis of this from an elite perspective, see Mauricio Tenorio-Trillo, *Mexico at the Worlds' Fairs: Crafting a Modern Nation* (Berkeley: University of California Press, 1996), 158–80.

75. Antonio Gramsci, *The Antonio Gramsci Reader: Selected Writings*, ed. David Forgacs (New York: New York University Press, 2000), 306–7.

76. Roseberry, "Language of Contention," 360–61.

77. Matthew Butler, *Popular Piety and Political Identity in Mexico's Cristero Rebellion: Michoacán, 1927–29* (New York: Oxford University Press, 2004).

78. These verses were compiled from the usual formulaic openings for the corrido folk song. The translation is:

> Friends, we are going to tell you,
> what happened to the fatherland,
> we will tell you many truths,
> of our glorious history.

PRIMARY DOCUMENT

Warfare and ideological strife marked the earliest decades of Mexico as a young nation. No figure dominated Mexican politics in the early to mid-nineteenth century as did Antonio López de Santa Anna. Serving as president, uncrowned king, or dictator on no less than eleven occasions between 1833 and 1855, Santa Anna used his charisma and political guile to lead the nation through a number of serious calamities including civil wars and foreign invasions. Of these, perhaps no event reshaped the course of national history more than the U.S. invasion, occupation, and annexation of Mexico (1846–1848). The country, plagued by civil wars between Liberals and Conservatives, proved a vulnerable target to the "Colossus of the North," losing half its national territory after the signing of the Treaty of Guadalupe Hidalgo. Christopher Conway analyzes the poetry of Mexican women during the occupation, and explores how these verses sought to shape, and perhaps reveal, people's views toward the U.S. invasion, the ephemeral regimes of Santa Anna, women's place in a changing nation, and the kaleidoscopic political systems introduced in the first half of the tumultuous nineteenth century.

"La Tempestad"[*]

Ya negros nubarrones oscurecen

El horizonte, y los terribles ecos
Del rayo estrepitoso, que intimidan

A criminales y cobardes pechos,
Imponen en los bosques silenciosos,
Resuenan en los cóncavos estensos
De las hondas cañadas, y parecen
Conmover de la tierra los cimientos.
Relámpagos vivísimos alumbran

"The Storm"

Already the black storm clouds
darken
The horizon, and the terrible echoes
Of the deafening thunderbolt, that
intimidate
Criminal and cowardly breasts,
Inspire awe in the silent woods,
Resounding in the vast hollows
Of the deep ravines, and seem to
Move the earth to its foundations.
Bright thunderbolts light

[*] Translation by Gustavo Pellón, from *The U.S.-Mexico War: A Binational Reader.* Reprinted by permission of Hackett Publishing Company, Inc.

Con la velocidad del pensamiento,
Las nieves que coronan la montaña,
El lago do se miran sus reflejos.

En las rocas vecinas se dibujan
Las sombra de los pinos gigantescos;
Y sus ramos se miran combatidas
Por el soplo encontrado de los vientos.
De la colina, baja ya el torrente
Que improvisaron fuertes aguaceros,
Y sus blancas espumas deleznables,
Desaparecen cual vapor ligero.
Estrecho va en su cauce el manso río;
Desbórdanse sus aguas, y soberbio
Arrastrando en su curso los peñascos,
Doblegando la yerba de su suelo,
Inunda la llanura cultivada;
Los prados en que agostan los corderos;
La selva hojosa, los fecundos valles
Que otras veces regaba placentero.

Amedrentado el toro, busca asilo
En las concavidades de los cerros;
Y el pobre labrador no puede hallarlo
En la cabaña de pajizo techo.
Hendiendo el aire, círculos describen
Las inocentes aves con su vuelo,
Y azoradas se vuelven a los nidos
Que vieron sus amores lisongeros.
¡Oh grandioso espectáculo! ¡sublime!
¡Digno del grande autor del universo!

With the speed of thought,
The snows that crown the mountain,
The lake where they see their reflection.

On the neighboring rocks are drawn
The shadows of gigantic pines;
And their branches find themselves attacked
By the clashing gusts of the winds.

From the hill, the torrent already falls,
Improvised by strong cloudbursts,

And its insignificant white foam,
Disappears like the lightest vapor.
The gentle river now strains its bed;
Its waters overflow, and arrogantly
Dragging boulders in its flow,

Bending the grass on the ground,
Floods the cultivated fields;
The meadows where the lambs graze;
The leafy jungle, the fertile valleys
That other times it sweetly watered.

Startled, the bull seeks refuge
In the hollows of the hills;
Nor can the poor farmer find it

In the thatched-roofed cabin.
The innocent birds in their flight,

Cut the air, describing circles,
And return flustered to the nests
That once saw their fond wooing.
Oh, grandiose spectacle! Sublime!
Worthy of the great author of the universe!

¡Que anonadas al hombre, que lo elevas,	That overwhelms man, and elevates him,
Desviando de la tierra sus afectos!	Turning his affection away from the earth!

Hacienda del Pabellon,
Septiembre 1846 Guadalupe Calderón
Josefa Terán
Una Zacatecana

Discussion Questions

1. What types of symbolic imagery does the author employ in this poem?
2. What do the symbolic images of the tempest and bull represent?
3. What does the author's use of imagery tell us about her views regarding the war?

CHAPTER ONE

Sister at War

Mexican Women's Poetry and the U.S.-Mexican War

Christopher Conway

One of the most promising areas of future research into literature and national identity in early republican Mexico is the literature of the U.S.-Mexican War of 1846–1848. Mexican literary responses to the United States' invasion of its territory, and to Mexico's continued defeats on the battlefield, constitute an invaluable archive for examining the emergence of Mexican nationalism. Indeed, during the war and its aftermath, Mexican writers recognized the value of national unity as they never had before, because they saw their defeat on the battlefield as a function of their political disunity. "A nation is nothing but a large family," wrote the distinguished *moderado* writer Mariano Otero in his 1848 assessment of Mexico's defeat, "and for this to be strong and powerful, it is necessary for all its members to be intimately joined by common interest and other feelings of the heart."[1] Such fraternal bonds did not take root between 1821 and 1848, when *pronunciamientos* and struggles between centralists and federalists, as well as *puro* and moderado federalists, destabilized the state.[2] Yet, the outbreak of the war, and the threat posed by the invading U.S. Army, afforded Mexican writers with a nationalist vision that transcended sectarianism. Literature, particularly poetry, gave writers an alternative to the highly partisan political tracts that populated Mexico's newspapers. As the stuff of individual feeling and sensibility, poetry enabled Mexicans to engage with their mythological or historical forefathers, imagine a collective victory against the northern aggressor, and evoke images of their nation's greatness.

In the largely forgotten corpus of Mexican poetry published during the war, women's poetry represents a particularly revealing dimension of this nationalist literary moment in Mexican history. [3] In fact, the war coincided with a rise in publications for women that blurred public and private spheres. Paradoxically, the marginality of women's voices in public affairs afforded them opportunities to define a platform from which to speak out. That is, women could express the horror and emotional anguish provoked by Mexico's military defeats and internal discord without explicitly compromising prevailing views of gender. Moreover, because combative and victimized women were dominant tropes in U.S. and Mexican discourses about the war, women writers discovered that they were already at the center of cultural representations of the deeper or symbolic meanings of the war. In the pages that follow, I trace the emergence of Mexican women's voices in the years leading up to and during the war, and the ways women poets understood and enacted their position as writers. Specifically, women poets cultivated a symbolic sisterhood through which they criticized Mexico's political failures and subtly challenged the separation of spheres that excluded them from political speech.

The Conquest of Mexican Women

Any study of Mexican women in relation to the U.S.-Mexican War must acknowledge how Mexican women were privileged as tropes by both U.S. and Mexican writers. In short, we begin the story of how Mexican women spoke out during war with how they were represented as symbols of triumph and defeat. Scholars such as Robert Johannsen, Shelley Streeby, Andrea Tinnemeyer, and Amy Greenberg highlight how gender and politics intertwine in U.S. literature about the U.S.-Mexican War, showing how writers used melodrama and its stereotyped characters to make arguments about race, nation, and sexuality.[4] In nineteenth-century popular literature, swashbuckling U.S. soldiers symbolized the virility and racial supremacy of the United States over Mexico, while Mexican men were caricatured as degraded and barbaric. When U.S. writers had their protagonists woo and fall in love with Mexican damsels threatened by their fathers or other Mexican suitors, they allegorized the conflict as a war of liberation against political tyranny. They also made the conquest of Mexico an analogue of sexual conquest that reinforced U.S. martial masculinity and the ideology of Manifest Destiny. This symbolically loaded damsel in distress love story was tempered by another kind of story: the recurring appearance of cross-dressing Mexican women who take up arms against U.S. forces during the war, as in the case of the female protagonists of *The Volunteer or, The Maid of Monterey* (1847) by Ned Buntline, *The Hunted Chief: Or the Female Ranchero* (1847) by Newton Curtis, and *The Secret Service Ship; or, The Fall of San Juan d'Ulloa* (1848) by Charles Averill, among others. These amazons helped to sustain the symbolic supremacy of Anglo American masculinity and to present Mexican masculinity as inferior, especially when the valiant señorita, who at first seemed to be a valiant male soldier, is unmasked and falls in love with the invader.[5] The different outcomes of these kinds of "international romances" stage a variety of arguments about the ways in which a subjugated Mexico can and should be positioned in relation to the triumphant United States.[6]

In Mexican print and oral culture, the relationship between Mexican women and invading U.S. soldiers was never figured as a romance, but as a violation. Mexican writers used representations of women as victims of rape and murder to whip up nationalist fervor and rally Mexicans against a common enemy that they saw as an existential threat. Popular nineteenth-century poet and journalist Guillermo Prieto uses vivid images of the violation of women to stir outrage in his 1847 poem "A Solemn Moment. To My Motherland." He represents Veracruz as the bloodied body of a queen who died as she hears "the 'hurrahs' of victory / from those who drenched her homes in blood!"[7] The prospect of defeat at the hands of savage latter-day conquistadors spurs Prieto to imagine the exile and dispossession of Mexican men. "Our anguish shall be their pleasure," writes Prieto, "the children of our love, their slaves; / and our women will give them comfort / alas, amid the remains of our brave men."[8] The victors from the North are cruel and avid panthers who gorge themselves on fleeing virgins and children. When Prieto addresses readers willing to surrender to the invader, he invokes the explosive image of the "violated bed / of the wife and the ravished virgin."[9] Other poems published in the Mexican press between 1846 and 1847 hit on the same themes, representing Mexico as a violated motherland, and using the horror of imperiled virgins and innocents to maximize calls for Mexican heroism and resistance to the cruel invader.[10] If U.S. representations of the war provided opportunities to exalt American virility over Mexican virility, Mexican representations were driven to horror over the potential failure of Mexican manhood to protect its motherland. Indeed, one of Mexico's most important poets of the first half of the nineteenth century, Manuel Carpio, called Mexico's defenders "shameless, effeminate sons" for losing Mexico in his poem "Mexico in 1847."[11]

The contest between Mexican and U.S. masculinities extended to popular culture as well, although it is much more difficult to trace because of the scarcity of print source material.[12] Thanks to the memoir of Antonio García Cubas (1832–1912), a nineteenth-century Mexican geographer and writer who was living in Mexico City during the United States' occupation, we have access to a corrido that sheds light onto how oral culture treated the intertwining of war and gender politics. Titled "La Pasadita," the corrido describes how Mexican prostitutes, known as Margaritas, mingled and danced with U.S. soldiers at the Bella Unión Hotel of Mexico City, where the occupiers spent their free time drinking, dancing, gambling, and carousing with women of ill repute. According to García Cubas, "La Pasadita" was sung by the "rabble of the city" who mockingly applauded the dancing between U.S. soldiers and Margaritas at the notorious hotel.[13] The word *pasadita* suggests two playful meanings. The first is a "quick visit," which in this context is an ironic refutation of the permanence of the U.S. occupation. Another more tactile and sensual connotation of pasadita is "to rub body parts together," which implied both dancing and sexual relations. The word "Margaritas" is also significant in the corrido; nineteenth-century Mexicans were familiar with the colloquial expression "*Echar Margaritas a los puercos*" (to cast pearls before swine), which referred to a passage in the Sermon on the Mount in which Jesus told his followers to not surrender what was holy to dogs, nor to cast their "pearls" (referred to as "margaritas" in the Latin Vulgate Bible) to the swine, "lest they trample them under their feet, and turn again and rend you." By calling the women who dance with the Yankees Margaritas, the corrido has some ironic fun with the idea that Margaritas are holy and pure (they are not), and also implies that the invaders are pigs.

Before exploring the complex, ironic, and biting treatment of the U.S. occupation in "La Pasadita," let's look at the full transcription of the song by García Cubas:

¡Ay! Amigos míos,
les voy a contar
lo que me ha pasado
en esta ciudad:
entraron los yankees
me arriesgué apedrear,
y á la pasadita,
tan-darín-da-rán.

Oh! My friends,
I'm going to tell you
what happened to me
in this city:
in came the Yankees,
and I threw some stones,
and on to La Pasadita,
tra-la-la-la.

Ya las Margaritas
hablan el inglés,
les dicen: me quieres
y responden: *yes,*
mi entende de monis
mucho gueno está
y á la pasadita
tan-darín-da-rán.

All the Margaritas
speak English now,
you say: do you love me
and they answer: *jes,*
I onderstan de money
ees very good,
and on to La Pasadita,
tra-la-la-la.

Sólo las mujeres
tienen corazón
para hacer alianza
con esa nación,
y ellas dicen: vamos,
pero no es verdad,
y á la pasadita
tan-darín-da-rán.

Only the women
are so kind
as to traffic
with that nation,
and they say: Let's go,
but it isn't true,
and on to La Pasadita,
tra-la-la-la.

Sólo de los hombres
no hay que desconfiar,
pues lo que ellos hacen
no lo hacen por mal:
suelen como el gato
también halagar,
y á la pasadita
tan-darín-da-rán.[14]

When it comes to the men,
there's no need for mistrust,
because what they do
has no ill intent:
just like cats,
they know when to fawn,
and on to La Pasadita,
tra-la-la-la.

At first glance, "La Pasadita" appears to condemn the Margaritas and women in general for being traitorous in comparison to men, who, like the proverbial cats, alternate between fawning with their tails and scratching with their claws. In a separate, extant version of the corrido, we see a more explicit expression of the idea that Mexican men are lying in wait:

Los yanquis malvados	The evil Yankees
no cesan de hablar	don't stop saying
que habrán de acabar	that they will finish
con esta nación,	with this nation,
yo les digo nones	*I tell them no no no*
el día llegará . . . [15]	*the day will come . . .* [emphasis added]

The juxtaposition of Margaritas taking Yankee cash ("Let's go") with Mexican men who bide their time to strike back, would seem to suggest that covert resistance belongs to men while collaboration and betrayal to women.[16] A closer look, however, reveals that the corrido is much more playful and ambiguous than this reading suggests. The refrain or chorus of *tan-darín-da-rán,* which Gustavo Pellón has translated here as *tra-la-la-la* to capture the phrase's musical function, may be read as a double entendre composed of the adverb *tan* (equivalent to the English adverb "so" in constructions that emphasize the degree or extent of a quality).[17] In turn, *darín* and *da-rán,* may be read as riffs on the verb *dar* (to give), especially *da-rán,* which is the third person plural in the future tense: [*ellos*] *darán* / [they] will give. The chorus, then, may allude to both the beating of bodies together (second stanza) and the aggressive action of "giving a beating" or "giving them hell" (the first, third, and fourth stanzas). When the women say "Let's go" to the yankees in the third stanza, the *corridista* sang "but it isn't true / and on to La Pasadita / *tra-la-la-la,*" suggesting that by having sexual relations with the Yankees ("beating" their bodies against them), the Margaritas are giving them something unwelcome, or resisting them in some other way ("giving them a beating").

The representation of Mexican women by U.S. and Mexican poets demonstrates that the U.S.-Mexican War was fought upon the symbolic body of voiceless Mexican women whose primary purpose was to project back the triumphant redemption or disgraceful perdition of U.S. or Mexican constructions of the masculine. Yet, elite Mexican women were not without words of their own. For several years before the war, some Mexican women had begun to speak out in newspapers and literary magazines, and the outbreak of war found them prepared to play a role in rallying Mexican armies to victory, in analyzing the failures of Mexican politics, and in exploring their fears about Mexico's defeat. It is to a few of these remarkable and largely forgotten women that we now turn.

In Search of a Voice

Although Mexican women took on prominent roles during the War of Independence as republican spies, smugglers, nurses, and conspirators, the years that followed the war saw the rise and consolidation of European notions of domestic femininity, particularly the construct of the *ángel del hogar,* known in the English-speaking world as the angel of the hearth.[18] According to the emergent bourgeois belief system that enshrined the ángel del hogar as an ideal feminine type, women constituted the weaker and more sensitive sex defined by motherhood and sensibility.[19] The prospectuses of Mexico's women's magazines in the 1830s and 1840s reinforce the role of the ángel del hogar. In the first issue, in 1841, of the *Semanario de las Señoritas Mejicanas*, for example, we find a staged dialogue between various men and women at a *tertulia* (gathering) over the merits of the prospectus of the magazine, which calls for the education of women. Some argue against women's education, seeing it as a threat to men, whereas others disagree, arguing that women need to be educated to strengthen marriage and motherhood.[20] One of the conversants, a woman called Doña Quitéria, playfully telegraphs the idea that women's education does not represent a threat to patriarchy: "*yo estoy pronunciada porque se reforme la educación mugeril*" (while all clamor for political reform, I am up in arms in favor of reforming women's education). [21] Doña Quitéria's use of the past participle of *pronunciar* (to rise up against, or to rise up in arms), is ironic considering that the pronunciamiento (military uprising) was very much the business of men, and the primary mode of regime change in early republican Mexico. Doña Quitéria has risen up (in arms) but only with regards to women's education, not Mexican politics. The ironic comment underlines that the "politics" of women are not about public affairs, but about nurturing women as better partners and mothers.

Despite these restrictive views about gender, Mexico on the eve of the U.S.-Mexican War also saw countercurrents that created openings for women to seize the word and publicly speak for themselves. Under the mantle of enlightened domesticity, women began to represent and share their experiences through poetry, thereby carving out a space for their voices to be heard by the educated women who constituted the primary readership of literary print material in Mexico.[22] There were several reasons for this loosening of strictures against women's writing and the idea of women as visible, public writers. The first of these was the influence of Romanticism. As Susan Kirkpatrick notes, the rise of Romanticism in Europe created a space for women to express themselves as subjects.[23] Kirkpatrick argues that the privileging of introspection as a source of knowledge about experience and nature, and of sensibility and emotion as the domain of a properly romantic imagination, afforded women a measure of authority to begin to construct a romantic literary tradition. "If feeling was a feminine specialty," writes Kirkpatrick, "if the loving and restorative spirit of the home was identical with the female psyche, then women surely had something to say in the forging of a language to represent the full range of subjective experience."[24]

The realities of a booming print culture at midcentury and the rise of Mexican women's magazines also played a role in promoting the self-expression of women. The introduction of lithography into Mexico in the 1840s led to the publication of the most handsome, illustrated periodical publications Mexico had seen up to that time in its history.[25] In particular, women's magazines such as *Semanario de las Señoritas Mejicanas* (1841) and *Panorama de las Señoritas Mejicanas* (1842), both of which were printed by Vicente García Torres, were predicated on valuing women and women's experiences as worthy objects of public discourse. Isidro Rafael Gondra's *Semanario* was conservative, with numerous articles emphasizing religious subject matter and the ideology of domesticity. *Panorama* was much more cosmopolitan and modern in its approach to gender, despite a prospectus that promised to downplay public affairs in favor of the themes of an enlightened domesticity.[26] In particular, many of the articles in *Panorama* provide historical precedents and philosophical and political arguments for women to step outside of the home into the public arena. For example, in 1842, the magazine reprinted a French article originally published in 1786 titled "Valor en las mujeres," which sings the praises of valiant women in history and myth, such as Queen Tomyris, who defeated the Persian ruler Cyrus the Great in 530 BCE; the Sabines, who fought against the Romans in 750 BCE; and the women of Saguntum, who in 219 BCE sacrificed their children and themselves instead of being taken as slaves by the armies of Hannibal.[27] Individual women were also singled out for celebration through a column called *Biografías de mujeres célebres*, which featured brief biographies of religious and historical heroines who are honored for their courage, sacrifice, and talents.[28]

Indeed, we can find some intriguing evidence of how such galleries of warrior women and women writers might have fostered female empowerment and nationalist engagement in a striking article titled "Invitación a los mexicanos" by María de la Salud García; the article was published on August 31, 1846, in the Mexico City newspaper *El Republicano*. Little is known about Salud García other than the fact that her short stories and a novel appeared in the women's magazine *La Semana de las Señoritas Mejicanas* in 1851.[29] In her article for *El Republicano*, Salud García explained that the urgency of Mexico's crisis empowered her to rise above the limitations of her sex and authorized her to call on the men of Mexico to restage, in the present war, their past triumphs against the yoke of Spanish colonialism. If Mexican men did not rise to the occasion, she threatened, the women, whom she calls the weak and useless half of the human race, will abandon their household chores to fight to the death in place of the men, like the poet Telesilla of Argos, who cross-dressed as a man and led an army of women and slaves against the warriors of Sparta. Salud García's argument that women could be transcendental historical actors and replace men in battle did not go unchallenged. Three weeks later, an anonymous respondent called "M" published a poem in *El Republicano* about Salud García's article, imploring her and other women to refrain from becoming warrior women and to instead weave laurels for the battered heads of their male liberators.[30]

Besides drawing inspiration from the heroines of the past, Mexican women readers and writers like Salud García also began to make horizontal connections between themselves and other Mexican women poets of their time. The construction of a lyrical sisterhood (to borrow a phrase from Kirkpatrick) becomes a frame for imagining a space through which women readers can become speakers and writers. For example, Mexican women poets explicitly dedicated poems to other women writers and to each other, and they used their art to explore their deep bonds. In 1845, Guadalupe Calderón published an elegy on the death of her brother, the distinguished poet and playwright Fernando Calderón, and dedicated it to her sister-in-law Josefa Letechipía de González. Josefa Letechipía de González, in turn, published an elegy about her friend Josefa Heraclia Badillo,[31] and published another poem dedicated to the Spanish poet Carolina Coronado (1851), in which she admiringly cites Sappho, Teresa of Avila, and Gertrudis Gómez de Avellaneda.[32] By writing to one other, invoking women writers of the past, and exploring their bonds of friendship, women poets made their plural voice a defining force within their own poetic subjectivity. In contrast, male authors of the romantic age such as José de Espronceda, Ignacio Rodríguez de Galván, William Wordsworth, and William Hazlitt did not have to frame their poetic self-expression in a collectivist manner; theirs was a Promethean poetry of the individual, of an exalted "author" whose identity was predicated on a solitary quest to know and celebrate the self.[33]

In addition to the ideology and aesthetic of Romanticism, and the rise of spaces for women's voices in Mexican print culture, class privilege and family networks constituted another way to authorize women's voices in print. Most of the women who achieved a modicum of literary recognition in the middle and second half of the century belonged to notable Mexican families, or to the families of the so-called *hombres de bien*.[34] The hombre de bien was a virtuous, honorable gentleman and "ideal citizen" belonging to an emergent middle class who prized public office, posts in the civil or military bureaucracy, and other professions associated with power and influence.[35] Networks of women's literary vocation and solidarity spread through the family ties of the hombres de bien, as well as through those of the urban and provincial elites. For example, one of the most celebrated Mexican poets of the first half of the nineteenth century was Fernando Calderón, and both his sister Guadalupe and his daughter Soledad were published poets.[36] In turn, Josefa Letechipía de González, apart from being Fernando Calderón's sister-in-law, was a close friend and collaborator of his sister Guadalupe, with whom she wrote poetry. Similarly, the daughter-in-law of Vicente García Torres, Josefina Pérez de García, was also a published poet, and Dolores Puigi de León, Catalina Zapata de Puig, and Albertina Puig all belonged to the same extended family, which included the novelist J. M. Puig Cassauranc.[37] Writing ran in families, and it was precisely in the families of the hombres de bien and the enlightened upper classes that women writers found a space to write, as well as the networks to connect with or mentor female relatives in the art of literary expression.

Lyrical Sisterhood and National Identity

Although prominent literary magazines intended for women readers and the publication of poetry by women had emerged by the 1840s, we have relatively few examples of poetry written by women about the U.S.-Mexican War of 1846–1848. One problem is that women poets had to compete for space in national publications with men whose patriotic poetry became increasingly visible during the war. Women's poetry was also often signed with initials only, when not presented anonymously, thus making attribution to women difficult if not impossible. For this reason, the poems I have recovered and selected for this chapter can be traced back to specific women's organizations and identifiable women poets of whom we have some biographical information. The poems illustrate the ways in which gender, voice, and literary convention shaped literary responses to a moment of grave national crisis and to the social status of women's voices.

Some poems by women about the war were printed in newspapers as marches or hymns, and although we do not know whether they were indeed sung, or to what music, or whether this labeling was just a literary conceit, their identification with song is significant because music was considered an extension of feminine refinement, sensibility, and beauty.[38] Poems inspired by musical form, such as "Marcha que la junta patriótica de Señoritas poblanas dedica al batallón de los libres" (July 5, 1846) and the "Himno dedicado a la sección militar que marcha a la villa del Paso a batir a los norteamericanos, por unas señoritas chihuahueñas" (October 18, 1846), also accent femininity insofar as they are put forward as works created by communities of women, a practice men did not share in this period.[39] The corporate nature of women's authorship may be seen in relation to politically sanctioned forms of women's service to the state in nineteenth-century Mexico, as in the case of women's charitable societies and patriotic juntas that supported the war effort. In 1846, for example, the government of Zacatecas sought to capitalize on women's willingness to aid the war effort by creating the Junta Patriótica de Beneficencia, through which its women members could solicit supplies, sew clothes and sheets, and support the stocking of hospitals and medical personnel at war.[40] Indeed, at least one of the women discussed here, Guadalupe Calderón, and possibly her coauthors, belonged to this junta.[41] The offering of a song to departing troops, then, may be read as yet another service, like the sewing of clothes and bandages, which women could provide to the war effort without compromising their domesticity.[42]

The authors of the "Marcha que la junta patriótica," the "Himno," and the individual author of the composition titled "Marcha guerrera, compuesta por una mexicana" (September 27, 1846), also published in *El Republicano,* all affirm a role for themselves as the inspiration and conscience of the war effort. Rather than directly challenging prevailing definitions of gender, these poets capitalized on their status as the "weaker" sex to inspire martial virility, demanding protection and promising recompense to men who were courageous in battle. The authors of the 1846 "Marcha que la junta patriótica," for example, conjured up the horror of the frail virgin transformed into the invader's concubine, situating women in the role of disempowered victim, along with children and the elderly: "The innocent child, and the weak elder / Already tremble as they watch the lost homeland; / The sinless virgin already hears the tyrant, / Collect the caresses of the surrendered slave."[43] This imagery, common in poetry by men, sought to instill horror in the reader and inspire a renewal of courage and self-sacrifice in the face of the invader.

If the foregoing poems deployed traditional definitions of gender to speak out on the war, one of two poems published on Friday, November 27, 1846, in *El Republicano*, provides us with a much more pointed and complex testimony about the war. Both poems, "A la patria" and "La tempestad," were signed by no fewer than three authors, which reinforces the idea of a lyrical sisterhood: Guadalupe Calderón (n.d.), Josefa Terán (n.d.), and "Una Zacatecana," the pseudonym of Josefa Letechipía de González (n.d.–1854).[44] Their names are accompanied by a line that reads: "Hacienda del Pabellón, septiembre 1846," which indicates that the poems were written in Aguascalientes, which was then a department of the state of Zacatecas.[45] Guadalupe Calderón, the sister of the writer Fernando Calderón, was a well-regarded poet in civic circles. Josefa Letechipía de González was the sister of both Manuela Letechipía, Fernando Calderon's wife, and Pedro Letechipía, whose valor in combat against the French twenty years after the U.S.-Mexican War garnered him a place in the *Rotonda de hombres ilustres*. Josefa Letechipía was active in the same circles as Guadalupe Calderón, reading patriotic and commemorative poems at public functions and providing support to the war effort against the United States.[46] The close relationship between the two women can be clearly seen in Guadalupe Calderón's elegiac farewell to her brother Fernando, "A la memoria de mi hermano," which was prominently dedicated to Josefa Letechipía and published in *El Museo Mexicano* in 1846. Letechipía's poetry, usually signed "Una Zacatecana," appeared on more than one occasion in *El Republicano*, and was also published in *El Album Mexicano* in 1849 and *La Semana de las Señoritas Mejicanas* in 1852. Because the Letechipías owned the Pabellón estate, it is fair to surmise that Guadalupe and Josefa Letechipía both resided there, along with the widow of Calderón, Manuela.[47] Less is known about Josefa Terán, but she was probably related to Jesús Terán (1821–1866), an Aguascalientes notable who came to national prominence as one of the ministers of Benito Juárez. In 1868 and 1871, doña Josefa and one doña Tomasa Terán took out loans in Aguascalientes, which suggests that Josefa managed her own household and financial affairs with Tomasa.[48]

The fact that "A la patria" and "La tempestad" were signed by three women, collectively, underlines their commitment to sharing a voice. In the brief and straightforward poem, "A la patria," the poets hit on the commonplace themes that characterized the vast majority of Mexican poetry written by men about the war, namely the Yankee invasion as a violation of the feminine homeland and the failures of Mexican unity. In contrast,

"La tempestad" breaks with contemporaneous poetry by men, by introducing coded criticisms of Mexico and Mexican masculinity. The poem takes the motif of the tempest, and its effects on a peaceful, pastoral scene, to allegorize the effects of the war on Mexico. The poem begins with the gathering of dark, stormy clouds, and the fearsome flashes of lightning and deafening sounds of thunder, which shake the earth to its foundation. The lightning, like the electric sparking of thought, illuminates the mind with peaks and reflections, diagramming ways of seeing and knowing the self in relation to the world. In these dramatic illuminations, the shadows of the branches of gigantic pine trees battle one another in the wind, evoking the image of warring antagonists. Then the rain comes in strong torrents, overflowing the river and destroying the fertile pastures and woods of yesterday, dragging heavy debris in its wake. The pastoral *locus amoenus*, with its cultivated fields and grazing lands, is overrun, drowned and crushed by boulders and water. In the poem's frame of personal subjectivity, the image of the destructive flood mirrors the power of uncontrolled emotion, which overruns the ordered self. This reading is corroborated by a later poem by Letechipía de González titled "A un rosal, el día de la partida de mi hijo," published in *El Album Mexicano* in 1849, in which the poet uses the same image of the torrent of water to describe the effects of sorrow on her heart upon the departure of her son.[49]

Yet "La tempestad" takes its exploration of the destructive power of the flood much further, ultimately linking it to the war, by suddenly introducing the image of a bull that has bolted into the hills, fleeing both the storm and its custodian, a "poor farmer" who finds his stable empty. The closing lines of the poem then amplify the image of absence and the experience of abandonment:

Hendiendo el aire, círculos describen	The innocent birds in their flight,
Las inocentes aves con su vuelo,	Cut the air, describing circles,
Y azoradas se vuelven a sus nidos	And return flustered to the nests
Que vieron sus amores lisongeros.	That once saw their fond wooing.
¡Oh grandioso espectáculo! ¡sublime!	Oh grandiose spectacle! Sublime!
¡Digno del grande autor del universo![50]	Worthy of the great author of the universe!

The flight of the bull, an archetype of masculine virility, mirrors the flight of love from the nests of the innocent feminine birds, whose abandonment leaves them flustered and uncertain, flying in circles. Abandoned to their empty nests, and to the destruction caused by the flood, the birds, like the orphaned women of defeated Mexico, mourn the loss of the earthly paradise of the motherland.

In "La tempestad," our poets have clearly indicted the martial virility of Mexico. Whereas their male contemporaries were quick to invoke the threat the United States posed to the safety of the virginal homeland as a propagandistic rallying cry, these poets represent the failure of Mexico and the abandonment of its women as something that has already occurred at the outset of the war. Indeed, the sublimity of the terrible scene in this poem allows for an unspoken margin of hope, as it is the very nature of the sublime to stir up the strongest emotions in the romantic subject. The form those emotions should take, and in what actions they should result, is not explicitly stated, but it may be safely surmised that self-sacrifice, valor, and resistance are the outcomes that the poets intended.

Josefa Heraclia Badillo's Dual Voice

Although the poet Josefa Heraclia Badillo (n.d.) was a very active poet during the war, appearing repeatedly in the pages of *El Republicano* between 1846 and 1847, much less is known about her than about Calderón and Letechipía de González. Letechipía de González's elegiac poem "Ofrenda a la memoria de la señorita Doña Josefa Badillo" indicates that the two women knew each other, or at least that Letechipía de González admired her poetry. Little else is known about her, other than the fact the she was a signatory of a women's petition against the "tolerancia de cultos" in 1856.[51] Of the six poems by Badillo that appeared in the pages of *El Republicano* between 1846 and 1847, only one, "Inquietud" (March 20, 1847), lends itself to an allegorical reading about the ongoing war.[52] In this poem, Badillo develops the theme of the tempest that we have seen already, but to a much more contradictory end, without criticizing the nation-state or the martial virility of Mexico. Rather, her poem uses the conventions of feminine sentimentality to map her struggle to find a coherent voice in a moment of national crisis. The resulting poem is split in two parts, each one designating a separate theme, problem, and resolution.

The poem opens with the poet affirming her sadness over the absence of her beloved, a sadness that is driving her to an early death. The poetic voice declares that it is her mission to suffer, to die of feeling, even going as far as to wish that she not be reunited with her beloved, because it would interrupt her defining sorrow: "I will not see you before I die, / because to see you again, I'd be glad / and my sad mission would not be fulfilled / if I expired less unhappy."[53] Her life is a "desert of thorns," whereas her beloved lives the easy life, picking flowers on the easy path he travels. She has given up on being reunited with this man and muses that she may be lowered into her grave very soon. Up to here, the poem fits comfortably in the well-established canon of sentimental poetry, particularly poems inspired by Germain de Stael's popular *Corinne, or Italy* (1807), in which the titular protagonist, a latter-day Sappho, famously renounces her happiness in a much-imitated, sorrowful farewell titled "The Song of Corinne."[54] The focus of "Inquietud," then, is the sorrowful, female self that seeks to immolate herself on the altar of her own suffering. Abandoned by her beloved, the poetic voice embraces melancholy and solitude to realize herself.

It is at this point that the poem splits in two, effectively twisting itself into a different kind of thematic formulation. With the conjunction *pero*, Badillo introduces the fear that the object of her love is in danger while on a sea journey:

Pero . . . [*sic*] tu acaso en este instante mismo	But . . . [*sic*] you yourself perhaps in this very instant
Te ves cercado de peligros mil;	Find yourself surrounded by a thousand dangers;
Y solo te separan del abismo	And nothing more than a plank and a mast [*sic*]
Un tablón miserable y el mastil! . . . [*sic*]	Separate you from the abyss! . . .

She imagined the tempest lowering a dark, threatening veil over his head and fear filling his previously peaceful heart, driving him to beg for clemency from the heavens. The poetic "I" calls out to the imperiled traveler, calling him "her good, her light, her love and her sweet brother," and then she sees him perish in the storm. There is little consolation in the fact that his death is only imagined, however, because the beloved is soon to depart on a sea voyage, and the poetic voice fears that harm will come to him. Specifically, she envisions a bandit with a bloodied dagger stabbing him in the breast. The poem closes with Badillo calling out to her beloved that she would rather never see him again than have him risk his life by leaving the homeland.

The duality of "Inquietud" is at first quite perplexing. In its first movement, the poem is anchored in the conviction that the mournful poetic voice has been abandoned by the male subject, whose life is lackadaisical. The "I" turns away from this betrayer to embrace the prospect of death. Yet the second part of the poem reconfigures this relationship significantly. Now the poetic voice situates herself not in opposition to her beloved, but as a caring and anxious protector who is consumed by anxiety over his safety. Her references to him as "her good, her life, and her brother," and her praise for his inherent goodness, introduce intensely amorous and fraternal feelings into the poem. Whereas in the first half of the poem, the poet had turned away from her beloved to embrace solitude, she now associates her beloved's presence with his safety and survival, and with her happiness. The focus is not on her own, solitary death, but on the prospect of her beloved's death at sea or at the hand of an assassin. The poetic voice turns away from death to embrace life, but this gesture is fraught with tension, with disquiet (hence the title of the poem), as terrifying visions of her beloved's death at sea haunt her.

One way to resolve the tension between the two parts of the poem is to read it as an unconscious revenge fantasy, in which the sorrow induced by the man in the first half of the poem results in a "tempest" and an assassin who threatens to exterminate him for his mistreatment of the speaker. Tempests are indeed a romantic figuring of emotion unleashed, and as such, "Inquietud" may be read in relation to a fundamental tension in the poem between repression (mournful sentimentalism) and unconscious rage (the apparition of disembodied, imaginary threats to the beloved). However, here I propose a more historical reading, one that maintains rather than resolves the tension between both parts of the poem through the suggestion of allegory.

When the poetic voice refers to her beloved as a brother, linking his endangerment to his departure from the "sweet homeland" and from the "patriot grounds" of Mexico, she begins to suggest that the emotional world of the poem has shifted from sentimental love to fraternal love and patriotic sentiment. The invocation of a sea voyage and a tempest as the matrix of her fear is also significant, because such maritime imagery has a long tradition of political symbolism, hearkening all the way back to Plato's *The Republic*, in which the Greek philosopher explored the question of educated elites and political power through the metaphor of the "Ship of State."[55] The image appears in other Mexican poems about the war as well as in a political cartoon published in the satirical newspaper *El Calavera* in February 1847, which shows a ship called *La República Mexicana* being tossed on its side by waves as a mournful figure with a skull head watches the shipwreck.[56] It is not a great leap to associate "Inquietud" with this more explicit body of war literature, especially when we consider that the Yankee invaders, commonly referred to as murderous savages and barbarians in Mexican poems about the war, are a good allegorical match to the cold-blooded bandit who appears in the poem.[57]

Unlike the other poets discussed here, Badillo does not use sisterhood as a predicate for lessening her alienation and suffering. Although she remains isolated and unsettled, her poem enacts an important questioning of the thematic conventions associated with women's poetry. Her poem documents a journey from a comfortable, predictable place in which suffering and death are not frightening, but rather are welcome, familiar, and fulfilling of the self's desires, to a terrifying position of uncertainty and very real fear. It is as if Badillo had traced the artifice of the conventions of a certain kind of controlled and formulaic elegiac poem associated with femininity, to contrast it with something more immediate and dynamic: dreams and visions of disaster, and of woman's essential powerlessness to protect life in a moment of national catastrophe. In other words, literature in the sense of artifice gives way to an act of witness that documents the interior landscape of fear. Badillo does not go very far to make her engagement with the war explicit or accessible, but her poem dramatically displays the predicament of a poetic voice constrained by thematic and stylistic conventions associated with femininity.

Conclusion: A Poetics of Negotiation

I have sketched the reasons women's voices began to emerge in Mexican print culture shortly before and during the U.S.-Mexican War, as well as the ways women poets addressed the conflict. It is clear that the war afforded an opportunity to test the boundaries of acceptable women's discourse and to symbolically intervene in debates about Mexican politics and the war. Despite the fragmentary record that documents their voices, the extant pieces of their works attest to deep convictions and to a commitment to express those views publicly, despite the constraints imposed on them by a patriarchal society and culture. Indeed, women writers reinterpreted the very constraints that limited them as writing subjects—such as the association of women with heightened states of sensitivity and fragility—to claim a sentimental, nationalist poetics for themselves. Yet it was a different kind of poetics than that which their male contemporaries shared. As mediated by their marginal position in the public sphere, and by their strong sense of sisterhood, women's poetry was best situated to go beyond hollow and predictable calls for victory and sacrifice. Their poetry was a poetry of negotiation, challenge, and plural voice; it was a form of discourse that was fully self-aware of its precarious authority in the arena of nationalist debate, and as such, more nuanced and conditional in its expression. The Mexican women writers of the U.S.-Mexican War were spokeswomen for Mexico but also for a vision of womanhood defined by solidarity, mentorship, and poetic creation.

Notes

A shorter version of this essay appeared in *Latin American Research Review* 47, no. 1 (2012): 3–15. Permission to republish here is gratefully acknowledged. I thank the anonymous peer reviewers of this book and LARR, as well as Áurea Toxqui for improving this chapter with insightful comments and corrections. I also thank Michael Matthews, Stephen Neufeld, Gustavo Pellón, and Rick Todhunter.

1. Mariano Otero, "Considerations on the Political and Social Situation of the Mexican Republic in the Year of 1847," in *The U.S.-Mexican War: A Binational Reader*, ed. Christopher Conway, trans. Gustavo Pellón (Indianapolis, IN: Hackett Publishing, 2010), 136–39.

2. See Pedro Santoni, *Mexicans at Arms: Puro Federalists and the Politics of War, 1845–1848* (Fort Worth, TX: Texas Christian University Press, 1995); and Michael Costeloe, *The Central Republic in Mexico, 1835–1846: Hombres de Bien in the Age of Santa Anna* (Cambridge: Cambridge University Press, 2002).

3. For the period spanning Independence and the Reforma Movement, twentieth-century Mexican literary histories privilege writers whose poetry and fiction were collected in book form after the U.S.-Mexican War of 1846–1848. See, for example, Julio Jiménez Rueda, *Historia de la literatura mexicana* (México: Polis y Cultura, 1928); Carlos González Peña, *Historia de la literatura mexicana* (México: Cultura y Polis, 1940); and David William Foster, *Mexican Literature: A History* (Austin: University of Texas Press, 1994).

4. See Shelley Streebey, *American Sensations: Class, Empire, and the Production of Popular Culture* (Berkeley: University of California Press, 2002); Amy Greenberg, *Manifest Manhood and the Antebellum American Empire* (Cambridge: Cambridge University Press, 2005); Andrea Tinnemeyer, *Identity Politics of the Captivity Narrative after 1848* (Lincoln: University of Nebraska Press, 2006); Robert Walker Johannsen, *To the Halls of Montezuma: The Mexican War in the American Imagination* (New York: Oxford University Press, 1985).

5. Streebey, *American Sensations*, 100.

6. See Streebey, 100: ". . . plots that foreground the crossing of gender boundaries and frustrated or successful international romances manifestly display fears about the boundaries of the white republic and U.S. expansion into Mexico."

7. Guillermo Prieto, "Un momento de formalidad. A mi Patria" [A Solemn Moment. To My Homeland], in *U.S.-Mexican War*, ed. Conway, trans. Pellón, 176–78; "los ¡hurras! de victoria / del que empapó con su sangre sus hogares!"

8. Prieto, "Un momento de formalidad," 178; "¡Serán nuestras angustias sus placeres" writes Prieto, "de nuestro amor los hijos, sus esclavos; / y les darán solaz nuestras mujeres / entre los restos, ¡ay! de nuestros bravos . . . violado lecho / de la esposa y la virgen ultrajada."

9. Ibid.

10. Notable examples of the trope of endangered women in Mexican poetry of the war may be found in several poems published in *El Monitor Republicano*: two poems by Guillermo Prieto titled "A mi Patria" (May 30 and June 3, 1846), "Gratitud eterna: Soneto" by P. M. G. (December 30, 1846), "Veracruz y el General Scott" (April 11, 1847), "Mi ruego a Dios" by Manuel Henaro (April 15, 1847), and "Al Ser Supremo" by A. N. (May 24, 1847).

11. Manuel Carpio, "México en 1847," in *Poesías del Sr. Dr. Don Manuel Carpio con su biografía escrita* (México: La Enseñanza, 1880), 242–47. The image of the violation of a feminine, unprotected Mexico takes center stage in a novel titled *El Monedero* by Nicolás Pizarro Suárez, published thirteen years after the war. In the novel, there's a graphic scene in which a U.S. soldier breaks into a Mexican home and uses his rifle butt to beat an old lady to death before raping her daughter.

12. Jesús Velasco Márquez argues for using print journalism as a voice of "public opinion." By "popular" culture, however, I am referring to cultural expressions not associated with print culture, but with orality. See Jesús Velasco Márquez, *La guerra del 47 y la opinión pública (1845–1848)* (México: SEP, 1975).

13. Antonio García Cubas, *El Libro de mis Recuerdos* (México: Imprenta de García Cubas, 1904), 439–40.

14. The English translations provided here are from "La pasadita," in *U.S.-Mexican War*, ed. Conway, trans. Pellón, 167–69; the original Spanish is from García Cubas, *El Libro de mis Recuerdos*, 439.

15. Alvaro Custodio, *El Corrido Popular Mexicano* (México: Ediciones Júcar, 1975), 31.

16. For more on this corrido, see Herón Pérez Martínez and Alvarez Pérez Ochoa, *Cancionero michoacano (1830–1840): Canciones, coplas y corridos* (Zamora: Colegio de Michoacan, 200), 107. The themes of resistance and mockery have made "La pasadita" an enduring corrido capable of retooling and adapting itself to a different war: the French Intervention of 1864. Other extant transcriptions of the corrido replace U.S. soldiers with French soldiers. See Laura Herrera Serna's *México en Guerra, 1846–1848: Perspectivas regionales* (México, D.F.: Consejo Nacional para la Cultura y las Artes: Museo Nacional de las Intervenciones, 1997), 83; Antonio Avitia Hernández, *Corrido Histórico Mexicano: Voy a Cantarles la Historia*, tomo 1 (México: Porrúa, 1997–1998), 77–85.

17. My reading of this corrido, specifically of its linguistic components and ambiguous treatment of gender is drawn from invaluable comments that Aurea Toxqui offered me on an early draft of this chapter.

18. See Silvia Marina Arrom, *The Women of Mexico City, 1790–1857* (Stanford, CA: Stanford University Press, 1985); Bram Dijkstra, *Idols of Perversity; Fantasies of Feminine Evil in Fin-de-siécle Culture* (Oxford: Oxford University Press, 1986), 3–24; Montserrat Galí Boadella, *Historias del bello sexo: La introducción del Romanticismo en México* (México: UNAM, 2002), 95–97.

19. See also William French, "Prostitutes and Guardian Angels," *Hispanic American Historical Review* 72, no. 4 (November 1992): 529–31.

20. Isidro Rafael Gondra, "Prospecto," in *Semanario de las señoritas mejicanas* (México: Imprenta de Vicente García Torres, 1841), 15.

21. Ibid., 14.

22. For circulation figures and discussion, see Emilie Bergmann and Seminar on Feminism and Culture in Latin America, *Women, Culture and Politics in Latin America* (Berkeley: University of California Press, 1990), 173–82.

23. Susan Kirkpatrick, *Las Románticas: Women Writers and Subjectivity in Spain* (Berkeley: University of California Press, 1989), 8–10.

24. Ibid., 8.

25. María Esther Pérez Salas C., "Nación e imagen. La litografía en busca de una identidad: 1837–1855," in *La construcción del discurso nacional en México, un anhelo persistente*, ed. Nicole Girón (México: Instituto Mora, 2007), 168–69.

26. Vicente García Torres, *Panorama de las señoritas mejicanas* (México: Imprenta de Vicente García Torres, 1842), 1–2.

27. Ibid., "Valor en las mujeres," 129.

28. Ibid., "Biografías de mujeres celebres," 289–94.

29. See María de la Salud García, "Invitation to Mexicans," in *U.S.-Mexican War*, ed. Conway, trans. Pellón, 114–15. For more on María de la Salud García, see Oscar Mata, *La novela corta mexicana en el sigo XIX* (Mexico: Universidad Nacional Autónoma de México/Universidad Nacional Autónoma Metropolitana-Azcapotzalco, 2003), 38; Galí Boadella, *Historias del bello sexo*, 375.

30. M, "A la señorita autora de una invitación a los mexicanos," *El Republicano* (20 Septiembre 1846), 3.

31. See José María Vigil, *Poetisas mexicanas* (México: Oficina tipográfica de la Secretaría de Fomento, 1893), 179–80.

32. For a discussion of women's friendships, poetry, and Sappho, see Galí Boadella, *Historias del bello sexo*, 377–85; Kirkpatrick, *Las Románticas*, 79–80; and Patrick Vincent, *The Romantic Poetess: European Culture, Politics and Gender* (Lebanon, NH: University Press of New England, 2004), 52–60.

33. See Daniel Shanahan, *Toward a Genealogy of Individualism* (Amherst: University of Massachussets Press, 1992), 94; Pablo Mora, "El sueño criollo: optimismo y desengaño en la poesía de la primera mitad del siglo XIX," in *Actas del XII Congreso de la Asociación Internacional de Hispanistas* (Birmingham, U.K.: Department of Hispanic Studies, 1998), 128–35.

34. Lilia Granillo Vászquez and Esther Hernández Palacios, "El siglo de oro de las poetisas mexicanas," in *La República de las letras: Asomos a la cultura escrita del México decimonónico*, vol. 2: *Publicaciones periódicas y otros impresos*, ed. Belém Clark de Lara and Elisa Speckman (México: UNAM, 2005), 121–52.

35. Michael Costeloe, *The Central Republic in Mexico, 1835–1846: Hombres de Bien in the Age of Santa Anna* (Cambridge: Cambridge University Press, 2002), 18.

36. Granillo Vásquez and Hernández Palacios, 134.

37. Ibid.

38. Galí Boadella, *Historias del bello sexo*, 187.

39. A thorough review of all of the poems published in the newspapers *El Republicano* and *El Monitor Republicano* during the U.S.-Mexican War supports this assertion. See "Marcha guerrera compuesta por una mexicana," *El Republicano* (27 Septiembre 1846), 3; "Marcha que la junta patriótica de Señoritas poblanas dedica al

After the Revolution of Ayutla (1855) ousted Santa Anna from power for the final time, Liberal leaders sought to transform the nation along principles enshrined in the Constitution of 1857. The constitution aimed to introduce liberal values that would undermine the colonial structures that remained such as *fueros* (rights and obligations designated to various social groups), communal property, and the power of the Catholic Church. The implementation of these reforms would be interrupted by the Conservatives and their newfound ally, Napoleon III, who installed the Austrian archduke Ferdinand Maximilian on the throne of Mexico between 1862 and 1867. After the defeat of the usurper emperor, Benito Juárez and his liberal followers went about implementing the spirit of their constitution, seeking to make the nation modern. In a period called the Restoration, between 1867 and 1876, leaders began a process of consolidating power and rebuilding Mexico. The liberal policies they introduced would reach their climax under the dictatorship of Porfirio Díaz (1876–1911). Examining the poetry and ballads written by military men early in this era, Stephen Neufeld shows that these individuals' verses often straddled a line between traditional and modern values and, at times, either celebrated or mocked the regime's nation-building efforts.

"A los valientes soldados del ejército de Occidente al regresar triunfantes a esta capital"

"To the valiant soldiers of the Western Army upon their triumphant return to this capital"

Soneto*

Tostado el rostro y con la frente erguida	Sunburned visages and with head held high
Regresa a sus hogares el guerrero;	The warrior returns to home;
El orgullo humilló del extranjero,	The foreigner's pride humbled,
Y humilló a la traición aborrecida.	And the treasonous dog humiliated.

* Anonymous, *El Globo* (August 8, 1867), 3.

De México infeliz cuanto querida.
Las cadenas rompió con fuerte acero,
Haciendo respetar del mundo entero
A la que antes se viera envilecida.

For unhappy Mexico, so dear.
The chains broken by strong steel,
Making the entire world respect
What was before debased.

¡Gloria al valor! ¡Al mexicano gloria!
Ciña el laurel la frente del soldado
Que al porvenir legara su memoria; . . .

Glory to the brave! To the Mexican glory!
Tighten the laurel to the soldier's brow
The future bequeathed to his memory; . . .

Que su nombre inmortal quede grabado
De nuestra patria en la inmortal historia;
Y en ambos continentes admirado.

That his immortal name remain engraved
In the immortal history of our patria;
And be in both continents admired.

Guadalajara, Junio 21 de 1867.

"A los heroicos soldados del ejército de occidente, en su entrada a Guadalajara"

"To the heroic soldiers of the Western Army, on their entrance to Guadalajara"

Soneto[*]

¡Qué diferencia cuando entraba un día
El francés opresor del mexicano,
Atando sus cadenas inhumano
A tus pies delicados, patria mía!

What a difference when he came one day
The French oppressor of the Mexican,
Tying their inhuman chains
To your delicate feet, my patria!

[*] Anonymous, *El Globo* (August 8, 1867), 3.

Entonces el soldado se veía
En la sierra luchar contra el
tirano,
Con esa fé y esfuerzo soberano
Que allá en el pecho de Guerrero
ardía.

El estranjero huyó; se alza
altanera
El águila de Anáhuac, y se
mece
Viendo a sus pies el monte y la
pradera,
Donde entre escombros el laurel
florece,
Y sacude su copa placentera
La tierna oliva que a su sombra
crece.

Then the soldier saw
Fighting in the hills against the
tyrant,
With this faith and sovereign effort
That burned in his Warrior
chest.

The foreigner fled; and haughty
rose
The eagle of Anáhuac, and he
sways
Seeing at his feet the mountains
and the prairie,
Where among rubble the laurel
blooms,
And raises his cup in pleasure to
The tender olive that grows in its
shadow.

Guadalajara, Julio 21 de 1867

Discussion Questions

1. How did these sonnet writers envision Mexico's place in the world changing with the defeat of Emperor Maximilian's forces?
2. What images in these poems invoke national pride through classical or indigenous elements?
3. What experiences do the poems refer to that might shape Mexican perceptions of foreigners, and how?

CHAPTER TWO

The Sly Mockeries of Military Men

Corridos and Poetry as Critical Voice for the Porfirian Army

Stephen Neufeld

The patio of the barracks rang with amateur song most ordinary nights in Mexico's late nineteenth century. Improvised and regimental instruments accompanied the enthusiastic men and women of the army as they entertained themselves performing corridos (folk songs) about life, love, and war. Meanwhile, in small chambers some three stories above, young officers set pen to paper creating verse and poetry as an exercise in cultivation and culture. Quiet reflections of their own were nonetheless interrupted or perhaps inspired by the boisterous tunes that floated up from below. The unique mixtures of these peoples, and their verses, sheds light on the inner worlds of the soldier and his society.

In an era of accelerated change, the military men of President Porfirio Díaz (1876–1911) expressed themselves in various ways, from poems about their lives to singing corridos in the barracks. In these ways they illustrated how they saw themselves, and how they understood *mexicanidad* (Mexicanness). In both genres, the military men expressed ideas about the nation's legitimacy and power, its genealogy and future, and the place of masculinity and sentiment in their society. Officers strived to portray themselves as both *hombres de espada* and *hombres de pluma*, men of sword and of quill.[1] They presented poems as homage gifts (*obsequios*) to their officers and wrote them in honor of important personages. Their writings awkwardly dealt with the need to preserve their view of history and tradition, while at the same time lauding modern changes and science. Like most of their countrymen, the military officers also grappled with making sense of new technologies, emerging classes, and increasing globalization, all of which had direct effect on the ways in which the army operated and saw itself. Likewise, ordinary soldiers sang along with early corridos, and used ambiguities in their lyrics to mock official army narratives.[2] The songs dismissed the ideals of the regime, and asserted a different, often lower-class, understanding of masculine norms, nationalist sentiments, and racial identities. By comparing the expressions of these different echelons an intriguing picture emerges on how the nation was imagined. On one side, the military as an institution officially dedicated its efforts to a project of positivist modernizing and secular order, yet on the other, an alternative vision from within the ranks demonstrated the distance between rhetorical modernity and actual circumstances. The verses in both forms also communicated a degree of shared experiences in their repudiation of foreign elements, and their adherence to expressing mexicanidad in the national tongue. The shared language conventions exposed a common vocabulary with a mostly unified imagining of the *patria* (fatherland) invoked in terms of shared historical experience.[3]

This chapter sets out an examination of nation formation between 1879 and 1903 around three thematic areas: the military's role in society, its construction of a historical genealogy and future, and its vision of gendered meanings. Verse as a form of collective memory wove these elements into a hybrid narrative. This was represented in a number of corridos that addressed identity and challenged official narratives. The tales told in the folk song reflected some ideas similar to the poetry, but in contrast added ideas about injustice that resonated more with the lower classes, *los de abajo*.[4] These performances revived the common soldier's understanding of issues of race, of mexicanidad, and of society through a reiteration, and often a mockery, of elite pretensions. Complementing this were officers' poems that sought to create a community based on shared ideas and traditions that attempted to define modern progress, and to define the place of the military against civilian life. The majority of these officers, it must be noted, did not represent a view from an elite or a top-down approach, but rather they held a less defined position as intermediary between "higher" culture and the troops.[5] Seeking definition, their poems revolved around a sense of identity locating Mexican circumstances within a long historical trajectory. They sought to set their lives against a historical memory of military exploits, tragic losses, and classical iconography. At the same time, they optimistically pointed to scientific progress as inevitable success.

These two genres worked together in expressing Porfirian society from the perspective of ordinary military men. If career officers demonstrated an aspiration to explain the nation from their own perspective, so too did the common trooper. Real, or even functional, consensus on the legitimacy and meaning of Mexico did not materialize until late in the Porfiriato, if then. The subtle undercurrents of humor and mockery, far more than mere weapons of the weak, defined the fault lines that created a persistent weakness in the national hegemony.[6] The corridos and poems bring out the particular preoccupations and pretensions of performers, audiences, and writers whose side of the story scholars have not yet examined. These verses are narrative structures that highlighted social values and fears; they bring to light the nightmares of the lettered city, a sentimental masculinity, and the opportunity for sly mockeries of social strata.[7]

Taken as private and public transcripts, verses in comparison reveal social relations of power, and moments of collective memory.[8] Within the verses lay disguised public dissent—areas of conflict with the process of forming hegemony. The hidden transcript is, in James Scott's words, the condition for resistance, not the substitute.[9] This tension, in its own right, makes up much of the nuance in nationalism and national identity. It forms a constructive element as it describes modernity, gender, and caste or race.[10] The voice from the lower echelons provides an inherent counterpoint to hegemony, but more significantly it preserves a group's collective memory, that which constitutes its identity. This preservation permits future resistance to power, and "makes modernity stutter" as elites haltingly deal with different interpretations and demands from below.[11] Where Scott contends that hidden transcripts primarily are holders of meaning "between revolts," here I contend that verses are an active part of a cultural process of reconciling a multiplicity of visions of history and nation.[12] In Mexico these represented a clash of postcolonial and neocolonial reactions articulated within genres of verse, reflecting different concerns and attitudes toward where the nation had arrived.[13] Where some poetry adhered to a postcolonial narrative that justified the overall national trajectory as moving beyond the Spanish colonial period into something new, other poems joined their voice to the corridos' more neocolonial outlook, one that questioned not the direction but the continuous experience of nationhood as one of continuing domination or exploitation. Together, these views summarized contemporary imaginings of mexicanidad.

The Songs and Verses of the Barracks

There was considerable contrast between these poems and songs, in how they were created, deployed, and performed. Problems abound in analyzing or comparing these sources. The officers published their works for a specific and often limited readership, and only occasionally read them aloud as public performance. At times, financial reasons motivated officers rather than sincere artistic aspirations. Moreover, the addition of music to live performances of the corridos potentially changed the meanings in subtle or powerful ways; sadly the counterpoint to lyrics is nearly impossible to uncover—each singer, each setting, each audience experienced the music differently.[14] Pace, volume, and emphasis in the music could alter meanings in ways that printed lyrics cannot capture. Equally, as Michael Matthews argues in this volume, the images on accompanying broadsheets also had the potential to change the messages of the music. Furthermore, while the poems generally are attributable and their circulation somewhat understood, Chris Frazer has pointed out that corridos prove much more elusive.[15] They were often anonymous and undated, and what records remain of the possible lyrics came from later publications and so these were likely different from the actual wording of those songs that troops sang in barracks.

That said, what can be drawn from these sources? Why set two so different genres side by side? According to James Scott's study of hidden and public transcripts, loaded sources such as these (as problematic as they may seem), in combination offer many insights into power relations, and as such, into the nature of collective memory and the fundamentals of national

Figure 2.1. La gorra del cuartel. José Guadalupe Posado.

identity. As genres, they also represent two specific frames of communicating that have been little studied in Mexico.

Music filled the Porfirian barracks by night. As tunes spilled into streets, neighbors recalled decades later how much they enjoyed the army bands.[16] The military bands also frequently performed for the public in arranged settings, but they were equally ready to accompany soldiers for less stilted material, chiefly corridos.[17] Whether with instruments or not, men sang in the evenings and free times in garrison or on campaign. Their sad songs of tragedy and betrayal, of bandits and bullfighters, brought the outside world into army life.[18] The music of the lower classes represented their stylistic taste, and also held deeper social meanings as they channeled rage and hostility into group solidarity.[19] Of course, there were occasional critics: one officer locked his band in a room and shot at their feet as a dance lesson, but his actions were likely due more to alcohol abuse than genuine critique.[20] But the songs that allowed men and women the taste of home gave sufficient reason to sing. They were an acceptable way to express emotions, to vent loneliness, and were an important measure of cultural capital—every unit desired a good singer. And further, in the repertoire certain songs held special appeal as they spoke to military life, and significantly, challenged it through subversive lyrics and subtle mockeries. Poetry built on this expression for a different audience, adding to a set of stories that articulated nation and gender.

Society considered the writing of verses as an essential element of cultural or social capital for men of the nonworking classes. That gentlemen of the middle classes, officers or not, would express themselves in poetry in the last years of the nineteenth century is hardly a surprise.[21] In their world of cultivated salon gatherings, poetry was part of an expected modern skill set. As one example, memoirs of officers such as Victor Salvador Alvarez spoke fondly of literary discussions in family settings and revealed a great breadth of reading materials that had shaped conversations between military men in a context of humor and erudite competition.[22] In contrast to the argument of Luis González, the distinction between men of the sword and men of the pen was never a neat, clear divide, and more of a political fiction of rivals vying for influence over the president.[23] Eschewing narrow political definitions that sorted all of the elite into either José Yves Limantour's *científico* or Bernardo Reyes's *militar* parties, one finds that officers generally represented a group of reasonably educated and literate men with significant interest and knowledge in modern sciences and literature.

Modern expectations of the officer classes included considerable schooling at the best military colleges of Mexico, or abroad in France, Germany,

Britain, and the United States.[24] As a matter of course the students learned mathematics, engineering, and logistics, but they also spent considerable classroom effort mastering languages and history. Guillermo Prieto's *Lecciones de historia patria* was among the many works assigned at the Colegio Militar that sought to instill in them a love of the nation rooted in a historical vision of liberal triumph, punctuated with his verses.[25] And from the ranks of these impressionable youths and from the army in general, great literary talents appeared, including authors such as Ignacio Manuel Altamirano and Manuel Payno. The writers also continued to emerge during the Porfirian era, as Francisco Luis Urquizo and Heriberto Frías attest.[26] For officers keenly aware of their social position, poetry provided a creative outlet where they could express their caste identity during a period when the army faced no external threat to justify its budget or importance.

The military poem went beyond the task of expressing sentimental masculinity for socially mobile officers, and helped construct an imagining of the nation, much as the corrido did for others.[27] Verse was a common feature in military journals and periodicals exchanged internationally with other armies and distributed nationally as required reading for officers. The mandatory nature of this appreciation may have lessened enthusiasm, but it signals a concerted attempt by the military to create a more cultivated or cultured officer class. By engaging in this literary production, Mexicans could give voice to an alternate vision of their nascent nationalism, whether this had been the military's intent or not.

In poem and corrido alike, artists looked to the past to inspire their progress.[28] They sought heroes and meaningful narratives, making history an ally for self-identification. As Matthew Esposito has demonstrated, these decades saw the creation of a state theater built around the deaths and funerals of the old guard of officers who were passing away almost daily.[29] These men would now be eulogized in poetry and monuments as a matter of course, and remembered in songs. As the elderly slipped into history, the regime sidled nearer to modernity. Their positivist-inspired public works and monuments were inaugurated with verses as equally tender as that of any general's funeral cortege. As a national project, this expressive ceremonial drive enhanced the apparent legitimacy of the regime and nation, and not coincidentally, featured at its visual and aural forefront the uniformed military men.

Writing verses for these carefully choreographed affairs gave young ambitious officers an opportunity to display their modern, cosmopolitan erudition. With education and eloquence, the new generation proved itself worthy of replacing or even surpassing the old guard of crude veterans now passing away. Ideally, the new officers no longer pissed in the palace or sketched dirty pictures on barracks walls.[30] A message of *civilismo*, belief in the civilizing ethos, accompanied the elaborate eulogy poems that remembered and celebrated the disappearing traditional world.[31] The poets wrote a narrative of change anchored in meaningful sacrifice; they found consolation in a shared commemoration of the dead, whose lives had permitted the patria to exist.[32]

Yet poetry and song was also an everyday affair. Not all had the skill or time to write long articles or essays, but a verse could be relatively quickly fashioned for any occasion and held the appeal of sentimental sincerity. Raw recruits, young cadets, and decrepit veterans alike shared verse as a way of commemorating and building a shared memory. These stories helped to cement bonds of solidarity between military men.[33] They bridged often-significant divides of social class and life experience where army politics and nepotism had at times created factions. They also connected those privileged to have fought formal wars against invaders to those whose experience was often of peacetime or quelling less glorious rebellions and uprisings. [34] As such, a type of hegemony often lacking at a national level might be mitigated by a show of military unity in shared literary work. In contrast to the corrido, some poets offered verses as homage (gifts referred to as "obsequios") to superiors, at times under a degree of peer pressure, under orders, or as a substitute for expensive cash payments expected from subordinates. As an artistic form, nonetheless, both genres comprised the staking out and making lines of community allegiance and emotional expression in an institution not known for such. The poems and the music published in the army at least represented an effort in civilized discourse.[35]

The verses that built a traditional military community relied strongly on conventions of language and history. They sought to inculcate or express a love of patria and the army, perhaps as counterpoint to the inculcation of hatred toward the "Other" common to the training at arms under hardened drill sergeants.[36] The verses' power derived in part from a shared vocabulary and the use of what might be called buzzwords, terms repeated from one poem to the next, as references that marked the poem and poet as martial. The shared language conventions exposed a common vocabulary with a mostly unified imagining of the patria, invoked in terms of shared historical experience.[37] This partially explains their frequent use of the idea of the classical world and its connections to the present as a show of education and respect for traditions, whether they be invented or not.[38] A class identity, or caste, was reinforced by the consensus on how to discuss themselves—even the occasional ironic twist merely added to the acceptance of the terms of discussion.[39]

Roughly, verses may be divided into those focused on the military community and its history, the rise of scientific modernity, and those that sought to connect soldier and society—although in all cases some overlap is inevitable. Tales of war and its effects appeared more rarely in poems than in corridos, but with a poignancy and sophistication in vast contrast to the occasional, and sometimes awful, love poems. Before discussing the development of a historic-national vision and the sentimental masculine underpinnings that challenged it, verses that directly established or rejected the regime's narrative provide some context.

Of National Narratives and Legitimate Violence

Governments throughout the nineteenth century had mostly proved unable to instill in the citizenry a strong sense of national belonging or identity, and had not manufactured a genuine consensus about legitimate rule in all corners of the country. For example, bandit stories, according to Frazer, demonstrated the inability at the highest levels of government to control the image and meaning of Mexico that reached foreigners, singers, and the poor.[40] Bandit literature may have failed in this endeavor throughout Latin America due to the nature of its subject and its inherent potential for interpretative use by the marginalized (for example, as critique of policing, or in the emergence of folk-hero brigands).[41]

In contrast to what Juan Pablo Dabove calls "the nightmare of the lettered city," officer poets participated in the creation (albeit amateur and halting) of a national counterdiscourse, or new hegemony, that sought to define mexicanidad for the dawning century.[42] The patriotic rhetoric and focus of most soldier-poets turned away from the teratological bandit tales and optimistically made the nation into a protagonist. The country became the sympathetic victor rising from troubled beginnings. Considering Mexico's turbulent nineteenth century, this also situated soldiers as those that forged the nation. Since the Porfiriato was relatively less violent, especially in terms of participating in formal wars and not simply putting down local rebellions, it seemed almost necessary for the writers to remind readers and listeners about the importance of military men. And in this vein, commemoration held powerful potentials. At the same time, verse could challenge official ideas of the military's importance. Some songs and poems wrestled with the contradictions between the regime's liberal rhetoric and its practiced ruthless oppression, particularly in the case of executions and massacres.

Tales of betrayal and injustice had particular appeal to the performers and audiences of corridos, and in the earliest years of the Porfiriato some songs directly criticized the perceived tyranny of the new regime. "De los mártires de Veracruz" (Of the Martyrs of Veracruz) depicted the aftermath of a small-scale naval mutiny in the port at Veracruz that forces under General Luis Terán brutally suppressed in 1879. The corrido, for its part, portrayed the uprising as brave resistance and saw the execution of the participants as nothing less than criminal and arbitrary:

El general Luis Terán,	The General Luis Terán
con inaudita crueldad,	with unprecedented cruelty,
por complacer a un tirano	to please a tyrant
ejecutó a unos valientes.	executed some brave men.
Infame gobernador,	Infamous governor,
dizque del deber cumplido,	saying his duty fulfilled,
con un corazón de fiera,	with a heart of iron,
mostrado en esa ocasión,	showed on this occasion,
no tendrá nunca rival.	he would have no rival.

The regime had no match in cruelty perhaps, but the song at least could challenge the legitimacy of the government by mourning the deaths of nine sailors. Why did they need to die?

Su delito fue atacar	Their crime was to attack
a un tirano presidente,	A tyrannical president,
que se mantenía en el puesto	who held his place
odiado de toda gente.	hated by all people.

Newly installed by coup d'état, President Díaz had no patience for resistance, although the corrido doubtlessly exaggerated both his not-yet-established tyranny and the hatred that people felt for him. Opposition to Díaz's reign had taken up arms in other states, and few supported his serving another term as president in 1880 since his revolutionary platform of "no reelection" had not yet been overturned. Nonetheless, as he was a dashing young war hero of the French Intervention, and a popular figure in states such as Oaxaca, many saw Díaz as a good choice for solving Mexico's instability. Yet the Liberal rhetoric that his government openly claimed in 1879 was quite at odds with the lack of respect for due process and individual rights that the Veracruz incident came to represent:

Juvencio Robles decía:	Junvencio Robles said:
—Esto parece inhumano,	—this seems inhuman,

que se les forme consejo,	they deserve counsel,
como a todo mexicano.	as do all Mexicans.

[But the general replied]:

—Es inútil objetar,	—It is useless to object,
que al cabo son malhechores,	that in the end, they are all criminals,
los hemos de ajusticiar.	that we should execute.

The president addressed the uprising with a style of ruthless pragmatism, which he later embodied and obscured. He sent a terse telegraph to the commanding officer, according to the corrido, "que se les mate en caliente," which has been commonly translated by subsequent critics and historians to mean "kill them on the spot," or "kill them in cold blood."[43] This interpretation lacks nuance, as the military dictionary of the time defines "matar en caliente" as "to kill in the heat of the action." Notwithstanding the clarity of wanting these men dead, Díaz preferred that the general take no prisoners and thus avoid possibly embarrassing open trials. For the young regime, it would be better if the mutineers died with guns in hand, and be forgotten as combat casualties:

Sin permitirles testar,	Without allowing them to testify,
los sacaron de mañana . . .	they took them out in the morning . . .
Murieron como valientes,	They died as brave men,
sin pedir gracia ninguna.	without asking any forgiveness.

The corrido ends with a more subtle challenge to the regime by asserting that the brave men asked no mercy of anyone, and pardons them for their honor and valor, as the secular state would not. After 1879, the tone of most corridos lessened in direct criticism and ceased the outright naming of officials as villains. Likely this reflected the increased stability and power of the regime to quell dissent, as well as at least a grudging acknowledgment of Díaz's accomplishments.

Most officially sanctioned poetry contrasted with this critical stance, building instead on ideals of Order and Progress, the motto of the regime. These poems assumed the positives of technological improvement and its corresponding effect on morality. The military, in their view, became the vanguard of a nation becoming modernized, secular, and European-like.

These poets further defined the army as a separated place where a new caste of men joined together like a great family, with Díaz as father figure.[44] This vision used a vocabulary of filial duty and servitude to set the military into a place of honor and prestige.

In "El brindis" we see an overt example of how the military as a community or perhaps as a family saw itself.[45] Corporal Fuentes clearly set out in his toast a view of the army and its values. He saluted the tired men on the march, the specialized sharpshooters, and lauds their endurance under the worst of conditions. Accepting hardship in all circumstances represented the chief ethos of the idealized soldier. The civilian remains soft, pampered, and clumsy, by contrast. But he saves the climax of the toast for the officer classes and military on an institutional level as those who deserve the best, himself included, as his last evocation was addressed to "us, as servants."

After a century of coups and betrayals this trope of responsible servitude held special weight in official writings. Now, the writers argued, Mexico as a modern nation would no longer be plagued by uncivilized military interventions.[46] The army in Fuentes's view earned this praise for having preserved national honor:

Cumplir lo que se ordenó	To comply with what was ordered
Y hacerlo con ligereza	And to do so swiftly
Sin preguntar quién mandó.	Without questioning who commanded.

A long legacy of supposed obedience was connected to a notion of honor and expectations of hierarchy with a thin veneer of culture, and this now tied closely to the assumption of Díaz's legitimacy. The sacrifice and self-abnegation of the military also carried an undercurrent of expectation. If the army was honorable, and the government legitimate, then there could be no question of civilian interference. The poem thus alluded to some long-held assumptions in the army that they deserved separate rights (*fueros*) and impunity.

A stark division therefore appears as the corrido and poem consider the rightful place of the army in a somewhat peaceful society. Where "Mártires" called the regime's legitimacy into question over its treatment of rebels, the toast presumed (a decade later) that total obedience trumped political concerns. The army's role, whether as dissident or servant, reflected a social and historical dividing point between these officers and the soldiers, one emphasized in verses describing Mexico's pedigree as nation.

Genealogies of National Sacrifice, Commemoration, and the Classical

A shared imagining of authentic collective identification, one that described the concept of nation, remained an elusive consensus in the late nineteenth century. Establishing a sense of self that all Mexicans could equally agree upon required, at least, a foundational and historical narrative of where the nation had come from and who mattered in it. This would also be needed before ideas of future development could be negotiated. A genealogical discourse emerged at this time in countries throughout Latin America that sought to explain the fictive parentage of racially mixed and post-Spanish nations.[47] Those who took part in this process, primarily elites, sought to reconcile a history of conquest and inequality with a contemporary situation that adhered to a mere façade of liberal ideology. Many poems published in army journals worked to build a genealogical narrative, while corridos tended to frame their ideas with current tales of racial injustice. The poems tended, therefore, to be part of a postcolonial discourse of hybridization and mimicry, while the songs spoke to a neocolonial sense of continued oppression.[48] Nonetheless, both types illuminate visions of a developing mexicanidad.

These imaginings were complemented with concise connections to other narratives, specifically historical name-dropping (e.g., Hernán Cortés, Napoleon, Caesar) that served to set verse into a diachronic context. In this revision of history, the military became the sole persistent feature of nation through centuries of struggle, and a linkage to a wider Western civilization or genealogy.[49] As Rebecca Earle argues, nascent nations of the fin-de-siècle drew extensively on a selective genealogical mythos to explain where they came from, omitting or altering the contributions or harms of indigenous, Spanish, or other influences.[50] Setting Mexico at the culmination of a long line of conquering warriors lent rhetorical weight and justified pride to narratives that the soldier-poet wrote. It also helped build resonance with an audience emotionally affected and hence complicit with a postcolonial enterprise of engineering *la patria* (the fatherland as object). The new nation, the poems implied, had a deep past worthy of empire and stood ready to enter the new millennium.

A key element of this was the poems that graced the pages of martial periodicals and worked to make sense of the tragic loss of soldiers' lives in war. The language of death and sacrifice, of ghosts and martyrs, pervades the poems of this sort. Among the many examples: "A mi patria" (To my Fatherland), "Cineraria" (The Crematory Urn), "Poesía en Chapultepec"

(Poetry in Chapultepec), and any number of elegies and eulogies that drew on loss to define progress.[51] The passing of the old generations in true positivist fashion led inexorably toward a new stage of nationhood, as Mexico evolved and built on the foundation that elderly warriors had laid. In this view of mexicanidad every victim and every old warrior became the savior of the patria and no death was ever a waste. And to the victors? Laurels, the crowning wreath of conquerors since Roman times, appear in nearly every poem written by military men. Their inclusion in these poems sought to make a history of bloody loss into a history of proud tradition.

Most military cultures do this. War must be explained, even after the fact, if warriors are to justify rewards and status. Verse is small consolation, but helps shape historical memory as it functions as a form of *trauerarbeit* (mourning work), and resolves a culture of loss into a meaningful narrative.[52] Communities of memory can flesh over the skeleton of these commemorative, fantastic projections. By discarding the negative aspects of Mexico's nineteenth century, a military history of lengthy civil wars and bloody foreign invasions, the poems leached the events of shame or blame. Quite to the contrast, the corrido worked to remember recent occurrences, to attribute unjust victimhood, and to deny official myopia. Commemoration, in itself, can set ritualized forms of memory to the purposes of national hegemony—if within limits.[53] As historians of memory have shown, the state cannot direct this reliably, and most often the communal memory that forms as "known history" does so in the hands of a broader popular impetus.[54] No verse by itself can reliably convince the masses that *dulce et decorum est pro patria mori*.[55] For the fatherland to matter, the children needed reassurance that they were, in fact, not bastards. Poetry helped to legitimate the historic genealogy.

Congressman Ignacio Luchichi read aloud his highly formal poem "Poesía" in Chapultepec Woods during a solemn September 8 ceremony, commemorating the beginning of the Battle of Mexico City against U.S. invaders in 1847. His work tied the Mexican military together with sinews of history both local and classical. He dedicated each verse of the first half to varying classic cultures: to Palas, to Greece, to Rome, and then leapt to France, Cuba, South America, and finally turned to Mexico. Laurels appeared with frequency here, perhaps fitting in a leafy forest, as he invoked Greek myth after Greek myth—thus demonstrating his classical education but also illustrating that the army's modern incarnation (far from the *Iliad*) nonetheless respected old traditions of the warrior hymn.[56] The Homeric tradition captured a particular idealization of the masculine in a far removed, and hence pure, invented past:[57]

Cantad; ¡oh pueblos todos! el indomable y fiero
valor de los Aquiles de la moderna edad;
cantad con la robusta entonación de Homero
los versos de "La Ilíada" forjados en acero
y haced con esos cantos un himno universal.

Sing; oh people! the indomitable iron
valor of Achilles for the modern age;
sing with the deep tones of Homer
the verses of the Iliad forged in steel
and make of these verses a universal hymn.

Warriors, rather than soldiers, proved themselves in battle for all to see and envy. Mexican soldiers, no longer the slaves of a postclassic Church, could take whatever European honors they wanted, posing themselves as the Achilles, Caesars, and Neros of the New World.

Thus, Luchichi's army became an institution connected to, yet distinct from, a tradition derived through the legitimizing forces of history. In this, "Poesía" called on seemingly every martial icon the author could summon including gods such as Mars, events like the French Revolution, and generals like Julius Caesar, Simón Bolívar, and José de San Martín. The Porfirian military somehow shared in the glories of ancient and recent warriors, borrowing recklessly from across time. The comparisons were specific if sometimes baffling, as the poem asked where Poland will get its Hidalgo,[58] asserted that the Niños Héroes fought like Leonidas at Thermopylae, and disdained Hernán Cortes as not yet Mexican and thus as a lesser man than Cuauhtémoc:

cantad esa jornada, poetas varoniles;
le gloria de Leónidas opaca la de Aquiles;
Cortés es menos grande
que el gran Cuauhtémoc.

sing this day, gallant poets;
the glory of Leonidas overshadows Achilles;
Cortes is less large
than great Cuauhtémoc.

In both poems and songs, it was Cuauhtémoc that received this lauding rather than, for example, Nezahualcoyotl, the ancient poet-king of Texcoco, possibly because the former was executed and it was the sacrifice that gave him meaning.[59] Likewise, Leonidas died at Thermopylae to protect his homeland, while Achilles represented arrogant aggression in wars abroad. Nonetheless, with no further context given, the author assumed that these

Figure 2.2. El Desertador. José Guadalupe Posado, in Antonio Vanegas Arroyo, 1901.

references were in the common repertoire of the readers' historical education, or perhaps he pretentiously included these to distance himself from his readers. If the former, they would form a rich mental connection between Thucydides or Herodotus and the soldiers that they saw every day lounging in cantinas around the *zócalo*.

At the heart of this narrative, the poet sets military sacrifices. During Luchichí's oration he claimed that the guns of U.S. generals Zachary Taylor and Winfield Scott (from the American invasion of 1846–1848) echoed through the forest around him—with a touch of poetic license he conveniently ignored Taylor's historical absence in those parts. Since the invasion by U.S. armies scarce decades earlier, and in the context of contemporary foreign economic neocolonialism, the antigringo attitude in the army was a common feature of patriotic poetry and a prime source for identity formation.[60] In poetry and corrido alike, soldiers found their purpose in deep feelings of hostile anxiety toward the United States, which ultimately represented the only real external threat to Mexico, notwithstanding a brief enthusiasm among some to invade Guatemala in the mid-1880s.

This antiforeign element reflected an important aspect of general culture in the army and Mexico more broadly, where the nation reflected on its identity. "Poesía" needs to be read as a postcolonial document in this regard.[61] Understanding the new identity of the nation, where "Mexican" culture would be valued and distinct, meant accepting or molding uncomfortable legacies from the Spanish, the Aztecs, and the Americans. The remnants of an uncivilized past or alien invasions made up part of the resultant hybrid of the postcolonial nation.[62] Formulating a new national identity entailed a contemporary reimagining of the present in terms of a past often made palatably fictional. The military poets made multiple references to their readiness to prevent any further incursions by the Colossus of the North, rarely lionized the New Spanish past, and proved highly selective in mentions of long-dead indigenous kings. This also reflected their historical training, especially from such texts such as Prieto's *Lecciones*.[63] The poets and songwriters nonetheless assumed that the audience understood the same reference base, which made them a co-performer complicit in constructing a mexicanidad through shared historical memory.

Poets invoked a potent and ambivalent symbol in this cultural framing when they used the Niños Héroes, eight teenaged cadets who died defending the last redoubt of Chapultepec castle against the U.S. Army in 1847. Persistent issues of memory complicated their tale. When their military college castle fell, the youths became somewhat troubling hero figures. They represented the military and yet at the same time, they ultimately lost, and the army itself had failed to unify against the invader. How did this become pride? Military defeat, particularly targeting apparent innocents, transforms into a narrative of sacrifice and caution against tragedy.[64] The youth of the boys only became a focus point for patriotic framing decades after the events, since in 1847 teenagers in the army would have been considered adult. For example, take the specific fate of Lieutenant Juan Escutia who purportedly wrapped himself in the flag and plunged from the parapet to deny it to the invaders. His gesture has been fashioned as the exemplary moment for the whole mishandled war in everything from artwork to textbooks and street signs.[65] Yet by the early twentieth century, these children, as children, could not fully satisfy the need for martial heroism, in the way that other nations made exemplary adult heroes of Horatio Nelson, Davie Crockett, or Giuseppe Garibaldi.

Students at the Military College that overlooked the Chapultepec forest were often contributors to the publication of military poetry that called on the exemplary Niños Héroes to commemorate their sacrifice each September. The poems "A mi patria" (To my Fatherland), "Cineraria" (Funeral Urn), and "13 de Septiembre," all written in 1890, expressed how Mexico had risen from its dark past, redeemed by the cadets' sacrifice.[66] The new generation fantasized in poetry about this secular martyrdom.

These poems were sincere, if sometimes crude. Written with less than subtle imagery, these amateur pieces also featured some simplistic stretches in the cause of rhyming, for example, "labio" with "gravio," and "mía" and "día," with "hidalguia." Fernando Rodríguez described the past as veiled in darkness from which slaves rose to make a patria. He, like other poets in this genre, was quick to point out that next time the United States invaded, Mexico would rise up to fight like lions, having learned their patriotism in the cradle:

Y si alguna otra vez viniere osado	And if some other time they dared
A insultarnos con ánimo altanero,	To arrogantly insult us,
Hasta en el niño encontrará un soldado	Even in the child will they find a soldier
Con alma altiva y corazón de acero.	With haughty soul and heart of steel.
. . .	. . .
Y tuvieron por cuna el patriotismo.	And they had patriotism for a cradle.

Of course, he and the others would be proven largely wrong some twenty-five years later during the Revolutionary chaos when the Marines easily took Veracruz from Victoriano Huerta in 1914 and Blackjack Pershing's expedition subsequently roamed the northern deserts in search of Pancho Villa in 1917. Other students took an even darker tone.

José Ceballos saw dead people. His poem invoked the ghosts and specters of vengeance that roamed those busy woods of Chapultepec where wars had raged since Aztec times:

Levantarse sangriento fantasma,	Rise bloody ghost,
Encubierto por blanco sudario,	Covered with white shroud,
Mudo espectro que pide venganza.	Mute specter that calls for revenge.

Likewise, the wilderness had always been seen as full of danger and devils, and Chapultepec continued to host hunting parties and suicide pacts alike. And yet, Ceballos seemed unsure at points whether the spirits were those of a warrior slain by foreigners, or of the foreigners who had put his people to the sword. There was an ambiguity here about who he saw as his own people, and whose spirits belonged. Yet simple antiforeign sentiments imbued the verses with a sense of what the young authors felt an appropriate tribute to the niños, and to their sense of martial duty.

Ignacio Iragorri's paean to the September 13 assault echoes the others but brought in further classical references as he elevated the niños to the status of demigods. Where Ceballos began his poem claiming he felt too choked up to speak, Iragorri outdid him by claiming the war was unspeakable, unprintable, and beyond paint to express:

Que no pueden pintarla la pluma ni el pincel.	It can not be painted with pen or with brush.

The discursive silencing and possibly unthinkable has more recently been ascribed to the Haitian Revolution, but it seems an intriguing thought here.[67] While the poet may more likely be working through writer's block or with hyperbole, the repeated hints of silencing and voice suggest an expression of habitus or discursive limits to the normal discussion of the past. To some degree, the invasion and relatively pointless deaths of a futile resistance became a memory to be avoided unless one spoke of the cadets. Clearly the trauma lingered or festered in the national psyche. How can the poet deal with this loss and redeem the failures of the mestizo army? One strategy was to posit a racial solution.

The good military students were the heirs to the old empire, inheriting the legitimacy of ancient indigenous glory: "they are the descendants of iron Cuauhtémoc." Just as in "Poesía," they could thus bypass the Spanish conquest, the long oppression of natives, and move on to an untainted genealogy by virtue of sacrifice and war.[68] Without becoming the cursed offspring (Cain, Ham) of the conquistador and the cannibal, the poets selected their own parentage. As scions of the tragically noble last Aztec emperor, with interceding centuries skipped, the Mexican of the turn of the century became untainted, un-Spanish, undefeated.

A powerful and often-deployed symbol for this poetry also comes into play here as Irragori claims: "Your heroism shines like the Sun." This seemingly innocuous inclusion held significant meaning. The sun as a sacred symbol represented an icon of light used to play to a pre-Columbian religious past in Mexico.[69] In the standard iconography, the masculine sun sat in opposition to the feminine moon. This also appeared in the stellar markings in the Virgin of Guadalupe's cloak.[70] Hints of the ancient religion could also allude to the cleansing and purification entailed in sunlight and sacrifices. And given the era, poets simultaneously employed the sun to allude to Enlightened Reason, the dawn of the modern age, and the twilight of an older generation.

In songs sung by common troops, the florid prose of postcolonial genealogy turned instead into a neocolonial accounting. Tradition, race, and religion were all depicted as threatened by the new order. In the corrido, the Spanish Conquest had now merely changed masks, and ancient heroism mattered little in light of contemporary violence and tragedy.

Ordinary soldiers often worried about the prospects of open warfare against the uprisings that continued to plague Díaz's nation. Chasing bandits or manning garrisons proved relatively easy duty in comparison with ongoing wars against the Yaqui of Sonora, or the Maya of the Yucatán. Their songs reflected pride in victory, but also had telling elements of concerns over fighting against their own (50 percent of soldiers were of indigenous descent).[71]

An early corrido, "De los Tomochis" (Of the Tomochis) told the tale of a battle against a millenarian movement in the largely mestizo town of Tomochic in 1893.[72] The townspeople had risen in revolt against the state government as a religious movement that venerated a local girl blessed with visions, Santa Teresa. The uprising quickly escalated, and the federal army sent to quell it initially failed, thereby staining the repute of the Díaz military apparatus:

A esos indios del Tomochic, yo los quiero	To those Indians of Tomochic, I like them
porque saben morir en la raya,	because they know how to die on the line,
todititos murieron en la playa,	all died on plowed field,
combatiendo al Once Batallón.	fighting the 11th Battalion.

The lyrics spoke of fighting against Indians on cultivated farmlands, even though the uprising rose among mestizos high in the mountains. Making the place of the event ambiguous, the singers could build on the generalized plight of the indigenous soldier, even in an apparently patriotic song. The songwriter admired that Indians knew how to die properly when the 11th Battalion went to war. The town, established as a military buffer against Indians in an important hub for mining traffic, was not populated by self-described Indians of any type. Where were all the Indians? Officers of the

11th Battalion had quite tellingly made up deficient numbers on the roster with aggressive conscription of Pima natives, and had also taken a number of Yaqui prisoners of war into their ranks. In comparison with the followers of Santa Teresa in the mountain town, the army was indigenous. When the battle turned against the ill-prepared federal forces, the "indios del Tomochic" did indeed run and die:

Salieron los indios pimas
peleando de tres en dos,
todos a una voz decían:
—¡Que viva el poder de Dios!
y que mueran los del Once
Batallón.

Salieron cinco tomochis
peleando de tres en dos.

The Pima indians came out
fighting in threes and twos,
all in one voice said:
—Long live the power of God!
and death to the 11th Battalion.

Five tomochis came out
fighting in threes and twos.

This corrido also made an oblique reference to executions. The Indians died fighting in twos and threes, shot down with the same two-three pattern that repeatedly appeared in corridos about firing squads (see discussion of executions later in this chapter). With this twist, the only Indians in Tomochic, actually federal conscripts, faced heroic executions in the cause of God against the guns of the government.

The popular lyrics and their interpretation of the fight ran contrary to the official military narrative of the campaign. The official story told of a secular modern nation quelling "savages" that threatened commerce, where initial setbacks were made right rationally and swiftly.[73] It spoke of a contrast, a contradiction between a backward or traditional identity in the highlands and the secular modern nation without. Yet, religion did not come into the public discussion until subversive novels emerged, and oddly worded corridos sung. The prime novel on the subject was originally penned under a pseudonym due to its sensitive politics, written by a young officer who witnessed the events.[74] Where the past seemed vaguely distant and the present politically troublesome, some poets instead worked on auguring a glorious future.

Connecting Past, Future, and Present

The deep angst over modernity drove poets to set pen to paper. Bound between the rhetoric of the "modern" and the practices of modernization, modernity entailed the elusive process of understanding new relationships and possibilities full of contradiction.[75] An observer at the end of the century saw a bewildering explosion of new technology from zippers and x-rays to automobiles and railroads, along with rapid cultural changes marked by the emergence of new social classes. Attempting to mediate these accelerating shifts became a central role for the government and intellectuals.[76]

Ramón Rodríguez Pena dedicated "Por la Patria" to Lieutenant Colonel Ignacio José Mendoza in 1901.[77] He likened Mexican life to forces of nature:

Como formó el Océano Atlántico	As the Atlantic Ocean forged
dos corrientes aonatícas, grandes	two great contrary currents,
que en el Golfo de México	that in the Gulf of Mexico
siempre	always
. . . con furia asaltando,	. . . furiously assault,
de igual modo en la vida moderna	similarly in modern life

The Atlantic made sense to the poet, connecting Mexico to Europe, the Mediterranean, and thus to a "Western" narrative of historical progress. By contrast, the Pacific offered little as Acapulco only linked to alien Asian countries of dubious value.

Science appeared prominently in Rodríguez Pena's vision of a positivist progression that remained somewhat mired by the warlike past, and he proclaimed the army to be caught between magnetic poles of calm and combat:[78]

así el mundo, por ley biológica,	so the world, by biological laws,
a pesar de soñados desarmes,	despite disarming dreams,
tienes polares extremos	has polar extremes

His invocation of science emerged from a military culture with significant investment in modern knowledge. The hundreds of technical officers in the army, highly educated by standards of the day, studied and trained in the sciences in the Military College, or abroad.[79] Grasping scientific principles and mathematics allowed the military an illusion of control over nature, and across the nation.[80] This also fostered a sense of Praetorianism in the army, as it came to understand itself as the only qualified institution to guide progress or save the nation from its own internal enemies.[81] Only, as this poem suggests, a scientific military can truly serve the patria.

Rodríguez Pena poetically described human progress and class struggle as evidence of positivist laws of evolution. Nations, he said, progress much as a youth moves from playing with toy guns to adults fighting as men in a patria perpetually in throes of cataclysm:

Tal estado perpetuo antagónico	Such a perpetually antagonistic state
se revela, potente, en las graves	reveals itself, powerful, in the serious
erupciones terrestres volcánicas;	earthly eruptions of volcanoes;
en los cuatro elementos vitales;	in the four vital elements;
en las luchas del alma y del cuerpo	in the struggles of soul and of body

An odd marriage of Comtean philosophy with pre-Hispanic religion, the mention of the volcano as holding back civility was significant. Anciently holy sites such as the volcano Popocatépetl loomed over the modern Mexico City. The unpredictable nature of the volcano, understood better as an act of a vengeful god than through the crude science of the late 1800s, suggests the possibility of a future science in which both civil wars and destructive eruptions might be solved by the intellectual. The optimism of positivist progress meshed neatly with the domination of nature that technology had promised.

If this utopia arrived, what role would remain for the military? He claimed that while the people have no respect or regard for law, per se, they all understand honor, power, and blood because their only true creed comes from armed strength:

La mejor religión es la fuerza;	The best religion is force;
la lealtad más eterna, el dios Marte,	loyalty most eternal, the god Mars,
el valor, la virtud más sublime;	valor, the most sublime virtue;
el honor nacional, el más grande;	national honor, the most grand;
la mayor dignidad, los laureles	the greatest dignity, laurels
para adorno del patio estandarte.	to adorn the flags of the parade square.

Perhaps one of the oddest panegyrics to the wonders of the modern age came in an 1899 poem read at the inauguration of the Military Library of the Artillery Corps by José Manuel Gutiérrez de Zamora.[82] His poem,

"Libro y espada" (Book and Sword), argued that science and war had to work together, to become "invincible allies" where the artillerist destroys and the engineer rebuilds in harmony. This accorded with the official views within the army, where influence and promotion greatly favored those branches. Unity suffered as elite families dominated the technical branches and their socially inferior peers in the officer class were relegated publicly to lead infantry battalions of the worst repute.[83] His poem suggests that the rewards for conquering, the laurels, would now belong to officers who were mathematically proficient rather than mere fighters.

Science and intellect, the condensed spark of the sun, trump the sword, which could not conquer ignorance alone. He prescribed that the best result would see book discussions in the barracks when the cannons were quiet:

Y mientras calla el cañón,	And while the cannons are silent,
Habla el libro en el cuartel!	The book speaks in the barracks!

To Gutiérrez de Zamora, the giants of science and war complemented one another; Christopher Colón, the Montgolfier brothers, Benjamin Franklin, Thomas Edison, and William Herschell (the man who discovered Uranus) would teach the soldier to live and die only for the patria. Like other poets, he demonstrated with this knowledge his distance from the uneducated reader, while assuming that at least some would understand his references. The enormously accelerated rate of technological change that the poet witnessed in his lifetime pointed him to this rather unconventional panoply of scientific heroes, none of whom had ever set foot in Mexico.

The library as repository of all of this wisdom permitted the poet a sort of optimism about his nation's future. As a cautionary note, he asserted that an unnamed "*ibero Capitán*" (the reader would identify this as Hernán Cortés) conquered the indomitable Cuauhtémoc, who could not read Spanish:

Pero el inmortal azteca	But the immortal Aztec
Cuauhtémoc ni leer sabía!	Cuauhtémoc knew not how to read!
Y asombro su bizarría	And his gallantry
Y su belicoso afán	And eagerness for war [Was overcome]
Al ibero Capitán,	By the Iberian Captain,
Su vencedor y verdugo	His conqueror and executioner

Common to Latin American nation building, many elites repudiated their savage indigenous collective past as justification for the Spanish intervention, while at the same time extolling the virtues of indigenous individuals long-since dead who fit an idealized genealogy. Theorists have described this contradictory stance as symptomatic of the inherently unstable position of the postcolonial nation-state.[84] Alongside Cuauhtémoc, Cortés becomes savage. Yet in other circumstances, he remained the heroic founder of the military narrative.

Thus, the poet combined several lines later a heroic Cortés (1520s), with the father of Independence from Spain Miguel Hidalgo (1810s), and the execution of Hapsburg emperor Maximilian at the Cerro de Campanas (Hill of Bells, 1867). These became the poet's crucial moments when Mexico overcame its oppressors:

Como lo admiró Cortés!	How I admire Cortés!
. . .	. . .
Desde el Grito de Dolores,	Since the Cry of Dolores,
Al Cerro de las Campanas,	To the Hill of Bells,
Las legiones mexicanas	The Mexican legions
Triunfan de sus opresores!	Triumph over their oppressors!

The identification of the "Other," in this case Spain and France, situated Mexico as an organic nation of people with common historical cause. As success stories, of a sort, the rejection of these colonizers seems instead to highlight the oppressor he missed—given that the U.S. occupation in 1847 was omitted from his historical summary. These invaders received, instead, an allusion in the final stanzas.

He ended by emphatically exclaiming that the next time Mexico was invaded, all citizens would fight to the last, dying like lions rather than fleeing ignominiously:

Contra extranjeras legiones,	Against foreign legions,
Sucumbamos cómos leones	we will fall like lions
Todos tus hijos guerreros,	All your warrior sons,
Y mueran tus artilleros	And all your gunners die
Pero al pie de sus cañones![85]	But at the foot of their cannons!

As with the niños poems and countered by the Tomochic corrido, this genealogy assumed that the sons of Mexico were no longer Indians, and would be transformed into mighty warriors as the patria needed. Technology and élan together would suffice to repel the dreaded gringo horde. His national imagining, a composite of scientific ideas and historical heroism, came together in the military library. In this sunny space of intellect, a new set of historical traditions could be invented in the best and most constructive sense of the engineered nation. At least in poetry, the invasions that had cost so much treasure and territory now represented lessons learned and the cost of the nation's birth.

A well-crafted corrido could challenge this interpretation by inserting sly mockery within celebratory lyrics.[86] One such was "De los indios Mayas del 28 Batallón" (Of the Mayan Indians of the 28th Battalion) from around 1900.[87] The song purported to tell the story of General Ignacio Bravo's defeat of the Maya uprising at Santa Cruz de Chemal. The army fought a decade-long campaign of counterinsurgency in the Yucatán jungle to destroy an enemy that knew the ground and had arms from British suppliers in Belize. Disease, climate, and terrain made the war highly dangerous and protracted. Thus, when victory seemed at hand, this song did reflect a certain degree of pride and some self-deprecatory modesty. At the same time, a closer reading of the lyrics reveals a subtle message of resistance that subverts the official military narrative:

Voy a cantar un corrido, pero no crean es de amor, es un corrido de historia, del Veintiocho Batallón.	I am going to sing a corrido, but do not believe it is of love, it is a corrido of history of the 28th Battalion.

The song played on the idea that the soldiers, rather than the Maya, were the protagonist Indians of the corrido. Its title suggested that the Battalion was, in fact, comprised of Indians, and the lyrics throughout imply that the emotions attributed to the enemy were those of the singers. The song also described the troops as mere cannon fodder, yet suggested their slyness through wordplay. Thus, the good but poorly forged soldiers became the Indians dying of fright:

Yo ya me voy, ya me voy, ya me voy con mucho gusto, porque ya los indios mayas se están muriendo de susto.	I am going, I am going, I am going happily, because the Mayan indians are dying of fright.
Cuando el fuego se rompió, los indios *nomás* gritaban; pero el Veintiocho valiente puras balas les echaba.	When the fire broke, the Indians cried "no more"; but the brave 28th poured on the bullets.

The song referred also to burnt fields, alluding figuratively to the homes the recruit had left behind. It mourned the warfare as the soldier yearned to leave all Indians and move inland or overseas instead of seeing the Hell all around him:

me voy pa' Guadalajara,
. . . .
Yo ya me voy, ya me voy,
al otro lado del mar,
que ya no tienen los indios
ni camino que agarrar.

I am going to Guadalajara,
. . . .
I am gone, I am gone,
to the other side of the sea,
that has no indians
nor a path to take.

Snidely commenting on officers, the corrido also explained how one was shot in the brain to no effect, but he died anyway. As Scott and Bhabha suggest, those in positions of relative weakness can attempt to assert some form of agency in cautiously worded criticisms, what the latter called sly civility.[88] In this case, the mocking of the sublieutenant might be simple fun, harmless teasing, yet it would still indicate a boundary being crossed by the subordinate singer in an institution where "murmuring" was a crime punishable by up to a year in jail:

Cuando el subteniente Lauro
ya la sangre corría,
porque la herida tenía
en la inmediación del cráneo.

El subteniente decía
que nada le había pasado,
pero si a los pocos días
quedó el pobre sepultado.

When Sublieutenant Lauro
ran with blood,
from the wound he took
right in the skull.

The sublieutenant said
that nothing had happened to
him,
but a few days later
the poor man lay entombed.

Finally, it ended with a veiled criticism of General Bravo, saying he made the Indians run but not specifying which Indians this meant:

Bravo de pronto llegaba
y el campo se levantó,
mandó poner la lumbrada
y a los indios los quemó.

Ignacio Bravo, el valiente,
los indios hacía correr,
y como buen combatiente
nunca se le vio agobiado.

Bravo soon arrived
the country rose in revolt,
he ordered it put to the torch
and he burned the indians.

Ignacio Bravo, the valiant,
made the indians run,
and they never overwhelmed him
such a great warrior.

Con ésta y no digo más,
tremolando mi bandera,
porque al Veintiocho en la guerra
no le han ganado jamás.

With this I say no more,
my flag trembles,
because the 28th at war
has never been defeated.

Were this simply meant as celebration, there would be no speechless trembling. The apparently proud final stanza also suggested a tragic interpretation of a relatively dirty war that at times relied on torture, hostages, and widespread destruction. One of the chief architects of this effective method was Victoriano Huerta who, as a young officer, maintained a daily correspondence with then Secretary of War Bernardo Reyes about the harsh campaign. The adoption of brutal tactics on the whole resulted from the debacle of eight years earlier in the mountains of the Sierra Madre at Tomochic, and the subsequent experience of the army in quelling the Yaqui of Sonora through increasingly draconian measures.

The ambiguous tone of this corrido reflected a collective memory of wartime horror as integral to the common understanding of Mexico. Verse dramatized the imagined world, and often the narrative that emerged set tragedy and sentimentality at the heart of mexicanidad.

The Sentimental Masculinity and Tragedy

Tragedy inherently criticizes. Where there is injustice and sadness, there is blame and regret. Whether in melancholic poems, or in corridos that dealt with the *fusiliamientos* (execution by shooting), sorrowful stories were potent affective devices enjoyed on their own terms, but they also contained sharp criticism of the status quo.

As a trope, execution narratives represented a common genre in the corrido, which spoke to masculinity, family, justice, and religion. They rarely gave much attention to the legal side of the trials, but rather focused on the inherent tragedy that real men faced as consequence of aggravated desertion, banditry, or murder.[89] The protagonists are not portrayed as villains, but as flawed men who face the inevitable firing squad bravely, piously, and with concern for their comrades and family. As Frazer has argued, the tragic suggests that the betrayal of the antihero had meaning, and was on some level a necessity for civilized life.[90] Similarly, newspapers frequently commented on all details of the execution cases with long narrative pieces describing the sad necessity of the affair. The executed soldier, in particular, becomes an almost holy sacrifice or secular martyr to the laws and institutions of the modern nation. This image was sharpened in the special attention that both corridos and newspapers paid to the religious angles of the ritual.

The inclusion of the priest and final rites in the process, the language of the honest self-sacrifice, the prayers of the family, all reframed the stark institutional rite into something more symbolically meaningful for the audience. And the most immediate audience was nearly always the soldier's unit, some of whom made up a firing squad while the others looked on as witnesses, making the event both official and educational by their presence. For the subsequent singers and listeners of the corridos, the lessons of honorable bravery, masculine norms, and institutional solidarity all lent to the popularity of these sad songs in everyday barracks settings.

The life of a soldier, with all of its hardships and injustices, is voiced in the song "Del desertor o Juan Soldado" (Of the Deserter, or Juan the Soldier), apparently a favorite in some garrisons.[91] Even the title suggests a dual vision, as it questions whether Juan embodies only a deserter or is instead a soldier—the possibility of existing as both was denied. The Porfirian conscript did not have an easy life; soldiers were generally locked into barracks that functioned in many ways more like prisons for the first three years of their service. There, they faced dangerous conflicts with fellow troops, deprivation of comforts, and harsh punishments from their officers. Even worse for many soldiers was the boredom rising from incessant routine. The combination, even without the specter of actual combat, resulted in a desertion rate that sometimes reached 50 percent.[92]

Still, Juan's fall from grace was not inevitable. Indeed, he had always wanted to be a soldier since childhood, lured by the pomp and music. He joined the army when taken by the *leva* (forced conscription) at age fifteen. Despite his lack of choice in this, he came to love his regiment, became a corporal (*cabo*), and rapidly rose to sergeant, but eventually chose to desert back to his land and his mother:

Ya no me gustó seguir la carrera y me deserté y me fui pa' mi tierra.	I no longer enjoyed to follow my career and I deserted and went back to my land.

His homecoming did not last long. Making matters worse for Juan, he was captured and then abused by a mounted patrol of the Acordada. This infamously callous paramilitary force was a colonial vestige, and its presence in this song hints at the corrido's long pedigree, since the Acordada had been replaced by a new (and of equally poor repute) paramilitary police called the *rurales* in 1867.[93] The cavalry beat Juan, and dragged him from his home in front of his poor mother:

Estando en mi casa	While in my house
con mi pobre madre	with my poor mother
llegó la Acordada	the Acordada arrived
tendiéndome el sable.	and took the saber to me.

Family was integral to the army. Soldiers sought wives, had children, received support (food and legal help) from parents, and went to great lengths to maintain relationships with family.[94] His mother's weeping becomes the repeated lyrical counterpoint to the chorus, as the indifferent military band "toquen y toquen" (played and played). Music framed Juan's experience in the army, and his mother's sobbing interjects. The juxtaposition of the music and the weeping emphasized the separate worlds of home and barracks.[95] Army periodicals often, in fact, asserted that the military was one Great Family with the president as father, suggesting that recruits might give up a past life and still retain this essential emotional connection, at least in theory. Yet Juan's two families did not easily coexist, and he could not legally abandon one, or emotionally leave the other:

Y lo van llevando	And he was taken
para su cuartel	to their barracks
y la pobre madre	and my poor mother
llorando tras él.	was crying behind him.

After brief trial, and convicted of desertion in time of war, Juan faced execution by a firing squad of seven rifles (one loaded with blanks) and a coup de grâce delivered to the head or heart by his immediate officer. The unfortunate man made his goodbyes and faced his fate:

¡Adiós, mi cuartel . . .	Goodbye, my barracks . . .
¡Adiós, compañeros	Goodbye, fellows
los de zapadores![96]	of the sappers!
Toquen, toquen, toquen . . .	Play, play play . . .
¡Adiós, mi teniente . . .	Goodbye, my lieutenant . . .
¡Adiós, mi sargento . . .	Goodbye, my sergeant . . .
¡Adiós, padre y madre,	Goodbye, father and mother,
adiós, hermanitos!	goodbye, my little brothers!
Aquí se purgaron	Here they will purge
todos mis delitos.	all of my crimes.

A shared colloquial language added meaning to lyrics beyond the mere obvious. A curious convention comes into play at this point. He faced death without blindfold or hesitation, and without blame for the men who did the shooting (and might have sung this later). He then was shot dead, with two bullets in the head, three bullets in the heart:

Tirar, compañeros,	Shoot, companions,
tirar con valor,	shoot well,
dos en la cabeza,	two in the head,
tres el corazón.	three in the heart.

This two-three combination defied the usual request to avoid the face, but also seems to have coded something deeper. The two and three strangely appears in corrido after corrido, especially but not exclusively in those about executions. It suggests perhaps a beat, reminiscent of current whistling *chin/ga-tu/mad/re* (fuck your mother), or perhaps some *albur* (colloquial double entendre) of the time. At the very least, it was a convention of language that made the tragic execution a standardized and shared trope that made the audience a participant in the song.

The corrido could also build on shared sentiments by elaborating on execution cases that received considerable press, such as the death of the soldier Bruno Labastida, a coronet player shot in 1890.[97] His tale likely inspired the corrido "De Bruno Apresa" (Of Bruno Apresa), in 1902 with another tragic execution taking place like "Juan Soldado" in the Second Regiment of Morelia.[98] His tale particularly emphasizes the notion of masculine pride and pins the blame for his actions in the first stanza on a woman (often the culprit)[99] who caused his execution:

Día veintinueve de abril,	The 29th of April,
señores aconteció	gentlemen accounted
que fusilaron a Apresa	that they shot Apresa
y una mujer lo causó.	and a woman caused it.
en mil novecientos dos	in nineteen hundred and two
fue por los diablos tentado	he was tempted by the devil
y un crimen cometió.	and he committed a crime.

Bruno and his sergeant both had relations with the same lady, but one night she brought a plate of food to the non-commissioned officer rather than the soldier.

This was quite in keeping with the barracks culture of women called *soldaderas* who provided food, comfort, vending, and even religion to soldiers not permitted to leave the garrison at night. They provided nearly all services beyond the scarce logistical capacities of the army as informal healers, beasts of burden, venders, and of course, morale, including sexual liaisons.[100] Scientific understandings of the female body and nature underlay the army's official policies regarding the military family, hygienic barracks, and racial discourses.[101] The soldadera was seen by military reformers as the inevitable instigator of soldier's indiscipline, and by military doctors as the unwanted carrier of contagious diseases. Yet it was the soldaderas, not the men, who chose whom they would be with, and they fought one another to establish hierarchies of power within the walls of the barracks. Bruno's femme fatale, the army audience would understand, was to blame for the troubles because a mere man could not be expected to resist temptation, and a soldadera should know better than to provoke such envy:

el enojo comenzó por un plato de comida.	the rage began over a plate of food.
[but the real cause beneath was that]	
—que ambos tenían relaciones de amor con una mujer.	—both men had amorous relations with one woman.
El señor don Bruno Apresa se encontraba haciendo guardia, cuando el sargento pasó le dió un balazo en la espalda.	Mister Bruno Apresa found himself on guard duty, and when the sergeant passed he shot him in the back.
También a un cabo lo hirió con el mismo proyectil, Al señor don Bruno Apresa a Santiago lo llevaron,	Also a corporal was wounded with the same bullet, So Mr. Bruno Apresa was taken to Santiago prison,

While on sentry duty, the enraged Bruno shot his rival in the back, but accidentally also wounded his corporal. The song suggested that the accidental wound led to Bruno's sentence, implying that murder of a rival would not suffice. While the military court might not agree, the common culture of the corrido audience likely felt this constituted a crime of passion and honor, equivalent in some respects to the elite practice of dueling.[102] Bruno's legal advice and the efforts of his family to clear his name then followed:

—un pretexto lo inventó diciendo que estaba loco, la autoridad no creyó.	—he invented an excuse saying that he was crazy, the authorities did not believe it.

—Entrando en la cartuchera	—Entering into the cell
lloraban sus dos hermanas,	his two sisters cried,
sus lágrimas que lloraban	the tears that they cried
ya todas eran en vanas.	were still all in vain.

With his legal options running thin, the soldier asked help of his lieutenant who would likely have been a man of similar age, but of even less experience. The corrido pokes some fun at his expense, making it clear that the young officer was both dishonest and ignorant:

—Pues ¿ Que irán a hacer conmigo?	—Well, what are they to do with me?
—Quién sabe. Yo no sé nada.	—Who knows? I know nothing.
Al ruido de los fusiles	At the sound of rifles
Bruno se puso a exclamar:	Bruno exclaimed:
—Ya están haciendo ejercicio	—The ones who will kill me
los que me van a matar!	are already practicing!

With the writing on the wall, poor Bruno finally turned to religion, asking for a priest, who proved quite happy to be involved:

tráigame *usté* al confesor.	bring me a confessor.
. . . al sacerdote	. . . the priest
que vino con gran contento.	came with great contentment.

With his soul covered, Bruno turned his attention to comforting his family:

Bruno dijo a sus hermanas	Bruno said to his sisters
con muchísimo dolor:	with great pain:
—No le avisen a mi madre,	—Don't tell my mother,
se los ruego, por favor.	I beg you, please.

Oddly, this part of the tale does not fit with the story of Bruno Labastida, whose mother received many lines in the newspaper accounts as being present and quite involved in the execution process. It might be in this case that the corrido emphasized what the singers deemed should happen, a mother spared the spectacle and terror, rather than the facts of what did occur. Nonetheless, Bruno was doomed either way. Hardly a speedy process, he spent a hard two years in jail (where his family would have to pay to feed him), before finally being taken to the firing squad. As with Juan, he gave his fellow soldiers a jaunty informal goodbye, alleviated their worried guilt, and calmly addressed a wider public. That crowds came, if indeed this was Labastida, was confirmed by newspaper reports of great mobs of lower-class spectators who lined the procession route for the execution. Once in place, he proved his manliness yet again by denying a blindfold:

Muy güenos días, mis amigos—, a todos les saludó.	Very good day, my friends—, I salute you all.
—¡Adiós, muchachos!—les dijo cuando el kepí se quitó; Bruno, con mucho valor, del público se despidió.	—Goodbye, lads!—he told them when he took off his hat; Bruno, with much bravery, bid the public farewell.
Llegó el capitán Guerrero, se arrimó para venderlo, Bruno Apresa respondió: —Déjeme mirar el cuadro.	Captain Guerrero arrived, he tried to blindfold him, Bruno Apresa responded: —Let me see the square.

An odd thing happened when they finally shot. The squad fired eight bullets, but could not kill him because he carried a holy talisman in his mouth. In counterpoint to his interaction with the gloating priest, Bruno had his own folk religious practices that ultimately proved to make him bulletproof:

Ocho balazos le dieron, pero morir no podía y era por una medalla que en la boca la traía.	Eight shots they gave him, but he could not die and it was because of a medallion that he held in his mouth.

He was not so fortunate, nonetheless, when his captain fired the final shots into his head at close range. The song thus demonstrates who was to blame, truly, for the soldier's tragedy. He ultimately fell at the hands of an officer, not a soldier, having been initially protected by folk religion, not by a priest's benediction. Army and Church shared guilt with the "bad" woman who started it all. Adding to the critique, for some reason his execution was witnessed by a foreigner, although the press reports of Labastida's death make no such mention. The strong anti-U.S. feelings of many Mexicans, still raw after 1848, continued to inform the public even in corridos absolutely unrelated to economics or politics in a formal sense. In the corrido, an American, impressed by the show of bravery, offered to buy Bruno's military cap (kepi or shako) for an enormous five pesos, intending it as a souvenir, but the captain refused to sell it. The tragic element of the execution was emphasized by hinting at an inappropriate foreign interest in the spectacle, and perhaps even another level of blame:

Un americano dijo cuando el kepí lo aventó: —Cinco pesos por el chaco, para conservarlo yo.	An American said when the hat rolled: —Five pesos for the shako, for I would keep it.

[But the captain declined, saying it was not fitting to sell]:

—para recuerdo de un hombre.	—for the memory of a man.

The corrido ended by repeatedly proclaiming Bruno's manliness. Tough, masculine, and not for sale to foreigners, the tragic figure of the soldier struck a chord and represented how the singers envisioned their own military ideal:

que hombre como Bruno Apresa en el mundo no le ha habido.	such a man like Bruno Apresa the world has never had.

Manliness though, was hardly the province of the executed alone. In poems and corridos, a romanticized and individual-focused masculinity worked to articulate ideas about appropriate gender behaviors.

Poems to Sex Both Fair and Foul

While young officers often wrote elegies and eulogies to please superiors in day-to-day service, sometimes poetic obsequios (gifts) crossed the military-civilian boundary.[103] A poetic homage was offered to the president's wife on July 16, 1897, for her birthday, from the army as a whole. Officers presented Carmen Romero Rubio de Díaz with an album measuring an enormous 86 x 60 cm in size, made with the finest imported Bristol paper, and colorfully bound.[104] The opening claimed it to be merely a "weak show of our admiration and profound respect" and complete with three watercolor paintings, it was a collection of letters, poems, and short rhymes (*rimas*).

Romero Rubio earned their efforts for a number of reasons: she was seen as the civilizing influence over a president known to come from uncouth origins; she brought a degree of refinement to the president's palace and ceremonies, and hence the nation; she was young, beautiful, and rich; and she was the beloved daughter of a genuine hero of Mexican foreign affairs, Manuel Romero Rubio, who died in 1895. Her family's contributions to earning Mexico recognition and support from abroad throughout the century, and in particular during the 1860s and 1880s, was certainly common knowledge among the officer corps. And yet their poems, perhaps predictably, focused on her beauty and feminine charms.

Carmelita thus represented the epitome of womanhood to be set on a pedestal. In one poem of this vein, by a Lieutenant Becquer, he skirted the edge of propriety as he alluded to a mystery woman who was ardent in passion, fair skinned yet dark (*morena*), and blessed with golden tresses:

Yo soy ardiente, yo soy morena,
yo soy el símbolo de la pasión:
. . .
Mi frente es pálida, mis trenzas
de oro,

I am burning, I am dark haired,
I am the symbol of passion:
. . .
My face is pale, my braids are
golden,

She was the composite of all mixes of woman, a blond fair indigenous mix. The poet suggestively exclaims that to such a woman he could endlessly . . . toast. With a hint of chivalrous love from afar, the troubadour's chansons de geste[105] from an earlier age, he laments that she is intangible, incorporeal, and so he cannot love her:

Yo soy un sueno, un imposible,
vano fantasma de niebla y luz.
Soy incorporal, soy intangible,
no puedo amarte, ¡oh! ven, ven tú.

I am a dream, an impossibility,
mere phantasm of fog and light.
I am incorporeal, I am intangible,
I cannot love you, Oh! come,
come you.

This is also a veiled reference to the supposed virginity of Carmelita, who in popular belief was thought not to have ever consummated her marriage to the much older Porfirio Díaz. Again, this would connect her iconographically to the perfected Mexican woman, the Virgin of Guadalupe, and suggests that while the nation might be moving away from religious dogma, ideals of female propriety failed to match that progress. Setting aside the possibly sexual evocation of the final line, Becquer set her up on a pedestal. The possibility of his love relied on her remaining an imaginary, disincarnated idea, and as such was as much constructive of proper masculine behavior as it was of idealized femininity.[106]

Numerous letters and poems continued the homage, with nearly all calling attention to Carmen Romero Rubio's angelic nature, her work with orphans and so-called unfortunate women, and her exemplary role in the patria. So soon after her father's sad death and the vast state funeral that ensued, she represented an equal, but feminine, model of public service. She could become surrogate mother to comfort and guide all who fell through the widening gaps of Porfirian society.

Tellingly, it was her idealized position as Angel of the Hearth that made her so worthy of the military's adulation in poems.[107] Corridos also made use of this simplified binary and sorted women into saintly mothers or sexualized perils, as with Bruno Apresa. Martial masculinity set against the domestic mother figure played to two poles of gendered simplification: she becomes the patria they would die to defend, and the secular Virgin de Guadalupe for a positivist age. As the paradoxically female patria, mother yet asexual, by representing an ideal, Carmelita could help the nation progress from religious backwardness. She could now embody the secular side of the patria, replacing the old hagiography with a new modern face.[108] As in corridos where the mother appears as last resort, weeping over her sacrificed martyr of a son, the president's young wife now stood in for the Virgin in a purely symbolic state.

Carmelita was not the only subject of such romanticism. Officers wrote other love poems that they published in military journals, and at least one of these was truly terrible. The *Revista Militar* published a poem in 1897 called "Tu y yo" (You and Me) by José Gabriel Malda.[109] It was crudely written, for example, as he rhymes "*vida*" with "*olvida*" but perhaps its worst sins were in what he mistakenly took to be romantic language. Throughout the poem harps and crystals clamor noisily amongst flowers as the protagonist first drunkenly dies from his love and subsequently (having been resurrected?) drowns in his love. All this, he proclaims, for the illusions of youth.

Aesthetics aside, this poem does erode the idea of a monolithic and emotionless military institution without genuine reflection and interests. The audience did not always see this in the journals, but the inclusion of maudlin verse suggests a human aspect to the officer caste. Just as much as the conscripted troops, officers faced long absences from family and loved ones. Young officers also may have read poetry with an eye to finding material to impress the ladies they courted.[110] If nothing else, the presence of poems of this sort demonstrated a less cynical or jaded readership than might be assumed of military men. If these types of romantic or obsequious poetry helped to lend the military a sense of gendered traditions and historical footing, others articulated an individualized and sentimental masculinity, in the style of *modernismo*, and questioned the costs of violence and warfare.

Sentiments of Masculinity at War

The certain defeat of foreign enemies aside, not all poems or songs of war were cut from the same cloth. Far from the poems of patriotic chest-thumping or obsequious tributes, some martial verse directly faced the experiences of war and its price. A human and emotional reflection of this experience is not surprising. The nineteenth century had devastated Mexico with near continuous civil warfare, indigenous revolts, secession movements, and at least five serious foreign invasions.[111] The damage this caused to society and civilians, let alone to soldiers, was tremendous.[112] Yet often the human element has been lost; these verses in some way help to recover the deeply intimate meanings for the victims of war. Even during the relative pacific Porfirian era a number of serious political uprisings appeared, banditry in the early years was endemic, both the Yaqui and Maya sustained lengthy rebellions, and war with Guatemala became a serious possibility. To be in a fighting army was not a strange or alien experience (even if somewhat more rare than in previous generations), and over 200,000 young men served as conscripts at some time during the Porfiriato.[113] Art at times tried to make sense of this turbulence.

The poem "La Guerra" by Julio Flores in 1900 takes the perspective of a young girl frightened by distant cannon fire.[114] She does not know, nor does it matter, whose army is shooting. She asks what the guns are saying, and her mother replies that it is "a rumor of war" and:

—El festín de algunos aves Y el luto del corazón.	—The feast of some birds and the grief of hearts.

Ending his poem on a distinctly anti-war note, the poet asks what soul could be serene hearing the cannons when:

Sí cada vez que resuena Se abre en el suelo una tumba?	Every time it roars It opens a grave in the soil?

The horrors of sacrifice here remained unjustified by any talk of honors, laurels, or patria. The mother and daughter caught in this war experienced simply horror. The poem does not, nonetheless, offer a similar image of frightened boys. Here fear was something specific to women, the expected masculinity of soldiers remains unquestioned as they exhibited male honor.[115] In contrast, the sacrifice made by women was psychological and, of course, also in the loss of their children and loved ones who served as soldiers. The poem opens readers to an option that wars may not necessarily be justified, despite politics or patriotism, if the popular view of combat was one of simple horror.

A less certain stance is evident in "Los voluntarios" by Miguel Francisco Barrós, published in *México Militar* in 1901.[116] He wrote of two brothers sitting in a cornfield looking up at the sky and thinking of their mother in a distant little house:

Sentados bajo la sombra de los tupidos maizales, . . . dos jóvenes, casi niños, de pensativo semblante, de mirada azul, y triste como el adiós de la tarde.	Sitting in the shade of the dense cornfields, . . . two young men, merely boys, with thoughtful countenance, a blue gaze, and sad like the end of the day.

They lay among the quintessential Mexican crop, pre-Hispanic and sacredly symbolic with its vivid gold and green imagery and a potent invocation of life and home. They had left their family for an uncertain future:

que á su madre, por la patria sin vacilación dejaron, cambiarán las dulces horas de caricias y de encantos, por las tristes y azarosas de la vida soldado.	That their mother, for the patria they gave up without hesitation, they would exchange sweet hours of caresses and charms, for the sad and random life of the soldier.

As in the earlier corridos and poems, the mother represented a holy figure to the patria and an important connection between soldiers and *patria chica* (regional homeland). Their nostalgia would be widely shared by the audience of the poem.

The boys now faced the hard life of a soldier, a sad routine that made them homesick. The poem, nonetheless, purposefully calls these recruits volunteers, hinting that the issues of conscription might be overshadowed in this case by the real anxiety caused by a wartime deployment. The poet asserted that while all this worry will fall away come combat, at the moment the boys could only think of their bodies lying rotting and forgotten on a battlefield. What kept them there, they asked?

tal vez el campo desierto	perhaps the empty wilds
después de ruda batalla	after a hard battle
guarde sus despojos muertos.	will keep the remains of the dead.
	[or perhaps] . . .
vuelvan sanos al pueblo,	they'll return healthy to the village,
donde corrieron sus años	where they spent years
entre risas y entre juegos,	laughing and playing,
donde su madre amorosa	where their loving mother
pide que vuelvan, al cielo.	begs to heaven for their return.

Ultimately the boys' hopes rest on their village, on their mother, and on heaven above.

Barrós's approach does not entirely reject the notions of patria or glory in battle, the mother and sons appear, at least, dutiful. Yet there is no sense here of wide political stakes or of history; these could be recruits to any army, anywhere, at any time. Moreover, rather than orating about bravery and valor, this poet admits outright the terror that war can bring, and the price to family that may be required. There is a human element to this poem that the honestly worried language emphasized. Few knew this ambivalence better than the next writer.

Some verses added weight to the sentimental visions of war. The author Heriberto Frías was a second lieutenant in the debacle-ridden campaign and fight against the village of Tomochic in 1893. Perhaps this experience informed a pessimistic view of war, and perhaps his poetry was autobiographic, though this remains unclear. Whatever his motives, in novels and in the following poem, Frías provided readers with yet another strong example of a military worldview quite capable of nuance beyond unexamined patriotism. His works built on an alternative vision of the military and its campaigns as barbaric in their own right. The legitimacy of armed violence belied the cost to the veteran and to the family. Frías saw the greed and callousness of the Porfirian elite as ultimately causing the degradations and immorality among the soldiers excoriated in the press:

> The miserable soldiers fought blindly for concepts as lofty and incomprehensible as national tranquility, order, peace, progress, and duty. What fault was it of the troops if they gave in to hunger, if they appropriated or snatched up whatever lay in their path? He understood now that these troops could not be blamed for acting out of hunger. It's what city people did out of perverse ambition, wearing their white gloves and affecting the best manners.[117]

The best proof that the author's writing entailed a threat to the official narrative, a sly mockery of the powers that be, comes from his prudent use of a pseudonym. Despite this precaution, the Díaz government sought to arrest him and his editor Joaquín Clausell for their novelization of the Tomochic campaign.[118]

Aside from his controversial book, he also published poetry that was apparently better received by officials since it appeared in their military journals. Frías's "Presentimiento" (Presentiment) from 1900 offers another poem from the perspective of a child, this time a son with his parents.[119] The protagonist flinched from the noise and clatter as a dusty regiment of cavalry passed through his little town:

Con horrido estruendo	With a horrid roar
Sonando los sables	Ringing of sabers
Golpeando los cascos	Striking of helmets
El suelo, al trotar,	The ground, at the trot,
Alzadas las bridas,	Raised bridles,
Cubierto de polvo	Covered in dust
Pasó el regimiento	The regiment passed
Como un huracán.	Like a hurricane.

He asked his mother where they went so fast and so late:

—Se van á la guerra	—They go to war
Ya no volverán!	They will not return!

Common distaste for the leva style of conscription added here to the popular perception that even if a recruit survived military service to return home, he was not the same person that had left. Much in common with barracks songs, the personal cost to soldier and family was more significant than some abstract or grandiose cause for war. Even peacetime took a toll on the recruited. Hard living in an alien barracks changed men.

Similarly, the poem hints that veterans continued to suffer into older age. The boy asked his father why the men would not return, but the man was silent, choked up. His emotional response seems to suggest that his stakes in the fighting might be personal, intimate:

Ahogó en su garganta	He [the father] drowned in his throat
Profundo golazo	A deep sob
Y nada me dijo . . .	And said nothing . . .
Se puso á llorar!	He started to cry!

He may quite likely have been a veteran himself, suffering the sorts of nightmares and flashbacks that historians have so rarely discussed for conflicts before the twentieth century. The father finally cleared his throat, but rather than speak, broke down. The tragic sense of this resonates with the horrors of war in the corridos about the Yucatán or Tomochic, and in a way with the ultimately senseless tragedies of execution songs. The experience of war does not make one an Achilles, and does not make Mexico great.

The poem ends with the anonymous regiment dying in distant rocks, departing "like a hurricane." A poignant and loaded poem, the presentiment of the title hints at war coming home, of disaster in wait. As with the last poems, in this there is little indication of glory and patria, where a nameless regiment rode off to die in a nameless place. While narratives of war can celebrate the nation and through this facilitate or create a sense of order, here the reader would find no inherent meaning or justification.[120] The clashing of sabres as the riders initially passed echoes in the last lines as they fall among rocks, suggesting perhaps the pointlessness of the war. The repetition and echo is empty of meaning and offers no agency to the dead.

Verses like this one brought together collective memory, masculinity, and an experience of history. They expressed an idea of national meaning, mexicanidad, on behalf of fallen warriors for the benefit of the still living. They preserved a worldview and shaped social expectations.

Conclusions

The contrast and continuity between forms and meanings in poems and corridos reflect that the distance between a young officer and a recruit singing in the barracks might not be so great. In the lyrical contradictions and interpretations of mexicanidad, often both groups of men were surprisingly similar. Where the two showed marked differences, they reflected their subject position. The common soldier took pride in different things, saw race as more important than history, gave voice to value in religion, and feared different sorts of injustices. At the same time, I contend that both forms of expression offered a sly mockery of military society as they defied official narratives or seized control over their nuances. Singing a corrido to an appreciative audience allowed popular classes to strike a blow against the iron cage of modernity that enclosed them. Rather than simply accepting new limitations to their choices and agency, the singer and audience could express alternative and popular perspectives on the issues that mattered to them. It afforded them a means to preserve their collective memory in the face of homogenizing pressures and social changes. Their refusals to bow to the official line on executions or on campaigns permitted them a degree of individual and group interpretation of the world, and one that better fit their senses of self.

Poems and corridos gave military men of the Porfiriato a forum to express a multitude of ideas about their lives and about the wider meaning of changes around them. Officers used poetry to build a social capital among like-minded military readers, or to maintain relationships through the obsequio or eulogy. They expressed a vision of nation in terms of imagined genealogies from classical pasts to a scientific future. They could also find opportunities to make a mockery of superiors, if done subtly. For others, it seemed that poetry allowed them a medium to address misgivings about the costs of war with poems that distanced their class from the activity, using instead proxies of children or parents to voice hidden anxieties. Similarly, many corridos engaged in a contestation with authorities through double entendre and wordplay that made sly mockery of their place as indigenous, as executed, as executioners, and as men. The verses in both forms communicated a degree of shared experiences in their repudiation of foreign elements, and their adherence to expressing mexicanidad in the national tongue. The rapidly accelerating changes in modern living that swept the country in the latter part of the nineteenth century created profound uncertainty as new classes appeared, vied for influence, and as new technologies like rail or electricity altered old habits. The great power of expressions in verse was that traditions and history could connect changing conditions to solid ground. Whether sly, clever, or just plain awful, the lyrical military verses helped define what it was to be Mexican in the advent of modernity.

Notes

Thanks to Steven Jobbit, Lynn Sargeant, and Carrie Lawson for helpful suggestions on this chapter. All unattributed translations are mine.

1. On the men of sword and quill see Luis González, "El liberalismo triunfante," in *Historia general de México*, vol. 2, ed. Daniel Cosío Villegas et al., 6th ed. (México: Colegio de México, 2005), 638–706; Pablo Piccato, *The Tyranny of Opinion: Honor in the Construction of the Mexican Public Sphere* (Durham, NC: Duke University Press, 2010), 4; Robert Martin Alexius, "The Army and Politics in Porfirian Mexico" (PhD diss., University of Texas at Austin, 1976); Guillermo Prieto, *Lecciones de historia patria: Obras Completas XXVIII* (México: CONACULTA, 1999), 41.

2. James C. Scott, *Weapons of the Weak: Everyday Forms of Peasant Resistance* (New Haven, CT: Yale University Press, 1985).

3. Sara Castro-Klarén and John Chasteen, *Beyond Imagined Communities: Reading and Writing the Nation in Nineteenth-Century Latin America* (Baltimore: Johns Hopkins University Press, 2003), xvii–xvix.

4. Chris Frazer, *Bandit Nation: A History of Outlaws and Cultural Struggle in Mexico, 1810–1920* (Lincoln: University of Nebraska Press, 2008), 14–15, 133–39.

5. Junior and mid-ranking officers were not quite in the elite; see James R. Kelley, "Professionalism in the Porfirian Army Corps" (PhD diss., Tulane University, 1971), 11–12.

6. On the weakness of Mexican hegemony, see Frazer, *Bandit Nation*, 10–11, 17–19; William Beezley, *Mexican National Identity: Memory, Innuendo, and Popular Culture* (Tucson: University of Arizona Press, 2008), vii–xii, 147–49; in Latin America more generally, see Miguel Angel Centeno, *Blood and Debt: War and Nation State in Latin America* (University Park: Penn State University Press, 2003), 24; for an analysis of hegemony, weapons of the weak, and nation, see William Roseberry, "Hegemony and the Language of Contention," in *Everyday Forms of State Formation: Revolution and Negotiation of Rule in Modern Mexico*, ed. G. Joseph and D. Nugent (Durham, NC: Duke University Press, 1994), 357, 360–65.

7. "Nightmares of the lettered city" refers to the fears of urban elites in Latin America regarding rural violence and disorder, particularly that rising from racial or caste differences; see Juan Pablo Dabove, *Nightmares of the Lettered City* (Pittsburgh: University of Pittsburgh Press, 2007), 1–7, 23–25; the notion of slyness is from Homi Bhabha, "Sly Civility," in *The Location of Culture* (New York: Routledge, 1994), 132–45.

8. Scott, *Weapons of the Weak*, 40–41; James Scott, *Domination and the Arts of Resistance: Hidden Transcripts* (New Haven, CT: Yale University Press, 1990), xii, 4–5, 19, 20.

9. Scott, *Domination and the Arts of Resistance*, 191.

10. Franz Fanon, *The Wretched of the Earth*, trans. Richard Philcox (New York: Grove Press, 1963), 97; Paul Ricoeur, *Memory, History, Forgetting*, trans. K. Blamey and D. Pellauer (Chicago: University of Chicago Press, 2004), 15–16.

11. Patrick Hutton, *History as an Art of Memory* (Hanover: University of Vermont Press, 1993), 6–8; John Kraniauskas, "Hybridity in a Transnational Frame," in *The Latin American Cultural Studies Reader*, ed. Ana del Soto, Alicia Ríos, and Abril Trigo

(Durham, NC: Duke University Press, 2004), 746–47; William Rowe and Vivian Schelling, *Memory and Modernity: Popular Culture in Latin America* (New York: Verso, 1991), 205, 228.

12. Scott, *Weapons of the Weak*, 25–29; Fanon, *Wretched of the Earth*, 177; Mauricio Tenorio-Trillo, "Essaying the History of National Images," in *After Spanish Rule: Postcolonial Predicaments of the Americas*, ed. Mark Thurner and Andrés Guerrero (Durham, NC: Duke University Press, 2003), 76.

13. Brooke Larson, *Trials of Nation Making: Liberalism, Race, and Ethnicity in the Andes, 1810–1910* (New York: Cambridge University Press, 2004), 11–15, 248–51; Darcy Ribeiro, "Excerpts: The Americas and Civilization," in *Latin American Cultural Studies*, ed. del Soto, Ríos, and Trigo, 58–82; Fanon, *Wretched of the Earth*, 2, 6, 163; Peter Fritzsche, *Stranded in the Present, Modern Time and the Melancholy of History* (Cambridge, MA: Harvard University Press, 2010), 8; see also Mabel Moraña, Enrique Dussel, and Carlos A Jáuregue, eds., *Coloniality at Large: Latin America and the Postcolonial Debate* (Durham, NC: Duke University Press, 2008), 7–12, and essays by Aníbal Quijano, Walter Mignolo, and Santiago Castro-Gómez in particular.

14. On corridos as a periodical for popular classes and as a political pamphlet, Mario Arturo Ramos, ed., *Cien corridos: Alma de la canción mexicana* (México: Editorial Océano de México, 2002), 13–15; on the genre, see Vicente T. Mendoza, *El corrido mexicano* (México: Fondo de Cultura Económica, 1954).

15. Frazer, *Bandit Nation*, 1, 131–68, 210.

16. Interview of Fausto Becerril (by Eugenia Meyer, 1974, Instituto Mora and INAH, Project of Oral History 1/61), who recalls listening to the music of the barracks across from Ildefonso, in downtown Mexico City; yet these tunes scarcely received academic interest, for example, only the briefest mention in Robert Stevenson, *Music in Mexico: A Historical Survey* (New York: Thomas Y. Crowell Company, 1952), 162–63.

17. For example, see official repertoire of 17th Battalion: AGN (General Archive of the Nation), Comandancia Militar del D.F., Caja 323, Personnel File of Cpt. Santiago Avadaño.

18. Heriberto Frías, *The Battle of Tomochic: Memoirs of a Second Lieutenant*, trans. Barbara Jamison (New York: Oxford University Press, 2006), 39, 114.

19. E. P. Thompson, *Customs in Common: Studies in Traditional Popular Culture* (New York: The New Press, 1993), 485: speaking of rough music but also of popular or lower-class music more generally, he points out that it often channels rage and hostility felt toward conditions of life.

20. AGN, Comandancia Militar del D.F., Caja 95, Personnel File of Cpt. Luis Delgado, 3/2/77: "dar cañonazos a banda."

21. Piccato, *Tyranny of Opinion*, 10, 11.

22. Victor Salvador Alvarez, *Memorias de Victor Salvador Alvarez, Tiempo Viejo* (México: E.D.I.A.P.S.A, 1940), 74–85.

23. Luis González, "El liberalismo triunfante," 638–75.

24. Mílada Bazant de Saldaña et al., *La evolución de la educación militar de México* (México: Secretaría de la Defensa Nacional, 1997).

25. Prieto, *Lecciones de historia patria*, 21, 27, 206, 448.

26. For example: Frías, *Battle of Tomochic*; Francisco Luis Urquizo, *De la vida militar mexicana* (México: Herrero Hermanos Sucesores, 1920).

27. See Mark S. Phillips, *Society and Sentiment: Genres of Historical Writing in Britain, 1740–1820* (Princeton, NJ: Princeton University Press, 2000), 19, 29, on evocations of sentimentality as a mediation of readers' and writers' experiences, which highlighted the individual mind and self-recognition; on masculinity in Mexican literature, see Robert McKee Irwin, *Mexican Masculinities* (Minneapolis: University of Minnesota Press, 2003), xv–xix, 4, 47–64.

28. Fritzsche, *Stranded in the Present*, 4; Phillips, *Society and Sentiment*, 26–27, 29.

29. Matthew D. Esposito, "Death and Disorder in Mexico City: The State Funeral of Manuel Romero Rubio," in *Latin American Popular Culture: An Introduction*, ed. William Beezley and Linda Ann Curcio Nagy (Wilmington, DE: Scholarly Resources, 2000), 87–103.

30. For example, as a cadet Victoriano Huerta apparently had a running tab at a cantina near Peravillo named Reforma del Niágara and drank heavily there, leading to numerous punishments, including confinement where he scrawled graffiti on his cell; see interview of Angeles Meraz, in Instituto Mora, Project of Oral History collection 1/31, 6.

31. On how civilizing meets nationalism, see Fanon, *Wretched of the Earth*, xix.

32. T. G. Ashplant, Graham Dawson, and Michael Roper, eds., *The Politics of War Memory and Commemoration* (New York: Routledge, 2000); Jay Winter, *Sites of Memory, Sites of Mourning: The Great War in European Cultural History* (Cambridge: Cambridge University Press, 1995); Lyman Johnson, ed., *Death, Dismemberment, and Memory: The Body Politic in Latin America* (Albuquerque: University of New Mexico Press, 2004), 6.

33. The intergenerational banter between Victor Salvador Alvarez and his cousin David seems to support this assertion; Salvador Alvarez, *Memorias*, 80–82.

34. See, for example, Piccato, *Tyranny of Opinion*, 4; and Juan Pedro Didapp, *Gobiernos militares de México; Los ataques al ejército y las maquinaciones políticas del partido científico para regir los destinos nacionales* (México: Tip. de J. I. Guerrero y Comp., 1904), passim.

35. Centeno, *Blood and Debt*, 2, 6–7; this discourse of civilization reached the highest levels of government. See, for example, James Creelman, *Díaz, Master of Mexico* (New York: D. Appleton and Co., 1911).

36. David Grossman, *On Killing: The Psychological Cost of Learning to Kill in War and Society* (New York: Little, Brown, and Company, 1995), 80–81.

37. Castro-Klarén and Chasteen, *Beyond Imagined Communities*; Hutton, *History as an Art of Memory*, 1, 2.

38. Eric Hobsbawm and Terence Ranger, eds., *The Invention of Tradition* (Cambridge: Cambridge University Press, 1983).

39. Antonio Gramsci, Quentin Hoare, and Geoffrey Nowell-Smith, *Selections from the Prison Notebooks of Antonio Gramsci* (New York: International Publishers, 1972); Mauricio Tenorio-Trillo, *Mexico at the World's Fairs: Crafting a Modern Nation* (Berkeley: University of California Press, 1996).

40. Frazer, *Bandit Nation*, 2, 97–99, 176–78.

41. Dabove, *Nightmares of the Lettered City*, 26–336, 210–211; Gilbert Joseph, "On the Trail of Latin American Bandits: A Reexamination of Peasant Resistance," *Latin American Research Review* 25, no. 3 (1990): 7–53.

42. Dabove, *Nightmares of the Lettered City*, 285.

43. For examples, see Paul Garner, *Porfirio Díaz: Biography of Power* (New York: Longman, 2001), 87; M. Meyer, W. Sherman, and S. Deeds, eds., *The Course of Mexican History*, 9th ed. (New York: Oxford University Press, 2010), 379; W. Beezley and M. Meyer, eds., *Oxford History of Mexico* (New York: Oxford University Press, 2010), 404.

44. This was not particular to Mexico; see also Leo Baudry, *From Chivalry to Terrorism: War and the Changing Nature of Masculinity* (New York: Vintage, 2005), 245.

45. D. Fuentes, "El brindis de una pieza" (Toast for an Artillery Piece), in *Boletín Militar*, vol. 2 (July 1900), 16.

46. Thomas Janvier, "The Mexican Army," *Harper's New Monthly Magazine* (November 1889): 812–27.

47. Abril Trigo, "The 1990s: Practices and Polemics," in *Latin American Cultural Studies*, ed. del Soto, Ríos, and Trigo, 356–61; for a brief overview of Michel Foucault's analysis of genealogical knowledge and critique as resistance, see Quentin Skinner, *The Return of Grand Theory in the Human Sciences* (New York: Canto, 1990), 76–80; and for this chapter, especially, see Rebecca Earle, *The Return of the Native: Indians and Myth-Making in Spanish America, 1810–1930* (Durham, NC: Duke University Press, 2007).

48. Bhabha, "Sly Civility," 19, 37; see also John Kraniauskas, "Hybridity in a Transnational Frame," 736–45.

49. It also excludes the so-called people without history; see Fritzsche, *Stranded in the Present*, 10.

50. Earle, *Return of the Native*, 2–18, 79–99.

51. Second Sergeant (of Students) Fernando Rodríguez, "A mi patria" [To my Fatherland], Student (1st class) José A. Ceballos, "Cineraria" [The Crematory Urn], in *Revista México Militar* (December 15, 1889), 3; Ignacio Luchichí, "Poesia en Chapultepec" [Poetry in Chapultepec], *México Militar* (September 1900), 186; on loss leading to progress, see Fritzsche, *Stranded in the Present*, 8, and Wolfgang Schivelbusch, *The Culture of Defeat: On National Trauma, Mourning, and Recovery*, trans. Jefferson Chase (New York: Picador, 2004), 4.

52. Schivelbusch, *Culture of Defeat*, 10–22.

53. Jonathan Vance, *Death So Noble: Memory, Meaning, and the First World War* (Vancouver: University of British Columbia Press, 1999); Paul Ricoeur, *Memory, History, Forgetting*, trans. K. Blamey and D. Pellauer (Chicago: University of Chicago Press, 2004), 56, 72–73; Johnson, *Death, Dismemberment, and Memory*; Fritzsche, *Stranded in the Present*, 169–172.

54. Pierre Nora and David Jordan, eds., *Rethinking France: Les Lieux de memoire*, vol. 1: *The State*, trans. Mary Seidman Trouille (Chicago: University of Chicago Press, 1999); Hutton, *History as an Art of Memory*; Maurice Halbwachs, *On Collective Memory*, ed. and trans. Lewis Coser (Chicago: University of Chicago Press, 1992).

55. "It is sweet and fitting to die for one's country" from Horace, *Odes* (III.2.13).

56. Baudry, *From Chivalry to Terrorism*, xix.

57. Ibid., 6–7; Hutton, *History as an Art of Memory*, 39.

58. *Polonia se retuerce doliente y oprimida; ¿adónde están Bolívar, Hidalgo, y San Martín?* [Poland twisted suffering and oppressed; where are Bolivar, Hidalgo, and San Martin?]—the so-called Polish Question loomed large in European discourse over the course of the nineteenth century. Poland had been partitioned between Prussia, Russia, and Austria at the end of the eighteenth century, and experienced a nationalist

"revival" over the course of the nineteenth century. Polish émigrés in Western Europe and the United States helped to make the Polish nationalist cause a "romantic" cause for non-Poles. Poland was held up as an example of a noble, historic people fighting for freedom from tyranny.

59. Johnson, *Death, Dismemberment, and Memory*, 13, 18, 212–15.

60. Eric J. Hobsbawm, *Nations and Nationalism since 1780: Programme, Myth, and Reality* (New York: Cambridge University Press, 1990).

61. Edward Said, *Orientalism* (New York: Vintage, 1979), 19–20; Moraña, Dussel, and Jáurengue, *Coloniality at Large*; Mark Thurner, "After Spanish Rule: Writing Another After," in *After Spanish Rule: Postcolonial Predicaments of the Americas*, ed. M. Thurner and A. Guerrero (Durham, NC: Duke University Press, 2003), 12–57; Tenorio-Trillo, *Mexico at the World's Fairs*, 58–86; John Beverly, "Writing in Reverse: On the Project of the Latin American Subaltern Studies Group," in *Latin American Cultural Studies*, ed. del Soto, Ríos, and Trigo, 625–35.

62. Bhabha, "Sly Civility," 37.

63. Prieto, *Lecciones de historia patria*, 40, 152, 358–59, 366.

64. For example, in textbooks intended for troops, see Jorge Suárez Pichardo, *Hechos ilustres de la clase de tropa del Ejército mexicano* (México: D. Hernández Mejía, 1909), or in Guillermo Prieto's text for officer cadets, *Lecciones de historia patria*, 366.

65. A more recent example from World War I made German losses at the battle of Ypres, mostly of young recruits, into a hero sacrifice narrative of the "Kindermord von Ypern"; see also Schivelbusch, *Culture of Defeat*, 29–30.

66. Lt. Ignacio Irragori "13 de Septiembre," all published in *Revista Militar Mexicana* (September 15, 1890), 3.

67. Trouillot argues that silencing the unpalatable played an essential role in marginalizing the Revolution's significance, bolstered the legitimacy of Western powers that continued in slaveholding, and was indicative of the West's failure to imagine a different sort of world, Michel-Rolf Trouillot, *Silencing the Past: Power and the Production of History* (Boston: Beacon Press, 1997), 72–74, 90–107.

68. Mark Thurner, "Peruvian Genealogies," in *After Spanish Rule: Postcolonial Predicaments of the Americas*, 141–75; Earle, *Return of the Native*, 79–99; Bhabha, "Sly Civility," 359–60.

69. This is also the case in the Andes; see Earle, *Return of the Native*, 44, 60–64, 73, 209.

70. Serge Gruzinski, *Images at War: Mexico from Columbus to Blade Runner (1492–2019)* (Durham, NC: Duke University Press, 2001), 98–104.

71. This estimate comes from Cptn. F. H. Hardie, "The Mexican Army," *Journal of the Military Service Institution of the United States* (1892), 1203–8. Official statistics on race in the army were not kept by the regime.

72. Mendoza, *El corrido mexicano*, 23, 24; on Tomochic see Frías, *Battle of Tomochic*; also Paul J. Vanderwood, *The Power of God against the Guns of Government: Religious Upheaval in Mexico at the Turn of the Nineteenth Century* (Stanford, CA: Stanford University Press, 1998).

73. It also confused the Yaqui and Tomochic campaigns in Mexico City newspapers; see Vanderwood, *Power of God*, 245.

74. Heriberto Frías is further discussed later in this chapter.

75. See Rita Felski, *The Gender of Modernity* (Cambridge, MA: Harvard University Press, 1995), 9.

76. Tenorio-Trillo, *Mexico at the World's Fairs.*

77. Ramón Rodríguez Pena, "Por la Patria," *México Militar* (1901), 275.

78. On the tension between science and poetic stories in nation building, see Fritzsche, *Stranded in the Present,* 1–6.

79. Bazant de Saldaña et al., *La evolución.*

80. For an example: Raymond Craib, *Cartographic Mexico: A History of State Fixations and Fugitive Landscapes* (Durham, NC: Duke University Press, 2004).

81. Kelley, "Professionalism In the Porfirian Army Corps"; Brian Loveman, *For the Patria: Politics and the Armed Forces in Latin America* (Wilmington, DE: Scholarly Resources, 1999).

82. Gutiérrez de Zamora, "Libro y espada," *Boletín Militar* 3 (April 20, 1899), 4.

83. Personnel files of the General Staff and technical branches (the Plana Mayor Facultivo) reveal very rapid promotion and advancement for the educated elite families over regular line officers (AGN, Estado Mayor, Expedientes Personales).

84. Moraña, Dussel, and Jáurengue, *Coloniality at Large*; Rowe and Schelling, *Memory and Modernity*; Thurner and Guerrero, *After Spanish Rule*; del Soto, Ríos, and Trigo, *Latin American Cultural Studies.*

85. In wars between the seventeenth and twentieth centuries, a sign of complete victory was the capture of enemy cannons, often by cavalry, but this was rarely possible if gunners held their ground or even sheltered beneath the barrels. This line implies that Mexicans would not abandon their guns in future.

86. On the various forms of cunning or sly transcripts within discourses, see Scott, *Domination and the Arts of Resistance,* 136–61.

87. Mendoza, *El corrido mexicano,* 21–23.

88. Scott, *Domination and the Arts of Resistance,* 41; Bhahba, "Sly Civility," 132–45.

89. Few crimes earned one capital punishment in the army, save aggravated desertion (during combat) or murder of a superior, yet there was also the possibility of *ley fuga,* the practice of shooting prisoners and claiming they had tried to escape. For bandits, the latter was applied frequently during these years.

90. Frazer, *Bandit Nation,* 131–68; see also María Herrera-Sobek, *The Mexican Corrido: A Feminist Analysis* (Bloomington: Indiana University Press, 1993), 16.

91. Francisco Urquizo, *Tropa Vieja* (México: SEDENA, 1984), 101: singing "Juan Soldado" in barracks; lyrics in Mendoza, *El corrido mexicano,* 147–50; Juan Soldado is the equivalent to GI Joe, a generic term to describe average soldiers. This corrido prefigured and was reused in 1938 in the case of Juan Castillo Morales, examined in Paul Vanderwood, *Juan Soldado: Rapist, Murderer, Martyr, Saint* (Durham, NC: Duke University Press, 2004), although Vanderwood's title subject was not an official execution, but shot after being forced to flee, and without trial (51).

92. Stephen Neufeld, "Servants of the Nation: The Military in the Making of Modern Mexico, 1876–1911" (PhD Diss., University of Arizona, 2009), 68–73; Vanderwood, *Power of God,* 242–45.

93. Vanderwood, *Power of God,* 40–42, 144–46.

94. On family, see Neufeld, "Servants of the Nation," 106–52.

95. On street versus home: Gilberto Freyre, *Casa-Grande & Senzala: Formação da família brasileira sob o regime de economia patriarcal,* 13th ed. (Rio de Janeiro: Olympio, 1966); Roberto da Matta, *A casa & a rua: Espaço, cidadania, mulher e morte no Brasil* (São Paulo-SP: Brasiliense, 1985); Peter Beattie, "The House, the Street, and the Barracks:

Reform and Honorable Masculine Social Space in Brazil, 1864–1945," *The Hispanic American Historical Review* 76, no. 3 (1996): 439–73.

96. Sapper, or *zapador,* is the archaic term for a combat engineer who originally undermined fortifications with tunnels and the burning of support beams, called saps.

97. See "El Coroneta Bruno Labastida," in *Revista Militar Mexicana,* tomo 2 (Nov. 1890), 660–62. The article reprints the reportage of an unnamed daily newspaper, telling of the sentencing, the defense, the arrival of his mother, his last dinner, his last goodbyes, his procession to the execution site, the execution itself, and the autopsy afterward. The article reports that the man was executed to fulfill the demands of rigid laws, a tragedy over which even the president "struggled against his sentiments." Labastida may well have been the protagonist of this corrido, with Apresa (synonymous with "arrested") used as a pseudonym to make the corrido more broadly applicable to later execution stories.

98. Mendoza, *El corrido mexicano,* 150.

99. Piccato, *Tyranny of Opinion,* 14–15, 216–19; Baudry, *From Chivalry to Terrorism,* 202–3; Herrera-Sobek, *Mexican Corrido,* xiii, 64.

100. Neufeld, "Servants of the Nation," 106–52; Elizabeth Salas, *Soldaderas in the Mexican Military: Myth and History* (Austin, TX.: University of Texas Press, 1990).

101. Neufeld, "Servants of the Nation," 127–52.

102. Piccato, *Tyranny of Opinion,* 250–51.

103. Sometimes these were somewhat sardonic and mocking too. A flattering elegy to General Pedro Hinojosa made reference, for example, to his snowcapped brow, even though the general had been quite bald for decades.

104. "Homenajes del ejército," *El Imparcial* 303 (July 16, 1897), 1.

105. Piccato, *Tyranny of Opinion,* 15; Baudry, *From Chivalry to Terrorism,* 82.

106. Baudry, *From Chivalry to Terrorism,* 103, 106–14, 202; R. Claire Snyder, *Citizen Soldiers and Manly Warriors: Military Service and Gender in the Civic Republic Tradition* (New York: Rowman and Littlefield, 1999), 3, 5.

107. William French, "Prostitutes and Guardian Angels," *Hispanic American Historical Review* 72, no. 4 (November 1992): 529–31; Herrera-Sobek, *Mexican Corrido,* 10–11, 33–34.

108. Gruzinski, *Images at War,* 130–31, 219; see also Mona Ozouf, *Festivals and the French Revolution* (Cambridge, MA: Harvard University Press, 1988), 7–8, 86–91, regarding society's need to forge a new sacrality around themselves for legitimacy. This is often done with religious—and hence familiar—iconography, and with mockery of the elite.

109. José Gabriel Malda, "Tu y yo," *Revista Militar Mexicana* (May 1, 1889); this was also the title of a popular salón song written at the time, and it is possible that he intended this as lyrics.

110. For example, see INAH Project of Oral History 1/61, interview with Fausto Becerril—for his discussion of the social aspects of being a young officer.

111. Stephen Neufeld, "Mexican Military and National Change, 1821–1920," in *A Companion to Mexican History and Culture,* ed. William Beezley (Boston: Wiley-Blackwell, 2011).

112. Jaime E. Rodríguez O., *Down from Colonialism: Mexico's Nineteenth Century Crisis* (Los Angeles: University of California, 1988); Centeno, *Blood and Debt.*

113. Neufeld, "Servants of the Nation," 72.

114. Julio Flores, "La Guerra," *El Universal* (February 18, 1900), 3.

115. On masculine norms, and the paradoxes of its sentimental expression, see Héctor Domínguez-Ruvalcaba, *Modernity and the Nation in Mexican Representations of Masculinity: From Sensuality to Bloodshed* (New York: Palgrave Macmillan, 2007), 2, 3, 5, 13, 29.

116. Miguel Francisco Barrós, "Los voluntarios," *Mexico Militar* 1, no. 16 (January 1901), 320.

117. Frías, *Battle of Tohomchic*, 11.

118. Ibid., xiii–xiv, xvi, xix.

119. Frías, "Presentimiento," *México Militar* 1, no. 15 (Dec. 1900), 284.

120. Dabove, *Nightmares of the Lettered City*, 247.

PRIMARY DOCUMENT

A defining characteristic of the long rule of Porfirio Díaz was the tremendous growth and development of the economy, especially after the 1880s. The country's newfound political stability enticed foreign investors to pour capital into the mining and railway sectors, both crucial to the export-led development championed by the dictatorship. While Díaz's policies more or less successfully promoted "order and progress," the social hardships faced by the majority of the population, the dictatorial rule of an oligarchy, and the domination of the economy by outsiders caused considerable opposition to the regime by its final years. Within this context, Michael Matthews investigates how songs and poems about railways and railway development reveal that popular sectors interpreted the arrival of the iron horse in both positive and negative terms. Far from being recalcitrant toward technological innovations, he shows that ordinary people discussed the locomotive's utopian potential in its untapped capacity to improve their lives, a vision that led to the formulation of sharp critiques against the government on the eve of the Mexican Revolution that would overthrow the long-time dictator (1910).

"El Camino de Ultratumba"

Los peregrinos en viaje
por nuestro ferrocarriles,
llevan los sustos á miles
y marchan como equipaje;
el maquinista es salvage,
los trenes huelen . . . no á flor,
(sucio, viejos. . . . ¡un horror!)
Por eso los accidents
son ahora tan frecuentes
que viajar causa pavor
Pregúntenselo á Maltrata,
que fué el último torneo,

"The Track from Beyond the Grave"[*]

The pilgrims travel
on our railways,
they experience frights in thousands
and are hauled like baggage;
the driver is a savage,
the trains smell . . . not like flowers,
(dirty, old . . . a horror!)
Because of this accidents
are now so common
that travel causes terror
Go ask those at Maltrata
which was the last such event,

[*] "El Camino de Ultratumba," in *El Diablito Rojo*, May 11, 1908.

donde un convoy de recreo
metió hace poco la pata;
mas cuando la Empresa mata
dice: "las manos me lavo;"
y si alguien cobra un centavo,
pidiendo indemnizaciones,
le gritan los gringos: ¡nones!
Y aquí le responden: ¡bravo!

where a recreation train
recently got screwed;
and when the Company kills,
it says: "I wash my hands;"
and if someone charges a penny
asking for compensation,
the gringos scream: no way!
And, here, they reply: bravo!

Discussion Questions

1. Why might religious pilgrims be the subjects of this song?
2. What does this song tell us about how Mexicans viewed the U.S.-owned railroads? According to the song, what were the consequences of foreign ownership?
3. What can this song tell us about popular views toward the government in the late Porfiriato?

CHAPTER THREE

The Track from Beyond the Grave

Challenges to Porfirian Policymaking in Popular Verse

Michael Matthews

The dictatorship of Porfirio Díaz (1876–1911) marked a period of rapid and expansive railway development. The growth of the country's transportation network, above all other infrastructural accomplishments undertaken by his regime, provided the most tangible example of material progress based on massive foreign investment. The year that Díaz came to power, the nation possessed only 640 kilometers of track. By 1884, the country witnessed that transportation grid expand to 5,731 kilometers and to 12,173 kilometers by 1898. In Díaz's final year as president, 19,280 kilometers of tracks, with another 8,000 in trunk lines, crisscrossed the nation.[1] This remarkable achievement did not only represent an economic and political project. It also provided policymakers and supporters of the regime with a success story. This they promoted in cultural venues to garner support for a dictatorial regime that had jettisoned its liberal credentials and disregarded the hallowed Constitution of 1857 that originally forbade presidential re-election. Through artwork, poetry, literature, and government-sponsored pageantry, elite groups celebrated the locomotive as the harbinger of civilization and modernity, and, in doing so, worked to legitimate Díaz's rule.[2]

Yet throughout the Porfiriato, and especially toward the final years of the regime, a wide range of groups—working-class penny presses, middle-class periodicals, Catholic newspapers, and liberal intellectuals—questioned the way that the government had promoted transportation development. These opposition groups often highlighted the dangers of travel (especially the possibility of the train wreck), the foreign ownership of the system, and the Americans who most often manned the machinery. This growing critical consciousness about policymaking decisions related to the country's infrastructure development was likewise expressed in cultural venues, especially in popular songs and poetry. A number of corridos, for example, implicitly and explicitly challenged government decision-making as it related to the country's railways.

These verses allowed a broad range of social groups to consider, question, and engage elite policymaking. In so doing, popular groups demonstrated a democratic desire to express a more meaningful political voice under a regime that denied them that opportunity. Yet they did so in sites beyond the earshot of the elite. More confrontational forms of opposition could draw the ire of those in power and lead to violence and repression.[3] The verses sung by these individuals reveal both awe and anxiety about the arrival of the iron horse, especially in the early years of transportation development. By the final years of the regime, the songs became more explicitly critical and made known a longstanding and percolating popular nationalism that lambasted the foreign ownership and operation of the country's railway system. These corridos were published in a number of different forms, ranging from inexpensive broadsheets to more costly songbooks. This considered, it suggests that different social groups with varying economic means participated in singing songs critical of the regime's policymaking while not necessarily gathered at the same social events. The corrido, in this way, crossed class boundaries and provided a unifying medium to express disillusionment with a number of issues related to railway policy. And, whether or not they accepted the viewpoint of the writer, and whatever their interpretation of the verses, the corrido created moments of shared reflection where the problems and possibilities of modernization and socioeconomic development found cadence in the rhythm and the rhyme of poetry and song.

The songs about railways that endured in the popular consciousness did so because they resonated with the values and beliefs of those individuals who bought the broadsheets, songbooks, and penny newspapers where they were printed, and with those who hired troubadours to perform at social get-togethers.[4] Moreover, the corrido's often colloquial language, its topics, and its infusion of Spanish and indigenous lyrical traditions, as noted by the renowned musicologist Vicente Mendoza, make it a popular cultural expression unique to Mexico that "constitutes an exemplar of the people's (*nuestro pueblo*) sensibilities."[5] The scholarship on corridos has provided a valuable overview of its origins, topics addressed, rhythm and meter, and social function.[6] Yet few studies have provided an analysis of their lyrics as discourses that shed light on the values, beliefs, and outlooks of the individuals who wrote, recited, and sang these verses. Ordinary individuals participated in the singing of these critical verses at social gatherings, on workshop floors, at cantinas, and on street corners. People partook in the singing of songs and the reading of poetry either as orators, active participants, or engaged listeners. In so doing, participants were permitted the opportunity to consider—perhaps often critically—the policymaking decisions of the elite and, in so doing, to voice challenges to official discourses from which they were excluded.[7]

The writers of corridos and penny-press poetry charted and denaturalized the assumptions of elite discourse by questioning the utopian promises offered by modernization. In this case, the ideological foundations on which Porfirian officials legitimated their rule—the securing of order, the attainment of modernity, the promotion of civilization, the celebration of cosmopolitanism—all came under attack in the words and images of broadsheets, songs books, and penny presses. These sources sought to expose the overly sanguine representation of modernity so often reproduced in elite discourse—whether in official policymaking or expensive illustrated magazines—through contestations of the supreme sign of progress: the railway.

Songwriters often used the language and symbols of elite discourse in framing their challenges, working within the confines of dominant discourse. This is not to suggest that these critiques reveal a "false consciousness" on the part of those individuals who wrote and recited these verses.[8] It was not that popular critiques about railway development failed to radically subvert the social, political, and economic order that marginalized peoples faced.[9] Instead, their critiques of the state of affairs implicitly suggested possible changes that could improve their ability to benefit from material progress. And, in this regard, the foreign control of the railway network became inextricably linked to the policy failures of the governing regime. These verses show, in the formulation of James C. Scott, that subordinate groups took seriously elite rhetoric of modernity's promises and stated their disillusionment when these visions failed to meet their everyday reality.[10]

In his examination of France's nineteenth-century press, Richard Terdiman argues that the dialectic interaction between dominant and oppositional presses reveals a clash of ideologies and sign systems.[11] While opposition groups critical of bourgeois society attempted to challenge and mock dominant discourse, the counterdiscursive strategies employed often worked *within* the very systems of representation that they sought to subvert. This provides a useful model for exploring the social and cultural function of the ballads and verses dealing with railroad development.

These lyrical and poetic verses represented counterdiscursive narratives that sought to challenge, question, and disrupt elite views of their successes in the realm of railway policymaking. Moving from implicit to explicit critiques articulated in popular verse, this essay examines the ways that ordinary individuals engaged issues related to political decision-making. It shows that they too believed in the railway's capacity to spur civilization and progress and the utopian promises of modernization more generally. The lyrics of ballads and poetry articulated nationalist concerns about the foreign operation and ownership of the countries transportation network. They also highlighted the gulf between the government's modernizing visions and the daily realities that ordinary people faced. These ballads, especially in the early years of the railway development, at the same time demonstrated a sense of allure and possibility as the locomotive provided increased mobility. Nevertheless, by the final years of the regime, critiques about railway policy in popular verse became more explicit and critical, culminating in the 1908 ballad "El Camino de Ultratumba" (The Track from Beyond the Grave), the final song examined in this study.

The Arrival of the "Foreign" Machine

Three corridos about the arrival of the railway demonstrate common concerns about the presence of foreigners in Mexico. While they revealed a sense of excitement about the coming of the iron horse, they also emphasized the "foreignness" of the machine, which played as a double entendre about the U.S. companies that constructed the lines. In this way, the songs stressed both the novelty of the machine's arrival, a feeling that evoked excitement, as well as its "foreignness," insofar as its builders and operators were not native to the country. A corrido distributed in 1880 for the inauguration of a line between Celaya and Salamanca, Guanajuato, conjured up images of U.S. companies buying up local lands. The opening verse offered a lighthearted but sarcastic take on the cost of railway development:

Ya los gringos ya llegaron
con mucha satisfacción,
para comprar los terrenos
y construir la estación.
Corriendo y volando
se va caminando;
pero ¡Ay caray!, qué bonito tren.

Now the gringos have arrived
with so much satisfaction,
to buy the lands
and build the station.
Running and flying
it marches away;
but, wow! What a pretty train.

The seeming uneasiness in the opening verse was furthered by a complaint about the price of tickets later in the song: "How much money does it cost from Celaya to Salamanca? / Seven *reales* and a quarter to only go by bench."[12] Nevertheless, the ballad offered a generally positive view about the opportunities offered by the arrival of the railway. The anonymous songwriter highlighted the impressive force of the locomotive as well as its capacity to offer a greater freedom of movement. The verses jokingly suggested that the singer could escape his quarrelsome mother-in-law by rail:

Dicen que el tren va a correr
yo ya me voy de esta tierra,
quiera Dios que ya no vuelva,
pa' no lidiar con mi suegra.[13]

They say that the train will be marching,
and now I'm leaving from this land,
God be willing that I don't return,
so that I don't fight with my mother-in-law.

The corrido demonstrated a two-fold reaction toward the possibilities that railway travel offered, discussed in both positive and negative terms, through an expression of the experiences of daily life that these songs so often addressed. The song made known the popular enthusiasm that surrounded the early years of railway development, a sentiment that would temper, and eventually turn, by the final years of the regime.

Juan Zavala's "Corrido del primer tren" (Ballad of the First Train) highlighted local people's excitement over the possibilities of the new technology while also suggesting an apprehension about the arrival of its Yankee operators. Zavala's verses captured the railway's ability to conjure up feelings of astonishment about how it brought the globe into closer communication while also highlighting its "foreignness." The song noted how the train's arrival awed spectators, something that the U.S. employees scoffed at:

Muy cuantioso y muy ligero se ve que viene corriendo, y por todo el mundo entero se ve que viene barriendo . . .	Very large and very swift it's seen that it comes marching, and it's seen that it comes sweeping across the entire world . . .
Con una trompa lucida por mayor, la pasajera, de lejos se oye el sumbido de la máquina extranjera . . .	With a shiny ear trumpet at best, the passenger, can hear the hum of the foreign machine . . .
Luego vide otros vagones donde van los pasajeros, 'onde van las niñas curras y también los gringos güeros. Se burlaron de nosotros los gringos ajoloteros, porque perdimos el habla de mirar tamaños fierros.	Then I see other cars where the passengers travel, where the girls of good stock travel and also the gringo whiteys. They mocked us the gringo salamanders, because we were struck dumb by looking at such a wondrous engine.

Zavala clearly disapproved of U.S. attitudes toward Mexicans, a common theme in corridos about railways, especially in those focusing on the experience of train wrecks. While the ballad acknowledged the universal aspect of modernization by noting the locomotive's spread across the globe, it nevertheless demonstrated considerable suspicion toward the "foreign" machine and the gringos who brought it to their state. This suspicion translated into concerns, seemingly about the newfound proximity that railway travel allowed between young Mexican girls and male American travelers. By stressing that the young women riding the train were of "good stock," the writer revealed an anxiety about the possible threat to their respectability through their presence in the public sphere, a presence that put them in intimate contact—that is, the close quarters of the train compartment—with foreigners who could not be totally trusted. In a society that privileged a form of patriarchy that often defined male honor through the control of women's sexuality, this concern also suggested a class critique against the elite, who by allowing, and perhaps even encouraging, their respectable daughters to travel with gringos undermined their family honor. The song discussed the fears about the foreign control of the railway in gendered terms that linked notions of honor, family, and national identity. Moreover, since U.S. railway investment had only recently begun, the song made known that fears over the U.S.-built network were not only shared by political elites in the Congress[14] but also articulated in popular verse from the outset of its construction.

The reference to American gringos as "*ajoloteros*"—the pink-skinned burrowing salamanders that inhabit Mexico—played both on the skin color of the "*güeros*" (whiteys) and their penetration into the nation, both in terms of economic control as represented by railway development but also, perhaps, a sexual penetration that could endanger the country's female youth. At the very least, comparing Americans to the ground-dwelling creatures (or perhaps an allusion to bottom-feeding) suggested more than a slight distrust of their close presence to the state's young women. The songwriter ended the ballad on a seemingly positive note, asking the doves to carry the news of the machine's arrival across the state:

Vuela, vuela, palomita,	Fly, fly little dove,
cuenta en Pinos esta nueva,	tell the news in Pinos,
que ha llegado el primer tren	that the first train has arrived
con su máquina extranjera.[15]	with its foreign machine.

Yet, as noted by Vicente Mendoza, the invocation of doves to carry forth the message of the corrido represented a common concluding feature that often sought to emphasize a moral or final message.[16] Here, and considering the songwriter's clear nationalist concern about the locomotive's arrival, the use of the literary trope served to warn listeners about its negative aspects, seeking to temper the enthusiasm so often spurred by people's first encounter with the iron horse.[17] The ballad thus demonstrated a tension between feelings of suspicion and possibility toward the new yet foreign. This tension resulted from the railway's ubiquity as a symbol of universal human progress and the opportunities that it might afford. The discursive limits of what the introduction of the railway could mean—national regeneration after the turbulent first half of the century, societal uplift through work and movement, cosmopolitanism insofar as Mexico had acquired a technology that spanned "the entire world"—constrained the composer. As a result, the song's lyrics avoided direct critique of the government's railway project and its dependence on foreign capital, machinery, and employees. The song, nonetheless, revealed serious anxieties at the very same time that it demonstrated awe at the machine's arrival.

The inauguration of the Mexican Central's Guadalajara trunk line in 1888 also inspired a corrido that emphasized the sense of wonder that people experienced in their first encounter with the locomotive while criticizing the so-called benefits that the machine offered. The writer chided *tapatíos* (residents of Guadalajara) for their excitement, telling them that the railway represented financial loss, social backwardness, and a "monster" looming over the state:

Por ahí vienen los gringos	Over there come the gringos
con mucha satisfacción,	with great satisfaction,
vienen echando medidas	they come taking measurements
pa' levantar su estación . . .	to raise their station . . .
Muchachitas de Jalisco	Girls of Jalisco
la máquina ya llegó;	the machine has arrived;
más valía que hubieran traido	it would be better to have been brought
la madre que les parió . . .	by the mother who bore you . . .
Pero cómo no se fijan	But how do you all not see
que ese nos viene a voltear,	that it comes to turn us around,
ese nos viene a dejar	it comes to leave us
lo de adelante pa' atrás . . .	turned upside down . . .
El tren es una tarasca . . .	The train is a voracious monster . . .
que hasta los olotes masca.[18]	it even eats the cobs of corn.

Referring to the train as a "*tarasca*," a mythical monster used to represent an insatiable voracity or a goal achieved at a great cost (much like a Pyrrhic victory), the songwriter articulated concerns about the national debts incurred through railway expansion, both economic and social. This idea was furthered in the song's final line, which stated that the railway even devoured the cobs of corn, a symbol of Mexican identity or, even, the people's souls. The song's symbolic language warned listeners that the arrival of the foreign-built and foreign-owned railway jeopardized national integrity, making the songwriter, and those who agreed with the song's message, individuals with a sincere interest in protecting their country. The writer demonstrated concern about what might be interpreted as a pacific conquest by American companies.[19] Those participating in the song could thus situate themselves as true patriots, in contrast to the government officials that had sold out the country in a fraught attempt to seek a rapid expansion of the country's transportation grid. And, in so doing, those individuals singing would be forced to question, or at least contemplate, the government's program of modernization and its heavy reliance on foreign investment.

While not targeting government officials or policies directly, it would be hard for listeners to miss the nationalist concerns expressed in the verses. The sardonic lines reversed the supposed socioeconomic value of the locomotive, stating that it would "turn us around" and "leave us / turned upside down." The opening line telling tapatío listeners that it would be better to be brought to Guadalajara by the "mother who bore you" clearly suggested a nationalist concern about the U.S. developers that had inaugurated the town's locomotive line. The ballad, while explicit in its nationalist concerns, also put forward an implicit counterpoint that stressed the need for the country to develop its own lines through native investment and construction. In this way, then, the songwriter simultaneously articulated nationalist concerns both implicitly and explicitly. On the one hand, the song clearly stated a mistrust of the Americans entering the state. On the other hand, that mistrust was expressed through symbolic language that highlighted patriotic concerns about the government's reliance on foreign capital and expertise to build the network.

The songwriter, as well as those who sang the verses, engaged in a broader political discussion about *how* policymakers should promote transportation development, a discussion most often elaborated in elite newspapers and congressional debates.[20] Ballads thus provided an outlet where popular groups could undertake discussions regarding matters of national progress and economic development, discourses from which the political system barred them. Porfirians, especially those from social groups that benefitted most from the government's policies fostering economic growth and development, agreed to sacrifice a meaningful political voice for social order and material progress.[21] Especially after 1884, the government replaced democratic participation with a paternalistic liberalism based on the administration of politics.[22] These verses demonstrate that popular groups found other avenues in which to express their own understandings of the strengths and weaknesses of government policymaking. They allowed normally powerless people to engage in important economic and political discussions of their own. And, as such, they reveal a democratic desire on the part of those groups for whom Porfirian progress had helped the least to express grievances about their quotidian experiences, and thus what they believed needed to change.

Together, these three corridos relied on both positive and negative claims about the possibilities offered by railway development and locomotive travel. While they could offer lighthearted critiques about the increased presence of foreigners or the cost of tickets, they also celebrated the power of the train and the increased mobility it offered. At the same time, corrido writers could exploit the railway's iconic power to stress the negative aspects of Porfirian modernization and question notions such as progress, economic development, and national sovereignty. Yet these corridos never explicitly discussed the government's role in railway development per se and instead vented their spleen against the U.S. companies that built the lines. The alleged threat posed by foreigners proved to be a lightning rod for xenophobic and nationalist outrage that also fostered a sense of class unity.[23] The critiques of the regime in these songs were implicit, oblique, and fatalistic. Moreover, they demonstrate an exchange between feelings of hope (in the mobility offered by locomotive travel) and fear (the increased presence of foreigners) that reveal contradictory impulses of anxiety and allure spurred by the regime's modernizing program. In this regard the songs intimate that the popular classes viewed railroads—like the process of modernization more generally—as out of control (at least *their* control), spurring changes that might be impressive and awe-inspiring but also destructive and alien.

The Railway Accident Corrido

While corridos about the arrival of the locomotive suggest conflicting understandings about the benefits of railway travel, the experience of train wrecks—the most common topic addressed in railway ballads—often fostered a sharp critique of Porfirian railway development. The train wreck represented a reoccurring theme in popular culture, as it was commonly the third-class passengers that were most often severely injured or killed when such episodes took place. Several wrecks moved songwriters to bring pen to paper. Train crashes in Zacatecas, El Paso, and the infamous

Temamatla wreck all inspired popular ballads that were printed and distributed as inexpensive broadsheets. These songs all shared common themes: lambasting the U.S. engineers who drove the trains; depicting—sometimes graphically—the violence of the wrecks; underscoring how those individuals riding in the second- and third-class cars were the most affected; and celebrating the selfless actions of Mexicans in assisting the victims.

The implicit critiques within these verses about government railway policy tended to emphasize American workers' disregard for passenger safety, juxtaposing this against the altruistic acts of Mexican citizens toward accident victims. The more explicit critiques expressed in corridos, in contrast, attacked the foreign-constructed and foreign-owned railway by highlighting specific failures in the network's operation. These attacks articulated the social and economic costs that buttressed railway development and highlighted how the writers of corridos held their own visions of what a nationally beneficial railway policy might entail.

In 1902, Antonio Vanegas Arroyo published a songbook of popular corridos accompanied by a lithographic image by José Guadalupe Posada. In the book's dedication, Vanegas Arroyo addressed the señoritas who he believed would sing the songs at dances. The book's title song was an abridged version of "El descarrilamiento de Temamatla" (The Temamatla Derailment), a corrido about the notorious 1895 train wreck that killed more than one hundred people, mainly religious pilgrims returning from the Shrine of Sacromonte in Amecameca, Mexico.[24] Vanegas Arroyo described the corrido as one of the most popular "modern" ballads of the day. Indeed, the famed collector of corridos, Vicente Mendoza, confirmed the song's haunting popularity, noting that listening to "El descarrilamiento de Temamatla" as a child had left an indelible impression "for days and weeks" and that he "could not forget the scenes referred to by the troubadour."[25] The song represented a shortened version of the original, providing twelve verses rather than the original twenty-four written by the song's anonymous composer. Along with the Temamatla ballad, the book presented ten other corridos and *coplas* (non-rhyming poetry) about love, the loss of love, and the daily lives of the poor, covering topics about their work, travels, and religious lives.

These songs were expected to be recited at *dancas* or popular celebrations. As such, these verses provided men and women the opportunity to engage in broader national discussions about policymaking, previously limited to the elite in official venues. Vanegas Arroyo's dedication explained that these ballads represented the most popular songs of the day, especially the book's title ballad: "El descarrilamiento de Temamatla." These types of cultural productions targeted working- and middle-class audiences, seeking to offer topics and perspectives that corresponded to their values and beliefs, thus making these songbooks, broadsheets, and newspapers marketable.[26]

The original, longer version of "El descarrilamiento de Temamatla" recounted the day's tragic events in almost journalistic fashion, recounting pilgrims boarding the train, the train departing and derailing, and the actions of officials once they arrived at the scene of the accident. The song then went on to blame the foreign operators of the train for the wreck:

Diez coches jalaba la locomotora	Locomotive number fifty-four
Número cincuenta y cuatro,	Pulled ten cars along,
Y su maquinista era un extranjero	And its engineer was a foreigner
Causa de tanto quebranto. [27]	Who caused all of this grief.

While placing the blame on the U.S. engineers who drove the train represented a common theme in verses about railway wrecks, "El descarrilamiento de Temamatla" countered the negligence of the foreign company and its employees by highlighting the acts of selflessness and care demonstrated by Mexicans and government officials. After blaming the "human hecatomb" on the company, in the following verse the song praised the work of doctors and soldiers in tending to the victims. The song went so far as to celebrate the actions of government officials and commended the quick actions of the military men who carried out the minister's orders: "The Minister of War / also gave his orders / those that the military / punctually fulfilled."[28] Furthermore, it celebrated how Mexicans united—through financial donations and the organization of a benefit concert to raise money for the victims—to take care of the many orphans that resulted from the wreck:

La sociedad alarmada	The alarmed society
Asegura con firmeza	Firmly assures
Que de esta horrible hecatombe	That for this horrible catastrophe
Tiene la culpa la empresa.	The company is at fault.
Familias enteras en triste orfandad,	Entire families, sadly orphaned,
Sin protección han quedado;	Have been left without protection;
Pero grandes sumas para protegerlas	But large sums of money have been collected
En México se han juntado.	In Mexico to protect them.

Funciones de beneficio	Benefit functions
En los teatros se anunciaban	Were announced in the theaters
Para auxiliar a las víctimas	To assist the victims
Que más lo necesitaban.	Who were most in need.

By highlighting the failures of foreign drivers—a group viewed to be protected by the national government[29]—and celebrating the altruistic actions of the people, the song's juxtaposition put forward a popular counternationalism that implicitly criticized the choice of policymakers in the early years of the Porfiriato to pursue railway development by any means necessary. Their style of modernization had allowed the national transportation network to be almost completely foreign owned and operated. Yet, at the same time, the song celebrated the actions of government officials in responding to the wreck. Through its indictment that the company bore the responsibility for the wreck and that the victims had been left without protections, the song made clear reference to the Interoceanic Railway Company and its executive board's decision to refuse any compensation to the victims. This declaration resulted in a media and public uproar that spurred a group of lawyers to offer to represent the victims at no cost and inspired a benefit concert organized to raise money for those individuals most affected by the accident.[30] Readers and singers of these verses would have understood them as a nationalist and patriotic celebratory response to the company's intransigence as well as to the government officials who were seemingly complicit in the decision to refuse financial indemnification to the victims. The Temamatla ballad was not as blatant or aggressive as some of the accusations against the elite's lack of true patriotism articulated in penny presses, critiques defined as expressions of "popular liberalism."[31] Its verses nevertheless championed ordinary Mexicans as the protectors of the people pitted against foreigners—referring to both the employees and owners of the railways—that undermined the poor's well-being and, at least implicitly, the government that had allowed those companies to control the country's transportation network. In so doing, this challenge targeted elite cosmopolitan nationalism centered on the desire to reach a level of material progress on par with the United States and Europe.[32] This desire had driven policymakers to pursue railway expansion in a manner that jeopardized national sovereignty, drawing the ire of many groups by the end of the Porfiriato.

It is worth noting that we find a similar sentiment articulated in other corridos. For example, the "Corrido del Héroe de Nacozari," told the tale of Jesús García, a Mexican engineer who sacrificed his own life to save the town of Nacozari, Sonora, as well as his coworkers, when a car carrying tons of dynamite caught on fire. García insisted that his coworkers save themselves as he drove the train a safe distance from the town where it exploded, killing García. This song remained popular among Mexican railway workers well into the 1950s and represented a marker of their identity as men and Mexicans.

Yet the criticism in the Temamatla ballad remained implicit. It did not attack the government or its policies directly, and it even commended the actions of certain officials. The song also presented the wreck as a lamentable byproduct of modernization to which the government had done its best in responding. The counterdiscourse engendered in the ballad thus accepted the necessity of railway development and, in so doing, revealed that it became a text determined by government policymaking and the ideology that buttressed it. This is not to criticize these sources for accepting the necessity of transportation projects; in the late nineteenth century anything else would have represented an anachronistic position. It shows the ubiquity of the locomotive as a symbol—something that emerged first in elite discourse—and demonstrates the restricted range of how oppositional voices could craft their critiques.

The song was nevertheless oppositional, especially when we consider the accompanying lithograph produced by Posada. Lithographic images represented, especially in their roughness compared to the images produced in elite publications, a medium of counterdiscursive illustration. As such, and in the formulation of Richard Terdiman, these images were necessarily of opposition, protest, and critique.[33] Vanegas Arroyo chose a striking image for the cover of the songbook: the destroyed locomotive surrounded by dead bodies and dismembered body parts, as well as a man and women mourning over the scene of the wreckage. The image's violence and fragmentation called into question the utopian promises of modernization so often espoused by the elite. Comparing Posada's image to those of the elite press, such as *El Mundo Illustrado* or *México Gráfico*, which stressed orderliness, teleological progress (for which the railway served as a perfect symbol), and civilization in their images of the locomotive, we find a perspective that disrupted the elite fetishization of modernity. Posada's lithograph demystified railway development by focusing on the human toll of the wreck, not allowing the locomotive to remain a fetish object. In the same way that the locomotive represented a symbol of the success of the government's developmentalist policies, the railway wreck became a symbol of the failures of that project. The emphasis on the dismemberment of bodies, both in the cover image and in the lyrics of the corrido, highlighted the possible violent consequences of modern technology. The lyrics and image thus put

Figure 3.1. Antonio Vanegas Arroyo's songbook: *El Descarrilamiento de Temamatla* (1903).

forward a vision of material progress in stark contrast to elite discussions that stressed the power of technology as a universal force for human betterment. In this regard, Posada's work reified the government itself. The lithograph's reification of railway development, embodied in the image of the wreck, worked within symbolic forms of representation that placed a locomotive as the signifier of progress, albeit, in this image, in its false promises.

The song and accompanying cover image also appeared to question the benefits of modernity itself. Until the arrival of the locomotive, so-called disaster corridos—a term used by Mendoza—focused on natural calamities such as earthquakes or floods. The railway disaster song discussed the train wreck, in a similar manner, as a phenomenon beyond people's control (at least for the passengers on board). The railway, as a modern technology that often symbolized order, timeliness, and progress, was undermined through the corridos that tackled the topic of the wreck. Like the natural disaster, the locomotive accident was beyond passengers' control and struck with randomness. Yet, at the very same time, the railway—as all technologies—represented the harnessing and control of nature. The accident corrido put forward a seemingly contradictory vision of the dangers of railway travel. The rapid progress experienced during the Porfiriato led to new forms of mechanized death, fostering a sense that the increased pace of life sped people toward their demise.[34] At the same time the railway accident engendered similar fears related to natural disasters in its unpredictability—even if harnessed by human ingenuity—and, in so doing, bridged seemingly contradictory experiences of controlled modern travel and the randomness of nature's violence.

The Temamatla songbook brings to light another important issue. Examining the works of Vanegas Arroyo and Posada, scholars have argued that these works targeted lower-class audiences. This claim has not been empirically proven through a systematic study of all the works that these individuals produced. Instead, scholars have based this assertion on the language, topics, and characters represented in the words and images they published.[35] Yet the critiques of government policy and the contradictions of modernity conveyed in their works reached more than lower-class audiences. As the song retells, the wreck's victims were overwhelmingly poor passengers, many of whom had been riding on the top of the third-class cars. Vanegas Arroyo's decision to place a middle-class couple in Victorian attire on the cover suggests that Posada's image, and the songbook, also sought to target middle-class consumers. Moreover, the higher cost of published songbooks, especially compared to penny presses and broadsheets, restricted their availability to people of lesser economic means.

Vanegas Arroyo's shortened published version of "El descarrilamiento de Temamatla" left in the original verse that asserted the culpability of the foreign engineer. The song omitted verses, most notably, that related how third-class passengers had borne the brunt of the wreck and how the people had rallied in support of the victims. Rather, the song included the verses that stressed the carnage of the wreck, especially the verses dealing with death and dismemberment. Vanegas Arroyo's choice to reproduce the verses that described the dismembered limbs, dead bodies, and broken families that resulted from the wreck matched well with the graphic cover art provided by Posada. By targeting the wreck's sensationalized aspects, Vanegas Arroyo focused on the macabre rather than the nationalistic, perhaps hoping to pique the interest of those individuals who could afford the more expensive songbooks. This might suggest a divide in what Arroyo interpreted as the different predilections of lower-class and middle-class customers, believing nationalist subject matter—that is, the emphasis on the good deeds of common Mexicans in aiding the victims financially—to be more working-class fare.[36] As Helia Emma Bonilla maintains, the works of Vanegas Arroyo and Posada did indeed target middle-class audiences, not only the poor and working class. This was especially true, according to Bonilla, because songbooks offered colored cover illustrations, used more text than images, and provided more "refined" subject matter on their covers. This more "refined" subject matter was denoted by the middle- and upper-class individuals who often graced the covers of his more expensive songbooks. For example, another Vanegas Arroyo songbook, *El Automóvil,* as well as his book of printed love letters, *Colección de cartas amorosas,* likewise depicted well-dressed individuals on their covers in a manner that did not disparage them, a marked contrast to depictions of the well-to-do in broadsheets and penny presses.[37] Both the original and shorter published versions of the Temamatla ballad reached a broader audience than scholars have so far considered.[38]

All these social groups, politically marginalized by the dictatorial regime, while perhaps not gathered together at social functions, nevertheless recited at least some of the same lyrics, allowing the policy critiques expressed to cross class boundaries. These corridos, in this way, provided a unifying medium to build solidarity between two newly created social classes. Moreover, it suggests that whatever the perceived differences between these two groups, they were largely of their own making, based on a self-identification with particular cultural and moral values. William French has shown how middle-class individuals sought to separate themselves from the working class by emphasizing their education, literacy, and morality.[39] Yet the popularity of these verses among different social groups suggests that they shared similar beliefs and concerns about the failures of the government's railway development policies.[40]

In the years following the publication of the Temamatla ballad, writers penned a number of songs that more explicitly articulated nationalist concerns about the foreign-owned railway system. For example, after a vivid description of the carnage caused by a 1904 accident near Zacatecas, the "Corrido del descarrilamiento del ferrocarril Central de Zacatecas" (Ballad of the Derailment of the [Mexican] Central Railway of Zacatecas), went so far as to name the foreign train drivers directly, faulting them for the accident. In the ballad, two U.S. railroad employees of the Mexican Central Railway Company, referred to as Lee and Moore, were blamed by the songwriters for the accident:

Casualmente el maquinista no salió nada de grave, a pesar de lo ocurrido en ese horrible resbalde.	By chance the driver did not end up gravely injured, despite what took place in that horrible wreck.
Ese maquinista Lee a la cárcel fue culpable y a pesar de ser güerito difícil es que se salve.	The engineer Lee was taken to jail guilty and despite being a whitey it will be difficult to save himself.
El conductor mister Moore en aguas se encuentra muy grave, y no es fácil, aseguran, que el pobre mister se salve.[41]	The conductor Mr. Moore finds himself in hot waters, and it will not be easy, they assure, for the poor mister to save himself.

These sentiments matched well with feelings in the local press, which, after the accident, reported that the passengers of the doomed train pleaded with the driver to slow down, a demand that fell on deaf ears. One newspaper exclaimed that Lee had more than likely been overcome by rage because that was a common occurrence among Americans who, according to the journalist, were "worse than savages."[42] In this regard, the ballad of the Zacatecas wreck was unique insofar as it engaged a specific discussion taking place in the press about the culpability of Lee and Moore. This discussion revolved around the issue regarding the need to have more Mexicans trained and hired as railway employees. The ballad thus introduced current political and economic dialogues taking place in the literate community to the social gatherings where these verses would be sung.

Like the original, longer version of the Temamatla wreck ballad, this corrido juxtaposed the failure of U.S. engineers to ensure the safety of passengers with the altruistic actions of the Mexican people as they united to help the accident victims. For example, the song noted that "The medics' train arrived / at seven at night / it arrived quite quickly."[43] The emphasis on the train's punctuality in its arrival to aid the victims, for listeners, would have stood in sharp contrast to descriptions of U.S. engineers in popular publications. Penny presses, for instance, often blamed foreign engineers for regularly departing late, an error that often forced them to drive too fast, endangering the lives of passengers.[44] Here, again, the song reiterated themes discussed in the Temamatla ballad that likewise stressed the punctuality of the soldiers who arrived to tend to the victims. In the following verses, the song would applaud the actions of medics who "took great care" in tending to the injured. Again, the lyrics contrasted Mexicans' concern for the plight of the people with the indifference of the Yankee operators. The song also related that the theaters across the nation's capital cities organized benefit concerts to collect funds to support the victims:

En muchos teatros de México y de otras capitals se preparan beneficios para remediar los males. Con los productos que salgan se atenderá a las familias	In many of the theaters of Mexico, and in other capital cities, benefits are being prepared to remedy the evils. With the money that is raised those families of the dead and injured
de aquellos muertos y heridos que del tren quedaron víctimas.	who became victims of the train will be helped.

Listeners to, and singers of, the ballad would surely draw connections between the song's lyrics and the failures of the government to provide financial compensation for the victims as the issue of indemnifications remained a lively topic of discussion in the government-subsidized, opposition, and penny presses.

Likewise, "El terrible choque y descarrilamiento del tren número 2 llamado El Paso" (The Terrible Wreck and Derailment of the Number 2 Train Called El Paso), about the 1907 Mexican Central Railway wreck near the Texas border, was published with an accompanying image and sold as an inexpensive broadsheet. Vanegas Arroyo produced the broadsheet and Posada crafted the image. The song, like its counterpart, provided listeners (and readers) with a description of the events and, likewise, and in no uncertain terms, blamed the American conductor for the disaster, who, according to the song, ignored orders to wait for another train to pass safely:

Dicen que el motivo ha sido porque el de carga siguió su trayecto a Aguascalientes, ¡culpable fue el conductor!	They say the reason was because the cargo train continued its way to Aguascalientes, the conductor was at fault!
La orden que dada tenía no la quiso obedecer, y era la de esperar en Santa María otro tren. Éste era el de pasajeros y se encontraron los dos, produciendo la catástrofe, como muy pocas, atroz. Vino el choque, en una curva, entre una y otra estación; fogonero y pasaleña fueron muertos ¡oh qué horror![45]	The order was given, he did not want to obey it, and it was to wait in Santa María for another train. This was the passenger train, and the two met, producing a catastrophe, like few others, atrocious! The crash came, at a curve, between two stations; the stoker and fireman were killed, oh what horror!

These verses echoed the same concerns and angers as did opposition newspapers that commonly placed blame for wrecks on the U.S. engineers who allegedly caused the accidents. The songwriter attempted to encourage listeners' nationalist outrage by reminding them that both the stoker and the fireman had died, both low-ranking employment positions most often held by Mexicans. In this regard, this song's lyrics connected the issue of the dangers of railway travel with another hotly discussed issue, especially among railway workers: namely, that the U.S. workers received better employment positions and higher pay than their Mexican counterparts.[46] The song's anti-U.S. tone matched the news reports of the day as well as the actions of local officials. A news report, for example, blamed the U.S. workers for the accident and related that, in the aftermath of the wreck, Aguascalientes police pursued the engineer and conductor of the cargo train who, presumably, attempted to get back the United States in order to avoid arrest.[47]

The accompanying image of a mangled ruin of train cars and strewn body parts put forward a pessimistic take on the civilizing capacity of modern travel. Thomas Gretton claims that the production of crude-quality lithographs, such as the image provided for the El Paso wreck broadsheet, was a conscious decision by Vanegas Arroyo and Posada. This choice allowed them to reject bourgeois art culture and, as such, made customers "feel their distance from the dominant processes of induction into markets, 'urbane' cultural comportments and 'civilised' mental universes."[48] The image, like the one provided for the Temamatla songbook, challenged elite assumptions about social and economic progress. It provided the opportunity for those individuals who purchased the broadsheets to consider the government's failure to live up to its own assertions about the benefits of its railway development program. These songs' emphasis on the errors of foreign-born drivers not only distanced the readers and listeners from the "mental universes" of civilized society, but put into question the very nature of official discourse that defined "civilization." The government's economic policies that promoted heavy U.S. investment, something that had allowed for the railway network to be overwhelmingly foreign operated,[49] became associated with symbols that undermined the notion of civilized order represented in locomotive travel. The fragmented images and the fatigue fractures on the image simultaneously emphasized the broadsheets' self-devaluation and the violent disorder of the railway accident. According to Gretton, Vanegas Arroyo's decision to devalue the appearance of his product allowed him to sell a commodity that could be produced because of "high-capitalist culture" at the same time that its appearance rejected that cultural milieu.[50] Moreover, the apparently conscious effort to make the broadsheets appear worthless through an array of printing techniques allowed Vanegas Arroyo to emphasize the affordability of these works for a mass audience. The image thus offered a broad critique to a large group of consumers who at once questioned the government's transportation policy, the U.S.-operated system, bourgeois values, and assumptions about the civilizing capacity of material progress.

Popular Verse and Challenges to Policymaking

The poetry and ballads produced in penny presses, especially *El Diablito Bromista, El Diablito Rojo, El Moquete, El Pinche,* and *Don Cucufate,* regularly focused on the dangers of railway and streetcar travel, targeting U.S. conductors and engineers with their ire. Again, troubadours and their audiences recited lyrics that underscored the failures of railway development caused by the U.S. companies that built the track. But, at the same time, these verses rarely focused on the government's role in securing those contracts. Beyond nationalistic critiques, those who penned the lines that filled the pages of the penny presses likewise took great joy in highlighting the failures, and more importantly, contradictions in government policymaking. One poem titled "Imparcialadas," published in 1908, used sardonic irony to contrast various government regulations that the author viewed as contradictory and wrongheaded, although not solely focusing on railway development. The poem lamented the plight of the poor, highlighting the daily experiences of danger and violence that intruded into working-class neighborhoods:

Veinticinco tirturadas	Twenty-five people crushed
Suicidas un montón,	A bunch of suicides,
Uno que otro cabezón	Every other pigheaded person
Dividido á cuchilladas.	Torn apart by stabbings.
Clausuras de pulquerías,	*Pulquerías* [drinking establishments] closures,
Descarillamiento en curva.	Derailment at the curve.
Así se ilustra á la turba,	That is how you teach the mob,
Con chismes y porquerias.[51]	With gossip and junk!

In the first four lines, the poem sketched out the streetcar deaths, suicides, and knife fights that represented daily realities for the readers of the penny presses such as *Don Cucufate*. In the next four lines, it directly questioned official attempts to regulate lower-class alcohol consumption at the same time that the problem of derailments went seemingly unaddressed. The poem's title clearly played on the government-subsidized newspaper *El Imparcial*—which could also mean impartiality (the ironic meaning) or indifferent (the literal meaning, at least in terms of what the author sought to convey). This undermined the celebratory discourse so often espoused in pro-government newspapers by placing official social policy (the closure of drinking establishments) against the realities of working-class social life, where experiences of industrial death (streetcars and trains) put into question the civilizing promise of modernization. The biting irony took to task the misguided priorities of the elite in regards to their concerns for social welfare. And, in this way, the counterdiscursive employment of irony becomes, as noted by Terdiman, the profoundest rhetoric of the real.[52]

Moving to the most explicit critique of government policymaking in popular verse, a corrido published in another penny press in 1908 directly addressed what writers viewed as serious failures on the part of the government. Lambasting both the U.S.-owned railways and the government's role in not holding the companies accountable for compensating victims, one corrido published in the popular penny press *El Diablito Rojo* offered a potent critique of the failures of Porfirian policymaking. Posada's print image,

Figure 3.2. The Track from Beyond the Grave. José Guadalupe Posada's "El Camino de Ultratumba" ("The Track from Beyond the Grave"). *El Diablito Rojo* May 11, 1908.

"El Camino de Ultratumba" (The Track from Beyond the Grave) accompanied the song. It showed a train flying off the tracks, tossing out religious pilgrims, while the devil and a Yankee looked on and laughed. The topic of compensation had produced a lively discussion in the press about the need to rewrite railway policies, placing them more in line with the laws in the U.S and Europe. Mexico did not have any formal rules regarding indemnification of accident victims, allowing recalcitrant railway executives to avoid paying out financial compensation to those individuals injured or to the families of those killed.[53] And, as shown earlier, some corridos had made implicit reference to the intransigence of foreign companies that failed to offer financial compensation to victims, a policy that sometimes led to the organization of benefit concerts to raise money for the poor individuals who were injured or had lost family. The song expressed this state of affairs by accusing the U.S.-owned railway companies of absolving themselves from their responsibilities and condemning the Mexican government for abetting this lack of action, an issue of social policy that became a serious point of contention after the Temamatla accident:

Los peregrinos en viaje	The pilgrims travel
por nuestro ferrocarriles,	on our railways,
llevan los sustos á miles	they experience frights in thousands
y marchan como equipaje;	and are hauled like baggage;

el maquinista es salvage,
los trenes huelen . . . no á flor,
(sucio, viejos. . . . ¡un horror!)
Por eso los accidents
son ahora tan frecuentes
que viajar causa pavor. . . .
Pregúntenselo á Maltrata,
que fué el último torneo,
donde un convoy de recreo
metió hace poco la pata;
mas cuando la Empresa mata,
dice: "las manos me lavo";
y si alguien cobra un centavo,
pidiendo indemnizaciones,
le gritan los gringos: ¡nones!
Y aquí le responden: ¡bravo![54]

the driver is a savage,
the trains smell . . . not like flowers,
(dirty, old . . . a horror!)
Because of this accidents
are now so common
that travel causes terror. . . .
Go ask those at Maltrata,
which was the last such event,
where a recreation train
recently got screwed;
and when the Company kills,
it says: "I wash my hands";
and if someone charges a penny,
asking for compensation,
the gringos scream: no way!
And, here, they reply: bravo!

The ballad put forward an alternative view of the railway, which clashed with elite representations of the locomotive as the harbinger of civilization. The account of ordinary people's travel experience clearly did not match those of the well-to-do. Religious pilgrims, overwhelmingly third-class passengers, suffered from the "filth" and stench of the train car that was driven by a "savage." The vocabulary of the ballad turned the regime's claims of modernization on its head, ridiculing the government's scientific concern about hygiene by contrasting those values with the unhygienic conditions that poor travelers faced. As has been noted, science emerged as a public discourse during the Porfiriato. The highly publicized drainage project that sought to stem the overflowing of Lake Texcoco as a means to mitigate the spread of disease, a project inaugurated in 1900, as well as the government's participation in World's Fairs, helped to popularize science through media reports of those events.[55] Furthermore, invoking matters related to hygiene reveals that the public dissemination of scientific discourse had not only gained prominence among the literate middle class, but also in the penny presses that targeted working-class audiences. Here, again, topics discussed by the elite found expression, albeit as they related to the experiences of poorer sectors of society, at public gatherings. These sources demonstrate that the writers of ballads hoped to draw popular audiences, through an entertaining and amusing medium, into a broader national discussion about economic and social policies limited to government (and, hence, undemocratic) decision-making, providing them with a more meaningful, yet clearly limited, political voice.

The song's focus on the plight of pilgrims also gave it a distinct concern with the poor, as its reference to the wreck near Maltrata suggests. That year pilgrims returning to Veracruz on the Mexican Railway after a two-day visit to Mexico City's Virgin of Guadalupe Shrine experienced an especially gruesome accident. Yet the deaths were not the consequence of a major wreck, as the song and image suggested. A cargo train leaving Veracruz, according to reports, failed to wait at the Garganta interchange track until the two trains replete with pilgrims passed. Allowing the first locomotive to pass safely, the engineer confused the order and set his cargo train in motion. As the cargo train approached the train carrying the pilgrims, the engineer slowed his velocity considerably and, as a result, the two trains experienced a minor collision and neither locomotive left the tracks. The impact, nevertheless, caused the engine's check valve to rupture. The check valve spewed fatal steam through the open door of a third-class passenger car connected directly to the engine. In the horrifying episode that followed, the steam that poured into the car caused thirty-six passengers to die from asphyxiation and burns.[56]

The song's emphasis on the religious devotees injured in the accident was a theme likewise articulated in the Temamatla ballad. Making pilgrim accident victims the subject of corridos allowed writers to counterpoise religious identity, a marker of authenticity, against the foreign identity of those ungodly individuals who caused the grisly incident. In a way, the song also suggested that tradition had become the victim of modernization. The accompanying image further emphasized the point by portraying a (presumably Protestant) Yankee in a conductor's outfit on the side laughing as religious pilgrims were thrown from the train. Above it all sat Porfirio Díaz, on his presidential chair, unperturbed. Using the image of Díaz, considering the song's message that "*they* [my emphasis] reply: bravo!" to the U.S. companies' failures to provide indemnification, was a not-so-subtle reference to the government. Together, by attacking the government's complicity in denying compensation for accident victims, and by highlighting foreign negligence, the song and accompanying image engaged serious policymaking matters related to national sovereignty and its relation to the U.S.-owned railways.

Yet while the song derided the gringo ownership of the country's rail network, the Mexican Railway where the Maltrata accident occurred was not an American-owned company. Instead it was Mexico's first major railway project to be completed—in 1873—years before U.S. investment came to dominate the nation's transportation network. British capital funded its construction along with subsidies secured from the government by the wealthy Veracruz merchant and financier Antonio Escandón, who owned the company.[57] The songwriter's choice to use the recent accident on the Mexican Railway might at first appear perplexing in its critique of the U.S.-owned network, since a Mexican family owned the company. Furthermore, one newspaper report of the Maltrata disaster referred to the train's engineer as Roberts (perhaps American or British) and its conductor as Sánchez (more than likely Mexican).[58]

In a number of ways, the song and accompanying image did not match the news reports that covered the wreck: the train did not leave the tracks and it did not toss accident victims from the train, as Posada's image detailed; the accident victims would not demand indemnification from gringos since Mexicans owned the railway; and the conductor of the train was more than likely not American, as the name Sánchez suggested. The song reveals that people associated any failure on the part of railway companies, whether American-owned or not, with the overwhelmingly U.S.–owned and operated network. Whether an error by the songwriter and Posada or not, "El Camino de Ultratumba" suggests either a conscious or unconscious racializing of the railway as gringo. This is not surprising, considering that U.S. interests owned most railways and American engineers and conductors, who often did not even speak Spanish, operated the system, an everyday reality that irked many Mexicans.[59] In this way, ordinary people who listened to or read the ballad came to view the railway as a symbol of American economic domination, even in cases where the lines were not in fact U.S.-owned.

More ironic still, at the very same time, the issue of national sovereignty vis-à-vis the preponderance of U.S. ownership of the transportation network had also come to preoccupy the decision-making of high-ranking officials, most notably José Limantour, the minister of finance. Likewise concerned with the nation's sovereignty, Limantour undertook a series of nationalist policy reforms. These included new laws that aimed to promote more European competition, to challenge U.S. monopoly capitalism through antitrust campaigns, to offer new contracts in infrastructure development and oil production to British companies and, most notably, to assume government control of the railway network.[60] By 1908, the government had purchased majority stock in the U.S.-owned railways, forming the National Railways of Mexico two months before this song was published. On the one hand, "El Camino de Ultratumba" demonstrates the gulf that existed between the popular perception that Porfirian policymakers acquiesced to the demands of U.S. companies and the actual actions the government took to mitigate their own fears about the possible economic consequences of too much U.S. control. On the other hand, the song put forward a bitter irony that, while the government Mexicanized the railway, people's travel experience nevertheless involved the continued presence of U.S. conductors and drivers as well as the continued failure to compensate accident victims.

The song's use of sardonic irony, as well as dark humor, assumed an audience that sought to divorce itself from the dominant system of values, in this case articulated through nationalist railway policy introduced by Limantour. This helps explain the rift between popular perceptions and government actions although they *both* shared concerns, albeit expressed over different issues, about the need to introduce more nationalistic economic policymaking. Yet, like the previous example, this critical discourse relied on the structural possibilities of the ideological framework that produced it. The critique, by using the textual protocols regularly employed in the elite press and by the government—the locomotive as an ubiquitous and elastic symbol that could represent an array of government policymaking decisions—showed itself fettered by the very language and practice of elite discourse it simultaneously subverted.

It also shows, in the formulation of James C. Scott, that subordinate groups do not necessarily produce radical, counterhegemonic ideologies in their opposition to the ruling elite. Instead, they take official narratives seriously and, in framing their critiques, put forward legitimate challenges to the ruling ideology.[61] In this case, the corrido took seriously elite discourse that framed railway development as an ontological necessity for the establishment of civilization and social advancement, making obvious the government's failure in that regard. The song emphasized the "savagery" of the engineer, the unsanitary conditions of third-class travel, and the failure of foreign companies to compensate accident victims. In so doing, it used the elite's own language and concerns to hold them accountable for a transportation network that, according to popular views, failed to deliver on the utopian promises of modernization so often articulated in official narratives. These verses, more generally, represented "hidden transcripts" that expressed popular challenges based on a sense of betrayal regarding the government's failure to implement railway policy in a manner that matched its own lofty rhetoric.

As demonstrated, lyrical attacks on the foreign-owned railway lines and their employees that manned the machinery represented the most common critique articulated in popular venues. These sources reveal that a pervasive sense of nationalism emerged during the Porfiriato. Historians of the

Mexican Revolution (1910) have emphasized the role of national outrage against foreigners as one of the chief causes of the popular rebellion. The Cananea strike of 1906 and the Río Blanco strike of 1907, for example, marked two important moments in the mobilization of workers against the regime, especially in regard to its support for foreign companies in the mining, industrial, and railway sectors.[62] The Cananea strike, where the Arizona Rangers entered Mexican territory to help restore order, unleashed a wave of nationalist outrage among the press and public, outrage that crossed political lines, upsetting both conservative and liberal dailies. Furthermore, the treatment of Mexican railway workers by U.S. bosses, as well as their poor pay compared to their American counterparts, even on railway lines under government control since 1908, enraged nationalist sentiment in the years leading to the Revolution.[63] Yet the number of songs and poems that expressed antiforeign attitudes (even if with subtlety in the case of Vanegas Arroyo's songbook), reveal that it was not only major moments of worker strife or moments of violence that radicalized people's patriotism. Instead there emerged a brewing nationalist sentiment, awoken and articulated through the lyrics of songs and the poetic verses printed in penny presses. The ideas espoused in these sources reached a wider audience than only the industrial working class. Through the singing of songs and the public reading of poetry (for example, among other places, at dances or drinking establishments), a diverse set of groups could have their patriotism sparked: women, unemployed laborers, people new to the city, urban workers outside the industrial sector, white-collar workers, among a host of others not considered as part of the traditional working class. This considered, I suggest that notions of popular nationalism confronted ordinary people in their daily lives and not only during major moments of crisis such as the Cananea or Río Blanco strikes. Instead, these ideas—whether or not individuals themselves agreed with the sentiments—were woven into the fabric of everyday life.

Mauricio Tenorio-Trillo claims that critical parodies of Porfirian policymaking, while important insofar as highlighting the failures of the regime in a number of arenas that affected lower- and middle-class groups, failed to reconceptualize an alternate form of modernization that challenged the "general ideal" on which those in power based their policies. As a result, he argues that revolutionaries, having ousted the undemocratic and corrupt regime of Díaz, would continue to attempt to forge a modern national image along similar guidelines.[64] The use of sardonic parody, and the challenges it posed to official discourse, also served to create the potential for conceptualizing different forms of social, political, and economic policy.

Thus, these verses helped produce a counterhegemonic discourse that disseminated, in the formulation of Terdiman, "a scandalous trace of a historical potentiality for difference."[65]

Conclusion

Corridos represented an important form of cultural expression that allowed ordinary individuals to consider, question, and engage one of the government's central state-building projects of the late nineteenth century: the expansion of the nation's railway system. While it is impossible to know exactly how the people who recited, or listened to, these lyrics interpreted them, partaking in social gatherings where troubadours and crowds uttered these lines provided the opportunity for people to reflect on the matters that the songs addressed. Sung at public settings such as dances, cantinas, shop floors, or street corners, among a host of other possible settings, these verses provided individuals with often critical interpretations of important aspects of policymaking that, although discussed in terms of railway development, connected to a myriad of other policy issues including foreign investment, indemnification laws, public hygiene, and public safety.

While these verses did, at times, reflect a sense of optimism about the new possibilities offered by the arrival of the iron horse, the majority of songs—either implicitly (during the early Porfiriato) or explicitly (during the late Porfiriato)—put forward critiques of the way that the regime had implemented its transportation policy. These verses, and the images that sometimes accompanied them in published books or on broadsheets, represented forms of counterdiscourse that disrupted, challenged, or subverted elite ideas about the railway's capacity to promote social and economic advancement, at least for the individuals who rode in the second- and third-class cars. In so doing, the songs had the capacity of arousing listeners' critical consciousness about the failures of the regime as well as having them consider possible alternatives to official policymaking. In a society in which the governing regime denied the vast majority of people a meaningful political voice, at times through state-sponsored violence, taking part in the singing of songs or recital of poetry allowed, in a limited way, individuals to engage important policy decisions from which they were excluded.

Above all, anti-Americanism represented the most common theme articulated in the songs about railroads. Thus in the nineteenth century, the development of a strong nationalism posed against the wrongdoings of U.S. companies and their American workers emerged as a popular discourse, a discourse that would remain exceptionally enduring into the twentieth century.[66] Ballads expressed this popular nationalism through a juxtaposition that often contrasted the negligence and disregard of American workers for passengers' safety—attitudes that resulted in railway wrecks, for example—against the selfless actions of Mexicans who came to the aid of accident victims in the wake of locomotive catastrophes. Yet this was not xenophobia for xenophobia's sake. The negative attitudes expressed in song about the foreign-owned and foreign-operated transportation system related to a number of policy issues debated in middle- and upper-class periodicals and among governing officials themselves. The issues of limiting foreign investment, providing better employment opportunities for Mexicans, securing public safety, improving public hygiene, and, generally, gaining better control of the country's infrastructure and resources all coalesced around the government's railway development project and, as a result, in the songs that people sang about railways.

The implicit and explicit critiques of government policymaking outlined in popular songs and working-class poetry often worked within the elite's discursive frameworks. They never blatantly articulated a radical revision of the existing economic order, of which railway expansion was the lynchpin. Rather, these counterdiscourses criticized and mocked the contradictions between the government's utopian promises of promoting modernization and the realities that most people faced. The verses of corridos and poetry, then, reveal that ordinary people took seriously the government's promises to promote "order and progress" and found ways to discuss and confront the failures of these promises as they experienced them in their daily lives. While these verses represent "hidden transcripts" uttered outside the earshot of authorities, they reveal an increasingly critical consciousness about the shortcomings of the Porfirian regime, a sense of disillusionment about the social and economic order that would express itself in the not-so-hidden transcript of the Mexican Revolution.

Notes

I thank the anonymous peer reviewers, as well as Clyde Ellis and Kirstin Ringelberg, for their help in improving this chapter. I also thank Natasha Varner for making me aware of important primary source materials that were unknown to me.

1. There is considerable literature on Porfirian railway development. See, for example, Francisco Calderón, "Los Ferrocarriles," in *La Historia moderna de México: El Porfiriato, La vida económica*, ed. Daniel Cosío Villegas (México: Editorial Hermes,

1955–1972), 7: 483–634; David M. Pletcher, *Rails, Mines, and Progress: Seven American Promoters in Mexico, 1867–1911* (Ithaca, NY: Cornell University Press, 1958); Sergio Ortiz Hernán, *Los Ferrocarriles de México: Una vision social y económica* (México: Secretaría de Communicaciones y Transportes, 1970); John H. Coatsworth, "Indispensable Railways in a Backward Economy: The Case of Mexico," *Journal of Economic History* 39 (1974): 167–87; John H. Coatsworth, *Growth Against Development: The Economic Impact of Railroads in Porfirian Mexico* (DeKalb: Northern Illinois University Press, 1981); Arthur Schmidt, *The Social and Economic Effect of the Railroad in Puebla and Veracruz, Mexico, 1867–1911* (New York: Garland Publishing, 1987); William French, "In the Path of Progress: Railroads and Moral Reform in Porfirian Mexico," in *Railway Imperialism*, ed. Clarence B. Davis and Kenneth E. Wilburn, Jr. (New York: Greenwood Press, 1991); Sandra Kuntz Ficker, *Empresa extrangera y mercado interno: El Ferrocarril Central Mexicano, 1880–1907* (México, D.F.: El Colegio de México, 1995); Kuntz Ficker and Paolo Riguzzi, *Ferrocarriles y vida económica en México, 1850–1950* (El Colegio Mexiquense: Universidad Metropolitana Xochimilco: Ferrocarriles Nacionales de México, 1996); Teresa Van Hoy, *A Social History of Mexican Railroads: Peons, Prisoners, and Priests* (Lanham, MD: Rowman and Littlefield Publishers, 2008).

2. Michael Matthews, *The Civilizing Machine: A Cultural History of Mexican Railroads, 1876–1910* (Lincoln: University of Nebraska Press, 2013).

3. For a discussion of the repression of the opposition press, see Daniel Cosío Villegas, *El Porfiriato, La vida política* (segunda parte), in *Historia moderna de México*, Cosío Villegas; Paul Garner, *Porfirio Díaz* (Harlow, England: Longman Press, 2001), 123.

4. In his examination of puppet theaters, William Beezley makes a similar claim about the need for performers to satisfy paying audiences by providing subject matter that resonated with their outlooks. See William Beezley, *Mexican National Identity: Memory, Innuendo, and Popular Culture* (Tucson: University of Arizona Press, 2008), x.

5. Vicente T. Mendoza, *El romance español y el corrido mexicano: Estudio comparativo* (México: Ediciones de la universidad nacional autonoma, 1939), 4, 115.

6. See Antonio Avitia Hernández, *Corrido histórico Mexicano: Voy a cantarles la historia*, vol. 1 (México: Editorial Porrúa, 1997); Mendoza, *El romance español*; Vicente T. Mendoza, *El corrido mexicano: Antología, introducción y notas* (1954; repr., México: Fondo de cultura económica, 2001).

7. For a discussion of the regime's anti-democratic tactics and the various ways that they undermined political participation, see Cosío Villegas, *La vida política*; Mark Wasserman, *The Native Elite and Foreign Enterprise in Chihuahua, 1854–1911* (Chapel Hill: University of North Carolina Press, 1984); William K. Meyers, *Forge of Progress, Crucible of Revolt: The Origins of the Mexican Revolution in La Comarca Lagunera, 1880–1911* (Albuquerque: University of New Mexico Press, 1994); and Allen Wells and Gilbert M. Joseph, *Summer of Discontent, Seasons of Upheaval: Elite Politics and Rural Insurgency in Yucatán, 1876–1915* (Stanford, CA: Stanford University Press, 1997); Garner, *Porfirio Díaz*, 102–10. For an examination of the use of city police forces, the *rurales*, and the military, see Laurence J. Rohlfes, "Police and Penal Correction in Mexico City, 1876–1911: A Study of Order and Progress in Porfirian Mexico" (PhD diss., Tulane University, 1983); Paul Vanderwood, *Disorder and Progress: Bandits, Police, and Mexican Development* (Lincoln: University of Nebraska Press, 1981); and Paul Vanderwood, *The Power of God against the Guns of Government: Religious Upheaval in*

Mexico at the Turn of the Nineteenth Century (Stanford, CA: Stanford University Press, 1998).

8. James Scott argues that subaltern groups' support for an idealized form of a reigning ideology does not mean that they passively accepted unequal political and economic relations that reproduced their subordination, a concept sometimes referred to as "false consciousness" in neo-Marxist scholarship. See James Scott, *Domination and the Arts of Resistance: Hidden Transcripts* (New Haven, CT: Yale University Press, 1990), 70–76.

9. Maria Elena Díaz, for example, questions the radicalism of working-class presses, arguing that they never articulated socialist or anarchist positions. This leads Díaz to conclude that working-class consciousness "was placed within the dominant discursive context of a reformist democratic liberalism." See Maria Elena Díaz, "The Satiric Penny Press for Workers in Mexico, 1900–1910: A Case Study in the Politicisation of Popular Culture," *Journal of Latin American Studies* 22, no. 3 (1990): 510.

10. Scott, *Domination and the Arts of Resistance*, 106.

11. Richard Terdiman, *Discourse/Counter-Discourse: The Theory and Practice of Symbolic Resistance in Nineteenth-Century France* (Ithaca, NY: Cornell University Press, 1989), 149–50.

12. "Cuánto dinero me cuesta de Celaya a Salamanca? / Siete reales y cuartilla tan sólo por ir en banca."

13. Antonio Avitia Hernández, *Corrido histórico mexicano: Voy a cantarles la historia*, vol. 1. (México: Editorial Porrúa, 1997), 166–67.

14. Matthews, *Civilizing Machine*, 38–40, 45.

15. Antonio Avitia Hernández, *Canciones y corridos ferrocarrileros: Ferrocarriles Nacionales de México, 50 años de integración nacional* (México: Ferrocarriles Nacionales de México, 1987), 5–6.

16. Mendoza, *El corrido mexicano*, xx–xxiii.

17. For a discussion of the unbridled, and often utopian, hopes inspired by people's first introduction to the locomotive at railway inaugurations and during railway travel, see Matthews, *Civilizing Machine*, especially chs. 2 and 3.

18. Avitia Hernández, *Corrido histórico mexicano*, 207–8; Mendoza, *El corrido mexicano*, 415–16.

19. As William Schell points out, a number of opposition groups, and especially Catholic periodicals, viewed the flood of U.S. investment in Porfirian Mexico as a "peaceful invasion." See William Schell, *Integral Outsiders: The American Colony in Mexico City, 1876–1911* (Wilmington, DE: Scholarly Resources, 2001), 113.

20. For a discussion of the political and congressional debates about whether Mexican officials should promote railway development through foreign or native investment, see Matthews, *Civilizing Machine*, ch. 1.

21. For example, Porfirian liberal Francisco Bulnes had long justified the dictatorial rule of Díaz as a practical means to avoid political chaos, and thus allow for material progress, comparing the president's rule to that of Caesar Augustus. See Charles Hale, *The Transformation of Liberalism in Late Nineteenth-Century Mexico* (Princeton, NJ: Princeton University Press, 1989), 11, 134.

22. Cosío Villegas, *La vida política interior* (segunda parte), xx; Garner, *Porfirio Díaz*, 100–110.

23. Chris Frazer, *Bandit Nation: A History of Outlaws and Cultural Struggle in Mexico, 1820–1920* (Lincoln: University of Nebraska Press, 2006), 141.

24. Antonio Vanegas Arroyo, *Descarrilamiento de Temamatla: Colleción de canciones para 1902* (México: Imprenta de Antonio Vanegas Arroyo).

25. Mendoza, *El romance español*, 124.

26. Elisa Speckman Guerra, "Cuadernillos, pliegos y hojas sueltas en la imprenta de Antonio Vanegas Arroyo," in *La república de las letras: Asomos a la cultura escrita del México decimonónico*, ed. Belem Clark de Lara and Elisa Speckman de Guerra (México: Universidad Nacional Autónoma de México, 2005), 397.

27. Antonio Vanegas Arroyo, *Descarrilamiento de Temamatla: Colección de canciones para 1902* (México: Imprenta de Antonio Vanegas Arroyo, 1902).

28. "El ministro de Guerra / también sus órdenes dió, / las que el cuerpo military / con puntualidad cumplió."

29. For a broader discussion of the Temamatla wreck, as well as how many sectors of press—both liberal and conservative—believed that the government shielded foreign companies from lawsuits, see Matthews, *Civilizing Machine*, 164–74.

30. See, for example, *El Noticioso*, April 12, 1895; *El Partido Liberal*, March 12, 1895; *El Tiempo*, March 7, 1895; *Gil Blas*, March 23, 1895; March 24, 1895; March 26, 1895; March 27, 1895; March 28, 1895; March 29, 1895.

31. See, for example, Robert Buffington, *A Sentimental Education for the Working Man: Mexico City 1900–1910*, ch. 1 (forthcoming).

32. Mauricio Tenorio-Trillo, *Mexico at the World's Fairs: Crafting a Modern Nation* (Berkeley: University of California Press, 1996), 8–9.

33. Terdiman, *Discourse/Counter-Discourse*, 152. In a similar vein, Thomas Gretton maintains that Posada's lithographs and prints were intentionally crude as a means to challenge or subvert bourgeois cultural frameworks. See Thomas Gretton, "Posada and the 'Popular': Commodities and Social Constructs in Mexico before the Revolution," *Oxford Art Journal* 17, no. 2 (1994): 36–37.

34. Claudio Lomnitz, *Death and the Idea of Mexico* (New York: Zone Books, 2005), 377–79.

35. Patrick Frank, *Posada's Broadsheets: Mexican Popular Imagery, 1890–1910* (Albuquerque: University of New Mexico Press, 1998), 9–10; Helia Emma Bonilla, "Imágenes de Posada en los impresos de Vanegas Arroyo," in *La república de las letras*, de Lara and de Guerra, 420–22.

36. This idea would support conclusions reached by Robert Buffington regarding the patriotism and popular liberalism that emerged as common themes in the publications targeting Mexico City's working class. See Buffington, *Sentimental Education*, ch. 1.

37. Bonilla, "Imágenes de Posada," 421.

38. For example, Patrick Frank asserts that the collaborations between Posada and Vanegas Arroyo "spoke for the urban lower-class mestizo." See Frank, *Posada's Broadsheets*, 10.

39. William French, *A Peaceful and Working People: Manners, Morals, and Class Formation in Northern Mexico* (Albuquerque: University of New Mexico Press, 1996), 66–67.

40. William French makes a similar point, stating that skilled workers often accepted and incorporated middle-class values such as their moralizing discourse. Moreover, he shows that they often sought to mimic middle-class culture by dressing like their superiors, attending night schools, and forming mutual-aid societies. See William French, "Progreso Forzado: Workers and the Inculcation of the Capitalist Work Ethic

in the Parral Mining District," in *Rituals of Rule, Rituals of Resistance: Public Celebrations and Popular Culture in Mexico*, ed. William H. Beezley, Cheryl English Martin, and William E. French (Wilmington, DE: Scholarly Resources, 1994), 206–7.

41. Avitia Hernández, *Corrido histórico mexicano*, 241–43.

42. *La Libertad*, July 2, 1904.

43. ". . . y el tren de auxilio llegó / a las siete de la noche / casi nada se tardó."

44. Matthews, *Civilizing Machine*, 184–95.

45. Avitia Hernández, *Corrido histórico mexicano*, 252–53.

46. See Rodney Anderson, *Outcasts in Their Own Land: Mexican Industrial Workers, 1906–1911* (DeKalb: Northern Illinois University Press, 1976), 89–90, 236–37. Maria Elena Díaz likewise demonstrates that penny presses often criticized the poor working conditions and discriminatory treatment that Mexican railway workers experienced. See Díaz, "Satiric Penny Press," 510.

47. *El Tiempo*, September 21, 1907.

48. Gretton, "Posada and the 'Popular,'" 36–37.

49. Anderson, *Outcasts in Their Own Land*, 89–90, 236–37. Sandra Kuntz Ficker seeks to temper this assessment by emphasizing that on the Mexican Central Railroad many of the mid-level employees were Mexican and that, by 1884, twelve of forty-nine engineers were Mexican. See Ficker, *Empresa extrangera y mercado interno*, 99. Nevertheless, there was a clear and vociferously expressed popular perception that Mexicans received lower-ranking jobs and lower pay than American workers.

50. Gretton, "Posada and the 'Popular,'" 35–36.

51. *Don Cucufate*, October 1, 1908.

52. Terdiman, *Discourse/Counter-Discourse*, 203–4.

53. Great Britain, for example, had begun to compensate accident victims with the passing of Lord Campbell's Act 1846 although it was not passed into law officially until 1864. See Wolfgang Schivelbusch, *The Railway Journey: Trains and Travel in the 19th Century*, trans. Anslem Hollo (New York: Urizen Books, 1977), 206, fn. 1; Jack Simmons, *The Victorian Railway* (Thames and Hudson, 1991), 279. Likewise, in the United States, Barbara Young Welke notes that by 1865 "courts had articulated all of the basic elements of a claim for negligence," although there was no universal law for accident injury. See Barbara Young Welke, *Recasting American Liberty: Gender, Race, Law, and the Railroad Revolution, 1865–1920* (Cambridge: Cambridge University Press, 2001), 83.

54. *El Diablito Rojo*, May 11, 1908.

55. Claudia Agostini, *Monuments of Progress: Modernization and Public Health in Mexico City, 1876–1910* (Calgary: University of Calgary Press, 2003), 122–53; Tenorillo-Trillo, *Mexico at the World's Fairs*, 171–75.

56. *Mexican Herald*, April 26, 1908; *El Tiempo*, April 26, 1908.

57. For a discussion of the tumultuous financing and construction of the Mexican Railway, see David M. Pletcher, "The Building of the Mexican Railway," *Hispanic American Historical Review* 30, no. 1 (1950): 26–62; Fernando Calderón, "La República Restaurada: La vida económica," in *Historia moderna de México*, vol. 7: *Cosío Villegas*, 4th ed. (México: Editorial Hermes, 1984), 614–22; Arthur Schmidt, *The Social and Economic Effect of the Railroad in Puebla and Veracruz, 1867–1911* (New York: Garland Publishing, 1987), 2–6.

58. *El Tiempo*, April 26, 1908.

59. Matthews, *Civilizing Machine*, 79, 180, 229.

60. Friedrich Katz, *The Secret War in Mexico: Europe, the United States, and the Mexican Revolution* (Chicago: University of Chicago Press, 1981), 21–27; Paul Garner, "La Compañia Pearson y el Ferrocarril Nacional de Tehuantepec (1896–1907)," in *Don Porfirio presidente . . . , nunca omnipotente: Hallazgos, reflexiones y debates, 1876–1911*, ed. Romana Falcón and Raymond Buve (México: Universidad Iberoamericana, 1998), 106–9; Richard Weiner, *Race, Nation, and Market: Economic Culture in Porfirian Mexico* (Tucson: University of Arizona Press, 2004).

61. Scott, *Domination and the Arts of Resistance*, 106.

62. See Anderson, *Outcasts in Their Own Land*, 326–28; John Hart, *Revolutionary Mexico: The Coming and Process of the Mexican Revolution* (Berkeley: University of California Press, 1987), 68–73.

63. Anderson, *Outcasts in Their Own Land*, 112, 327.

64. Tenorio-Trillo, *Mexico at the World's Fairs*, 177–78.

65. Terdiman, *Discourse/Counter-Discourse*, 343.

66. In his analysis of over one thousand corridos, especially those written after 1920, Merle E. Simmons argued that "*corridos* reveal profound dislike and even hatred to be the basic traditional attitude of the Mexican *pueblo* toward the United States and its people." See Merle E. Simmons, "Attitudes toward the United States Revealed in Mexican Corridos," *Hispania* 36, no. 1 (February 1953), 34.

PRIMARY DOCUMENT

The 1910 Mexican Revolution unleashed a wave of violence that engulfed the nation for decades. Originally sparked by the politically idealistic, if not naïve, beliefs of Francisco Madero that the people needed liberty and not bread, the country would erupt into multiple civil wars after Madero's short-lived presidency and eventual assassination. Briefly, the presidency fell into the hands of the ambitious soldier Victoriano Huerta before forces across the country, along with U.S. support, defeated him and left the nation without clear leadership. The victory of the more moderate Constitutionalists—led by Venustiano Carranza, Álvaro Obregón, and Plutarco Calles—over the Conventionist forces—led by the popular leaders Emiliano Zapata and Francisco "Pancho" Villa—would allow the victors to introduce the Constitution of 1917. This crucial document included radical land and labor reforms, among others, and sought to placate the former followers of the defeated and end the endemic fighting that had ravaged the nation. Nonetheless, the wars had left the country in ruins, with up to two million dead in a country of only thirteen million. Yet in the midst of all the devastation, life and love went on. William French analyzes *coplas* and amorous letters written during these years of strife, to consider how people understood love, marriage, familial relations, and gendered expectations at a time of national division.

Tu eres buena, ¡Ah! ¡Antonia del alma!*	You are so good, Oh! Antonia of the soul!
¿Dónde nos podemos ver?	Where can we see each other?
Para saber si tú me amas	To know if you love me
Y sabes corresponder;	And know how to return my love/write;
Cuando vaya a traer agua	When you go to get water
Allá te daré un papel	There I'll give you a letter/paper
En el dicho papel te diré	In that said paper I'll say to you
Que eres mi pálido flor	That you are my pale flower
Que te traje del jardín	That I brought you from the garden
Donde te ofrendí mi amor	Where I offered you my love

* Copla 1081, *Cancionero*, tomo 1, 138.

Dime si me amas a mí:	Tell me if you love me:
Te daré mi corazón.	I'll give you my heart.

Discussion Questions

1. What does this copla tell us about love and courtship in early twentieth-century Mexico?
2. What does the symbolic language employed in these lines suggest? What are the possible sexual innuendos being put forward?
3. Why would the writer recite orally the contents of a written message, to which this copla alludes?

CHAPTER FOUR

"I'm Going to Write You a Letter"

Coplas, Love Letters, and Courtship Literacy

William French

Papeles son papeles	Papers are papers
Cartas son cartas	Letters are letters
Palabras de mujeres	The words of women
Todas son falsas	Are all deceptions

The preceding stanza of popular lyrical poetry serves as a brief introduction to some of the interrelated themes taken up in this chapter as well as to the source used to do so, a form of nonnarrative verse known as the *copla*. In contrast to its much better-known relation, the corrido—a narrative form that tells a story about an event or occurrence by means of a series of stanzas that are related to each other, and in which the story emerges out of the entire piece that forms a single coherent entity unto itself—the copla is comprised of stanzas that are more or less independent of each other, at times combined into different songs, often brought together by chance or circumstances rather than with a definite or defined order. In the copla it is the stanza (also referred to as a "copla") and usually, but not always, comprised of four lines, each of eight syllables, that stands as a coherent entity in its own right. Music or the melody often provided coherence to any single performance of multiple stanzas, or coplas, although these very same stanzas could, in modular fashion, be sung to different melodies and/or combined in different and original ways all depending on region, circumstances, and the wont of the individual performer.[1]

As for the themes being addressed, although it may not seem so upon first reading, the copla that begins this chapter plunges the reader into the gendered dynamics of courtship, in particular, while hinting, more generally, at a tension not only in that relationship but in that between the written word, beckoned through the references to papers and letters, and orality, associated with the words of women. That this reading of the introductory copla is not immediately apparent but one subject to interpretation that depends on context, in this case, previous knowledge about the workings of courtship and understandings of romantic love, is also precisely the point. It is important to realize that multiple readings of any single copla are possible, and to embrace and explore the interpretive ambivalence associated with the genre, as I try to do here, in a way that makes my assumptions apparent, rather than wish such ambiguity away or ignore it completely. In fact, it may be this interpretive slippage, common in almost every form of poetry, that makes the copla particularly useful in teasing out for inspection and discussion of various practices associated with courtship and writing, in this particular case, as well as for expressing commonly accepted truisms and generalizations associated with such a relationship. It might also make it possible not only to express through this genre expectations about the way the world supposedly worked, but also to poke fun at or even, at times, challenge such truisms in a manner that may or may not be direct.

Meanings of coplas, then, may be suggestive rather than fixed, with verses taking on new and additional nuances according to the context and circumstances of their particular performance (although this can be a problem, as such details are not always available, even if the coplas themselves have been collected). It is also the case that listeners must often fill in much of the context themselves, as it is assumed that those listening to the verse would share in the collective understandings within which every performance is situated. This chapter draws on my previous research into popular writing about love and courtship, especially the composition of love letters in northern Mexico in the late nineteenth and early twentieth centuries, as a means of providing one such context. I read coplas about love and courtship against or through love letters, using the written word to reflect on and think about what is being sung in the coplas, while at the same time using the coplas themselves to reflect upon and tease out some of the dynamics and interactions surrounding courtship and romantic love being expressed in love letters. The chapter concentrates for the most part on coplas, using evidence from them to confirm, challenge, or modify conclusions generated elsewhere regarding love letters and the written word. It ends with a discussion of actual letters, as a means of offering a brief glimpse at one role that writing could play in courtship.

Attempting to use coplas to reflect upon romantic love, courtship, gender relations, and the relationship between orality and the written word (or, any other themes for that matter), means necessarily attending to the circumstances surrounding their collection, organization, and the principles and assumptions motivating such an archiving. The copla that introduces this chapter and, in fact, all the coplas consulted in its writing, have been gathered and published in a collection entitled *Cancionero folklórico de México*. It has now been almost forty years since a group of investigators at the Centro de Estudios Linguísticos y Literarios at El Colegio de México, under the direction of Margit Frenk Alatorre, began publishing this collection of coplas, the labor of their extensive investigations that had begun even earlier, in the late 1950s, and a work that would grow to five published volumes by 1985.[2] The hope was that the collection of such "folkloric poetry" would stimulate further study, a promise that has been fulfilled with the recent publication of *La copla en México*, in 2007. In this work, a number of contributors under the direction of Aurelio González, some of them members of a new generation interested in coplas, and others linked to the publication of the original multi-volume work, answer Frenk's call to continue the research. This includes the study of the poetic resources available to those composing coplas as well as the relationship between the various genres of Mexican literary folklore.[3]

For Frenk and, by extension, those contributing to her many volumes, "folkloric poetry" is defined as a bringing together of modes of poeticizing that pertain to the knowledge of a community, transmitted through space and time, even, on occasion, through many centuries. Only coplas satisfying these criteria, that is, those that form part of a flow of poetic resources known and employed by many and transmitted over a long period, qualify as belonging to the "popular poetic tradition" and, thus, merited inclusion within the *Cancionero folklórico*. In all, the team under Frenk gathered and published some 10,000 coplas in these volumes, many in multiple versions, providing particulars as to the place and date of their collection, when such information was available. These coplas were taken from a number of written and oral sources, including manuscript collections, old song sheets, and broadsides sold in fairs and at newsstands, and from records and tape recordings made before 1975 by investigators in many parts of the country. The aim of the collection is comprehensive, both in terms of geography, with coplas representing the entire country, and in terms of time, the work taking as its purview the entire twentieth century up to when the volumes were published in the mid-1970s.[4] Encompassing all of twentieth-century Mexico, the *Cancionero folklórico* seeks to claim a place for the copla as a particularly national passion and, perhaps, to piece together or sing, even if in printed form and one modular stanza at a time, an ode to the nation in which all share a common tradition and in which all can chime.

To use the copla as a means of reflecting upon romantic love is to acknowledge the centrality of that theme to the genre itself. Of the ten thousand coplas gathered to form the collection, nearly six thousand—filling two full volumes, the first and the second, as well as part of the third—are concerned, in one manner or another, with the theme of romantic love. Yet, this reduced number of coplas is still too large to be considered in a single chapter. In order to make the task at hand more manageable and to provide thematic coherence, the chapter focuses on a smaller subset within the amatory coplas, those concerned specifically with writing and the written word, particularly but not exclusively the love letter. It is my argument, then, developed in the rest of the chapter, that such coplas have a great deal to tell us about a particular kind of literacy associated with romantic love and courtship, as well as about the place of the written word within courtship and romance. Coplas, however, offer more than a means of gaining insight into courtship and romantic love—they also help us understand the meaning and impact of love letters, in particular, and the written word, in general, to those who may have fallen under its spell.

The Written and the Oral

If you turn once again to the copla that introduces this chapter, it is apparent that it expresses a particular point of view, an avowedly masculine one. Here, the voice in the copla offers a generalization that frames gender relations as conflictive, one in which men seemingly need to be wary of women, who cannot be counted on to tell the truth. One might even wonder what prompted the editors of the *Cancionero* to include this particular copla in the section of their collection dealing with love, given that the verse seems to have little insight to offer into this state of being. Yet, perhaps it does after all, especially if one juxtaposes the first two lines of the copla, those dealing with writing (papers and letters) with the final two, concerned with words, or, perhaps, orality, a world the copla associates with women. Looked at across this divide, the copla seems to establish a series of parallel binaries—if the world (and word) of orality is gendered female, that of writing is male; if orality is associated with falsity, writing must represent the truth; and, reversing the order of causation here, as much as papers and letters are unchanging or permanent, the realm of the oral seems fleeting, unfixed, and not subject to verification.

Introducing even more ambivalence, the copla might also be read as a warning to all men that, regardless of the format (written or oral), nothing women express, in any medium, can be believed, especially when it comes to love. Yet, in order to argue convincingly that the copla is indeed dealing with love, further contextualization is essential. If one begins with the understanding that letters represented a privileged form of communication in many courting relationships, helping to compose or bring into being the ideal couple that was exchanging them, then such an interpretation is more easily supported. In fact, even the arrival of a letter announced a courtship, with its acceptance marking its beginning just as the return of all letters announced beyond doubt its termination. Letters also served as a form of promise-making that, under some circumstances, especially in the case of a written promise of marriage from a male, could be legally enforced. While this copla, then, suggests what might befall a male suitor who gives his heart to a woman, it might also be doing so within the context of a courting relationship in which each gender had different access to and command over the use of the written word.

Regardless of which reading you find most convincing, this copla forces us to consider the relationship between the written word (papers and letters) and orality (words), how these might be gendered in particular ways, and, more generally, to think about the place of writing and the written word within the genre of the copla itself. It is one of the great strengths of Frenk's approach to the genre of coplas in her collection that she rejects what she refers to as the "false conception" that characterizes folkloric poetry as a purely oral form. Instead, she finds that writing or script, in both print and manuscript form, has contributed to supporting and renewing the genre of the copla. Nor does Frenk locate coplas exclusively in the rural setting; she finds the copla being sung in the city as well as in the countryside, and influenced by the spread of mass forms of communication. Frenk also refutes the assumption that considers coplas to be the exclusive preserve of the lower classes or the "people," finding instead that a constant process of moving back and forth between the various social strata in Mexico had helped enrich the genre.[5]

If Frenk and her contributors have been reluctant to subscribe to a written/oral divide in the case of the genre of the copla, others have been more insistent as to the existence of such a division, at least in general terms if not in this particular case. Indeed, debates over the relationship between oral and literate culture, ongoing for decades, received added impetus in the early 1980s, just as the last volumes of the *Cancionero* were being finished, with the publication of Walter Ong's work *Orality and Literacy: The Technologizing of the Word*. Ong, in that book, made broad claims about literacy's supposed impact on such things as memory, understandings of and constructions of the self, senses of privacy, time, and the conceptualization of history, all characteristic of what he referred to as the "chirographic mentality." "More than any other single invention," he claimed, "writing has transformed human consciousness."[6]

All have not agreed with this characterization of Ong's work. A recent review of the debate that the publication of *Orality and Literacy* helped generate and that it contributed to, for example, argues that Ong does not and never did support the idea that a "great divide" separated oral and literate cultures.[7] Regardless of how one reads Ong, many recent writers have taken great care to distance themselves from any approach premised upon such a "great divide." Laura Ahearn, for example, in her recent study of the relationship between literacy, love letters, and social change in Nepal, critiques the "autonomous" model of literacy, an idea that she associates not only with Ong but also with such authors as Jack Goody, a model that claims that the advent of literacy results in the same changes in every society. Such a claim, she argues, replicates the binary of primitive/civilized created by an earlier generation of anthropologists, merely substituting the poles "oral" for primitive and "literate" for civilized. Instead, Ahearn draws from an extensive body of research that stresses the importance of studying literacy as a social practice, paying close attention to the contexts in which literacy occurs and to being specific about the changes that actually take place and under what circumstances.[8] Scholars refer to this as an "event-centered" approach to literacy and they often focus their analysis on one particular social setting or context to ask how such a literacy, in that particular instance, derives its meanings from the broader contexts in which it is practiced. The "event-centered" approach leads to a concern not with literacy, in the singular, but with literacies, in the plural, each one associated with different domains of life, different social groups, different institutions, different genders, and each shaped by and helping to shape power in different ways.[9] Each literacy, as well, becomes a subject in need of investigation rather than the fulfilling of a trajectory already set out, as in the "autonomous" model, where the result is already seemingly known in advance. This chapter utilizes the event-centered approach to literacies to argue that love-letter literacy was one such event, one about which coplas have a great deal to tell us.

The focus on power in event-centered approaches to literacies is also of critical importance, both to the present chapter and more generally. Utilizing this approach, literacies can be regarded as exchanges that take place between classes, races, genders, and other groups, each in need of analysis. Although I have introduced only one copla to this point, my hope is that you will have already gotten a sense of how that copla might be pointing to one of the potential differences characterizing love-letter literacy, that dividing the genders. Power is also implicated in the ways that scholars define orality and literacy; often, only one, literacy, is defined, while the other, orality, becomes all that literacy is not. For Michel de Certeau, for example, "writing" or the "scriptural" is a practice that produces a text and produces society as a text. It is an activity, he argues, that constructs blank space, in the form of a page, onto which to inscribe, and then to construct a text in this space that has authority over the very thing that it represents. Of greatest significance, he asserts, is the intention of the text to dominate or transform that very object it inscribes. As part of this process, writing is given a definition, that which separates itself from the supposedly magical world of voices and traditions, while orality becomes that which writing is not, a background from which so-called legitimate practices associated with the scriptural, like science, education, and the law, can differentiate themselves.[10]

Within the Latin American context, it has been Angel Rama, writing at about the same time as de Certeau, who has done the most to focus attention on some of the ways that power must be part of any discussion of the relationship between literacy and orality. In *The Lettered City*, published posthumously in 1984 and then translated into English in 1996, Rama traces the close relationship between power, the ability to manipulate the written word and other signs, and the urban center in Latin America.[11] For Rama, the lettered city was the site where the extensive production of texts took place, through which the independent countries of Latin America were brought into being and ruled, and through which that rule, along with the hierarchies and values essential to it, was justified. It is when he turns his attention to the period after 1870, in a chapter he titles "The Modernized City," that his work seems directly applicable to the present discussion. Pointing to the impact of what he refers to as the "ever-expanding circuits of the written word," the spread of urban educational standards, and the accelerating arrival in the countryside of cultural substitutes originating in the city, Rama charts what he sees as the destruction in rural areas of living memory and oral traditions. This was premised precisely upon their dependence on oral communication, along with a concomitant appropriation of those very traditions by *letrados*, those producers and consumers of the written word, and the "fixing" or solidifying of these traditions in the service of the creation of national literatures and national histories. Speaking of rural culture, he concludes: "To the degree that this dying cultural universe depended on unwritten traditions and oral communications, one might say that urban letters came to its rescue, but only to hold its funeral services in writing."[12]

Much as with those subscribing to the "great divide" approach to the relationship between orality and literacy, a number of binaries undergird Rama's interpretive framework. For him, whereas oral culture is traditional, literate culture is modern; whereas change is slow in oral cultures, it is much more rapid in those characterized by "literacy" (and much more amenable to individualization, which leads to literature, which might, perhaps, be opposed to folklore, although Rama does not use that term); whereas oral culture might be seen as a continuum, the written is susceptible to rapid change. In short, the rural becomes constructed as the opposite of the urban, whose characteristics Rama is interested in identifying. With regard to the discussion being developed in this chapter, it is important to note that Rama does not see the complete elimination of rural cultures under the impact of the city and its writerly ways; rather, he sees a process of selection and adaptation at work, in which rural cultures absorb and utilize what is deemed useful, in responding to the changing circumstances being brought about by the modernizing city. As part of this process, new forms of rural culture, characterized by the mixture of orality and writing, emerge. As this is not Rama's main interest, however, he does not spend much time developing his ideas on these new, mixed forms that were both urban and rural. At the same time, merely acknowledging the existence of these forms does not solve the issues identified by those opposed to the great divide version of the orality/literacy debate.[13]

Rather than agree with Rama's views and, thus, accept the broad claims about the power of literacy, in the singular, to transform the world of orality, or, to see coplas and other mixed forms as exceptions or hybrid forms, perhaps always or inevitably in transition toward the literate, I treat courtship and romantic love as a "literacy event." It represents one specific and particular type of literacy among many forms of literacies, one characterized by such forms of writing as love letters, inscriptions on photographs, other kinds of letters (including those asking for permission to marry), and coplas, and one situated within particular historical circumstances that shaped it as it helped shape power in particular ways. Readers may object that I have included an ostensibly oral form, the copla, as one of the forms that characterize romantic literacy. As I spend much of the rest of the chapter justifying this choice, for the moment I limit myself to saying the following: the fact that coplas help illustrate the role of the love letter and the written word within courtship and romantic love qualifies them for such inclusion. In fact, at times, in the writing of this chapter, it seemed that had there been no love letters available as a means of contextualizing and historicizing romantic love, and the role of the written word in it in the late nineteenth and early twentieth centuries, coplas might have done just as well. Moreover, coplas offer a means not only of gaining insight into romantic love but also of understanding the importance of love letters, in particular, and the written word, more generally, to those who may have had the pleasure (or, in some instances, the trauma) of having fallen into its embrace.

At least one problem is immediately apparent with this research strategy. Although the love letters that I encountered in the archives and through which lens I read the coplas (as I use the coplas to reflect back upon them) were exchanged among everyday folk in northern Mexico that included artisans, workers, *campesinos*, and women, these letters date to the last few decades of the nineteenth century and the first two decades of the twentieth. The coplas that appear in the *Cancionero folklórico*, on the other hand, were gathered in the 1950s, 1960s, and 1970s, and may have been specific to the region of the country in which they were collected. These coplas, then, may have changed considerably over the years and may reflect a different reality than the one in which the love letters were written. It is certainly a fact that coplas change constantly, responding to the circumstances of their immediate present; their humor and insight often work because of their close association with the particular context in which they are being sung. This disjuncture would indeed be a major problem if my goal were to identify or chart changes over time in the practices, attitudes, and behaviors associated with courtship and romantic love—fortunately, it is not. Rather, I argue that coplas have a great deal to tell us about courtship and romantic love of an earlier period because they offer a glimpse at past practices that still resonate with many in the present.

Central to this is the intriguing way that coplas have of dealing with time. Although they are situated in a present in which they comment on events, practices, or behaviors contemporary to their singing, they also seem to transcend time by calling to mind previous instances when they may have been sung or heard, recalling earlier performances, perhaps by family or other members of an older generation in, or away from, one's community, or by harkening back to an earlier time in one's own life when a particular copla was heard. Like other songs and sayings that come to make up a shared repertoire, coplas foreground the various instances of their hearing (or singing) while, simultaneously, relegating all other events to a distant, or hazy, background. Bringing such performances into sharp temporal focus while washing out all intervening events can create a sense of time that transcends the tyranny of days, hours, and minutes to one that links the present with past performances of any particular song. This sense of time has the potential to be quite powerful, even transformative. Under the influence of what might be called "copla time," it might be possible to imagine a new narrative trajectory for one's self or to reestablish an older, perhaps seemingly forgotten one, all in the lilting cadence of an eight-syllable line and four-line verse, a rhythm that, in its own way, offers an additional means of accessing such a structuring of temporality.[14]

Finally, although my aim in this chapter is not to offer a history of changes in the practices associated with courtship and the meanings given to them (as this history remains to be written for twentieth-century Mexico), it must be acknowledged that some of the activities that could characterize courtship, and that are discussed in this chapter, did indeed become less prevalent over time or, if they continued, took on new and different meanings. The abduction (*rapto*) of young women by their suitors from the household of their parents or guardians, often, but not always, occurred for the purpose of getting the woman's family to agree, even if grudgingly, to their marriage in hopes of saving the woman's along with the family's honor. While not disappearing completely, rapto became less acceptable over the course of the twentieth century and thus less prevalent. And, even though lovers continued to exchange letters, the absolute centrality of letter writing to love diminished, Carlos Monsiváis has argued, a casualty of the arrival of the telephone and other forms of mass communication. That these changes were taking place simultaneously with the advent of a growing interest in Mexican literary folklore is also readily apparent. Even though such interest predated the Mexican Revolution, that process gave it added impetus, as it did for the collection and celebrations of all kinds of Mexican traditions, reflected in the publication of various collections of popular poetry in the 1920s, as well as the formation of the Folkloric Society of Mexico in 1938, the year in which that society also began publishing its journal. In the face of this (re)discovery of "deep" or traditional Mexico, and the accompanying changes in practices associated with romantic love, a nostalgic view of such practices emerged as the practices themselves faded, especially in the cities. Mexico's passionate past reappeared, not as a threat to the honor of families but as a means such families could use to portray themselves as both distant from and, yet, heirs to such practices. This they represented in artistic forms such as the paintings hung on the walls of their living rooms, to remind them of what they had ceased to be but yet as they wished to be remembered.

"I wrote it with my own hand" / "Yo con mi mano escribí"

To use coplas as a means of gaining insight into courtship as a literacy event necessitates coming to terms with two things simultaneously: on the one hand, with the phases of a courting relationship and, on the other, with understandings or assumptions of the time period concerning the role of writing and the written word within this process. The following copla has much to say about both courtship and writing:

Señorita, bien comprendo	Señorita, I know very well
Que no merezco su amor	That I'm not worthy of your love
Por ser pobre y mi color	Because I'm poor and of color
Considero que la ofendo	I think that I offend you
Pero yo ¿qué culpa tengo	But I, how can I be blamed
De quererla tanto asi?	For loving you so?
Y desde el día que la vi	And from the day I first saw you
En usted vivo pensando;	In you I live thinking;
La carta que le mando	The letter I'm sending you
Yo con mi mano escribí[15]	I wrote it with my own hand

To begin with, this copla mimics some of the qualities of a letter, especially the first or introductory letter a male suitor would send to a prospective *novia* or intended. It is full of polite and formal language, like "señorita" and "Ud," and the author apologizes for daring to write, the extent of his indiscretion being equal to the depths of the feelings of love that drove him to do such a thing. This copla, then, is a letter in oral form, a letter being sung out loud. That the two genres might even be interchangeable is, at times, played within coplas, as in the following copla that serves as another introductory or first letter from the male suitor, even though, again, it is being delivered in oral form. Instead of writing a love letter, the copla refers, playfully, to the writing of a *décima*, or poem, that serves the same purpose as a letter, that is, it hopes to initiate a courting relationship:

Si tú me quieres a mí	If you love me
Contéstame por favor	Answer me please
Esta décima de amor	This ten-line poem of love
Que yo para tí escribí[16]	That I wrote for you

While both the previous coplas are a particular and recognizable form of writing, that of the first or introductory letter, that can be located within the broader category of courtship literacy, the initial copla is remarkable for a number of other reasons as well. To begin with, the male narrator mentions his poverty and "race," characteristics only occasionally remarked upon in this genre, as well as how those factors created inequalities of class and, perhaps, of station between the writer (or singer) and his intended. The narrator's love is inappropriate, even forbidden, by virtue of these social rules, he seems to be saying, a claim that also serves to highlight the extent of his love, as only someone truly in love could even hope to transcend such social chasms. The differences in social status also serve to draw attention to another quality the writer/singer possesses: his command of the written word. In fact, the narrator is adamant that, despite the fact that his class and "race" may lead many to assume that he lacked the ability to read and write, he himself composed the letter/copla with his own hand.

The need to make authorship clear, to claim it for oneself as the narrator does, suggests that it might be entirely common, at least among certain social strata, to send letters composed by others. In fact, as you will see at the end of this chapter, authorship in the late nineteenth and early twentieth centuries, in many parts of the country, was often accomplished by a group rather than by an individual. It would not have been unusual, for example, to have someone else, or even a number of people, cooperate in order to write a letter, for another to read it to one's intended, and for another to take down a response. Alternatively, scribes, still found at the entrance of many public markets in many parts of Mexico, might be employed to accomplish the task of writing a letter. The following copla hints at how the relationship between writing and reading within courtship literacy might not only be accomplished by bringing together a number of people with various levels of skill in writing and reading, but might also be gendered, with men having more access to or command over such skills than women, although, here, the novia's female friend possesses skills that she herself does not:

La carta qe te mandé	The letter that I sent you
Ya tendrás quien te la lea:	Now you'll have someone read it to you:
Una amiga de confianza	A girlfriend you trust
Que te diga lo que sea	Who'll tell you whatever it says
Esa amiga de confianza	This girlfriend you trust
Mándame decir quién es	Let me know who she is
Para mandarle una carta	So I can send her a letter
Con las letras al revés[17]	With the letters all backwards

The final line referring to the "letters all backwards" is most likely a reference to the use of a kind of code so that, if the letter were to fall into the wrong hands, it would be difficult or impossible to decipher or understand. I came across a love letter written in a similar manner when working in the judicial archives in Parral, Chihuahua, Mexico, a number of years ago. After a day and a half of trying to decipher a very short letter I finally discovered, almost by accident, that if I read the letter out loud and switched the order, not of every letter, but of every syllable, actual words rather than what seemed to be random sounds appeared and the meaning of the letter became clear. Both the above copla and my own experience help show that, as much as coplas might be letters in oral form, letters could be highly oral, that is, contain many elements of speech as well as be better understood when read out loud. The use of code also illustrates that courtship might be a dangerous time, with real consequences for the discovery of a relationship, for reasons you will see shortly.

Mine was not the only experience of understanding a letter only when reading it aloud. As many letters were often read to their addressee, they must be considered as much an oral genre as coplas are a written one. Many letters, including those not in any code, were written in syllable, rather than word form, and lacked punctuation, making it difficult to understand them unless reading them aloud or having someone else do so. Letters and coplas also shared many of the same expressive strategies, playing across the supposed oral/written divide. Coplas, for example, often borrowed or copied set phrases that commonly appeared in love letters, phrases such as "I'll never forget you," or, as in the following copla, deploying a variant of the familiar closing in a letter, the "you know who":

Yo no te digo mi nombre
Para que no corra fama;
La que te quiere, te adora y te ama
Ya sabes cómo se llama[18]

I'm not telling you my name
So that it won't get around;
The one who wants you, adores you and loves you
You already know their name

Likewise, in the following copla, one of the most playful, simply because of the rhyming pattern in Spanish, the surprise attendant upon the last line seems to mimic, if not a letter, then another written genre, that of the telegram:

Blanca flor de garambullo,
Hermosa flor de pitaya
Te escribo de Tacubaya:
Punto, punto, raya, raya.[19]

White flower of the garambullo,
Beautiful flower of the pitaya
I'm writing you from Tacubaya:
Dot, dot, dash, dash.

Another imaginative form that could be employed in both love letters and coplas was the acrostic; whereas, in love letters, the writer often formed the poem out of the letters of the name of their correspondent or significant other, in coplas "love" itself might provide the first letter of the first word in each line, or the last, as in the following:

Estoy herida por la "A"
Por la culpa de la "M"
Y el gran golpe de la "O"
Puso en mi pecho una "R"[20]

I'm wounded by the "A"
The blame goes to the "M"
And the great blow of the "O"
Puts in my breast an "R"

The acrostic seemed particularly useful for expressing one's passions, whether in coplas or in letters, regardless of whether the letters were amatory or political, as in the following acrostic, sent in a letter to Álvaro Obregón, then president of Mexico, in 1921:

A dmirando el valor, mi pensamiento
L evanta el vuelo y llega a vuestra altura
V a desnudo de ritmo y galanura

Admiring courage, my thought
Takes flight and arrives at your heights
Unadorned of rhythm and elegance

A	rendir homenaje a un gran talento;	To bear homage to a great talent;
R	endir ese homaje yo quisiera	To bear this homage I would like
O	das formando llevasen bellas:	To offer odes their beauty carry:
O	livos y laurels con estrellas	Olive branches and laurels with stars
B	ienes sin fin y dicha verdadera	Riches without end and true happiness
R	ecibidlo, señor, cual si tuviera	Receive them, sir, which if you had
E	sos dones que os quiere enviar mi mente	Those gifts that my mind wants to send to you
G	rande teneís el alma e indulgente	Great would be your soul and indulgent
O	ireis este cantar de alma sincera	You would hear this song from a sincere soul
N	o mirándolo pobre y deficiente[21]	Not seeing it as poor and lacking

While the inclusion of an acrostic to honor President Obregón situates us in the immediate aftermath of the violent decade of the Mexican Revolution (1910–1920), it is the form and language of this copla, its poetics, rather than its particular politics, that is so compelling. Drawing on the same resources as those composing coplas and writing love letters, the writer of this acrostic stresses the affective nature of the link to the Revolution and its promises, as embodied in Obregón, a Revolutionary hero who became president. As you will see later on in the chapter, just as proving one's manliness might compel certain acts during courtship, participation in the Revolution might be motivated by and conceptualized in precisely the same terms, that is, the desire to "be a man" and act to back up one's word. In all cases—political participation, writing to a president, and in love letters—the language of politics and the language of love might be intertwined, making courtship more than an episode in one's personal life, and politics more than policies, programs, and proclamations, but also imbued with passion.

If a man sending a letter (or décima, as you have seen) to ask if one's love was reciprocated was the accepted way to initiate a courtship, the next step was for the woman, the prospective *novia*, to respond, preferably by writing a letter of her own, that might read something like the following copla:

Señor, ayer recibí	Sir, yesterday I received
Su perfumado papel	Your scented letter
Con atención le leí	With great care I read
Lo que estaba escrito en él[22]	What was written there

In this copla, the prose is cautious, much more reserved, just as it is in many of the letters women wrote when responding to the first letters sent by their epistolary suitors. Etiquette manuals, addressing what some authors have referred to as the "epistolary pact," the claims and expectations that go into sustaining any correspondence, were quite specific about what to do when receiving a letter: not answering a letter was impolite, they stated, even rude. So, for many, an answer was forthcoming. Yet, one can only wonder what a suitor must have made of this response, so devoid was it of any commitment, as it is expressed here in copla form. Such a guarded, even noncommittal, response was not unusual, however. The dynamic in most courtships required the woman to take this role, one of demanding ever greater proof as to the commitment and sincerity of the love being offered, of being convinced, through letters and other steps that together made up the dance of courtship, that the other's love was true and not feigned.

The narration of a copla from a woman's point of view is noteworthy for another reason as well—that it is there at all. Although not completely absent from the collection of coplas, women's voices are so seldom heard that they leave one wondering how or even if women may have given expression to their romantic sentiments. The preponderance of the masculine voice and perspectives in the coplas has already been established. Yet, as Frenk confirms, even many of the coplas that are supposedly narrated from a woman's point of view coincide in content and tone with the rest of the (masculine) copla genre. The following copla seems to bear out this observation. Although it expresses a woman's preference for death over losing her *novio*, or boyfriend, this is a theme that seems of particular importance to male narrators, both of coplas and in letters, as you will see later in the chapter:

Mi novia me dio una carta	My girlfriend gave me a letter
Donde me manda decir	In which she said to me
Que si no la sigo amando	That if I stopped loving her
Ella prefiere el morir	She'd prefer to be dead[23]

Warning readers not to draw too many conclusions from her observation as to the predominance of the masculine voice in coplas, Frenk explains it as a result of the origin of the genre that dates back to the inception of courtly love poetry in the twelfth century and one in which authorship and masculinity were synonymous.

Despite Frenk's warning, one conclusion that does seem immediately apparent is that, given the solitary (masculine) voice in which most coplas have been sung, the genre will be of limited use in gaining access to expressions of women's points of view in relation to the dynamics of courtship and the meaning of writing to romantic love. In this regard, coplas seem quite different than letters, despite the mixture of writing and orality that characterizes both genres. Although work on this subject in the Latin American context is limited, research elsewhere suggests that writing gave women a measure of power, even if of the epistolary variety, enabling them to make claims, under certain circumstances, to such things as greater equality in gender relations, even if with uneven results.[24]

Proof of Love / *Pruebas de Amor*

Given that the copla might serve as a kind of surrogate letter and that the letter might be imagined, just as easily, as a surrogate copla, it is not surprising, perhaps, that both genres tell a similar story concerning the stages and characteristics found in a courting relationship, at least from a masculine point of view. As you have seen, courtship was often initiated with the arrival of a letter (or décima) that, once accepted, then involved an escalating process of assuring the other that one's feelings were true and not feigned, while demanding ever-greater demonstrations that the other's feelings were likewise straight from the heart. Eventually, all the prose (or songs) in the world were insufficient for the task at hand and more substantial proofs were required. Such proofs were known as tokens or gifts, called *prendas*, that often took the form of photographs, embroidered handkerchiefs, and rosaries, although a kiss might do as well; letters themselves, valued as material objects that stood in for the absent other, could also serve as prendas, their status as objects surpassing the transitory echoes of a song or recited poem. In this case, letters might be more suitable than coplas as evidence of a courting relationship that was proceeding along the path to matrimony.

Letters, then, had symbolic properties, a quality that is not addressed in the debate over how to conceptualize the relationship between orality and literacy. While much of this debate focuses on the "meaning" of the writing, that is, what the actual words in the letter are saying, there is also the "magic" of the letter, that is, its ability to somehow stand in for the writer, to pass on the writer's touch, to deliver the very composer of the letter to its recipient.[25] Letters, in addition to being performative, that is, objects that helped to compose the very relationship that they referred to, might also be described as fetishes. They function as venerated objects that seem not only to symbolize the beginning of a courtship or to mark its end by their return to the original sender, but also to conjure the author out of paper and words, to somehow extend the physicality of the act of writing, the result of a hand touching the page. Critical in accomplishing this was the existence of a metaphorical relationship between the letter and the human body, an aspect of the written word in letter form that is captured by a number of coplas, as in the following:

Si los sospiros volaran	If sighs could sail
Como vuela el pensamiento	Like thoughts take flight
Una carta te mandara	A letter I would send you
Con el corazon adentro	With my heart inside
Escrebido por mis manos	Written by my own hand
Y sellada por el viento[26]	And sealed by the wind

In the case of this copla, the heart, likened to a page, is metaphorically enclosed within the envelope as a symbol of one's love. The heart, however, was only one of the organs composing a kind of figurative or sentimental anatomy common to both the letter and the copla. Other organs and bodily fluids circulated in both as well, as the language of love joins together the body of the letter with the body of the lover in a sensual, if textual, embrace:

Si mi mano fuera tinta	If my hand were the ink
Y mi corazón tintero	And my heart the inkwell
Con la sangre de mis venas	With the blood of my veins
Te escribiría: "Te quiero"[27]	I would write to you: "I love you"

If, as in the previous copla, veins and blood enable circulation through the sentimental anatomy, other coplas referred to yet more of its organs and attributes. Will or *voluntad* was another essential component of the body in love, expressing in ideal terms the manner in which love was meant to conquer all. The exercise of free will could also be the very measure of one's status as an adult, as many young people in love faced parental opposition to the choice of their partners or their desire for marriage. The focus on voluntad, as in the following copla, highlights the fact that marriage was, ideally, to be based on mutual desire rather than arranged or controlled by one's family:

No ruego porque me quieran	I'll not plead because they want me to
Ni pago por su amistad;	Nor pay for your friendship;
La que me quiera deveras	She who truly loves me
Ha de ser por voluntad	Must do so because of her will[28]

The soul, or *alma*, was yet another constituent part of the body in love, common not only to the copla and the letter but also implying a spiritual dimension to love itself. The copla that follows this paragraph not only introduces the soul but also illustrates how letters might be an integral part of courtship even when those in love, as in this copla, were able to meet face to face. It is interesting to speculate on why the narrator here also feels it necessary to recite orally the contents of the written message he plans to give his intended. Is it, perhaps, because she will not be able to read its contents? If so, does this not provide further evidence of the letter's symbolic properties, highlighting its status as a material object that symbolizes a promise of marriage and true love rather than the meaning of its words? As you read the copla, you also might note that it refers to a chore that was very common for women in the late nineteenth and early twentieth centuries in many parts of the country, that of fetching water for household use. As attested to by the existence of many cases in the judicial archives that begin by describing such an activity on the part of women, it was also a chore that left them either alone and able to see their lover or vulnerable and susceptible to abduction and/or the initiation of sexual relations, depending on the circumstances and on how one interprets the testimony accompanying such cases:

Tu eres buena, ¡Ah! ¡Antonia del alma!	You are so good, Oh, Antonia of the soul!
¿Dónde nos podemos ver?	Where can we see each other?
Para saber si tú me amas	To know if you love me
Y sabes corresponder;	And know how to return my love/write;
Cuando vaya a traer agua	When you go to get water
Allá te daré un papel	There I'll give you a letter/paper

En el dicho papel te diré	In that said paper I'll say to you
Que eres mi pálido flor	That you are my pale flower
Que te traje del jardín	That I brought you from the garden
Donde te ofrendí mi amor	Where I offered you my love
Dime si me amas a mí:	Tell me if you love me:
Te daré mi corazón.[29]	I'll give you my heart.

The previous four or five coplas provide evidence of the existence of a metaphorical relationship joining the letter and the body; they also introduce a highly sentimental or metaphorical language that characterized love. Whether in the copla, the letter, or, indeed, in other forms of verse and popular music such as the bolero, this was the language of courtship, nurtured and sustained by each of these interrelated genres.[30]

Letters, then, served as excellent prendas or tokens because of their ability to stand in for the absent other, that is, by their ability, somehow, to extend the reach of the other by passing along their touch, the promise of their presence made manifest. Other objects possessed the same capacity. In fact, in both letters and coplas, the term "prenda" could refer both to the actual person as well as to the object that stood in for them, whether it be a handkerchief, a rosary, or a photograph, as in the following copla that is really a letter meant to be sung, complete with the salutation, "Estimada," very common to letters:

Amada prenda querida	Loved one darling my love
Estimada jovencita	Esteemed dear young woman
Quiero que Ud. me reciba	I want you to take from me
Con voluntá esta cartita[31]	Of your own will this little/dear letter

Nor was it unusual for a suitor to ask directly for a prenda, as the narrator does in the following copla, only this time sampling from an inscription on a photo instead of from a love letter, still within the context of a stanza that would be sung:

Si cariño me tuvieras	If you had love for me
Me mandaras tu retrata	You would send me your portrait
Con un letrero que diga:	With an inscription that said:
"Eres dueño de mi amor."[32]	"You are the one who possesses my love."

Such prendas, however, at some point in the courtship, no longer seemed sufficient to assure suitors that the love they were being offered was indeed true; it was at this point that prendas yielded to demands for more tangible proofs of love, again, often directly asked for by the suitor:

Porque te amo con exceso	Because I love you so much
Y te adoro con fervor	And adore you with devotion
Dame de tu boca un beso	Give me a kiss from your mouth
Que es la prueba de amor.[33]	As a proof of love.

As with the term prenda, the word *prueba* (or proof) often appeared, as it is in the final line of the previous copla, as part of the phrase "prueba de amor" or "proof of love." Prueba took on particular meanings within the context of courtship, depending, additionally, on such things as time, place, class, and gender. If asked about the phrase "prueba de amor" nowadays, people in many parts of Mexico might smile and, like the singer of this copla, associate it with asking for a kiss. The meaning of this term was often very different at the turn of the twentieth century, at least among everyday folk in the Mexican north. At that time, courtship among workers, artesans, campesinos, and others often turned around a specific transaction, the terms of which were acknowledged by both men and women: in exchange for receiving from the man, in writing, a promise of marriage at a future date, the woman agreed to the initiation of sexual relations, often to confirm to the man's satisfaction her status as a virgin. This fragment, from a love letter written by a man in 1903, illustrates, although somewhat euphemistically, the terms of this bargain being struck: "This letter is the last in which I swear to you and obligate myself to marry you if you accept my desire this very same day today I'll wait for you at the time you decide and I hope no one will know what is going on. I swear to you that as soon as what I desire happens we'll get married and we'll be happy as I've already told you."

The letter that this quotation has been taken from is more than just a love letter, however. Under certain circumstances, letters like this one could become legally binding promises of marriage, simply because of the fact that they had been written out. This has to do with the particular status of the written word in law. Criminal codes in the late nineteenth century and up through the early decades of the twentieth century differentiated between written and oral promises of marriage, providing some legal backing for the families of women under the age of majority who had received a promise in writing like the one above. Although the crime of rapto (the abduction of an underage woman from parental authority) was not affected by the existence of a written promise of marriage, the related crime of *estupro* (the initiation of sexual relations with an underage woman) was. Under certain circumstances, if the initiation of sexual relations was compelled by means of a written promise of marriage, penalties were forthcoming if the marriage was not. Such a privileged status for the written word distinguishes letters from coplas while offering a compelling explanation as to why coplas might be preoccupied with the written word. Not only was the letter closely associated with the rituals of courtship, even for those who might not necessarily read or write, letters were part of the world of official circuits of power that sanctioned relationships based on the written word, the influence of which could be brought to bear, to compel men to honor their word (as long as it was written out).

Coplas, by contrast, were not part of these circuits. Regardless of their preoccupation with the written word and despite the fact that they were as imbricated in writing as letters were in orality, coplas, while sustaining the vocabulary of love, might be powerful in helping compose or give expression to such feelings, but useless when it came to enforcing any legal consequences that followed. Perhaps coplas referred to writing in order to bask, as if by reflection, in its power, one that came by way of its role in facilitating the working of the state and its various institutions, like the judicial system. Coplas, sung out loud in order to be remembered, their repetitive verses, rhymes, and cadences circulating knowledge and common-sense understandings in such matters as love and courtship, made pointed comments, at times. They described the dynamics of the courting relationship as understood by men, expressing in song its tensions, its delights, and its dangers, while, all the while, referring to the importance and power of the written word, even if in oral form.

Given the legal consequences of offering a promise of marriage in written form and the fact that courting often swirled around the exchange of such a promise for the initiation of sexual relations, references to "proofs of love" in coplas take on new meanings, as in the following:

No tengo hora de contento,	I don't have an hour of relief,
Ven a quitarme esta vida,	Come and relieve me from this life,
Para que veas lo que siento;	So that you can see what I'm feeling;
Quiero de ti una prenda	I want a pledge from you
En pruebas de casamiento	In proof of marriage

En pruebas de casamiento	In proof of marriage
Y de mi cariño fiel;	And of my true love;
Para que veas qué contento	So that you can see what happiness
Ahí te mando este papel,	There I'm sending you this paper/letter,
Mira lo que lleva adentro	Look what it has inside it
Mira lo que lleva adentro	Look what it has inside it
No te cause novedad:	It shouldn't be anything new:
Es una flor que en el centro	It's a flower that in its center
Va grabado mi amistad	My friendship is etched
Que me diste hace un tiempo.[34]	That you gave me a while ago.

Although this copla, like many, is subject to interpretation and capable of supporting various readings, it gathers together many of the components of a courting relationship, all charged with responsibilities, tensions, and promises. Here love seems to be something that is suffered, made bearable with a gift or token that serves also as a proof of love. In exchange, a written promise of marriage is offered. The letter itself seems to hold, perhaps metaphorically, a flower in which the narrator has engraved his love, linking paper, heart, body, and now another living entity, a flower, together. Readers will have to decide for themselves what, if anything, is really being requested or referred to in this copla.

While in the previous copla, inscription takes place on a flower, in the poetics of romantic discourse, common to both the copla and the letter, writing is inscribed on the body itself, especially the masculine body. Just as the letter might extend the touch of the body or stand in for it, the body could be the text bearing the message of love, in writing:

Si en mi pecho	If in my breast
Yo escribí tu nombre	I wrote your name
Nadie lo puede borrar	No one could erase it
Aunque se sienta muy hombre[35]	No matter how much of a man they thought they were

The sense of the permanence of the written word, inscribed on the male body and backed up by force in defense of it, is also captured in the next copla, in which the impossibility of achieving permanence of fixity by means of writing becomes the very measure of the extent of the man's love. In this copla, only if they could conquer the elements themselves (wind, water) through imposing writing on them, could anyone stop the narrator from loving his intended:

Tengo una manzana de oro
Madúramela en el viento.
Dicen que me han de quitar
De tu amor mi pensamiento
Sólo que escriban en la agua
Y echen firmas en el viento.[36]

I have an apple of gold
Ripen it for me in the wind.
They say they have to take from me
Your love from my thoughts
Only if they could write in water
And sign their names in the wind.

Being a Man

Given the link between writing and legally enforceable promises and the centrality of proving trust and truthfulness in a courting relationship, questions of character or moral values became paramount, for both men and women. While the male voice in coplas praised women's honor as the most prized quality sought in an ideal mate, it was no less concerned with claiming its own gendered prerogatives, often seeking to reassure women not only of the man's proper intentions but also of his standing as someone whose word could be trusted, a particularly valued and defended attribute. Such gendered ideals are introduced in the following copla:

Lo que te digo y te cumplo
Conmigo no hay reventada;
Yo te prometo quererte,
Porque eres mujer honrada.[37]

What I tell I'll do I do
With me there's no breaking;
I promise to love you,
Because you are an honorable woman.

As in the previous coplas, this one is also amenable to various interpretations, depending on how much one cares to read into such things as word usage. While the "breaking" in the second line above could refer to the man going back on his word, it might also be a reference to the woman's honor, often measured by the intact state of her hymen; it could also refer to the man's promise not to demand proof of virginity from an "honorable" woman. As for the man's word, keeping it is the very definition of being a man, as in the following:

Del cielo cayó una rosa
Del palo blanco una carta:

From heaven a rose fell
From a palo blanco tree a letter:

"¿De qué te sirve ser hombre,	"Why is it even worth being a man
Si la palabra te falta?" [38]	If you can't keep your word?"

Backing up one's word, however, was often not an easy matter, especially in the face of threats of violence from the male members of the woman's family, which are hinted at in the following verse:

Si me llegas a querer,	If you should come to love me,
Escrito te doy mi nombre,	In writing I'll give you my name,
Si algo te quieren hacer,	If they want to do something to you,
No te asustes, no te asombres	Don't be afraid, don't be surprised
Que no es la primera mujer	It's not the first woman
Que su amor pone en un hombre[39]	Who's given her love to a man

As coplas help spell out, courtship might best be imagined as taking place along a continuum, one end of which was marked by violence, with men, at times, acting on their word to remove the woman from her parental home and initiating sexual relations in an attempt to force the woman's family as well as, perhaps, the woman herself, to agree to marriage. The threat of such behavior often compelled male family members to act in defense of their perceived honor, lodged in their ability to maintain the virtue of the female members of their family, making novios, at times, the targets of violence and courtship itself into a struggle between men over women.

Such courting practices have left a documentary record in the archives of the judicial system in Mexico. As you have already seen, up until well into the twentieth century, men in courting relationships might be accused of or commit the crimes of rapto and estupro. The range of practices and behavior that actually took place, however, all encompassed within the categories of rapto and estupro, could be staggering. On some occasions, for example, it is apparent that the young women arranged for their own abductions, often as a way of forcing parents to go along with their choice of a marriage partner. Only in this way, through marriage, that is, could honor be saved after an abduction and the initiation of sexual relations that had presumedly taken place. In this scenario, abduction becomes a kind of elopement, with women as full participants:

Dime si te vas conmigo	Tell me if you can leave with me
Y la fecha me pondrás	And the date you'll set for me to do it

Para venir con Cúpido	So I can come with Cupid
Porque soy hombre capaz	Because I'm a man who's capable
De sostener lo que digo[40]	Of backing up what I'll say I'll do

At other times, however, women's agency is not as easily identified, although, as in the following copla, the woman is still envisioned as having a choice in the matter:

Campanitas, campanitas,	Bells, bells,
Las que repican por ahí.	Those that peal over there.
¿Que dices, mi alma, nos vamos	What do you say, my darling, shall we go
Para San Luis Potosí?[41]	To San Luis Potosí?

Finally, in the next copla, the woman's choice seems to be secondary to the particular performance of masculinity that is involved in carrying her off:

Soy Eduardo Magallón	My name is Eduardo Magallón
De la nación Mexicana:	Of the Mexican nation:
Si tú me quieres, morena,	If you love me, morena,
Te llevo, aunque sea mañana[42]	I'll carry you off, even though it might be morning (or, tomorrow)

As with many of the coplas included in this chapter, the meaning of the stanza emerges out of context, in this case, shared understandings of courtship and what it might mean to leave home with one's suitor. It is precisely this shared or common knowledge that gives the next copla its punch, stating out loud, as it does, what many parents must have feared, without necessarily saying so directly:

Y yo sé que tus padres se enojan	And I know that your parents are angry
Porque vengo a tus puertas a cantar;	Because I come to your doors to sing;
Anda, diles que ya no se enojen	Go, tell them now not to get so angry
Que a la noche te vengo a llevar.[43]	That in the night I'll come and carry you off.

While serenading or singing at the doors of a woman, implying a courting relationship, might have been annoying enough (from the parents' perspective), the real danger to which the previous copla refers is the potential abduction of the daughter, pitting suitor against parents, especially the father, in the struggle over women. In other coplas, as in the one that follows, the potential for violence in such a struggle is all too clearly stated:

Tu papa carga cuchillo	Your father carries a knife
Yo también cargo puñal;	I too carry a dagger;
Nos tiramos tiro a tiro,	We'll fight if we ever cross paths,
Nos tiramos a matar.[44]	We'll fight to kill.

Love and Death

Given this emphasis on violence and the ability to back up one's word with action, it should come as no surprise to learn that the figure of death seems to stalk love and courtship and, thus, the copla as well as the letter, and in a number of guises. For some men, death formed part of the poetics of courtship, serving as the ultimate means of expressing the extent of one's love and commitment. It was not unusual, for example, for men to end love letters with phrases such as "Yours until the grave." Many lovers also referred to "eternity" in an effort to assure their intended that their love was true and that they would never waver in it. Other men, following the logic set out in the exchange of prendas or pledges, found in one's life or the willingness to give it, the ultimate prueba de amor:

Mientras las olas del mar	As long as the waves of the sea
Se vistan de azul celeste	Dress themselves in heavenly blue
Te he de querer, te he de amar	I'm going to want you, I'm going to love you
Aunque la vida me cueste[45]	Even though it could cost me my life

Here, the final line is ambivalent, capable of sustaining a number of readings. On the one hand, it could simply be stating the obvious, that a potential for violence at the hands of male relatives existed. A more sinister message may lurk here, however, turning the line from a mere statement of possibility into a veiled threat as to what might happen. On rare occasions, the couple getting together one last time to return the love letters each had received from the other, thus marking the end of the courtship, the male killed the woman before killing himself. Read through the lens of this outcome, the line could refer to this unlikely but, nevertheless, possible scenario, warning the woman and all within hearing range that male honor was not something to be trifled with and that death would be the ultimate consequence of doing so, a theme the following copla sets out even more clearly:

Si crees que vas a burlarte	If you think you're going to make a fool of me
De mi cariño sincero	Of my sincere love
Antes habré de matarte	Before that I'll have to kill you
O yo en la raya me muero	or I in the end die
Pero tengo que enseñarte	But I'll have to teach you
A respetarme primero[46]	To respect me first

Murder and then suicide was a rare occurrence, however. In most coplas, it was the male relations of the novia or intended who were to be feared most. At the same time, however, willingness to face them could become the very measure of the extent of a man's feelings:

Voy a escribirle una carta	I'm going to write you a letter
A mi chata, no muy tarde	To my little pug nose, very shortly
A ver si se compadece	To see if she'll take pity on
De este corazón cobarde	This cowardly heart
Y si no me la contesta,	And if she doesn't answer,
Mejor me voy a ir	Better I'm going to go
Si me matan a balazos	If they gun me down
Por tu amor voy a morir[47]	For your love I'll die

Finally, in some cases, rather than male relatives it was love itself, if taken in large enough doses, that could prove fatal:

La noche le quita al cielo su luz y plata	The night takes from the heavens its moonlight
Y tú me quitas la vida	And you take from me life itself
Dejando sangrar la herida	Leaving to bleed the wound
Que por tu amor me mata.[48]	That because of your love is killing me.

More than just a possible consequence of courting, death seemed an active and constant presence, as it is evoked in the copla that follows. It seems to suggest that love, far from a unparalleled joy, might be drenched in the idiom of death and courtship, in the end, best undertaken by those manly enough to do so:

Por ahi dicen que la muerte	There they say that death
Me anda siguiendo los pasos	Walks after me following my footsteps
Y yo digo que la muerte	And I say that death
Me ha de llevar a tus brazos:	Has to carry me to your arms:
Entonces podré besarte	Then I'll be able to kiss you
Aunque me den de balazos[49]	Even though they may gun me down

Courtship certainly could be a time of violence. This violence could be didactic—instructing women on their supposedly "appropriate" behavior and men in how masculinity was to be understood and performed—as well as instrumental, that is, used to police the borders of women's options and to defend masculine prerogatives during courtship. It would be a misrepresentation, however, to end any discussion of love and courtship with death about to claim the lives of one or both of those involved in such a relationship. Despite the rhetoric of dying for love and the real violence that sometimes occurred, men and women mostly got married or formed informal unions, depending on the region, the time period, and their social status. It seems more appropriate, therefore, to end this chapter with the promise of a beginning, a request from an erstwhile, and highly creative, suitor to the male relatives of a young woman, asking for their permission for him to marry her. Ending in this way means introducing yet another type of written document, one as much a part of courtship as love letters, that of the petitioning letter, which ended up as evidence in a judicial procedure of rapto in the late nineteenth century. It is my hope, by briefly returning to the written word, that my argument concerning the relationship between orality and literacy and the role of the copla in helping to write a history of the ways that love, courtship, and the written word were intertwined will become clearer.

Although Liberato, our protagonist in this brief romantic interlude, had already been civilly married, that detail did not stop him from writing both love letters to María, his fifteen-year-old novia, and a letter to her older brothers petitioning for her hand in marriage. Well, not quite marriage, as his previous marriage made a union recognized under the law impossible, but, as Liberato stated in his letter, something very much like marriage. Actually, Liberato, a twenty-three-year-old campesino living in a rural community in northern Mexico, had not actually written the letter himself, he told judicial officials in his testimony, as he was unable to write. Instead, he had asked his brother-in-law to do it for him. Nor could María read or write "even one letter," she told authorities, getting others to read the love letters to her. Love letters, then, even though written, might sometimes be dictated and then delivered orally, much like coplas. As you might imagine, María's brothers were very upset, as they knew he had already been married, making it impossible for him to "cover the honor" of their sister, or, marry her civilly, as they explained it. In fact, it had been the arrival of "amorous messages" (three in August and one in September) that had tipped them off about their sister's relationship, and Liberato's petition later in September asking for their sister's hand in almost-matrimony that had confirmed it. "I'm now looking for a companion so that I can be happy," Liberato explained to them, "and I believe that, for me, [María] has all the qualities that would make for the happiness of a man like me. . . ." He offered to provide support for the young woman until the day he died, "the same as if we were married." Readers can only wonder what the brothers made of this petition. At any rate, they would have to have had someone else read it to them, as they could neither read nor write nor sign their names either. In the meantime, captivated by Liberato's letters, María had gathered up some of her clothes and left home to be with him, leading Liberato to be charged with carrying her off, as in the coplas above, the kind of abduction in which she herself had been a willing participant. As the legal charge was eventually dropped, there is no indication in the records as to how the situation may have been resolved, although it was possible to pay what was referred to as a "dowry" to recompense the loss of honor that the abduction represented, the honor, that is, of the brothers, who would be the injured parties in the case, not María.

Having read some of the preceding coplas, it is easy to anticipate the violence that Liberato was likely to face from male relatives or to imagine him acting to demonstrate his masculinity, backing up his word through the use of force. However, rather than illustrating assertions of masculinity within courtship, it is Liberato's creative deployment of form that I find most noteworthy. It was the written word itself, in the form of love letters and a petition, that carried the day, and through which he attempted to give his actions a pretense of legitimacy where none really existed. The love letters that seemed to fascinate María signified commitment, regardless of what they actually said, and convinced her to leave her home, while the petition was an attempt to justify his actions and somehow give them more permanence just by turning them into text, by expressing them in written form.

Nor did the fact that none of the parties could read or write serve as a barrier to the flow of the written word between them. As with many other couples, courtship literacy in this case was accomplished not by individuals but through the participation of many, with varying skills of reading and writing, acting together. Even in the absence of such skills in particular individuals, love letters still signified the existence of a courting relationship in which promises were being made, promises that might be legally binding under certain circumstances.

It was this latter factor that separated coplas from letters. Certainly, coplas, like Liberato's letters, were meant to be delivered orally, to be sung out loud, perhaps to a group larger than the two individuals involved in the courting relationship. Performed in this manner, coplas brought into being an audience that shared, debated, laughed at, and, perhaps, lamented or longed for many of the claims of masculinity and courtship being expressed therein. Given the power of the written word, its "magic" as much as its "meaning," however, it is little wonder that coplas are shot through with writing, letters, and the use of written forms. Because of this characteristic, they enable the telling of a partial history of courtship, from a masculine point of view, as they often resonated with actual behavior and attitudes that still echoed years after they had ceased being common practice. Even though coplas borrowed the forms of the letter as much as the letter was often grounded in those of speech, they could never be used to compel any male to make good on his promises, as could those delivered in writing. While differing in this respect, coplas, as much as letters, formed a part of courtship literacy, a literacy event in which men often enjoyed greater access to and command over the written word than women and in which writing, especially letters, functioned as much "magically" as through the meaning of the words themselves. Courtship was also a series of practices where masculine prerogatives, whether expressed in written or oral form, might be defended through violence and in which a man's word, whether given in writing or orally, might be worth defending with one's life.

As for our lovelorn couple, how much simpler it might all have been had Liberato not already been married. One can imagine him giving his word, that is, promising marriage, in written form, as stated in the final copla included here, even if his letter had to be read to María by someone else, or perhaps sung to her as it would have been in this copla:

Esta carta te dirijo	This letter I direct to you
Perdona mi atrevimiento	Pardon my daring
Pues en ella yo te doy	Well, in it I give to you
Palabra de casamiento.[50]	My promise of marriage.

Notes

Copla 4760, Margit Frenk Alatorre (coordinadora), *Cancionero Folklórico de México*, tomo 2, *Coplas del amor desdichado y otras coplas de amor* (1975; repr., México: El Colegio de México, 1998), 310.

1. Margit Frenk Alatorre, *Cancionero folklórico de México*, tomo 1, *Coplas del amor feliz* (México: El Colegio de México, 1975), xvi–xxi.

2. The five volumes were published between 1975 and 1985 and contain more than ten thousand coplas from all over Mexico; they are entitled as follows: Tomo 1, *Coplas del amor feliz*; Tomo 2, *Coplas del amor desdichado y otras coplas de amor*; Tomo 3, *Coplas que no son de amor*; Tomo 4, *Coplas varias y varias canciones*; y Tomo 5, *Antología, glosario, y indices*.

3. Aurelio González, ed., *La copla en México* (México: El Colegio de México, 2007); see the brief introduction by Aurelio González.

4. It is not clear why a century represented for the editor a useful or meaningful unit of analysis as no reason is given for such a periodization.

5. Frenk, *Cancionero*, tomo 1, xxi.

6. Walter J. Ong, *Orality and Literacy: The Technologizing of the Word* (London: Metheun, 1982), 78. On the "chirographic mentality," see 172. According to Ong, writing made possible "increasingly articulate introspectivity" (105); was a major factor in the development of personal privacy (130); it also led to a different conceptualization of "history" itself, in fact, it was responsible for "creating" history (172).

7. Taking stock of the impact of Ong's book twenty-five years after its publication, Paul A. Soukup concludes, ". . . Ong's work does not support a dichotomy between oral and literate cultures." See Paul A. Soukup, S. J., "Orality and Literacy 25 Years Later," in *Communication Research Trends* 26, no. 4 (2007): 17.

8. Laura M. Ahearn, *Invitations to Love: Literacy, Love Letters, and Social Change in Nepal* (Ann Arbor: University of Michigan Press, 2001), 47–48.

9. For an author concerned with an "event-centered" approach to literacy or "literacy events," see Niko Besnier, *Literacy, Emotion and Authority: Reading and Writing on a Polynesian Atoll* (Cambridge: Cambridge University Press, 1995).

10. As de Certeau puts it: "The 'oral' is that which does not contribute to progress; reciprocally, the 'scriptural' is that which separates itself from the magical world of voices and tradition." See Michel de Certeau, *The Practice of Everyday Life*, trans. Steven Rendall (1984; repr., Berkeley: University of California Press, 1988), 134. James Collins and Richard K. Blot also discuss the "literacy thesis" and de Certeau's contribution to the literacy debate; see James Collins and Richard K. Blot, *Literacy and Literacies: Texts, Power, and Identity* (Cambridge: Cambridge University Press, 2003), 30–32.

11. Angel Rama, *The Lettered City*, trans. John Charles Chasteen (Durham, NC: Duke University Press, 1996), first published as *La ciudad letrada* (1984).

12. Ibid., 62. For a discussion of the role of the written word in "fixing" or "immobilizing" an oral culture that he sees as in permanent transformation, see ibid., 63–64; brief quotation about the "ever-expanding circuits of the written word," ibid., 63.

13. Ibid., 67.

14. This relationship to time is not unique to the copla but seems to characterize much of what might be called ritual, its aural as well as visual and performative forms. I was reminded of this when hearing a hymn sung at a funeral I recently attended.

Not only did I remember all the words to the song from my youth, but I could distinctly "hear" or remember my grandmother's voice singing it, despite the fact that perhaps forty years separated the contemporary recitation with those of my past.

15. Copla 3237 in Frenk, *Cancionero*, tomo 2, 66. Although, at times, I attempt to translate to capture the rhyming as well as the meaning, I have been unable to do so for this particular copla.

16. Copla 1082, ibid., tomo 1, 138.

17. Copla 3142a, ibid., tomo 2, 52.

18. Copla 1005, ibid., tomo 1, 129. Accompanying notes reveal that a version replaces the first line with the following line: "No te pongo la firma" or "I'm not signing this."

19. Copla 4875, ibid., tomo 2, 337. The "garambullo" is a type of cactus and the "pitaya" is often called dragon-fruit.

20. Copla 2137, ibid., tomo 1, 283. An acrostic found in a love letter is discussed in William E. French, "'Te amo muncho': The Love Letters of Pedro and Enriqueta," in *The Human Tradition in Mexico*, ed. Jeffrey M. Pilcher (Lanham, MD: Rowman and Littlefield, 2002).

21. "Acróstico" Dedicada al Sr. General Don Alvaro Obregón, Presidente de la República Mexicana," in María del Carmen Nava Nava (editora), *Los abajo firmantes: Cartas a los presidentes, 1920–1928* (México: Secretaría de Educación Pública/Editorial Patria, 1994), 49.

22. Copla 531, Frenk, *Cancionero*, tomo 1, 68.

23. Copla 2442, ibid., tomo 1, 323.

24. Jennifer Cole and Lynn M. Thomas, eds., *Love in Africa* (Chicago: University of Chicago Press, 2009), 13.

25. James Collins and Richard K. Blot contrast the "meaning" of the letter with its "magic"; see Collins and Blot, *Literacy and Literacies*, 21.

26. Copla 493, Frenk, *Cancionero*, tomo 1, 63. The two spelling "mistakes" are as they appear in the collection.

27. Copla 499, ibid., tomo 1, 64.

28. Copla 2713, ibid., tomo 1, 363.

29. Copla 1081, ibid., tomo 1, 138.

30. Carlos Monsiváis argues that romantic song, especially the bolero, helped sustain the romantic vocabulary and understandings of such things as love and sentimentality as expressed in the love letter; see Carlos Monsiváis, *El género epistolary: Un homenaje a manera de carta abierta* (México: Miguel Angel Porrúa, 1991), 37.

31. Copla 510, Frenk, *Cancionero*, tomo 1, 66.

32. Copla 1245, ibid., tomo 1, 159.

33. Copla 1409, ibid., tomo 1, 181.

34. Copla 1203 bis, ibid., tomo 1, 154.

35. Copla 1892, ibid., tomo 1, 247.

36. Copla 1876c, ibid., tomo 1, 245.

37. Copla 341, ibid., tomo 1, 44.

38. Copla 4216, ibid., tomo 2, 218.

39. Copla 1718, ibid., tomo 1, 223.

40. Copla 1285, ibid., tomo 1, 164.

41. Copla 1308 bis-1, ibid., tomo 1, 167.

42. Morena refers to a dark or brunette woman; Copla 1291, ibid., tomo 1, 165.
43. Copla 1900, ibid., tomo 1, 248.
44. Copla 3858, ibid., tomo 2, 156.
45. Copla 1836, ibid., tomo 1, 240.
46. Copla 3882, ibid., tomo 2, 160.
47. Copla 2276, ibid., tomo 1, 301.
48. Copla 2833, ibid., tomo 2, 12.
49. Copla 1842, ibid., tomo 1, 240.
50. Copla 1204, ibid., tomo 1, 154.

Of all the radical reforms outlined in the Constitution of 1917, perhaps none spurred as much animosity and contention as those targeting the Catholic Church. The constitution's anticlerical provisions sought to—once and for all—divest the Church's power, seen by many Revolutionary leaders as a prime cause of the nation's backwardness and lack of progress. As a result, the country again fell into the grips of civil war, this time between the new Revolutionary National government and Christian rebels (known as *cristeros*). The latter, tens of thousands strong, opposed the heavy-handed policies that disbanded religious processions, exiled foreign priests, and closed Church schools, convents, and monasteries. The Cristero Rebellion (1926–1929) introduced a new bloody episode to the nation where the indiscriminate killings of officials, teachers, and priests revealed that opposition to the constitution was not solely religious, but also based on agrarian grievances and attacks on local autonomy. Temporarily called to truce after the assassination of President-elect Álvaro Obregón, the cristeros would rise up again in the mid-1930s. Stephen Andes investigates the corridos written and sung by these Catholic rebels, and explores how they created alterative and developing Christian identities in so doing.

"Corrido de la Contestación a las Estupideces del Bandido Rito Betancourt"*

"Ballad of Response to the Stupidities of the Bandit Rito Betancourt"

Vuela, vuela palomita y no dejes de volar; vuela y dile a los del Valle que ya viene Quintanar.	Fly, fly little dove and don't stop flying; fly and tell those of El Valle that Quintanar is on his way.

* Unknown, "Corrido de la Contestación a las Estupideces del Bandido Rito Betancourt," in *Corrido Histórico Mexicano: Voy a cantarles la historia (1924–1936)*, tomo IV, dir. Antonio Avitia Hernández (Mexico City: Editorial Porrúa, 1998), 42–43.

¡Ah qué bandidos del Valle, tan faltos de dignidad! pues que por bandido tienen a don Pedro Quintanar. [. . .]	Ah what bandits are those in El Valle, so lacking in dignity! and a bandit is what they claim don Pedro Quintanar to be.
¿Qué nos ofende diciendo fanáticos con medalla? a nosotros no nos manchan las babas de la canalla.	Do you think you've offended taunting fanatics with medals divine? we'll never be upended by the drivel of swine.
Estas beatas que así veis, tan cultas y silenciosas, no se parecen en nada a vuestras viejas babosas. Bolcheviques sin bandera, sin Patria y sin religión; vil lepra que sólo causa un poco de compasión. [. . .]	These holy women that you see in us, so piously educated and soft spoken, are nothing in the least like your idiotic old ladies so broken. Bolsheviks without flag, without country and without religion; vile leper that only arouses such little compassion.
Vuela, vuela palomita, párate en aquel placer ven a ver a los del Valle temblando como mujer. [. . .]	Fly, fly little dove, alight in that place come and see those in El Valle trembling like a woman.
¡Qué susto nos han metido!, (decía Fidel el Panzón) la verdá me dan torzones al pensar en Castañón. [. . .]	What a fright we've been given! (said Potbellied Fidel) truth is it hurts my stomach in thinking of Castañón [a cristero leader].
Que si son deveras hombres y deveras valientitos, que salgan a conocer, a sus meros papacitos.	If true men you would be, and if valiant laddies, then come out to meet, who's really your daddies.

Vuela, vuela palomita,	Fly, fly little dove,
párate en aquel palmar	alight on that palm tree afar
anda y dile a los del Valle	go and tell those in El Valle
que su papá es Quintanar.	that their dad is Quintanar.

Discussion Questions

1. How does the writer of this corrido characterize his enemies? What symbols and specific language does the writer employ?
2. How would listeners of this song interpret the use of gendered language in attacking their enemies in verse?
3. Why would the writer of this corrido characterize cristero enemies as Bolsheviks without country or flag?

CHAPTER FIVE

Singing for Cristo Rey

Masculinity, Piety, and Dissent in Mexico's Cristero Rebellion

Stephen J. C. Andes

Mexico's epic civil war known as the Cristero Rebellion (1926–1929) was less than a year old when a contingent of Catholic insurgents led by Pedro Quintanar established control over the region of Huejuquilla el Alto, Jalisco. From their stronghold in Huejuquilla, *cristero* rebels attacked federal troops and pro-government militias (*agraristas*) in many of the country's central-western states: Zacatecas, Jalisco, Nayarit, and Durango.[1] The constant raiding by Quintanar's soldiers won praise and plaudits from cristero allies and sympathizers. However, it enraged, infuriated, and generally exasperated local anti-cristero agraristas in Valparaíso, Zacatecas, a town just thirty miles away from Huejuquilla. The rivalry between cristeros and agraristas in the area resulted in back-and-forth fighting throughout the conflict. The opposing sides used song as a medium to vent their hatred for each other. One agrarista, Rito Betancourt Luna, fired the first wordy salvo in 1927. As a native of Valparaíso, which locals referred to as El Valle, Betancourt penned a corrido condemning the cristeros as fanatics. He made fun of the religious medallions they wore and poked fun at what he viewed as their austere piety; he also called them *beatas* ("holy women"), in essence questioning cristero manhood. Moreover, he accused them of being bandits who had cruelly robbed Valparaíso and its citizens.

Not to be outdone, of course, the Catholic rebels in Huejuquilla shot back with their own ballad, descriptively, and perhaps humorously, titled "Corrido de la Contestación a las Estupideces del Bandido Rito Betancourt" (Ballad of Response to the Stupidities of the Bandit Rito Betancourt). The song was anonymous, although Antonio Avitia Hernández attributes it to Lidio Pacheco, a famous cristero *corridista* from the area.[2] The balladeer had this to say regarding Betancourt's insults of cristero religion:

¿Qué nos ofende diciendo
fanáticos con medalla?
a nosotros no nos manchan
las babas de la canalla.

Estas beatas que así veis,
tan cultas y silenciosas,
no se parecen en nada
a vuestras viejas babosas.[3]

Do you think you've offended
taunting fanatics with medals divine?
we'll never be upended
by the drivel of swine.

These holy women that you see in us,
so piously educated and soft spoken,
are nothing in the least like
your idiotic old ladies so broken.[4]

The song provides a clear apologia of cristero manhood, valor, and piety, and rejects accusations of weakness, treachery, and fanaticism. The cristero balladeer also hurled his own insults, calling the soldiers of El Valle "Bolsheviks" without loyalty to country and without religion. The corrido continued with a flurry of lyrics dedicated to undermining the courage and masculinity of the troops in Valparaíso, even calling one agrarista "Fidel el Panzón" ("Potbellied Fidel"). The song casts anti-cristero leaders in El Valle as timid, valiant only because they drank before battle, and "trembling like a woman" with fear in the face of combat. The corridista finishes with a flourish, which modern-day aficionados of the English-language taunt "Who's you're daddy?" might appreciate:

Que si son deveras hombres y deveras valientitos, que salgan a conocer, a sus meros papacitos.	If true men you would be, and if valiant laddies, then come out to meet, who's really your daddies.
Vuela, vuela palomita, párate en aquel palmar anda y dile a los del Valle que su papá es Quintanar.[5]	Fly, fly little dove, alight on that palm tree afar go and tell those in El Valle that their dad is Quintanar.

The ballad provides an earthy, witty—at times even comical—snapshot of the cristero struggle. It also reveals constructions of masculinity by which cristeros and their enemies sought to define themselves vis-à-vis their opponents. Catholic rebels certainly fought with guns and bullets when available, and they especially became available in victory, as dead federal soldiers could offer no complaint to their ammunition being requisitioned for new purposes. But even in that first year the war fought for Cristo Rey (Christ the King) began to carry a tune: Catholic rebels used rhyme, rhythm, and verse against their enemies. They immortalized their heroes with ballads and recounted their exploits in songs of battle. Anti-cristero troops likewise extolled their own cause in lyrical verse, denouncing the religious crusaders as cruel, villainous miscreants. And although scholarship on ballads written during the period has rightly noted the historical value of the ballad genre, it has overlooked the usefulness of corridos in illuminating the color, quality, and characteristics of religion practiced and lived by Catholic militants.[6] Mexican corridos became avenues for popular news and for the preservation of memory. Yet, as artistic compositions, they also reflected more than merely the nuts and bolts of history: they not only chronicled important dates and names, but also created arenas in which identities were represented, performed, and interpreted. The ballads of the Cristero Rebellion therefore add nuance and depth to historical scholarship on Catholicism in Revolutionary Mexico (c. 1910–1940).

Popular balladeers composed their verses within a distinct context of religious and social upheaval that transformed early twentieth-century Mexico. The Cristero Rebellion, alternatively called the Cristero War or Cristiada, was a local and regional rebellion fought by lay Catholics against government anticlericalism. It was also a diplomatic and political struggle between Church and state elites. Between the years 1926 and 1929, rural

Catholic militants rose to contest anticlerical legislation incorporated in the Constitution of 1917. The most troublesome articles for Catholics included a ban on religious primary education (Article 3) and monastic orders (Article 5); restrictions on public worship (Article 24) and the nationalization of all ecclesiastical property (Article 27); the constitution also reinforced state control over clerical ministry, which required priests to obtain government-issued licenses, prohibited clerical garb in public, and enabled governors to set the maximum number of priests within state boundaries (Article 130). The legislation threatened community values, traditions, and autonomy, most notably in areas where clerical religion had the strongest foothold, especially in the west-central region, which was, in effect, Mexico's Catholic heartland. It was there that fighting spread across approximately thirteen states and took the lives of some ninety thousand Mexican combatants. However, even within the clerical center-west, local communities each had their own historical and cultural character that largely determined whether militants joined the pro-Church movement or took up arms against the cristeros. Varying relations with long-term government land policies, with the local Catholic hierarchy, and with neighboring towns were crucial factors in why communities just miles apart, such as Huejuquilla el Alto and Valparaíso, found themselves on opposite sides of the battlefield. Internal feuds and longstanding rivalries within these two towns compelled many to join one side or the other. The geographical, communal, and culturally embedded nature of Mexican Catholicism in the center-west provided the specific contexts from which arose a diversity of political allegiances.[7]

By 1929, Church and state elites brought the local rebellion to an end. In June, United States ambassador Dwight Morrow helped negotiate a Vatican-backed modus vivendi between Church and state. The American government desired to bring about internal peace in Mexico while the Mexican government viewed the cease-fire as an opportunity to end a costly insurgency.[8] The accords led to a momentary alleviation of hostilities, but did not fundamentally solve the religious conflict. Cristero veterans only begrudgingly accepted the Church's mandate to lay down their arms. The hierarchy's temporizing policy led to a rift between Catholic militants and Church leaders in Mexico. By the end of 1931 the Church-state battle reignited once again, and renewed anticlericalism led to another Catholic uprising (though far smaller) known as the Segunda (1934–1941).[9]

Research on the Cristero Rebellion and on religion in general during the Revolutionary period has undergone something of a revival. On the one hand, a new generation of scholars has expanded our view of the period. Local religion has received special attention, as well as the role of women and gender.[10] Where once the pioneering works of Jean Meyer and Alicia

Olivera de Bonfil stood out as the relatively sole exemplars giving voice to voiceless cristeros, a veritable historical choir of new studies has been published.[11] Each has added depth and tone, pitch and resonance to our understanding. Yet, the new historiography has not focused on cristero musical production. On the other hand, a growing number of scholars have focused on cristero corridos, but much of this work does not relate it to the new historiography of the religious conflict, especially in terms of gender and local religion.[12] This chapter represents an initial step in that direction, describing how the ballads produced during the period expressed cristeros' desire for local autonomy articulated through gendered lyrical compositions. The essay then provides examples of religious dissent voiced in ballads written by non-cristeros, as well as how cristero ballads could display ambivalent responses toward official Church policy, especially the unpopular Church-state cease-fire of June 1929. Corridos produced during the rebellion became avenues through which Mexicans voiced their political affiliations, expressed beliefs about religion and the Church, and revealed their convictions regarding the gendered nature of Catholicism.

Corridos of the Cristero Rebellion

What becomes abundantly clear when reading or listening to ballads written by cristeros is that they said very little about the larger political context of the era. This is not surprising, as many popular ballads from the Revolutionary period likewise did not provide broader context. Generally, Mexican corridos often focused only on specific battles or the deeds (and even misdeeds) of heroic individuals. In fact, a large number of ballads we might include as distinctly cristero—because of their content or authorship—are not unlike non-cristero songs. Corrido scholars Vicente Mendoza, Merle Simmons, and Américo Paredes spent a large part of their careers defining a genre of Mexican ballads they referred to as epic/heroic, which reached its florescence between 1910 and 1930, roughly covering the Revolutionary era. A specific formula characterized these epic/heroic corridos. They usually consisted of an introduction ("Voy a cantarles un corrido"); verses that set the time, place, and date of the events narrated; the entrance of the protagonist, as well as the hero's words, which were set up by formulaic phrases used in countless ballads; then followed the heroic deeds of the protagonist, usually concluding in his death (it was often, but not always, a man); and finally, the *despedida* (farewell) of the corridista ended the song.[13] A large portion of cristero corridos fit within this epic/heroic formula. At least in terms of form and style, nothing differentiated a cristero ballad such as the well-known "Corrido de Valentín de la Sierra" from one written about a non-cristero subject. The ballads of the Cristero Rebellion therefore form part of a much larger corpus produced over three decades of revolutionary upheaval and national reconstruction. Cristero corridos are found embedded within the *cancioneros* (songbooks), unedited collections, and loose broadsides of the period; many of them were only preserved orally, sung by the regional *cantantes* in locales where they were first composed.[14]

A recent study by Antonio Avitia Hernández has nevertheless endeavored to catalogue the corridos from the cristero uprising, extracting them from the general corpus of Revolutionary ballads. Avitia has collected sixty-nine such corridos, the majority of which originated in locations where the rebellion took place and evidence popular authorship. These songs naturally do not represent all of the cristero corridos written during the period. For example, Olivera de Bonfil and Jean Meyer cite the titles of cristero ballads that Avitia did not include in his study, an oversight that stems from the fact that a copy of these songs could not be located.[15] Many of the cristero corridos were in fact saved from historical oblivion through the intrepid work of scholars who ventured into the sierra to record local musicians playing songs unknown out of their immediate region. Irene Vázquez Valle and José de Santiago Silva preserved nine cristero corridos from Los Altos region of Jalisco and from Zacatecas, releasing them on a 1976 vinyl edition produced by Mexico's National Institute of Anthropology and History.[16] Avitia notes that in the case of two corridos he included in his list ("Corrido de Maximiliano Vigueras" and "Corrido del Conflicto Religioso y Los Arreglos"), the ballads were first recorded in Los Angeles, California, and San Antonio, Texas, respectively, revealing that corridos traveled as people did.[17] These two cities received large influxes of Mexican emigrants between 1920 and 1930, especially from the western-central region where the cristero uprising resulted in massive unemployment and community dislocation.[18] As Julia Young argues, although not all of these Mexican emigrants held cristero sympathies, both Los Angeles and San Antonio (as well as other cities such as El Paso and Chicago) saw the creation of many local pro-cristero organizations, and also played host to exiled lay militants and other religious emigrants who actively promoted the cristero cause in writing, religious processions, and marches: priests, nuns, monks, seminarians, bishops, and archbishops who fled Mexico or were deported in the course of hostilities.[19] While the exact reason these two ballads were recorded in the United States remains unclear, cristero corridos likely found a welcome audience among Mexican immigrants with cristero sympathies, providing yet another vehicle for popular expression and solidarity with their coreligionists in rebellion. However, within Mexico, many songs chronicling the rebellion remained within the regions where the events took place. Only rarely did the ballads become known—or even more rarely, popular—in Mexico more broadly. The relative freedom of movement and expression afforded to Mexican immigrant communities in the United States, as well as their transfer via recordings, probably allowed for the wider diffusion of the ballads north of the border.

Avitia's collection of cristero ballads displays a good deal of geographic diversity, split temporally between the two cristero uprisings. Of the sixty-nine corridos he located, forty-eight refer to events during the first Cristero War (1926–1929) and twenty-one to the Segunda (1934–1941).[20] The states of Jalisco and Durango produced the most, with eighteen a piece. Yet, many other states in which the rebellion happened also elicited ballads: Zacatecas (seven); Guanajuato (six); Michoacán (six); Aguascalientes (three); Colima (one); Mexico State (one); Nayarit (one); Oaxaca (one); Querétaro (one). In four cases, two states are listed, revealing how the events of the conflict often spilled over state boundaries: Jalisco/Zacatecas (one); Guanajuato/Michoacán (one); Aguascalientes/Zacatecas (one); Querétaro/Guanajuato (one). Although no battles took place in Mexico City, Avitia includes one corrido on his list that originated in the Federal District, as its cristero protagonist (Maximiliano Vigueras) hailed from the capital and was captured, tortured, and executed there. The remaining two ballads have no geographical connection, although they appear to reflect popular attitudes toward the Church strike and the *arreglos* ("Aniversario del cierre de las iglesias" and "Corrido del Conflicto Religioso y Los Arreglos").[21]

A number of other corridos from the era might be worth adding as well, especially as their themes touched on the Church-state conflict generally (i.e., "Corrido del Convención," "Atentado contra el General Obregón," "La muerte del General Obregón," "El Jurado de Toral," "El fusilamiento de José de León Toral," "Corrido de Tomás Garrido Canabal," "Corrido del General Cárdenas"). These ancillary corridos expose the problematic nature of deciding which songs should be included and which should not. Although they might have been written by well-known "official" corridistas from the capital, especially in the case of Felipe Flores, who wrote several, they certainly appear to reflect popular sentiments about the religious conflict, even if they do not narrate specific battles of rebellion like the majority of the other ballads. Including these compositions would bring the number to approximately seventy-six. A majority of the cristero corridos that have been located by Avitia display a clear pro-cristero perspective (forty-six). The remaining ballads showcase an anti-cristero bias (twenty) or a neutral position (three).[22] The ballads of the Cristero Rebellion reflect the complexities of the political and religious conflict and express a range of vantage points, from piety and dissent, to rancor and ambivalence.

Masculinity and Devotion to Cristo Rey

Religious motivations alone (though important) do not wholly explain why Mexicans chose to fight as cristeros or as agraristas.[23] Matthew Butler argues that socioeconomic historical realities and local religious traditions created by and through the specific context of the nation's center-west helped form political identities.[24] A quest for local autonomy, mediated through a fight over religious practices, became a key factor in why many Catholics chose to rebel. Cristero corridos reflect these complex motivations, where issues of religion and autonomy were articulated through gender representations. By analyzing performances of gender in cristero corridos we discover how contested understandings of Mexican masculinity often became the battleground on which cristeros fought for political power, national inclusion, and community autonomy.

Masculinity is a concept that bears some discussion. Scholars are unanimous in differentiating biological sex—the physical characteristics shared by men or women—from social gender, or the "collection of behaviors, attitudes and attributes [men or women] may or may not exhibit (but that, perhaps, they ought to)" according to societal conventions.[25] Biology is natural; gender is learned within specific historical contexts that change over time.[26] Thus, "femaleness" and "maleness" are terms used to describe physical states, while "femininity" and "masculinity" depict a spectrum of learned behaviors, enacted in day-to-day circumstances, that are dialectically engaged, and embedded within popular cultural productions. Recent scholarship has stressed the performative aspect of gender, as femininity and masculinity are "determined more by the judgments of others than by an intrinsic quality."[27] Men and women perform their gender identities in relation to other men and women, who are then judged more or less "masculine" or "feminine" by a set of assumed, or even imagined, characteristics. In the case of Mexico, the "violence-prone, overly emotional, fatalistic *machos*" or the "overly religious, fearful, conservative, family-obsessed" women are some of the well-worn gender stereotypes.[28] Yet these imagined categories reveal how definitions of the masculine are constructed in relations of power: with women, between heterosexual men and marginalized male sexualities, and through ethnic, racial, and class-based dichotomies. The masculine self is known by what it rejects, thereby making the study of excluded others integral to the study of masculine gender identities. Corridos from the Cristero Rebellion likewise present masculinity in relation to these "others." Even as they present a picture of the ideal cristero (virile, loyal, courageous), they reflect that masculinity was defined through actions, that masculinity could be won or lost by what one did (or failed to do). The ballad genre became a stage on which to perform the ideal, where cristero men could be found wanting and cristero women were vindicated.

Masculine identities in Mexico have been intricately linked to debates over national identity. This is not peculiar to Mexico; Roman "manliness" (*virtus*) was defined in relation to one's service to the Republic.[29] And so too, definitions of what it meant to be a man in Mexico have historically been included in a larger discussion of what it meant to be authentically Mexican. As Robert Mckee Irwin argues: "the imagined communities constructed in nineteenth-century literature were communities of men."[30] Interactions between men—"homosocial bonds"—symbolized national unity. By the turn of the twentieth century however, the threat of homoeroticism, transvestism, and effeminacy called into question the homosocial "allegory of the nation."[31] Most notoriously, the 1901 scandal of the transvestites ball, the so-called famous 41, where police raided a private Mexico City gathering of cross-dressed men, projected male effeminacy and homosexuality onto the popular imagination as "both the other that would define a macho heterosexual national model and an other that in fact was itself intrinsically Mexican."[32] Gender scholar Héctor Domínguez-Ruvalcaba writes that in early twentieth-century Mexico, "effeminacy constitut[ed] a device for emasculating political enemies" and that effeminacy was itself represented as antinational.[33] During the Revolution, representations of the hypermasculine male came to symbolize nationality to a new degree. As Victor M. Macías-González and Anne Rubenstein note, insurgents such as Pancho Villa and Emiliano Zapata "tacitly accepted the Porfirian conflation of nation, state, family honor, and male power."[34] The "exaggerated masculinity" of Revolutionary militants seemed to "make up for their lesser class and ethnic status, marking them as true citizens of the nation they were hoping to remake."[35] Cristero constructions of masculinity likewise associated national inclusion with male power, although cristeros further intertwined piety with notions of the sexualized heroic man (e.g., the repeated reference to cristeros as "papacitos"), ready to die for Cristo Rey and *la patria* (the Fatherland), who flaunted government authority and fought for autonomy from a corrupt paternalist state. The Revolutionary state embodied a failed patriarchy to cristero militants: a godless state could neither model authentic masculinity nor promote a durable Mexican national identity when it rejected Catholic faith and ritual.

An excellent starting point in analyzing masculine identities articulated in cristero corridos is the devotion to Cristo Rey, which became extremely popular during the rebellion. The cult was not entirely new. It developed as an adaptation of the devotion to the Sacred Heart of Jesus. Seventeenth- and eighteenth-century French visionaries—Marguerite-Marie Alacoque being the most famous—claimed to have seen Jesus, spoken with him, and observed his loving heart, exposed and wounded by human disobedience and scorn. The message of the visions was that the faithful had a role to play in repairing Christ's wounds, through intercession to the Virgin Mary and consecration of the family, the home, and even the nation to Jesus's divine and sacred heart.[36] European Jesuits popularized the cult and Society missionaries spread the devotion across the seas to Asia, Africa, and the Americas. New French missionary congregations also brought the devotion to Latin America. For example, by 1900 over three hundred nuns of the Congregation of the Sacred Heart of Jesus and Mary (Picpus Fathers and Sisters) worked throughout the region.[37] French missionary societies, including a variety of those dedicated to the Sacred Heart, "saw the missionary challenge as a struggle against secularization and liberalism, even though that battle was far from over within France itself."[38] Moreover, the devotion received support from the Vatican. Pope Leo XIII (1878–1903) exhorted the Catholic world in his encyclical *Annum sacrum* (1899) to take part in consecrations to the Sacred Heart because these pious acts could "establish or draw tighter the bonds which naturally connect public affairs with God."[39] The individual's indifference to Christ's commands did not alone account for wounding the Sacred Heart, according to the Pope. Christ's afflictions had also been caused by a general societal apostasy, represented in the rise of secular pretentions to authority that had little regard for the Church or religious legitimacy. Catholic anxieties regarding the expansion, consolidation, and vehemence of secular nation-building in the twentieth century provided much of the impetus for the adaptation of the Sacred Heart devotion, transforming the depiction of Jesus from suffering servant to conquering king.

Latin American Catholics quickly took up Pope Leo's call for dedications to the Sacred Heart of Jesus in the early twentieth century. Pious societies, especially women's associations, organized crusades of consecration, where an icon of the Sacred Heart would be enthroned in family homes.[40] While the official cult of Christ the King was not exclusively Mexican, the country's Revolutionary context created national tones to the devotion. Mexican Catholics, with the blessing of the counter-Revolutionary dictator

Victoriano Huerta, consecrated the nation to the Sacred Heart in 1914. Thereafter, the devotion to Christ the King rose in popularity. In 1923, Catholic militants in Mexico planned the erection of a large statue of Christ outside Guanajuato on Cubilete Hill. The event provoked the ire of President Álvaro Obregón (1920–1924) and resulted in the expulsion of the apostolic delegate, who had taken part in the public ceremony inaugurating the statue's construction. Dedications soon included the act of enthroning the Sacred Heart, an adaptation that lay at the root of the new Cristo Rey devotion.

Pope Pius XI (1922–1939) established the worldwide feast of Christ the King in his 1925 encyclical *Quas primas*. Pius selected the last Sunday of every October as an annual day of celebration, when the Church Universal would proclaim the temporal reality of Christ's reign on earth. In other words, Christ was not to rule simply in heaven, but also in the here and now, through a rechristianized society evidenced in respect for Church authority and Christian values. The evolving cult to Cristo Rey proclaimed the "socio-temporal" reality of Christ's Kingdom, which embraced "all mankind" and announced the Church's "independence from the civil power" (cf. *Quas Primas*).[41] Clear confrontational overtones were expressed in the bold proclamation of Christ's royalty. If Christ was king, then all earthly "Caesars"—including President Calles—were not. The annunciation of Christ's authority carried the implicit proclamation that Jesus's divine power trumped all other claims, especially from secular government rulers. In essence, the masculine, even virile, nature of Jesus represented an ideal type, a legitimate form of paternal authority that, according to devotees, dwarfed dysfunctional government paternalism in Mexico. In the first two decades of the twentieth century, the often feminized late nineteenth-century Jesus of the Sacred Heart variety grew into the masculine "Christ the King," reconquering society through an organized army of active lay Catholics.[42]

Allegiance to Cristo Rey in Mexico came to represent a rejection of ungodly government authority embodied in President Plutarco Elías Calles. The "Christ-Caesar" binary was easily applied to Mexico: Calles was often called "Nero" or a "Turk" by cristeros.[43] One rebel wrote: "Comrades, I have come to raise the banner of Christ the King, because we are tired of the constant tyrannies of the Turk Plutarco Elías Calles."[44] In the "Corrido a la Hacienda de San Juan Capistrano," written by Father José Adolfo Arroyo in 1927, Calles was depicted as a "heretic" whose impious machinations to destroy religious faith were impeded by *Cristo Rey*:

Si podrá, Calles hereje, acabar con nuestra Patria,	If he could, Calles the heretic, would destroy our Nation,

pero Dios que nunca muere guardará nuestra fe santa.	but God who never dies will protect our holy faith.
Esos pocos combatientes que tú ves, de mala traza, no combaten en su nombre, su Rey Cristo los ampara.[45]	These few fighters that you see, so ill-equipped, do not fight in their own name, their King Christ helps them.

Despite the small number of troops, which were ill equipped for battle, Father Arroyo claimed that their victory came because Christ the King had aided them. The holy cause for which they fought assured divine intervention to preserve the Catholic identity of the nation.

The title "cristero," in fact, stemmed from the battle cry "¡Viva Cristo Rey!" ("Long Live Christ the King!"), which Catholic militants used during the rebellion, as well as in less violent arenas like public manifestations and in pro-Church propaganda. The phrase became a mark of loyalty to the cause and a proclamation identifying the individual as a defender of religion. Cristeros, government troops, and agraristas in the field used the phrase as a kind of litmus test in determining one's political affiliation. "¿Quién Vive?" ("Who lives?"), the first group of combatants might enjoin. And if the response came back "¡Viva Cristo Rey!," the opposing sides commenced fighting.[46] Devotion to Christ the King became a sign of rebellion as well as a model for Christian manhood and sacrifice. In President Calles, the rebels perceived a corruption of national fatherhood that had endangered Mexico's holy and patriotic family. As cristero Ezequiel Mendoza wrote: "I think it is better to die fighting for Christ the King and the Virgin of Guadalupe and all Their family, and not take a single step against the one true God, even if the Devil is angered."[47]

Throughout cristero testimonies and, as evidenced in their corridos, invocations to Christ the King and the Virgin of Guadalupe dominate; specialist and local saints are less common, although they do appear, such as Saint James ("Santiago"; see below). The predominance of Christ the King and Guadalupe, perhaps peculiar on the surface, given that local religious cults were so important to many Mexican villages, finds an analogy in William Christian's research on local religion in sixteenth-century Spain: "like Mary, Christ was consulted as a divine generalist, and he took over a combination of problems from the specialist saints," especially in times of drought, calamity, and economic stagnation.[48] Moreover, many communities in the central-western region where the uprising took root had strong links to the institutional Church (for example, high rates of sacramental participation and frequent contact with priests and other religious officials), which heavily promoted the "official" cults of Christ and Mary. Evidence for the influence of a Hispanisized, institutional variety of Catholicism on cristero identities can also be found in the interesting fact that the official battle hymn of the cristeros was sung to the tune of Spain's national anthem, the "Marcha Real."[49] It appears that cristeros appealed to the Virgin of Guadalupe and Christ the King as national symbols, who might be enlisted to assist even in the local/regional conflicts that precipitated the rebellion. While local cults dedicated to the Virgin Mary, for instance, continued to be venerated (e.g., the Virgin of Zapopan in Jalisco), Guadalupe and Christ the King became the preferred divine intermediaries of the cristero struggle and represented the ideal models for a cristero gendered Catholicism.

Santiago Bayacora: Authority and Fatherhood

Themes of authority, masculinity, fatherhood, and nationality all played important roles in the experience of cristeros from Santiago Bayacora, Durango. Francisco Campos wrote that the decision of the townsfolk to rise against the government was forged through community consensus. In July 1926, a notice appeared on the door of the local church, stating that fines would be levied against anyone ringing the bells of the *templo*, teaching their children to pray, for keeping saints in one's home, or for wearing any religious medals.[50] Jean Meyer notes that the announcement probably did not exist in the form Campos described, but that it captured the sense of moral outrage at the government's attempt to regulate religious practices.[51] "Well, after seeing that manifesto," wrote Campos, "certainly we felt that the government is to be respected, but in these and other circumstances, this did not sit well with us and the people would rather be smashed to pieces than conform with what the Government said."[52] The president's reform of the penal code in 1926, which enacted the religious articles of the Constitution of 1917 (e.g., fines and/or imprisonment), represented a clear attack on the religious traditions of Santiago Bayacora. Many in the town gathered to deliberate on a course of action. All those present were asked their opinion. And according to Campos's account, "to defend Religion," everyone agreed to "fight to the death."[53] The town chose Trinidad Mora as its military leader and Francisco, along with his brother Agapito, pledged their support. Government officials sent to facilitate the transfer of the town's church to a group of laymen in accordance with the new ordinances were beaten by angry *santiagueros*. On September 29 a detachment of federal troops was dispatched to quell the unrest. Knowing the beatings and insults delivered to the government functionaries would bring official retribution, Trinidad Mora gathered weapons and those willing to fight. When the soldiers arrived, the rebels managed to gain the upper hand, ambushing the federal troops. Campos thanked God, Saint James, and the Virgin for helping them gain victory.[54]

Campos related the events of one early battle with government troops in a ballad he wrote titled "Corrido del Combate del Puerto de la Arena" in 1926. The rebels of Santiago Bayacora had received word that Federal General Ismael Lares asked President Calles if he could be sent to put down the uprisings in Durango. Campos recounted that a rumor began circulating that General Lares had boasted he would "bring all of us in the sierra back bound and tied up."[55] The general and his troops traveled from operations in Chihuahua to the sierra of Durango. The federal troops soon discovered the cristeros led by Trinidad Mora at Santa Elena, a hacienda near Puerto de la Arena. Thinking that only a few rebels were holed up in the house built on the hacienda, General Lares approached the door: "Inside boys we've arrived," he said standing outside. The second-in-command, a coronel, turned to Lares and suggested they wait: "Listen my General, let's leave the fighting until tomorrow because it's getting late." Meanwhile, inside, Mora had instructed Campos and the other men to wait until he gave the signal, and then fire with everything they had. "There's nothing to fear from these boys," replied Lares to his subordinate. "¡Adentro!" repeated Lares taking a few steps forward. Mora then gave the signal and the cristeros opened fire, Lares unable even to take out his pistol before falling dead. Mora and his troops pursued the retreating force, which according to Francisco Campos comprised 250 men and a mule (which died in the firefight). The rebels took a cache of weapons, jewels owned by Lares, and a bag of money that contained a thousand pesos.

Campos explicitly linked religion and masculinity in his ballad, intoning "General Lares died a Mason and man of no consequence."[56] Real men were not freemasons, according to Campos. Catholic faith inspired the virtue of valor, and without that faith, a man was of no consequence. The remainder of the corrido did not mention religion explicitly. However, Campos taunted President Calles, likening physical violence with sexual domination:

Vuela paloma y no te vayas a caer	Fly dove and don't let down
handa dile a Calles	go and tell Calles

que aquí están sus papacitos	that his daddies are here
que lo quieren conoser [*sic*].[57]	who want to get with him.

Calles, the father of the nation, had met his match in the victorious troops of Santiago Bayacora: the defeat of government troops, specifically the murder of Lares, who had been reportedly commissioned by Calles himself, represented a vindication of cristero masculinity and religion. Campos asserted cristero masculinity through the implicit act of homosexual sex (the phrase "who want to get with him" is a reference to copulation), where cristeros overpowered and violated federal troops.[58] According to Irwin: "contests of wit, authority, or brute force produce symbolic relations of sexual penetration, in which the loser cracks, gets fucked, and is feminized by the winner, who, in this way, enhances his masculinity."[59] In a postscript to the corrido, Campos further emasculated General Lares by comparing him to an animal and an Indian ("sprawled out like an animal, the old Indian"), which were both subjects that could represent feminized identity because of their purported passivity in hierarchies of power (man dominates beast; white man dominates Indian man).[60] Campos represented the cristero battle with federal troops as a symbolic sexual encounter where, because of their virility and masculinity, the rebels from Santiago Bayacora had bested General Lares and delegitimized the authority of President Calles. The symbolic sexual violation of the federal troops called into question the very paternalism of the state.

Quintanar's Brigade: Loyalty and Betrayal

Ballads from the Cristero Rebellion praised the heroic deeds of individuals who remained loyal to the cause of Cristo Rey. However, they also told the story of betrayal. The uprising led by Pedro Quintanar began in August 1926. A rancher with a good reputation in the south of Zacatecas, Quintanar had been leader of the defenses against Villista attacks after 1914. He had military skill and experience leading men. He only reluctantly entered into the rebellion, his decision prompted by the arrest and execution of a parish priest and other townspeople from Chalchihuites.[61] Another small-time cattle breeder from the area, Aurelio Acevedo, approached Quintanar earlier that summer about a planned uprising on August 1, but Quintanar demurred, waiting to see what would happen. The arrests in Chalchihuites compelled Quintanar to act and he mobilized a small force in an unsuccessful effort to free those taken prisoner. After their execution, Quintanar rode into Huejuquilla el Alto, his hometown, with one hundred men to shouts of "¡Viva Cristo Rey!" Although at first hoping to come to terms with the government on the religious question before the incident in Chalchihuites, Quintanar no longer hesitated: "I've made a commitment to the Virgin of Guadalupe,"[62] he reportedly told his wife. Acevedo joined Quintanar's troops, later being promoted to general and even acting as the governor of Zacatecas when cristeros controlled the region. After the rebellion, Acevedo would become the main chronicler of cristero testimonies, promoting their stories in the publication *David*, a monthly periodical that ran from 1952 to 1968.[63]

Quintanar's victory in Huejuquilla established the cristero troops in the region. The town held strategic value, as Quintanar feared that established agrarista militants in Valparaíso would take the region if they did not. By 1927, when cristeros and agraristas were writing ballads about each other, Quintanar had established control over the south of Zacatecas and north of Jalisco.[64] In 1928, the new supreme commander of the cristero forces, Enrique Gorostieta, appointed Quintanar head of a brigade composed of five regiments: "Libres de Huejuquilla," "Valparaíso," "Guadalupe," "Castañón," and "Libres de Chalchihuites."[65] At least three thousand troops were under his command.[66] Moreover, other regional cristero militias, such as Trinidad Mora and the Campos brothers from Santiago Bayacora, formally looked to Quintanar for leadership, but often operated autonomously.

The zone controlled by Pedro Quintanar and his troops produced one of the most iconic corridos of the Cristero Rebellion. The song narrated the death of Valentín Avila Ramírez, more famously known as "Valentín de la Sierra." The original ballad, written by Lidio Pacheco in 1928, recounted how Valentín was captured by agraristas and provided information on the whereabouts of Quintanar's troops. Thus, Valentín betrayed his fellow cristeros in order to save his own life. The corrido quickly became popular, not only among cristeros, but also with federal soldiers, and therefore it gained a wider audience outside of Jalisco and Zacatecas.[67] Federal troops probably liked the song because it told the story of a traitorous cristero, providing them with material to malign the Catholic rebels.[68] The ballad became an early radio hit, and because of the demands of the medium (the average song needed to be three minutes), the ballad itself was shortened to eight stanzas from its approximate original of twenty-five.[69] In addition to being cut, the radio version represented a complete inversion of the corrido's original meaning: Valentín de la Sierra was recast as a hero, who was executed by agrarista troops from Valparaíso because he would not provide information on the location of Quintanar's Brigade. The popularity of the ballad even led to two films about the so-called historical Valentín (*Valentín de la Sierra* and *El caudillo*, both in 1967). But here again, the films further changed the original context of the events, locating the action to the 1910 Revolution and not the Cristiada.[70] Thus, the most recognizable cristero ballad from the era, symbolizing the valor of a hero facing his death, began as a song describing the tragic consequences of disloyalty to the cause of Cristo Rey.

Avitia has reconstructed the historical events behind the corrido. Valentín Avila came from San Cayetano, a small pueblo near Huejuquilla el Alto. Before the rebellion he worked trading goods in the mountains of the region, which provided his nickname, Valentín de la Sierra. He joined the uprising and operated under the orders of Quintanar, working as a spy, guide, and message courier. He probably operated in a unit of no more than fifteen men, stationed near the hacienda de Los Landa (which later was changed to "Holanda," "los Andas," or "Rancho de Holanda"). As seen in the "Corrido de la Contestación," the agraristas from Valparaíso were the main enemies of the cristeros in the region. The ballad mentioned two: a captain of the agrarista militia, Epigmenio Talamantes, and J. Encarnación "Chon" Salas, who had assumed leadership of the town council of Valparaíso under agrarista control. During the back and forth fighting between Huejuquilla and Valparaíso, captured agrarista leaders were always released, until in January 1928, in an apparent move to take firm control over the region, five agraristas were executed. By the end of that year, the agrarista forces had regrouped and were in search of cristero detachments. In one of these expeditions, Talamantes invited Valentín to join the agraristas, as he seemingly did not know Valentín was attached to cristero forces in the region. His true identity was questioned by a woman who knew of Valentín's cristero affiliation. The discovery led to an interrogation by Talamantes and Chon Salas, demanding that he give up details of where cristero detachments were located, or else face execution. Valentín provided information on the whereabouts of a group of rebels, offering the information to settle a score with a cristero named Ignacio Serrano, who had offended Valentín. The agraristas then thought better of the deal they made with Valentín, saying that if he had betrayed his friends, why would he be loyal to us? Before executing their prisoner, Chon Salas offered Valentín amnesty once again, if he would provide the location of the "curato" ("curacy," or where clandestine masses took place, which later versions of the song changed to the nonsensical "jurado," or "jury," perhaps in order not to implicate Valentín in naming where sacraments were given out in secret, which would only underscore his betrayal) as well as information about a "Justo" (which referred either to Justo Jaime, a rich cristero supporter in the region, or Justo Avila, an assistant to General Gorostieta). Realizing his situation, Valentín sought to redeem himself, denied the offer, and faced death instead of giving up further information.[71]

Authentic masculinity in the "Corrido de Valentín de la Sierra" was defined by the protagonist's failure to exemplify loyalty and valor. The ballad exposes these weaknesses through a gendered comparison with two women who appear in the song. Both women demonstrate masculine ideal characteristics, thereby emasculating Valentín in the process. The first, an unnamed woman, arrives in company of muleteers and "was part of Quintanar's people." She reveals Valentín's cristero identity, yet the ballad does not describe the woman's actions negatively:

Se sentaron en el suelo, juntos con el capitán, y una mujer lo entregó, que era de la gente de éste Quintanar.	They sat together on the ground, together with the captain, and a woman turned him in, who was part of Quintanar's people.
Muy antes de Huejuquilla, la mujer lo señaló, iba con unos arrieros y, en esto, la tropa llegó y lo cercó.[72]	Before arriving in Huejuquilla, the woman singled him out, she came with some muleteers and, with this knowledge, the troop arrived and drew near to him.

Although speculative, the balladeer might have been suggesting that Valentín had ignoble motivations for joining the agraristas, either as a way to avenge his feud with Ignacio Serrano, or simply to save his own neck after the agraristas pressured him to join their troops. Refusing the invitation might have opened him to suspicions of a cristero affiliation. Valentín's masculinity was first questioned insofar as a woman forthrightly declared the truth about his identity, while Valentín's motivations remained unclear, murky at best. Moreover, Valentín did not show courage when interrogated, but rather the corridista claimed he gave up the information due to fear: "very scared he told them everything," which further served to feminize the antihero. When "Tiva," the second female character, enters the narrative, she mistakenly yells ("comenzó a gritar") that Valentín would be killed for his religion, which highlights his duplicity, emphasizing the distance between the cristero ideal of martyrdom in imitation of Christ and the reality of Valentín's treachery against his former allies. Tiva was the nickname for a woman named Natividad González González, who led the clandestine support efforts of the Saint Joan of Arc Feminine Brigade in the region. Immediately after the entrance of Tiva, the balladeer says that "Valentín wanted to cry," showcasing his timidity and lack of masculine courage. Filling the Judas archetype, Valentín had sold out the cristero cause and, in the process, lost his masculinity. Although in the last instant, he refused to give up any more information, the corridista claimed that Valentín's story was that of a "man traitor."[73] The ballad, in its original form, presents a cautionary tale where loyalty, honesty, and courage made one a true cristero, not simply one's sex.

The ideal cristera, who constantly worked to bring ammunition and supplies to the rebels, as well as acting as intermediaries and message couriers, would be lionized in several other ballads: "Corrido de la Generala," "Corrido de Agripina," and the ballad "Combate de San Clemente." In the first two, a woman is the sole protagonist, while in the third a long list of Feminine Brigade women are mentioned by name. The corridista intoned that "many young women" had risked their lives to bring provisions, clean clothes, ammunition, and even candies to those on the field:

Estas valientes muchachas,	These valiant girls,
unidas a las Mireles,	united the Mireles girls,
las Velasco y García de Alba,	the Velasco and García de Alba,
trabajaban de verdá,	worked in truth,
y era tan grande su audacia	and so great was their audacity
y las argucias que empleaban	and chicanery that they employed
que, hasta sus perseguidores,	that, even their persecutors,
de su valor se admiraban.[74]	their valor they admired.

The valor, and audacity, of these women served to reinforce the masculinity of cristero soldiers. Men such as Valentín de la Sierra could be emasculated in comparison to courageous women. Especially in context of the mother-son relationship, cristeras urged their children to "man up": "Sons, don't be cowards, rise up, and defend a just cause!"[75] What is more, femininity was used to define what authentic manhood meant for cristeros, as well as for agraristas, where both sides taunted each other using gendered language: "If you don't surrender, we will bring out our women to bugger you good and proper" and "If you let them, that means you are not men, and long live Christ the King, son of a whore!"[76]

On the one hand, women served to reinforce constructions of masculinity when cristeras acted out ideal "manly" attributes: courage, audacity, loyalty, self-sacrifice. Yet, on the other hand, if women showcased these characteristics too much, or even more than men, it could serve to feminize men (for example, female cristeras sexually violating agrarista men). Even in the highly gendered world of Mexican Catholicism, masculinity and femininity were elastic categories. Gender identity depended less on biological sex than on the performance of masculine and feminine ideals.

Los Altos de Jalisco: Roosters in the Henhouse of the Nation

President Calles notoriously commented to the governor of Jalisco in 1926 that nothing should be feared from the Catholics of that state, as Jalisco was the "henhouse of the nation" (*gallinero*). The phrase had a long history of attribution to men in the region of Jalisco, referring to alleged same-sex attraction, masculine religious fervor, and a supposed lack of marital potency.[77] Yet, as one cristero from the region wrote: "from within this henhouse emerged nothing but roosters that wore him out."[78] The gendered language reflects the representation of authentic nationality, associated with virility and sexual prowess. Calles' comment implied that Catholic piety feminized its male practitioners and became a strategy for exclusion from national unity. Cristeros, in addition to their claims of autonomy and critique of corrupt paternal authority, also sought to include piety in the homosocial bonds that tied Mexicans together. Just as Christ the King became a model for authentic Christian manhood evidenced through sacrifice, cristeros themselves, through extreme valor and bravery, became models of authentic masculinity, who represented the ideal Mexican man. Models of cristero heroic virtues were immortalized in popular ballads and exemplified in legendary figures. This becomes abundantly clear in the legend that arose around Victoriano Ramírez, better known as "El Catorce" ("The Fourteen").[79] El Catorce the legend presented one ideal type of cristero man, which many Catholic rebels often endeavored to emulate. But in the course of the rebellion, competing ideals of cristero manhood would also gain a following. Domínguez-Ruvalcaba notes that "the border between hate and desire outlines power relations."[80] The struggle to define authentic cristero manhood became a fight for power within cristero ranks.

Born March 23, 1892, in San Miguel el Alto (Jalisco), Victoriano Ramírez came to represent an idealized cristero masculinity, both in terms of his companions in war as well as in the popular legend that grew around him. His decision to rebel arose from respect for the *padrecitos* (little priests) that the government was persecuting, but yet, also, he claimed he had scores to settle, to avenge wrongs that had been left unresolved. He respected the Church and its hierarchy. He went to Mass, and took off his hat when hearing church bells and when passing sacred places. Ramírez would not back down from a fight, according to the legend, but also refused to kill prisoners in cold blood.[81] He earned his nickname before the rebellion. He had been arrested and jailed on charges of murder in his hometown of San Miguel; Ramírez managed to escape and local officials sent a posse in pursuit. When the manhunt caught up with the fugitive, Ramírez stood his ground, defeated them, and left all fourteen of the men tied up. He gathered up their weapons and sent them back to San Miguel with the message that the authorities should not send so few men to look for him next time.[82]

The romantic masculinity of El Catorce included a well-known sexual prowess, keeping at least one wife and several lovers. On this point, he departed from Church teaching and he knew it, but he had no shame about it. Heriberto Navarrete, a twenty-six-year-old cristero who fought with Victoriano Ramírez and later became a Jesuit priest, recalled one conversation he had with El Catorce on the subject of women and marriage:[83]

> "Hey, Victoriano, what is your wife's name?"
>
> "Which?"
>
> "Your legitimate wife."
>
> "¡Hum! any of them are legitimate."
>
> "That can't be. You're Catholic and now belong to the soldiers of Christ the King. You can't ignore that the Church condemns concubinage."
>
> "Look, these are different things. I am Catholic and as often as I could I went to church; and it enrages me that the condemned Government persecutes the Priests and robs the churches. And I know how to pray ('Y sé rezar'). But all this about being Catholic. About man's use of women, what does that matter?"
>
> "It matters a lot. The abuse of this faculty that God created to conserve the human race, it's sin."
>
> "That depends, my friend. If you told me I violate girls by force, or that the ones that take up with me do so against their will, I would say yes. But these abuses will come back to you! And more than that, a woman that I fancy, I always support with the necessities of life. I don't show favoritism."

Valentín was a masculine contradiction to Navarrete. He respected the valor, virility, and courage of Ramírez, attributes he desired, writing in his memoirs that had been witness to his fame among the people, his serenity in combat and his "superb marksmanship."[84] "In reality, without passing into the realm of the marvelous, his steady hand never failed," noted the young cristero.[85] But Navarrete's attraction to the dynamic charisma of Ramírez was tempered by his apparent lack of a disciplined interior piety. "Victoriano, along with other cristero leaders, [. . .] lived their rebel adventure making great sacrifices, without considering it. They never took much (or even a little) care in perfecting their private life in paths of austerity."[86] Like gender identity, notions of piety were fluid, elastic concepts, contested and performed by Mexicans during the Cristero Rebellion.

The dynamic tension between desire and rejection was showcased in Navarrete's role in El Catorce's execution by cristero forces in 1929. Ramírez commanded his own soldiers in the Los Altos region called "Los Dragones de El Catorce" ("The Dragoons of The Fourteen").[87] Technically under the immediate orders of the rebel priest Aristeo Pedroza, Valentín's unit, because of the fame of its leader, operated in semiautonomous fashion. As Enrique Gorostieta, the new commander of the troops in the region, began to consolidate the hierarchy of the cristero regiments under his own authority, Ramírez presented a problem for the new professionalization of the troops. El Catorce's detachment was decommissioned in the process. Moreover, one of Gorostieta's assistants, Mario Valdés, butted heads with Ramírez over the new policy of extracting money from the local population in 1929. Gorostieta instructed Valdés, along with Navarrete, to use the popularity of El Catorce as leverage for raising monetary contributions.[88] According to Valdés and Navarrete, Ramírez did not like the new arrangement, because up to that point, he had kept the money for himself. Further exacerbating tensions, Gorostieta placed Valdés and Navarrete in charge over the region.

Navarrete's esteem for El Catorce turned increasingly to frustration. Gorostieta, Father Pedroza, and Father Vega represented a new order, intelligent and disciplined. In this order Navarrete found his own star on the rise, promoted first to major and second-in-command over the region, and then later as Gorostieta's personal assistant. Ramírez, whose "most developed fighting skill rested in his personality," presented a threat to the new orderliness.[89] Navarrete recounted that during the decommissioning of Ramírez, the troops, under Valdés and himself, now stood at attention, in silence awaiting their command. "We were heading in the straight direction of organization," he wrote.[90] In contrast, the wild, untamed Ramírez mounted his horse, "giving his acts a theatrical seal" and "elegantly" rode away with his personal guard, which the cristero leaders allowed him to keep.[91] Navarrete later explained that "the period of irresponsibility had passed, of the initial chaos where the whims of a chief were almost sacred law in his tiny fiefdom."[92] Despite the bravado and courage that so attracted Navarrete, Ramírez had no place in the organized army of Cristo Rey, an army he hoped would establish the nation on a foundation of godly and ordered principles. Moreover, marginalizing El Catorce was a pragmatic effort to maintain unity among cristero troops, eliminating his challenge to rebel leadership.

A personal scandal added to Navarrete's disillusionment with Ramírez. Valdés and Navarrete made romantic advances toward two sisters of one of El Catorce's lovers. The women apparently rebuffed their advances and Valdés, in particular, held a grudge against Ramírez. The account was noticeably absent from Navarrete's memoirs, yet Jean Meyer writes that the situation was well known among cristeros from the region.[93] In revenge, Valdés conjured up a supposed letter written by Ramírez to a federal commander, making it look like El Catorce had entered into correspondence with *callista* forces, presumably to betray the cristeros. Whether General Pedroza took the bait and believed Valdés, or simply used it as a pretext to marginalize Ramírez, is unclear. Nonetheless, Pedroza demanded that El Catorce respond to the charges in person, which he failed to do. Cristero troops rode into San Miguel el Alto in March 1929, and during a celebration held by the town, Ramírez appeared with his personal retinue. Pedroza ordered his arrest, which was carried out by another cristero leader, Miguel Hernández. Pedroza held an impromptu trial, where both Valdés and Navarrete spoke against Ramírez. Pedroza made the decision to execute Ramírez, which took place before dawn.[94] Popular outrage ensued, and some troops even abandoned the rebellion over the affair.[95]

General Gorostieta, Father Vega, and Father Pedroza all met their deaths during 1929; popular opinion in Los Altos held that it was a sign of "punishment from heaven" for having executed their beloved El Catorce.[96] The corrido in honor of Victoriano Ramírez reflects the rift within the cristero forces. Moreover, the anonymous balladeer wrote that El Catorce had been executed to please the government, perhaps an effort to make sense of an event that appeared unfathomable to many:

Señores, de que me acuerdo, ganas de llorar me dan; que a Victoriano El Catorce ya lo van a fusilar.	Gentleman, when I remember, it makes we want to weep; that Victoriano El Catorce they are going to execute.
Válgame el Santo Niñito ya también el Padre Eterno,	Help me Holy Child also the Eternal Father,

mataron a Victoriano	they killed Victoriano
por darle gusto al Gobierno.[97]	to please the Government.

El Catorce's masculinity was central to his popularity. The balladeer's lament was thus an implicit vindication of the cristero manhood he embodied. After the execution, Navarrete's rebellion continued for only a few more months. When the cease-fire of June 1929 came, he sought amnesty and later entered the Jesuit order. After Navarrete rejected the unbridled masculinity he perceived in El Catorce, he pursued a model of piety found in the priesthood, which extolled the virtues of prayer, sacrifice, and celibacy.[98]

Between Piety and Dissent: The Corridos of the Cristero Rebellion

The religious sentiments expressed in corridos from the Cristero Rebellion were diverse, multifaceted, and complex. If ballads from the period could articulate beliefs about authentic Christian manhood they could also voice dissent and even anticlericalism. A few ballads radically attacked the clergy or religion in general. Still others communicated an implicit dissatisfaction with actions of Church officials. In examining sentiments of "Revolutionary anticlericalism" in these corridos, it is important that we differentiate corridos written by cristeros and their sympathizers from ballads penned by non-cristero combatants or other observers. We begin with a discussion of ballads written by non-cristeros, agraristas, or other Mexican observers, and then follow with an analysis of what we might call popular cristero dissent.

Not all anticlericalism during the Revolution conveyed the same meaning.[99] Adrian Bantjes argued for a disaggregation of the term: "'anticlericalism' which specifically refers to opposition to clericalism, must, of course, be distinguished from anti-Catholicism, anti-Christianity, deism, irreligiosity, and atheism."[100] Ben Fallaw has identified three types of Revolutionary anticlericalism: radical iconoclasm, moderate reformism, and popular forms.[101] Non-cristero corridos from the period reflect all three types of Revolutionary anticlericalism, though Jacobin iconoclasm shows up in relatively few ballads. An isolated example comes from Concha Michel, a radical activist, former Communist Party leader, and an organizer in the Revolutionary women's movement:[102]

No queremos religiones,	We don't want religions,
ni más leyes con engaños.	nor laws with deception.

¡Vivan los trabajadores!	*Long live the workers!*
¡Viva el pueblo proletario![103]	*Long live the people's proletariat!*

Michel equated religion with restrictive and deceptive laws that kept the working class bound in false consciousness. Still, even Michel managed to differentiate between Christianity and what she refers to as the corrupting influence of the clergy:

¡Maldito, maldito clero	Infernal, infernal clergy
que con engaño y maldad	who with deception and wickedness
las enseñanzas de Cristo	the teachings of Christ
nos ha venido a cambiar![104]	have come to distort!

The corrido was not an attack on Christ's teachings, but a critique of the clergy. Thus, although radical iconoclasts did indeed use ballads to express vehement anticlericalism, it was confined mostly to Revolutionary ideologues, who were concerned less with antireligion than with exposing the crooked behavior of priests.[105]

Where anticlericalism does appear in non-cristero corridos of the 1920s and 1930s, it more often reflects Fallaws's second and third categories: either moderate reformism, or popular forms. It comes as no surprise that appeals for religious reform were often expressed in ballads dedicated to avowed radicals, such as in "La muerte de Felipe Carrillo Puerto," written in honor of the Revolutionary governor from the state of Yucatán. The corridista claims that the Virgin of Guadalupe has been taken prisoner by priests and needed to be liberated:

Presa te tienen los curas,	The priests have you held captive,
libre el pueblo te venera;	free, the people would venerate you;
¡deja tus retablos! vente	leave your altars! and come
por los llanos y las sierras.[106]	through the plains and mountains.

Corridos such as this one allude to the battle for a Mexican "laicity." Roberto Blancarte describes laicity (from the French *laïcité*) as a political notion, "a system of association whose political institutions are no longer legitimated by the sacred or by religious institutions but by popular sovereignty."[107] Thus we find in a ballad titled "Los recuerdos de ayer" that the singer cries out with a mournful "Ay! Qué dolor!" when describing the root of the religious conflict: a battle between dueling sovereignties; on one side, the clergy invested with their traditional authority; on the other side, the Constitution of 1917 rooted in profane power.[108]

A ballad dedicated to Lázaro Cárdenas from the 1930s shows that perhaps the revolutionaries fighting for Mexican laicity had made little progress. Francisco M. Chávez's "Corrido del General Lázaro Cárdenas" esteems the president for "fighting for the campesinos," and for "teaching men justice and reason." But why is Cárdenas able to govern, according to the singer? After mentioning the president's "great intelligence" and his "manner of thought," characteristics assisting him in battling his rivals, the balladeer made clear that "The Eternal One sent him to save the Nation." Moreover, the song articulated that, in fact, "God let him govern and will take him to glory."[109] Cárdenas might have called for radical reforms, in essence, but the sovereignty of God was still the source of his political power. Non-cristero ballads from the period provide evidence that political power remained rooted in the sacred, even when current officials, presidents, or governments claimed otherwise. Songs written by many non-cristeros contained anticlerical calls for moderate reformism. However, these usually differentiated the faith of the people, defined as veneration for the Virgin of Guadalupe, other popular devotions, and idealized Christian teachings, from corrupt ecclesiastical officials.

But what of ballads written by cristeros or their sympathizers? I have yet to find a corrido expressing radical iconoclasm in a ballad written by a cristero, which comes as no surprise. Cristero memoirs, such as the one written by Francisco Campos from Santiago Bayacora, repeatedly stated that Catholic rebels fought for religion.[110] Counterintuitively, however, the ballads produced by pro-Church insurgents did contain sentiments critical of official Church policies. These attitudes appear to fit best within Fallaw's third type, described as popular forms. Two examples reflect the extent to which cristero songsters questioned Church policy. The first comes from a ballad titled "Aniversario del cierre de las Iglesias," written to commemorate the beginning of the religious struggle in 1926, when the Mexican hierarchy declared the cessation of the sacraments. The decision resulted in a Church strike where the nation's priests stopped administering the Eucharist, and performing marriages, confirmations, and baptisms in the nation's houses of worship. The corridista sings that the clergy made the decision and the president accepted it, implying that the faithful had no role in the transaction other than as passive recipients of the order. The people, with "pain and affliction" responded "with devotion and fervor" praying for God's pardon. They prostrated before the altar, participated "in continuous procession," and sought to make reparations to the Virgin of Guadalupe for the nation's sins, which many felt had brought on the callista persecution. But, as floods, misery, and adversity continued, the balladeer asked where had the clergy gone?:

La gente, con grande amor, y cual parvada de abejas iban en busca del pastor que dejaba sus ovejas.	The people, with great love, like a flock of bees went in search of the shepherd that had left his sheep.
Adios, padres, que dejaís sin pastor vuestro rebaño; quiera Dios pronto volvaís y la halléis sin ningún daño.	Goodbye fathers, that left without a shepherd your fold; grant that God helps you soon return and that you find it without any harm.

The ballad then ended on a sullen note, unsure whether the Church's decision would be for the best of religion in Mexico: "if it is or isn't defendable; / history will be the judge."[111]

A second example of popular cristero dissent comes from a ballad written in 1929, celebrating the reopening of the churches and the end of the Cristero Rebellion. The anonymous author of the corrido narrated the religious conflict, beginning with the decision to rigorously apply the religious articles of the Constitution of 1917 to the rebellion inspired in protest against limitations on the liberty of conscience. The result of this conflict, declared the singer, was that the faith of Mexicans had not been destroyed. Yet, a certain satire was evident in the refrain, when the corridista exuberantly announced the outcome of the Church-state accords:

Ya no hay tiros ni trancazos, toditito está arreglado, ¡ora sí puedo casarme, por la Iglesia y el Estado![112]	The shooting and fighting has ceased, everything has been fixed, Now I can get married, by the Church and the State!

The chorus underscored the disaffection felt by many cristeros at the time. The church strike had been called in protest of what many Catholics felt were unjust laws. Until these laws changed, the battle needed to continue. Nevertheless, the 1929 modus vivendi agreed to by the hierarchy and the president left the same laws in place, and demanded that the cristeros surrender their weapons and give up the fight. The chorus thus lampooned the fact that nothing had changed, the battle of sovereignties continued without solution, leaving the Mexican people caught in the middle. True liberty of conscience had, in fact, not come to Mexico; Catholics had not gained the right to choose whether to be married by either the Church or the state. Everyday life continued to be dictated by forces outside the immediate control of many individuals. These examples therefore conveyed popular forms of dissent expressed through music produced by cristeros or their allies. They offered a popular critique of ecclesiastical decision-making, which produced little in terms of a fundamental reconfiguration of official Church-state relations.

Cristero Masculinity, Piety, and Dissent in Verse

The musical production of the Cristero Rebellion opens a window on the gendered aspects of Mexican Catholicism. The devotion to Cristo Rey, rooted in Marian practices and the Sacred Heart of Jesus—two religious traditions with a long history in Mexico—developed as a crucial moniker of rebellion. Adhesion to Christ the King signified a rejection of corrupt earthly authority incarnated in President Calles. Calles represented a mirror image of Christ: as a man loyal to the Virgin and Mexican traditions, as a virile warrior, and a just leader. The gendered invocation of both Christ and the Virgin ("Long Live Christ the King!" "Long Live the Virgin of Guadalupe!") depicted the cristero ideal of traditional family on which the nation should be constructed. Many Catholics perceived that anticlerical laws had challenged that order, which needed to be preserved through action and suffering. Christ became a model of cristero manhood: as Christ remained loyal to his Mother, so too cristeros should persevere for the Church and the community in which that institution was rooted. The rebels in Santiago Bayacora defended these ideals. Trinidad Mora claimed to wage his war against the government "by his triple title as a Mexican, a Catholic and a parent [. . .] against the Nero that was persecuting the Church."[113] Francisco Campos asserted cristero religious autonomy through performance of masculine violence. Cristeros took on the role of "papacitos" who violated their enemy, feminizing the passive victim through racial epithets ("the old Indian").

Corridos of the rebellion reveal that even if gender binaries (Christ and the Virgin) represented ideal types, they were often contested. Valentín de la Sierra offered an inversion of masculine and feminine forms, where the man (Valentín) was emasculated by courageous cristero women. In addition to confirming that all notions of what "makes a man" demands comparison with constructions of femininity, the "Corrido de Valentín de la Sierra" collapses the boundaries between the world of men and women.[114] Even in a supposedly segregated world of war and violence, women were ever-present during the Cristero Rebellion. Just as during the 1910 Revolution, Catholic women (mothers, wives, sisters, daughters) participated in the uprising and, because of their actions, even performed "masculinity" better than some men in particular. And yet, women remained the foil for defining the masculine, often reinforcing the gender hierarchy. Mothers wished martyrdom for their sons and exhorted them to valor. However, if women were perceived to be too mannish to an enemy, cristeras held the potential to emasculate Catholic men ("If you let them [bugger us], that means you are not men, and long live Christ the King, son of a whore!").

Cristero corridos expose the conflict between an ideal imitation of Christ and desire for the sexualized hero. Homosocial interactions play an important part in the legend and corrido about Victoriano Ramírez, El Catorce. Domínguez Ruvalcaba has shown that autobiographical accounts of the 1910 Revolution (*El águila y la serpiente* and *Memorias de Pancho Villa*, both by Martín Luis Guzmán) "present us with the image of the hero as a desirable body, a body composed by the gaze that euphorically venerates the great men of the nation."[115] Heriberto Navarrete's account of El Catorce echoed a similar desire: to ride with elegance, to be beloved by women, feared by enemies, and courageous in battle. And yet, homosocial relations are constrained by "fear of effeminacy."[116] Navarrete's rejection of El Catorce as a model of masculinity coincided with his promotion in the cristero hierarchy, where he was put in charge of virile bodies, commanding his new regiment to attention ("¡Atención! . . . ¡Regimiento! . . . ¡Firmes! . . . ¡Presenten! . . . ¡Armas! . . . ¡Firmes! . . .").[117] The erratic, erotic, and chaotic sexualized hero was rejected in favor of the organized, controlled masculinity represented in Christ the King and the cristero army. In the "Corrido de Valentín Ramírez," El Catorce was a popular vindication of the hero, revealing that masculine religious identities were contested within the cristero ranks. Aurelio Acevedo, cristero to the end, commented that "in this period the masculine element predominated in acts of worship."[118] However, the "masculine element" was always plural, disputed, and challenged.

Ballads of the Cristiada diversify our comprehension of religious dissent. The binary of faith versus impiety collapses as ballads from the period are examined through the prism of gendered expectations and ideals. A spectrum of political identities found voice through the words of the corridista. Non-cristeros were not all alike in their attitudes toward the religious struggle. The soldiers for Christ likewise used song as a platform to express their dissatisfaction with Church policy, often defining their cause as separate from that of the ecclesiastical hierarchy. Cristeros lauded their heroes, taunted their enemies, and memorialized their momentous struggle in song; their music revealed that cristeros were "engendered and engendering" beings, who fought for national inclusion as Catholics, but also as men and as women.[119]

Notes

Special thanks are due to David Seng and Katie Nisbet who provided valuable research assistance in preparing this chapter.

1. The agraristas were irregular militias recruited by the federal government in order to put down the Catholic cristero insurgency. Agraristas were so-named because many of them benefited from the Revolutionary government's "agrarian" policy, consisting of the redistribution of communal land (*ejidos*) to villages; see Jennie Purnell, *Popular Movements and State Formation in Revolutionary Mexico: The Agraristas and Cristeros of Michoacán* (Durham, NC: Duke University Press, 1999).

2. Antonio Avitia Hernández, *Corrido histórico mexicano: Voy a cantarles la historia (1924–1936)*, tomo IV (Mexico City: Editorial Porrúa, 1998), 42.

3. Quotes in ibid.

4. Unless otherwise noted, all translations are mine.

5. Avitia Hernández, *Corrido histórico mexicano*, tomo IV, 43.

6. Vicente T. Mendoza, *El romance español y el corrido mexicano: Estudio comparativo* (Mexico: Universidad Nacional Autónoma, 1939); Mendoza, *El corrido mexicano: Antología, introducción y notas* (Mexico City: Fondo de Cultural Económica, 1954); Merle E. Simmons, *The Mexican Corrido as a Source for Interpretive Study of Modern Mexico (1870–1950)* (Bloomington: Indiana University Press, 1957); Américo Paredes, *"With His Pistol in His Hand": A Border Ballad and Its Hero* (Austin: University of Texas Press, 1958).

7. Matthew Butler, *Popular Piety and Political Identity in Mexico's Cristero Rebellion: Michoacán, 1927–29* (Oxford: Oxford University Press, 2004), 2–13, 214; Jean Meyer, *La cristiada*, 3 vols. (Mexico City: Siglo XXI, 1973–74); and Christopher R. Boyer, *Becoming Campesinos: Politics, Identity, and Agrarian Struggle in Postrevolutionary Michoacán* (Stanford, CA: Stanford University Press, 2003), ch. 5.

8. The Cristero Rebellion exhausted at least 25 percent of the national budget; see José de Jesús López Nieto, *Diccionario histórico de México, 1800–2000* (México: Ediciones Quinto Sol, 2004), 310.

9. Approximately 7,500 cristeros took part in uprisings from 1934 to 1941 in Mexico's central western states; see Meyer, *La cristiada*, 1: 367–68. By 1938, most cristero

militants had disbanded, although a small minority continued to fight. The last corrido of La Segunda details events from Durango in 1941 ("Corrido de Federico Vázquez").

10. Adrian Bantjes, "Religion and the Mexican Revolution: Toward a New Historiography," in *Religious Culture in Modern Mexico*, ed. Martin Austin Nesvig (Lanham, MD: Rowman and Littlefield Publishers, Inc., 2007), 223–54; Edward Wright-Rios, *Revolutions in Mexican Catholicism: Reform and Revelation in Oaxaca, 1887–1934* (Durham, NC: Duke University Press, 2009); Patience Schell, *Church and State Education in Revolutionary Mexico City* (Tucson: University of Arizona Press, 2001); Kristina A. Boylan, "Mexican Catholic Women's Activism, 1929–1940" (PhD diss., Oxford University, 2000); Robert E. Curley, "Slouching Towards Bethlehem: Catholics and the Political Sphere in Revolutionary Mexico" (PhD diss., University of Chicago, 2001); Patience A. Schell and Stephanie Mitchell, *The Women's Revolution in Mexico, 1910–1953* (Lanham, MD: Rowman and Littlefield Publishers, Inc., 2007); Jocelyn Olcott, Mary Kay Vaughn, and Gabriela Cano, eds., *Sex in Revolution: Gender, Politics, and Power in Modern Mexico* (Durham, NC: Duke University Press, 2006); Ben Fallaw and Terry Rugeley, eds., *Forced Marches: Soldiers and Military Caciques in Modern Mexico* (Tucson: University of Arizona Press, 2012).

11. Alicia Olivera de Bonfil, *Aspectos del conflicto religioso de 1926 a 1929: Sus antecedentes y consecuencias* (Mexico City: Instituto Nacional de Antropología e Historia, 1966); Jean A. Meyer, *The Cristero Rebellion: The Mexican People Between Church and State (1926–1929)*, trans. Richard Southern (Cambridge: Cambridge University Press, 1976).

12. A lone exception to this is the brief feminist analysis of a few cristero corridos, see María Herrera-Sobek, *The Mexican Corrido: A Feminist Analysis* (Bloomington: Indiana University Press, 1990). The best recent analysis of cristero corridos, but which does not include gender analysis, is Antonio Avitia Hernández, "La narrativa de las cristiadas: Novela, cuento, teatro, cine y corrido de las Rebeliones Cristeras" (PhD diss., Universidad Autónoma Metropolitana, Unidad Iztapalapa, 2006). The late Jaime Nicolopolus, assisted by his students at the University of Texas, Austin, produced a web page dedicated to corridos of the Cristero Rebellion, "Corridos de la Cristiada," http://www.laits.utexas.edu/jaime/cwp5/crg/index.html, accessed September 25, 2012.

13. Simmons, *Mexican Corrido*, 17.

14. Avitia Hernández, "La narrativa," 635.

15. Meyer, *La cristiada*, 406–10; Alicia Olivera de Bonfil, *La literatura cristera* (Mexico City: Instituto Nacional de Antropología e Historia, 1970).

16. Irene Vázquez Valle and José de Santiago Silva, eds., *Corridos de la rebelión cristera* (Mexico City: Instituto Nacional de Antropología e Historia, 1976). A compact disc version was released in 2002.

17. Avitia Hernández, "La narrativa," 641.

18. In Los Angeles between 1920 and 1930, almost 37 percent of adult male Mexican immigrants came from the center-west, while in San Antonio during the same period, a large number of the 21,000 Mexican émigrés came from the same region; see Julia G. Young, "Cristero Diaspora: Mexican Immigrants, the U.S. Catholic Church, and Mexico's Cristero War, 1926–1929," *The Catholic Historical Review* 98, no. 2 (April 2012): 276; see also Richard A. García, *Rise of the Mexican American Middle Class: San Antonio, 1929–1941* (College Station: Texas A&M University Press, 1991), 28.

19. Young, "Cristero Diaspora," 278, 286, 288.

20. Avitia Hernández, "La narrativa," 639–40. Avitia's list of corridos number only 69, although the author says he collected 70, an apparent editorial oversight.

21. Ibid., 637–42. The term "arreglos" (Spanish for "fixes") referred to the Church-state modus vivendi, which ended the Cristero Rebellion in June 1929.

22. Ibid.

23. Like Butler, other scholars see the motivation for revolt more sharply in the convergence of local identities with sociocultural and political forces: see Purnell, *Popular Movements*; and Boyer, *Becoming Campesinos*, ch. 5.

24. Butler, *Popular Piety*, 214–21.

25. Robert McKee Irwin, *Mexican Masculinities* (Minneapolis: University of Minnesota Press, 2003), xvii.

26. Many scholars of sex and gender argue against strict sexual dimorphism. Thus, even biological differences between men and women are better conceptualized along a continuum. Matthew C. Gutmann cites work by Anne Fausto-Sterling, who "provides evidence of the existence of at least five biological sexes (hermaphrodites, male pseudohermaphrodites, female pseudohermaphrodites, females, and males"; see Matthew C. Gutmann, *Changing Men and Masculinities in Latin America* (Durham, NC: Duke University Press, 2003), 8.

27. Irwin, *Mexican Masculinities*, xviii.

28. Victor M. Macías-González and Anne Rubenstein, eds., *Masculinity and Sexuality in Modern Mexico* (Albuquerque: University of New Mexico Press, 2012), 13.

29. Myles Anthony McDonnell, *Roman Manliness: "Virtus" and the Roman Republic* (Cambridge: Cambridge University Press, 2009), xiii, 2.

30. Irwin, *Mexican Masculinities*, xvii.

31. Héctor Domínguez-Ruvalcaba, *Modernity and the Nation in Mexican Representations of Masculinity: From Sensuality to Bloodshed* (Houndsmill, Baginstoke: Palgrave Macmillan, 2007), 2.

32. Irwin, *Mexican Masculinities*, xii.

33. Domínguez-Ruvalcaba, *Modernity and the Nation*, 3.

34. Macías-González and Rubenstein, *Masculinity and Sexuality*, 11.

35. Ibid.

36. Raymond Jonas, *France and the Cult of the Sacred Heart: An Epic Tale for Modern Times* (Berkeley: University of California Press, 2000), 2.

37. Claude Pomerleau, "French Missionaries and Latin American Catholicism in the Nineteenth Century," *The Americas* 37, no. 3 (January 1981): 360.

38. Ibid., 351.

39. Claudia Carlen, ed., *The Papal Encyclicals, 1878–1903* (Raleigh, NC: McGrath Publishing Company, 1981), 451–54.

40. Gertrude M. Yeager, "In the Absence of Priests: Young Women as Apostles to the Poor, Chile 1922–1932," *The Americas* 64, no. 2 (October 2007): 207–42.

41. Claudia Carlen, ed., *The Papal Encyclicals, 1903–1939* (Raleigh, NC: McGrath Publishing Company, 1981), 271–79.

42. See Matthew Butler, "Trouble Afoot? Pilgrimage in *Cristero* Mexico City," in *Faith and Impiety in Revolutionary Mexico*, ed. Matthew Butler (London: Institute for the Study of the Americas, 2007), 152–53.

43. Many Catholics who opposed the president's policies associated his paternal name "Elías" with the influx of Middle Eastern, especially Lebanese, immigrants in

Mexico; thus, the epitaph "el turco" ("the arab") became a popular slur, linking his anticlericalism to a supposed non-Christian heritage. In fact, Plutarco's paternal family clan was founded by a Catholic of low nobility named Francisco Elías González, who emigrated from the province of La Rioja, Spain, in the colonial period. As an illegitimate child of Plutarco Elías Lucero, Plutarco Jr. was raised by his uncle, Juan Bautista Calles, from whom he took the surname "Calles." Only later in adulthood would the president incorporate his biological father's surname, endeavoring to play up the Elías clan's more notable standing in Sonora; see Jürgen Buchenau, *Plutarco Elías Calles and the Mexican Revolution* (Lanham, MD: Rowman and Littlefield Publishers, 2006), 8–10.

44. Meyer, *La cristiada: I*, 311.

45. Avitia Hernández, "La narrativa," 677–78.

46. Jean Meyer, *El coraje cristero: Testimonios* (Mexico: Universidad Autónoma Metropolitana, 1981), 20.

47. Meyer, *Cristero Rebellion*, 185.

48. William A. Christian, Jr., *Local Religion in Sixteenth-Century Spain* (Princeton, NJ: Princeton University Press, 1981), 22.

49. See the documentary film, *Cristeros, Soldados de Cristo* (2007). The cristero flag was emblazoned with the Virgin of Guadalupe. Thanks to the anonymous reviewer who highlighted this detail.

50. Meyer, *El coraje cristero*, 11.

51. Ibid.

52. Ibid.

53. Ibid.

54. Ibid., 11–16.

55. The following account comes from Meyer, *El coraje cristero*, 19–21.

56. Quoted in Meyer, *El coraje cristero*, 84.

57. Ibid., 85.

58. The use of homosexuality to define masculine power relations in early twentieth-century Mexico was widespread. For recent research on homosexuality and the definition of criminality, see Pablo Piccato, *City of Suspects: Crime in Mexico City, 1900–1931* (Durham, NC: Duke University Press, 2001); Robert Buffington, *Criminal and Citizen in Modern Mexico* (Lincoln: University of Nebraska Press, 2000).

59. Irwin, *Mexican Masculinities*, xxiii.

60. Quoted in Meyer, *El coraje cristero*, 85; Irwin, *Mexican Masculinities*, xxix.

61. Meyer, *La cristiada: I*, 107.

62. Ibid., 108.

63. Ibid., 395.

64. Ibid., 202.

65. Enrique Gorostieta, ex-Porfirian officer, was recruited by the League for the Defense of Religious Liberty in 1927 to take command of cristero rebel forces; see Marta Elena Negrete, *Enrique Gorostieta: cristero agnóstico* (Mexico City: Ediciones El Caballito, 1981).

66. Meyer, *La cristiada: III*, 106.

67. Antonio Avitia Hernández, "La verdadera historia de Valentín de la Sierra," *Aztlán* 22, no. 1 (Spring 1997): 73–90.

68. On the multiple uses of corridos by Mexican soldiers, see Stephen Neufeld, ch. 2 of this volume.

69. Avitia Hernández, "La narrativa," 688–93.
70. Ibid., 681.
71. Ibid., 685–87.
72. Ibid., 689.
73. Ibid., 693.
74. Herrera-Sobek, *Mexican Corrido*, 100–101.
75. Meyer, *La cristiada: I*, 121.
76. Meyer, *Cristero Rebellion*, 174–75.
77. Thanks are due to one of the anonymous reviewers who pointed out the rich history of the term "gallinero."
78. Meyer, *La cristiada: I*, 171–72.
79. Valentín Avila Ramírez and Victoriano Ramírez had no relation.
80. Domínguez-Ruvalcaba, *Modernity and the Nation*, 5.
81. Victor Ceja Reyes, *El catorce y la guerra cristera* (Mexico City: Editorial Universo, 1983), 22–23, 31, 77.
82. Heriberto Navarrete, *Por Dios y por la patria*, 4th ed. (Mexico City: Editorial Tradición, 1980), 178–79.
83. The following dialogue is quoted in ibid., 180–81.
84. Ibid., 179.
85. Ibid.
86. Ibid., 182.
87. Ceja Reyes, *El catorce*, 45.
88. Meyer, *La cristiada: III*, 222.
89. Navarrete, *Por Dios*, 183.
90. Ibid., 188.
91. Ibid.
92. Ibid.
93. Meyer, *La cristiada: III*, 222.
94. Navarrete, *Por Dios*, 190–205.
95. Meyer, *La cristiada: III*, 222–23.
96. Ibid., 223–24, n. 72.
97. Avitia Hernández, *Corrido histórico mexicano*, 114.
98. Navarrete entered the Jesuit order on October 2, 1933; see José Gutiérrez Casillas, *Jesuítas en México durante el siglo XX* (Mexico City: Editorial Porrúa, 1981), 621.
99. See in the special issue of *The Americas*: "Personal Enemies of God: Anticlericals and Anticlericalism in Revolutionary Mexico, 1915–1940," *The Americas* 65, no. 4 (April 2009).
100. Bantjes, "Mexican Revolutionary Anticlericalism: Concepts and Typologies," *The Americas* 65, no. 4 (April 2009): 468.
101. Fallaw, "Varieties of Mexican Revolutionary Anticlericalism: Radicalism, Iconoclasm, and Otherwise, 1914–1935," *The Americas* 65, no. 4 (April 2009): 482; and Knight, "The Mentality and Modus Operandi of Revolutionary Anticlericalism," in *Faith and Impiety*, ed. Butler, 23.
102. Jocelyn Alcott, *Revolutionary Women in Postrevolutionary Mexico* (Durham, NC: Duke University Press, 2005), 1, 3, 93, 106.
103. Quoted in Simmons, *Mexican Corrido*, 409.
104. Ibid.

105. Fallaw, "Varieties of Mexican Revolutionary Anticlericalism," 494.
106. Quoted in Simmons, *Mexican Corrido*, 394.
107. Blancarte quoted in Bantjes, "Mexican Revolutionary Anticlericalism," 477, n. 40.
108. Simmons, *Mexican Corrido*, 390.
109. Quoted in Avitia Hernández, *Corrido histórico mexicano*, 205.
110. Quoted in Meyer, *El coraje cristero*, 22.
111. Quoted in Avitia Hernández, *Corrido histórico mexicano*, 44.
112. Ibid., 147.
113. Meyer, *La cristiada: I*, 379.
114. Gutmann, *Changing Men and Masculinities*, 19.
115. Domínguez-Ruvalcaba, *Modernity and the Nation*, 57.
116. Ibid., 74.
117. Navarrete, *Por Dios*, 188.
118. Quoted in Meyer, *El coraje cristero*, unpaginated original description on photograph titled "Comunión General."
119. Gutmann, *Changing Men and Masculinities*, 19.

The Mexican Revolution reached its most sweeping period of reform during the presidency of Lázaro Cárdenas. Redistributing more land than all his revolutionary predecessors combined, enforcing the labor laws of the Constitution of 1917, and nationalizing the foreign oil companies and the railways, his presidency marked the climax of socialist and nationalist policymaking. Cárdenas also introduced an impressive program of rural and socialist education that dedicated more federal expenditure toward schooling than ever seen before in the country's history. While he would steer the Revolution to the left after years of unimplemented reforms, by 1938, economic challenges facing the nation convinced Cárdenas to support his conservative Secretary of War Manuel Ávila Camacho for president, moving the nation down a new path of policymaking. It within this context that Elena Jackson Albarrán analyzes the poetry of Jesús Sansón Flores who, patronized by the Cárdenas administration, produced a collection of verse that introduced the "Proletarian Child" as a new social category and a symbol of the shortcoming of Revolutionary policymaking.

"Los Niños Pobres"*

Los niños pobres no saben
de princesas encantadas;
a sus pocilgas obscuras
no llegan nunca las hadas.

No hay duendes ni pulgarcitos;
no hay historias de Estambul;
ignoran los pobrecitos
el cuento de Barba-Azul.

Allá en los estercoleros
¡tan sólo el hambre los mata!

"The Poor Children"

The poor children don't know
of enchanted princesses;
to their obscure pigsties
the fairies never come.

There are no elves or Tom Thumbs;
there are no stories of Istanbul;
the poor little ones don't know
the tale of Blue Beard.

There in the dung heaps
Hunger only kills them!

* Jesús Sansón Flores, "Los Niños Pobres," in *El niño proletario: Poemas clasistas* (México: Ediciones Ala Izquierda, 1936).

los hijos de los obreros
no empuñarán en sus manos
espadas de hojadelata.

El hijo del campesino
no tiene corcel de palo
corriendo por los trigales,
ni soldaditos de plomo;
pero miró los caballos
del viejo patrón obeso,
y ha visto a los federales
llevando a su padre preso.

Sólo serán sus juguetes
el azadón y el arado;
y no verá otro automóvil
que el Packard color de cielo
de la hija del hacendado.

Los niños pobres no tienen
historias color de rosa
ni muñecos de aserrín;

no saben que existen hadas
ni princesas encantadas
por los llanos de Merlín.

the children of workers
will not wield tin-can swords
in their hands.

The son of the peasant
does not have a hobby horse
to ride through the wheat fields,
nor toy soldiers;
but he saw the horses
of the old obese *patron*,
and he has seen the federal soldiers
carrying his father off to prison.

Their only toys will be
the hoe and the plow;
and they will see no other car
than the skyblue Packard
of the hacendado's daughter.

The poor children don't have
rose-colored stories
or sawdust-stuffed dolls;

they don't know that fairies exist
or enchanted princesses
along Merlin's plains.

Discussion Questions

1. How does this poem characterize the lives of poor children?
2. Why does the author of this poem repeatedly use images of children's toys? What effect does this have on the reader?
3. What is the author's view of the social outcomes of the Mexican Revolution?

CHAPTER SIX

El Niño Proletario

Jesús Sansón Flores and the New Revolutionary Redeemer, 1935–1938

Elena Jackson Albarrán

My muse will suckle hungry children. My Numen will inoculate their breasts with a boiling virulent protest against Capitalism. Because within every proletarian child resides a Messiah making birds from clay. The birds of an ideal future pecking at the cages of the bourgeois system.

—JESÚS SANSÓN FLORES, 1936

With this stark imagery, radical poet Jesús Sansón Flores closed the introductory remarks to his volume *El niño proletario: poemas clasistas* (*The Proletarian Child: Classist Poems*). A young, self-designated "revolutionary poet" from the state of Michoacán, Sansón Flores had published widely since the 1920s on social and political issues, garnering a reputation as an ardent defender of the oppressed classes. A book of children's poetry hardly stood to launch him into international literary fame. Little more than a cardboard-bound pamphlet of fifteen simple didactic verses for children, this collection nevertheless captured the essence of Sansón Flores's Marxist social critique at a moment in his life that coincided with a brief radical socialist experiment in the Mexican political milieu. In his collection of poems, Sansón Flores translated centuries of historical violence into succinct and visually compelling terms for a child audience, described the colonial abuses of power that persisted in the countryside in terms they could understand, and charged them with assuming the mantle of class struggle in order to redeem—and avenge—their ancestors.

Even as Sansón Flores penned his poems, his fellow *michoacano*[1] Lázaro Cárdenas undertook measures to radicalize the Revolution from the national stage, perhaps most significantly through the implementation of a socialist education program. Leninism fortified the labor sector, and the art community elevated the proletarian mestizo as a national icon. In this context, the "Niño Proletario" emerged as a reified image in the public sphere, a reminder of the continued injustices that remained unaddressed by Revolutionary reform, and a justification for the urgency of political radicalization. The national fascination with the Proletarian Child as a metaphor for the Revolution received a boost from the sensationalized reports of the plight of Republican children in the Spanish Civil War. Sansón Flores, thanks in part to his longstanding personal ties to Cárdenas, assumed a public role in this conflict, which was literally transported to Mexico with the arrival of five hundred Spanish child refugees in 1937. Not long after these events—the publication of *El niño proletario*, the socialist education experiment, and the Spanish Civil War—both Sansón Flores and the Mexican Revolution slipped into ideological malaise. The convergence of these three phenomena revolved around and relied upon the rhetorical construction of the metaphor of the Proletarian Child.

This chapter examines the personal and political intersections that contributed to the heightened visibility of the Proletarian Child archetype, with an eye to the international forces that contextualized its position in the Mexican Revolutionary discourse. It also marks an important contribution in the recent Latin American historiographical trend to examine the role of children—both as historical agents and as semiotic devices—in processes of nation-building and state formation.[2] First, an overview of the socialist education experiment of President Lázaro Cárdenas (1934–1940) and the curricular and iconographic references to the Proletarian Child that this program yielded provide the political context. Second, a presentation of the literary career of Jesús Sansón Flores and an analysis of his political poetry for children suggest the rhetorical value of the Proletarian Child. Finally, a discussion of the ideological impact of Spanish Civil War realities reveals a political climate that put Sansón Flores's personal convictions to the test, a phenomenon reflected on the national stage with the arrival of "real" proletarian children from Spain to Mexico. In the final analysis, the redemptive power of the metaphorical Proletarian Child evident in Sansón Flores's poetry diminished when confronted with reality.

Teaching National Archetypes and *Historia Nacional* Through Textbooks

The new Revolutionary archetype emerged on the heels of a longer cultural tradition of constructing codified national types. Beginning in the late nineteenth century and inspired by Liberal secularization campaigns, the state began promoting national heroes, civic holidays, and official art to supplant traditional religious calendars and saints. Following two consecutive Conferences of Public Education (Congresos de Instrucción Pública) held from 1889 to 1890, and 1890 to 1891, a generation of Liberal, scientifically oriented pedagogues emerged that sought to modernize the Mexican education system by infusing it with nationalist content, with the goal of producing a universally recognizable set of historical narratives and cast of national heroes. The subsequent publication of Justo Sierra's history textbook *Historia patria*, widely considered a standard classroom text by 1905, marks a watershed moment in the pursuit of uniformity in primary school textbooks, insofar as it married nationalist content with basic reading skills.[3] While still preoccupied with the scientific molding of the child into a desirable product, close readings of late nineteenth-century primary textbooks reveal the aperture of a more child-oriented educational culture: the style, language, font, format, and illustrations included in these curricular materials demonstrated the authors' awareness of the child reader.[4] While many of the Porfirian-era textbooks still betrayed a bias toward a middle- to upper-class urban readership, a tendency did emerge in Sierra's volumes to raise awareness of the plight (and malleability) of working-class children—a social group not yet politicized as "proletarian."

The technological advances in printmaking and mass media that marked the years following the Revolution accelerated the dissemination of newly articulated national history, or *historia nacional*.[5] The readily identifiable costumes of *charros* and *chinas poblanas*, *tehuanas* and *toreros*,[6] enjoyed heightened visibility in textbooks, theaters, and the graphic media from the 1920s as part of a concerted official effort to forge national identity around a set of common symbols. Ultimately, these types fulfilled the call issued by Ramón López Velarde—upheld by José Vasconcelos as the national poet—in 1921 to create a self-referencing visual culture intended to promote neither historical revisionism nor political agendas, but rather to paint an intimate portrait of the nation.[7] They eclipsed the overtly French and North American cultural references that had been the vogue up until the Revolution, and provided Mexicans with a stamp of their own, one that corresponded to the popular and mixed-race majority. While the 1920s saw the construction of a visual panorama of romantic national types largely devoid of political meaning, officially sponsored identity formation grew increasingly politicized with the onset of Cardenista social reforms.

In this context, the Proletarian Child briefly joined its less political counterparts in the pantheon of nationalist icons during the Cárdenas administration. Like its fellow archetypes, the Proletarian Child corresponded to the popular classes and elicited largely sympathetic responses. But unlike the cheerfully dressed china poblana, the dashingly svelte charro, or the comically styled *negrito* (black man), the Proletarian Child was less of a visual trope and more of a rhetorical device. His contours were sketched through bellowing speeches by politicians like Plutarco Elías Calles, or through the linguistic stylings of literary figures like Sansón Flores. Unlike the Revolutionary nationalism burgeoning in visual culture, Mexicans were free to use their imaginations to construct an image of the Proletarian Child—perhaps he looked like one's child, one's godson, one's paperboy, oneself. Drawing from a political culture that leaned heavily on the welfare of children as a justification for political maneuvers and policy formation, Sansón Flores helped to make this idealized symbol visible through his powerful, if not elegant, verses.

Heeding the observations of sociologists of childhood, we would do well to attend to the rhetorical power of "the child," but not to confuse this singular device with the conditions and experiences of children; in most cases, political references to "the child" bore little resemblance to any individual child's life.[8] The emergence of an idealized, singular, and male Proletarian Child should therefore always elicit images of the hundreds of thousands of living (male and female) children that this monolithic symbol came to preclude during the years of its iconic national status.[9]

The Socialist Education Experiment in Revolutionary Mexico

While children occupied the center of nation-building projects since the late nineteenth century, Porfirian educational policymakers saw them as objects rather than agents of reform. Scholars attendant to the history of Mexican education acknowledge that textbook authors, schoolteachers, editorial houses, and educational administrators focused their energies on cultivating future citizens by "protecting, educating, and disciplining him."[10] But the Revolution ushered in a discursive shift among educational officials, who, drawing inspiration from new international pedagogical models, sought to harness the energy and ingenuity in the moment rather than wait to harvest children's potential in their adulthood. Rather than scientific overtures to redeem the child, then, for a brief space, the child was poised to redeem the nation.

The Proletarian Child was born out of education reform that evolved in the first decade and a half after the Revolution to take on a decidedly socialist nature by 1934. Ideas about introducing socialism at the elementary school level had been percolating long before Cárdenas made it a state mandate in 1934. At a 1915 Pedagogy Conference (Congreso Pedagógico) in Mérida, promoters of a new Rationalist School (Escuela Racionalista) excoriated the traditional pedagogical approach, which they dubbed the "school-prison" system. At its core, the Rationalist School promoted an educational environment that would be secular (and actively antireligious), science-based, student-directed, coeducational (*mixta*), and oriented toward productivity. It struck a balance between nineteenth-century positivism's attempts to perfect humankind, and a modern economic structure that valued physical labor and nationalist production.[11] Article 3 of the Constitution of 1917 made provisions for a free, obligatory, and secular education roughly along these lines, but did not designate the Rationalist School as the official state curriculum. Beginning in 1917 and throughout the 1920s, Rationalist Schools dotted twenty-one states across the nation, to the celebration of some and the consternation of others. Indeed, the secularization of the education system met with impassioned, staunch resistance from many Catholic parents. A 1922 endorsement of the schools by the left-wing national labor union, the Regional Confederation of Mexican Workers (CROM), established the political orientation of their unique pedagogical approach. In a statement issued at the union's convention, a delegate proclaimed that the Rationalist School promoted collective over individual will, and espoused a model of socialization based on solidarity, with an ideological emphasis on uplifting the conditions of the working classes—presumably by reflecting the structures of their lives in the curriculum.

Much of the impetus for a radical restructuring of education came from the south of the country, and the resulting reforms gained the most traction in the states of Yucatán, Campeche, and Tabasco. Yucatán's governor Felipe Carrillo Puerto (1922–1924), headed the Socialist Party of the Southeast and the peasant Leagues of Resistance, and gave free reign to the Rationalist School in his state. In nearby Tabasco, the "laboratory of the Revolution," Governor Tomás Garrido Canabal (1922–1935) led the most strident reform program, characterized by excessive anticlerical measures. In 1929, Garrido Canabal published "The Socialist ABCs" for rural schoolchildren, a primer of sorts that defined their position as exploited members of the working class, and warned against the rapacious advances of capitalism, priests, and alcohol.[12] In this document, he directly addressed the Proletarian Child: "You, who have been born in this century of liberties and compensations, must obtain for the proletarian family the right to enjoy all that which you produce."[13] Tabascan teachers took their charge seriously and literally; they eschewed school competitions (in such areas as essay and spelling contests) as fostering jealousies and emulation, a departure from the Rationalist School's self-guided learning.[14]

The assault on religious instruction continued as the Rationalist School gained currency. In the throes of the *cristero* backlash against such secularizing tendencies, in 1928, the National League of Rationalist Teachers sent a petition to the national legislature to amend Article 3 to implement the system nationwide, based on an insistence that the school should be "free of dogmas, prejudices, and fanaticisms."[15] They saw the child as the agent best poised to hoist the nation out of centuries of entrenched superstition. On September 6, 1934, Cárdenas expanded upon the vigorously funded rural education system championed by predecessors Obregón and Calles, by branding it for the first time as "socialist education" through a modification of Article 3 of the Constitution.[16] The premise of the socialist turn during the first half of the Cárdenas administration was that the Revolution had not yet reached the protagonists of the armed movement: the glorified, anonymous Proletariat. While this designation lasted only until 1945, suffered hazy definition, and elicited strong negative reactions almost from its inception, the choice of terminology signaled Cárdenas's ideological position toward the nation's youth. Ironically, the institutionalization of socialist education crushed its organic momentum, and galvanized its opposition among the religious sector, effectively guaranteeing its demise after a few short years. The emphasis here, then, lies in the brief span during the Cárdenas years in which socialism, and its idealization of the proletariat, enjoyed state sponsorship in the national spotlight.

The emergence of the Proletarian Child as a part of nationalist discourse was not a wholly Mexican phenomenon; it had parallels around the world in the interwar period as nation-states cast around for domestic, self-determining solutions to the rising threat of authoritarianism in global politics. Soviet children's literature, following the Russian Revolution, glorified modern machines as a way to elevate the worker's potential while captivating the child audience. By positing industrial labor as a positive, modern, and productive force and by including compelling visual representations through avant-garde illustrations in children's books, the Soviet child came to see him- or herself as an important character in the national narrative. Tellingly, even as the Soviet project began to lose traction, depictions of the proletarian child became even more stylized and propagandistic.[17] In the United States, beginning in the 1920s, the Communist Party promoted the Young Pioneers as a politically active children's organization intentionally opposed to the capitalist state-run school system and the decidedly middle-class Boy Scouts movement. By the time the Great Depression struck, shifting public attention to poor children as metaphors of national crisis pushed the symbol of the proletarian child from the marginal left to the square center of national discourse, most famously evidenced by Lewis Hines's striking photography of industrial child labor and Dorothea Lange's iconic "migrant mother" portrait from the Oklahoma dustbowl. As Julia Mickenberg has demonstrated, the American left mobilized and normalized romantic notions of the innocent child as a "redeemer of corrupt adulthood."[18]

As part of the new educational campaign, official Secretary of Public Education (SEP) pamphlets, textbooks, magazines, and broadsides filtered their way into the national school system and infused the countryside with socialist vocabulary and symbols through anthems, marches, art, and activities. American pedagogue John Dewey, renowned for his creation of the Action School, visited Mexico, and lauded the rural education initiative that he witnessed as truly revolutionary, "one of the most important social experiments in the world."[19] Unlike the case in the United States, in which radical or progressive authors took advantage of the relatively uncritical approach given to the genre of children's literature, to covertly disseminate anticapitalist values left of the mainstream,[20] Revolutionary Mexican official culture embraced children's literature as a space in which to foment class consciousness and political activism among its youngest citizens. Textbooks, magazines, and primers all enjoyed liberal dissemination through an educational system designed, at least in principle, to deliver free, obligatory, and secular education to the entire population. Notably, the children's book *Fermin*, illustrated by Diego Rivera and used as a staple in the primary classroom, constructed for its readers a new, positive, national identity that conflated youth, indigeneity, and rural work as the new "biography of millions of Mexican children whose existence we ignore or try to forget," in the words of author Manuel Velázquez Andrade.[21]

Cardenista officials worked to sacralize the pedagogical turn as part of a new national ethos. While textbooks were not uniform or guaranteed in the rapidly expanding Revolutionary education system, certain publications enjoyed government sponsorship and publicity (such is the case with the text by Sansón Flores discussed below). The daily practice of reading and writing alone was seen as an important tool in raising children's class consciousness, through primers infused with a new vocabulary: "compañero," "camarada," "comité."[22] SEP publications such as *El Sembrador, Simiente,* and *El Maestro Rural* promulgated the "new proletarian morality" (*la nueva moral proletaria*) among rural workers, parents, teachers, and children. This new moral code cloaked traditional family values and work ethic in socialist rhetoric.[23] An April 1935 memo to teachers of elementary and normal schools proposed that May Day (May 1) commemorations be used to solidify international proletarian identity among schoolchildren through speeches and reports on social conditions in their communities. Accompanying the memo, a song titled "Revolución," by Juan Orca, codified the Mexican Revolution as socialist:

Cinco millones de camisas blancas	Five million white shirts
Como flores	Like flowers
Siembran de margaritas el áspero terruño;	The rough terrain sown with daisies;
Cinco millones de hoces en el puño	Five million sickles in fists
Brillan al Sol!.	Shining toward the sun!. . . . . .
Ha callado sus voces el tambor	The drum has quieted their voices
Triqui-trac ¡Revolución!	*Rat-a-tat*, Revolution!
El bronco penco ya en descanso	The wild bronco now at rest
Sorbe el agua apacible del remanso;	Laps placid water from the pool;
El soldado se volvió pastor,	The soldier-turned-shepherd
Cuida ovejas traviesas en el llano. . . .	Watches playful sheep on the plains. . . .
Ha callado sus voces el tambor!	The drum has quieted their voices!
Triqui-trac ¡Revolución!	*Rat-a-tat*, Revolution!
Y con árduo tesón	And with ardent determination
El Soldado, el Obrero, el Agrarista!	The Soldier, the Worker, the Agrarianist
Mexicano, paria, hermano;	Mexican, pariah, brother;
Con hierro, cerebro y piedra	With iron, brain, and stone
Se forjan los cimientos de una patria major	Are forged as the cement of a better nation
Triqui-trac ¡Revolución! [24]	*Rat-a-tat*, Revolution!

The imagery of this song reflects the concurrent emerging visual culture, most particularly that of the social realist art movement. This particular verse, likely penned by a schoolteacher and submitted to the SEP offices to promote broader circulation, assigns nation-building duties to the same archetypical figures—the Soldier, the Worker, the Agrarianist (or politicized peasant)—that cropped up in Diego Rivera's contemporary murals. The anonymity (five million shirts, sickles, and fists, but not faces) evoked in the verse reflects the visual technique employed by David Alfaro Siqueiros in his Revolutionary art of suggesting consensus through the repetition of the crowd. The "Revolution" referred to in this verse is not the moment of taking up arms, but rather the reconstructive phase of nation-building, in which soldiers return to the land and engage with their compatriots in churning out national productivity. This verse, then, precisely reflects the official narrative of the Revolution: the drum signals not a call to arms, but rather a call to work. Even though many teachers did not implement the curriculum to the letter, and most probably never saw this song, as we will see, many students became literate in the official rhetoric. Through government-produced literary and visual material such as this, distributed through the Socialist School, the redemption narrative characteristic of Christianity and associated with the spiritual realm was being transferred to the contemporary political Marxist discourse of class struggle. The sin was capitalist exploitation, and the burden of national redemption fell upon the proletarian masses.

While official propaganda of socialist education and its intended product, the Proletarian Child, were steeped in the cultural milieu of the late 1930s, it bears emphasizing that popular response did not always absorb the ideological infusion. As Mary Kay Vaughan, Elsie Rockwell, and Engracia Loyo B. remind us, rural schoolteachers subjected the national curriculum to significant modifications according to local realities and practices.[25] Religious education persisted—albeit sometimes surreptitiously—and received substantial support from the Catholic urban middle classes.[26] A religious publication from the conservative city of Puebla, *La Defensa del Hogar: Salvemos a la Patria Salvando a la Niñez*, excoriated the "traitorous school," decrying the "hate poison" and "brute materialism" to which the socialist educators subjected their children. The religious opposition made nationalist appeals to bolster their case, claiming that children in socialist classrooms learned allegiance to the red and black Communist flag and the lyrics to "The International," leaving behind the *tricolor* and the national anthem.[27] Socialist education, then, forced its way through embattled territory, and rarely achieved full implementation despite the backing of an ideologically committed administration.

Educational officials struggled to disabuse the public of their apprehensions about the new national curriculum. Ignacio García Téllez, the first

Secretary of Education appointed by Cárdenas, made a concerted effort to appease the agitated conservative sector. At a January 1935 inauguration of the socialist Escuela Horacio Mann in Mexico City, García Téllez directly addressed the Padres de Familia (a prominent Catholic parents' organization), reminding them that by supporting the teachers, they would contribute to improving the overall national economy. Furthermore, he reminded them that labor was not a biblical sin nor a punishment, but rather a virtue and of great national benefit.[28] Gonzalo Vázquez Vela assumed the leadership of the SEP in 1935; for his first act on the job, he ran a series of full-page essays on the back covers of *El Maestro Rural* that summer, with eye-catching red headings to offset the black-and-white text. These overviews described the basic tenets of the Socialist School, and urged young people to consider teaching as a noble profession in the service of the country. In these missives, Vázquez Vela seemed most preoccupied with assuaging the doubts of the *maestros*, the group most immediately affected by a new curriculum and a relatively new ideology being foisted upon them. "Socialist Education. Ideological Unity. Help for the Proletarian Child. Affordable Textbooks," read the subheading of his published declaration.[29] Here, as elsewhere in official promotions of the socialist education program, a public official deployed the trope of the Proletarian Child as an inviolable mascot of educational reform.

"If Society Does Not Need its Proletarian Children, It Should Find the Courage to Kill Them"

In a substantial semiotic shift, the public visibility of poor children transformed from signaling problems to suggesting promise. Prior to the concerted official efforts to elevate the Proletarian Child as a secular Messiah, popular responses to the visibility of poor children flowed from the nineteenth-century child-saving paradigm. When a social type of the Proletarian Child emerged in public discourse, defined by his relation to the dominant economic system, it was as a victim of capitalism and a subject of pity. As Susana Sosenski has demonstrated, the creation of the Juvenile Court (Tribunal de Menores) in 1927 sought to create a swift, bureaucratic mechanism through which to whisk problematic children from public view, normalize their behavior, regulate their work, and diminish the symbolic power of their presence in the streets.[30] Some editorials served up downright hyperbolic predictions about the ability of this fragile sliver of Mexican society to tip the national scale toward glory or decay. "Society needs its proletarian children," posed one editorialist for *El Universal* in 1934. "If society does not need its proletarian children, it should find the courage to kill them," a practice customary, he presumed, in tribal cultures.[31] Clearly the author wrote sarcastically, his ridiculous proposal intended for his readers to make a contrast between primitive and modern societies. Drawing on an extreme characterization of poor children as degenerate vagrants who frequented bars, brothels, hospitals, and jails, the author declared it to be the Revolution's responsibility to save these children. In this case, he gendered the Revolution as female, relying on Liberal allegories of the nation as a woman, and extending the metaphor of the citizenry as her children. Nevertheless, he identified a social group that needed to be activated lest dire consequences ensue. In this author's eyes, Mexico's very civilization depended on its ability to rescue its impoverished children and thus its own reputation as a modern nation.

In a second example, a mild editorial about the need for preschool education derived from international models, the author also drew upon the Proletarian Child as a social type in need of state-sponsored protection. He posited his argument from the position of "the problem of the protection and education of the child, especially the proletarian children who desperately need [this state-sponsored education] because they have not been able to receive it in their poor homes." He saw state-sponsored preschool as the best way to assimilate "rural [*campesino*] and indigenous children . . . little by little to the national culture."[32] In this case, as in the one previously cited, these children's class conditions were seen as problems to be solved by the state. Yet in a very short span of time, this interpretation of proletarian conditions was inverted in official culture. Far from being a cesspool from which antisocial and counterproductive behaviors were bred, the proletarian home was seen as fertile Revolutionary ground, and its children were the seeds that would bring new life to the nation's future. While this transformation of the social type of the Proletarian Child does not follow a neat, linear trajectory, much of its metamorphism can be situated in the reformist agenda of the middle years of the Cárdenas administration.

It is hard to exaggerate the rhetorical emphasis placed on the device of the Proletarian Child as the key ingredient to the Revolution's success. By the mid-1930s, the Proletarian Child was becoming a mainstay of the Revolutionary collective imaginary, on par with the rehabilitated *indio* (indigenous) for his moral incorruptibility. Scholars have demonstrated the contested strategies employed by *indigenistas* to replace religious figures with social archetypes by infusing history books, textbooks, the civic calendar and official art with positive—though essentialized—references to the noble, indigenous past as a site of inspiration for the modern, Revolutionary present.[33] In fact, the elevation of the indio as a model citizen, a process described by Alexander Dawson, overlaps significantly with emergence of the Niño Proletario, even protagonized by many of the same public officials and intellectuals of the Revolutionary period (Moisés Sáenz, José Vasconcelos, Dr. Atl, Adolfo Best Maugard, among others). Like the indio, these men ascribed to the Proletarian Child inherent qualities that paved the way for model citizenship: they were both naturally egalitarian, socially conscious, virtuous, socialist-minded, and possessed of a highly civilized moral code.[34] Conceptually, they overlapped these categories by infantilizing indios, assigning them to the same intellectual plane. Moisés Sáenz noted in 1929 in an observation of a rural literacy campaign that both parents and children absorbed the presentation with childlike fascination and naivety.[35]

In the 1930s, Cardenismo accelerated the merging of the indio and the niño into the politicized lumpenproletariat; class and culture came to trump race in the Cárdenas years as useful ways to define social categories that needed assistance.[36] Yet as political symbols, the two figured differently in Cardenista populist politics—Indians were subjects *redeemable* for the above-mentioned qualities, valuable as a vast social sector that would boost the voting majority. Children, on the other hand, while not yet participants in electoral politics, stood in as *redeemers* of society. For Revolutionary officials, children represented the uncorrupted, easily malleable, yet still-dependent proto-citizen that could best absorb and perform the new moral code of the Revolution, thus eradicating the patterns of oppression learned over centuries. The possibilities were endless; though not all Mexicans claim Indian heritage, everyone is born a child, and therefore possesses these redemptive traits at least fleetingly. The inclusion of the Niño Proletario as a national type vastly expanded the "national stock" that Vasconcelos envisioned as the base for model citizenry.[37]

During the Cárdenas administration, monuments cropped up across the nation that recast military, independence, and insurrectionist heroes as children to underscore the moral justification for their actions. The monolithic Niño Pípila statue towered on a hillside overlooking Guanajuato's Alhóndiga to commemorate the alleged actions of young Juan José de los Reyes in Father Miguel Hidalgo's independence uprising of 1810. This folk hero, who supposedly tied a flat stone to his back to avoid gunfire while carrying a torch with which he set fire to the Alhóndiga, if he existed, likely was a young man, but he entered into the textbooks as a niño.[38] Primary school textbooks included (and still include) the requisite anecdote of Benito Juárez, as a child, trekking forty miles from his rural Zapotec hometown of Guelatao, Oaxaca, to the seat of the presidency and to immortality, driven from his shepherding by an incorruptible moral sense of duty to his nation. Likewise, the Niños Héroes de Chapultepec, military cadets popularly credited with leaping to their deaths cloaked in the Mexican flag rather than surrendering to the invading U.S. forces in 1847, were styled unquestioningly as pure patriots and, not coincidentally, "children."[39] Nevertheless, as Stephen Neufeld underscores in his contribution to this volume, their reputation as children underscored the purity of their motives, and thus catalyzed this historically nebulous episode as a foundational fiction in the construction of the Mexican nation. At the Second Children's Anti-Alcohol Assembly in 1940, the head of the Department of Public Health under Cárdenas, José Siurob, trotted out the Niños Héroes along with the fabled *niño inmortal* of Cuautla, who saved Morelos's life in battle. The ceremony thus conflated nationalism, morality, and childhood into a single demonstration of unity. In his speech, after evoking the heroic acts of the patriot children of lore, Siurob implored Mexican children to save the nation, reminding them that "of you, we expect everything; you are the balm for our pain . . . you are the citizen that Mexico needs," possessed of the "clean consciences and powerful potential." [40] These national myths, recast by government officials, conflated childhood with moral impunity, and paved the way for the Proletarian Child to occupy a moral center for the Revolutionary regime.

The anonymous Revolutionary Messiah got a public face in 1935. As an offshoot of the seventh Pan-American Conference on the Child, held in Mexico City in 1935 and host to professionals in child-related fields from across the hemisphere, SEP officials sponsored the First Proletarian Children's Conference during the first two weeks of March. The goals of the conference, as stated by SEP Secretary García Téllez, were to understand the point of view of the Proletarian Child, to convert him into a productive member of society, to study his methods of organization, and to provide him with the skills and platform for articulating his vision for change in the school system.[41] Child delegates from around Mexico City organized, presented, and moderated panels on social issues within the school system, all under the spotlight of the national press. Most certainly coached and groomed by the schoolteachers that selected each delegate, they performed their public role flawlessly, offering to the nation (and not coincidentally to the hundreds of international Pan-American Conference on the Child attendees) an idealized prototype of class-conscious, politically active, Revolutionary Mexican proletariat. That they *appeared* to act independently attested to the supposed innate purity of children's political conscience. In one instance, young delegates proclaimed that teachers would be afforded neither voice nor vote in the proceedings, and relegated them to the observation seats at the edges of the auditorium.[42] In another session realized at that Santa Anita Farm School, urban working-class children met with children of campesinos in a discussion of their respective conditions and mutual problems, and ended with both groups of children signing a "socialist pact."[43]

Their uncorrupted fervor became a public spectacle for the two weeks of the conference, as journalists and bystanders hovered around the proceedings for a glimpse of the ideological purity that had issued forth from the institutionalized Revolution. Perhaps the public fascination stemmed from a sense of nostalgia for the heady days of the Revolution that had characterized the audience's youth. Perhaps the pitch-perfect ideology spilling from the mouths of babes struck the public as a novelty. Regardless, the child conference format proved popular for a brief spell, and the 1935 Proletarian Child's Congress triggered a rash of state and regional conferences along the same ideological lines.[44] Whether intended to organize the Proletarian Child, the socialist child, or the rural child, these state- or school-based events raised the visibility of this new young protagonist as the new face of real reform.

The conference saw most of its publicity through the education magazine for rural schoolteachers, *El Maestro Rural*. While the photographer of these images remains anonymous, the images are in keeping with the style typical of Revolutionary photography of the day popularized by Tina Modotti, the Italian Communist expatriate who created a visual vocabulary for the Mexican Revolution. John Mraz has described Modotti's contributions as "historiciz[ing] Mexican emblems by linking them to the international socialist movement."[45] In the case of the propaganda for the upcoming proletarian children's conference, the children themselves are rendered emblems of the nation, embodiments of national culture as organic as corn or as ethnic as a sombrero. In other cases, the framing of the photographs clearly aggrandizes the children, grounding them in the tools of their trade (a book or a speech clutched in their able hands), even as the celestial background suggests that they possess otherworldly, exceptional qualities.

Notwithstanding their exclusion from the spotlight, socialist pedagogues occupied ample space in the media coverage swirling around the phenomenon of the self-actualized fledgling citizens. In editorials and interviews, teachers contextualized the seemingly spontaneous emergence of the Proletarian Child for foreign and national audiences, in effect mobilizing the archetype for political impact. Traditional ideas about the inferiority of the child, said Professor J. J. de la Rosa P., had prevented children

Figure 6.1. Primer Congreso del Niño Proletario. *El Maestro Rural,* tomo VI, Núm. 7 (1 abril 1935). Courtesy of AGN, Mexico.

from achieving their full potential; any attempt by the child to express himself independently had been met with hilarity or indifference by adults who believed themselves to have children's best interests at hand. De la Rosa insisted that the Conference of the Proletarian Child offered adults an opportunity to observe proletarian children in their element: how they act, think, sound, see, and attempt to resolve those issues that have previously only been tackled by adults.[46] It is hard to overlook the voyeuristic tone that de la Rosa assumed, and which cloaked the entire conference, as the carefully selected children performed their identities as proletarians before an audience desperate to see them succeed.[47]

But one message resonated clearly from the official sector: the Proletarian Child would be the savior of the Revolution. In the face of demonstrated

Figure 6.2. Primer Congreso del Niño Proletario. *El Maestro Rural*, tomo VI, Núm. 7 (1 abril 1935). Courtesy of AGN, Mexico.

self-interest, fanaticism, and hatred that marked adult implementation of reform, educational officials turned to the child—believed in the Lockean sense to be a blank slate, but also to have an inherent grasp of social justice—to restore the nation's productivity. In particular, the working-class child, as showcased through the events surrounding the First Conference of the Proletarian Child, when provided with space and resources, ought to be able to model strategies and methods for moving forward that eluded the jaded minds of adults. All that remained, according to de la Rosa, was to sit back curiously and watch the ideology unfold into praxis.[48] Perhaps fearful of the erosion of ideological fervor, Cardenistas believed that the emergence of a generation of proletarian children—ideologically pure and morally justified in their demands for social justice—could galvanize an increasingly fragmented population. As symbols, the proletarian children were irresistible: to the press, to their parents, and to the international community of child specialists descending upon Mexico for the conference.

Jesús Sansón Flores and the Construction of the Proletarian Child in Verse

Against this cultural backdrop, Jesús Sansón Flores published a book of poetry for this newly identified sector of society. Of humble origins, Sansón Flores tied his fortunes to Cárdenas's ascending political star.[49] In his home state of Michoacán, Sansón Flores saw his class consciousness piqued as a young student at the Colegio de San Nicolás, a famed germination bed for a generation of Revolutionary intellectuals.[50] Before long, he earned a name among the bohemian-Revolutionary class of intellectual elites in the early 1920s through his publications in the magazine *Juventud* in support of the local labor union struggle. After taking part in a controversial takeover of a prominent Catholic temple in Morelia to convert it into a library in 1927, Sansón Flores found himself in the midst of a heated public political scuffle, and went into a brief self-imposed exile in Tampico. He was beckoned back the following year, 1928, when Lázaro Cárdenas assumed the governorship, and joined the social and political ranks of Morelia's Revolutionary elite. The experience that most galvanized his radical politics was his militant involvement as a journalist, since its foundation in 1929 in Pátzcuaro, Michoacán, for the Revolutionary Labor Confederation of Michoacán (Confederación Revolucionaria Michoacana del Trabajo), or CRMDT, under the slogan "Unity, Land, and Labor."[51] Sansón Flores published his first and perhaps most acclaimed book of poetry, *Clarinadas*, in 1932, commencing in earnest his career as a poet.

Sansón Flores expressed his dismay with the aesthetic priorities of the Revolution at the expense of its economic advances in an essay he penned for an official Partido Nacional Revolucionario (PNR) newspaper: "We have built more statues than schools, and we have distributed more speeches than land . . . the *Científicos* and new rich have risen again . . . We were poor administrators of our own dreams and we were the unprepared inheritors of a blood fortune left to us in this new cycle of our history."[52] Implicit in this critique was the same message that educational officials expressed more directly in the socialist education publicity: the generation of adults alive in 1934 had been damaged and disillusioned by the bloody Revolution. Only a new generation of children, free of the brutal images that marred the collective memory, could step in and salvage the Revolution's originally stated goals of eradicating divisions between social classes and retrieving the Mexican economy from the hands of foreigners and the wealthy.

Sansón Flores gave literary expression to the rhetoric, gaining currency in official circles, which looked to the child as the nation's salvation. He was not alone in crafting nationalist verses; Sansón Flores joined a cadre of poets who added literature to other cultural expressions that lauded indigenism, provincialism, socialism, or a host of other Revolutionary-isms.[53] By his own admission, and a claim supported by his biographers, the 1936

Figure 6.3. Cover image of *El niño proletario*, by cartoonist Antonio Arias Bernal, 1936. Courtesy of Biblioteca Lerdo de Tejado.

publication of *El niño proletario: Poemas clasistas* represented the apex of his ideological commitment.[54] In it, he echoed the themes swirling about the political milieu that served to reify the child—the Proletarian Child—as the redeemer of the Revolution. The book's cover set the tone for its content; a simple black and white line drawing by prominent cartoonist (and later World War II propagandist) Antonio Arias Bernal features a (boy) child, wearing worker's overalls, lurching forward even as he turned back to beckon unseen followers with a raised fist. He brandishes a red flag that bears the volume's title. He is undoubtedly a leader. While the spare line drawing does not clearly mark the child's race, he appears to be phenotypically on the whiter end of the mestizo spectrum, and his overalls serve as an internationally recognizable signifier of his socioeconomic class as an urban laborer.[55] Ostensibly directed toward urban working-class children as his audience, Sansón Flores effectively defined the social archetype through his fifteen poems:

Desde que en el fértil vientre
    tu vida
	From the moment your life
	    became

se hizo carne;	flesh within the fertile womb;

Se fecundó tu condición de
    esclavo, . . .
	Your condition as a slave was
	    fertilized, . . .

¡Ni siquiera eres dueño . . .	You are not even master . . .
de la tierra que pisas!	of the dirt that you tread!
¡Naciste ya vendido! [56]	You were born already sold!

In this first poem of the collection, Sansón Flores informed the eponymous "Niño" of his oppression, and thus politically activated his child audience. He identified the source of the persistent poverty that plagues their class: no ownership over their means of production. In the poem, he spoke to a child. Yet the lofty language employed suggests that he was equally concerned with establishing the metaphorical connection between children and the proletariat to an adult audience, signaling the double oppression of both social groups. He both infantilized the proletariat (situating them as powerless "children" of a patronizing landlord), and empowered the children (lending them the tools for developing class consciousness even within the womb). In making this parallel, Sansón Flores drew on a long history of politicians from across the ideological spectrum, identifying children as the tabula rasa upon which their respective administrations would inscribe their vision for society.[57] Although he defined the Proletarian Child's condition as predetermined, a marked slave since conception, he continued on where others might have left the child in that resigned position to make a damning statement about class-based oppression. For Sansón Flores, poetry served as a vehicle not only to draw attention to the Proletarian Child's plight, but as a revolutionary tool of consciousness-making (*concientización*), the oppressed child's first glimpse in a mirror and realization of self.

The poems in the volume define the systems of oppression against which the child must revolt. But the poet also made it clear that the parents, society's adults and traditional political actors, have been rendered powerless and demoralized by a lifetime of servitude. In one verse, titled "Question" ("Pregunta"), a father has a conversation about class identity with his son, styled as very young, with a toddler's childlike speech (he confuses his consonants, saying "palde" instead of "padre," and "linelo" instead of "dinero"). Using this linguistic technique to mark the boy's extreme youth, Sansón Flores returns to the assumed irreproachability of the line of questioning that followed in the poem. This stereotypical rendering of the boy's lexicon echoes popular transcriptions of a Nahuatl speaker (Nahuatl has no "r" sounds) trying to speak Spanish. The effect is actually overdone in the poem, as Sansón Flores comes dangerously close to obfuscating the child's voice through his heavy documentation of the speech impediment. Similar linguistic strategies prevailed to mark ethnicity in literature and eventually cinema as well (a codified pidgin Spanish that stood in for visual markers of ethnicity, or in the case of cinema, when the actors did not look convincingly indigenous).[58] Again, then, we see the conflation of indigeneity and childhood as parallel signifiers of both innocence and righteous indignation. In the poem, the boy asks his father why the hacienda owner took the wheat that his father had harvested:

—Palde: ¿pol qué lecole l'amo	—Father: why does the boss harvest
El tliguito que semblaste?	The wheat that you planted?

After a brief lesson about the evils of the bourgeoisie, the father concedes that there is nothing he can do about his status as a peon, but looks to his son for vindication:

—Hijo: cuando seas grande	—Son: when you grow up
Tendrás una pistol "dedeverás";	You will have a "for real" pistol;
Tuya será la bala que taladre	Yours will be the bullet that pierces
El corazón de piedra de esas gentes	The heart of stone of those people
Que hoy viven del trabajo de tu padre.[59]	Who today live off of the labor of your father.

Youth and innocence notwithstanding, the child protagonist of this poem is not a victim. Sansón Flores situated the young boy as the actor, seeking out the pistol of justice, while his emasculated father faded back among the ancestral generations of the oppressed. Sansón Flores resurrected virility and Revolutionary potential in the figure of the toddler son. In this poem, the Proletarian Child reacted immediately and viscerally upon gaining class consciousness.

Sansón Flores intended to nudge the politicization of his child audience along, stirring their innate sense of justice at a level that corresponded with childlike concerns. He did not approach this task elegantly. The poem "Little Boy" ("Niñito") administered a jolt of terror, narrating in second person the story of police carting off the boy's father, suggesting that perhaps in the middle of some night they might kill him, or worse: "What will the soldiers do with your father, campesino?," he menaced in the final line. While this poem did not direct the child reader to a specific action, it left the child in a desolate landscape unpopulated by any moral authorities. Not even the erstwhile heroes of the Revolution, the soldiers, represented a safe adult refuge for the boy in this verse. The implied appropriate response to the moral vacuum can be found in the companion poems such as "Pregunta": recourse to violent retribution. Other strategies to politicize the child can be found in "Poor Children" ("Los Niños Pobres"), in which the poet enumerated the Western-style toys and fantasy stories that inhabit the homes and heads of well-to-do children. His blunt contrasts twisted the knife cruelly:

El hijo del campesino	The son of the peasant
no tiene corcel de palo	does not have a hobby horse
corriendo por los trigales,	to ride through the wheat fields,
ni soldaditos de plomo	nor toy soldiers
pero miró los caballos	but he saw the horses
del viejo patron obeso,	of the old obese *patron*,
y ha visto a los federales	and he has seen the federal soldiers
llevando a su padre preso.[60]	carrying his father off to prison.

Sansón Flores effectively employed symmetry here: toy horses cavorting through wheat fields compared with live ones straining beneath the weight of the greedy land boss; innocuous tin soldiers contrasted with flesh-and-blood agents of oppression. These direct parallels served to animate a child audience's imagination.

The poem "The Three Wise Men" ("Los Magos") plied at children's natural jealousies with an ideologically infused call to action. Sansón Flores reminded his reader that although the Three Wise Men brought toys and candies to rich children, the trio of Lenin, (Emiliano) Zapata, and Marx would leave a flag and a weapon in the hands of the poor child (when he was grown). Small solace for a young reader? The poem in its entirety is composed of two stark, parallel verses:

Melchor, Gaspar y Baltasar, al niño rico, en noche buena le dejaran, cuando amanezca, muchos juguetes y bombones, en el zapato colocado sobre un helecho del pretil;	Melchior, Gaspar, and Balthasar will leave for the rich child, on Christmas Eve, when he wakes, many toys and sweets in the shoe he has left over a fern upon the mantel;
pero Lenín, Zapata y Marx, al niño pobre, cuando crezca, le dejarán entre las manos una bandera y un fusil. [61]	but Lenin, Zapata, and Marx, will leave for the poor child, in his hands, when he is grown a flag and a rifle.

The parallel structure allowed Sansón Flores to swap out the religious figures of the three kings for a new set of secular and nationalist deities. Rather than the trite instant gratification of candy, the poor child received lasting gifts on the mantel of national identity (the flag) and the means with which to vindicate himself (the rifle). The child in this poem did not have to work to obtain these items; he appears to have been entitled to them by virtue of his socioeconomic status, so long as he educates himself accordingly.

Even as the social realist murals began to codify the mestizo or indigenous laborer as the incarnation of the Revolution in the nation's collective imaginary, the presence of the barefoot child underscored this trope in the streets. Even as the shoe in the previous poem, "The Three Wise Men," signaled wealth, and figured literally as a receptacle for material goods bestowed by the visiting kings, the absence of shoes pointed to the impoverishment of the masses, and thus the lack of so much as a receptacle in which to receive any potential gifts (the Three Wise Men left gifts in shoes, rather than stockings). As Susana Sosenski tells us, the street boy or "*muchacho callejero*" became an increasingly visible and talked-about presence in the Revolutionary decades, as he ran unsupervised and unshod between marketplaces and doorstops conducting his own extralegal business.[62] The *papelero*, or paperboy, was perhaps the most visible of this dubious social category, and his shoeless presence came to be a somewhat conflicted visual trope in the print media, a quaint national symbol that reflected mixed messages about the welfare of the nation. Barefoot paperboys plagued the Revolution's reputation by evading the education and welfare institutions designed to encourage social conformity. At the same time, as Alberto del Castillo Troncoso argues, these paperboys were the purveyors of the very images of social conformity printed in the daily news—officially sanctioned photographs of children as aesthetic anecdotes to the Revolutionary narrative of prosperity.[63] Notwithstanding the fact that barefoot children had always characterized urban thoroughfares and rural pathways, public intellectuals like Sansón Flores politicized the social type as a way to push the urgency of a more radically Revolutionary program. In the quest for a set of codified images to establish the child as a metaphor for the proletarian condition, the poet chose shoelessness as a starting point:

¡Cada vez que te mires	Each time you look at your bare feet,
con las plantas desnudas,	you think that you have never had,
piensa en que no has tenido ni tendrás patria! [64]	nor will you have a homeland!

The bare feet served as a reminder, not only to the rest of the world, but also to the child himself, of the great failures of the nation to fulfill Revolutionary promises. Again, shoelessness represented another feature shared by indigenous people and this sector of the child population—a distinct marker of ethnicity, poverty, or marginality. Sansón Flores's papelero embodied this social problem. Drawing from the established characterization of the paperboy as a mischievous pariah, the poet reinterpreted the archetype of the paperboy from one signaling social danger to a symbol of tragedy. The paperboy that he directly addressed did not flaunt his disregard for authority—rather, he epitomized liminality:

Papelero, papelero, yo te quiero, yo te quiero por tramposo y por ratero, papelero, papelero.	Paperboy, paperboy, I love you, I love you As a mischief-maker and a thief, Paperboy, paperboy.
Tu primer sueño fue un día aquel pedazo de pan.	Your first dream was one day [to aquire] that piece of bread.

Llevas un primer recuerdo que dos voces lo alumbraron las llamas de cuatro cirios.	You carry with you a first memory illuminated by two voices the flames of four candles.
Tienes por padre el suburbio, por madre la soledad.	The suburbs are your father, solitude your mother.
Tal vez porque te miraron sin zapatos los tres reyes los reyes no te llevaron juguetes ni chocolates.	Perhaps because the Three Kings saw you without shoes, The Kings brought to you neither toys nor chocolate.
Granuja tramposo y bueno: el hambre te dio sus tretas; la gente pisa los sueños que dejas todas las noches untados en las banquetas.	Mischievous and good rascal: hunger played its tricks on you; the people step on your dreams which you leave spread each night upon the sidewalks.
Papelero, papelero, yo te quiero, yo te quiero por tramposo y por ratero.[65]	Paperboy, paperboy, I love you, I love you as a mischief-maker and a thief.

Again, the shoelessness of paperboys rendered them unable to receive the holiday goodwill taken for granted by middle-class children. The extralegal or socially dangerous activities in which paperboys infamously engaged (stealing, drinking alcohol, visiting brothels, street fights) remain unnamed by Sansón Flores, who relegates them to the category of childhood indiscretions. That he showed open affection for the paperboy ("I love you, I love you") demonstrated uncharacteristic tenderness by the poet, especially since he adhered to the unflattering characterization of the paperboy as a "ratero," or common thief. These sins, then, can be forgiven of the paperboy, as they merely represent everyday forms of equalizing the socioeconomic field. In this poem, he restored the reputation of the paperboy and returned him to childhood, a fragile social category to which by many measures most paperboys of the time no longer really belonged. In so doing, the paperboy could join the ranks of the Proletarian Child and the Indian—victims of historical oppression with the potential for productive Revolutionary action.

The politicization of the Proletarian Child mirrored the transformation of the "indito" from a comic stereotype to a figure to be taken more seriously as a subject of national integration in the 1930s.[66] But while the "indito" represented a figure that needed redemption, Sansón Flores and his cohort of educational reformers poised the Proletarian Child to be the *redeemer* of the nation. This anonymous, barefoot child was the generation born of iconic Revolutionary Messiahs such as Pancho Villa and Emiliano Zapata. The responsibility for the nation's salvation fell to these children of the Revolution's mestizo protagonists; Sansón Flores demonstrated repeatedly the powerlessness of their parents. After proclaiming that the Proletarian Child hails from an ancestral line tarnished by rags and death, he suggests that the key to breaking the cycle might lie with the spontaneous conscientization of the child inspired by his natural surroundings:

¡Quién sabe si algún día, niño, quién sabe!
veas la hoz descansando en un martillo
en lo alto, al ondear de una bandera
clavada en el pezón de cada surco;
. . . y un desfile de hambrientos y de esclavos
al mundo entero con las manos coja;
¡Quién sabe si algún día, niño, quién sabe
mires que dora los trigales nuevos
la luz sin patria de una aurora roja![67]

Who knows if one day, child, who knows!
You'll see the sickle resting upon a hammer
up on high, and with the wave of a flag
staked to the crest of every furrow;
. . . and a parade of the hungry and enslaved
seize the whole world with their hands;
Who knows if some day, child, who knows
you'll see the new wheat fields made golden
by the international red dawn.

The theme of forging, rather than simply inheriting, a better and more just world runs through the *poemas clasistas* of this volume. These sentiments were echoed elsewhere at the time too, as we have seen in the events of the First Proletarian Child Congress that shone a spotlight on children as vocal political beings in the conference proceedings, however staged those events might have been. Other literary figures echoed Sansón Flores's language of redemption and disseminated it further. A nationalist reading primer by Adolfo Ornelas Hernández, destined for the titular *El Niño Rural*, featured a poem (titled "Al Niño Rural") that glorified the bronzed, strong, rural child (descendent of Nezahualcoyotl and Cuauhtémoc, of course, to further perpetuate the myth of Aztec exceptionalism characteristic of early twentieth-century indigenism). In it, the author reminded his young readers of their historically charged responsibility:

No olvides: en tus manos tienes depositado un tesoro de energías nuevas; empléalas en mejorarte cada día más física, moral e intelectualmente. México necesita una nueva raza más apta para la lucha y el trabajo.[68]

Don't forget: in your hands has been deposited a treasure of new energies; use them to improve yourself every day physically, morally, and intellectually. Mexico needs a new race better adapted for the struggle and for work.

Yet not all of Sansón Flores's poems empowered the child reader. The poet devoted so much space in the small volume to the description of the misery in which his subject (and presumed audience) wallowed. For instance, "Lullaby" ("Canción de Cuna"):

"Duerme, hijo mío, duerme," que el cadaver del fuego calentó nuestro hogar; y los niños cautivos también pueden, a veces dedicarse a soñar.	"Sleep, my child, sleep," the cadaver of the fire heated our home; and captive children can also, sometimes try to dream.
¡Ya se abre el hocico de la noche enseñando los dientes del invierno que hizo al viento del norte su emisario! pero toma la esencia de mi aliento para que se acurruquen y perfumen tus sollozos de niño proletario.	The night is opening its muzzle showing its wintry teeth with the north wind its emissary! But take the essence of my breath let it sweeten your sobs of a proletarian child and curl up in sleep.
"Duerme, hijo mío, duerme," que el fantasma del AMO va cruzando el potrero y al mirarlo, quién sabe si se espante tu sueño.[69]	"Sleep, my child, sleep," for the ghost of the MASTER is crossing the field and who knows, if looking at it it will frighten you in your sleep.

Not even the sleep of the Proletarian Child remains free of the specter—and responsibility—of class consciousness that Sansón Flores so doggedly reiterates in this volume. In this case, the genre of verse serves as an effective counter to other interpretations of proletarian sleep emerging in visual culture. A panel of Diego Rivera's mural cycle in the Ministry of Education headquarters in Mexico City completed between 1923 and 1928 (and the widely disseminated lithograph of the same subject that the artist drew in 1932) depicted a proletariat family deeply and peacefully sleeping, against a background of round-the-clock productive activities in which this newly politicized group had been engaging (cottage industries, manual labor, education). For Rivera, proletarian sleep appeared deep, dreamless, and restorative. For Sansón Flores, proletarian sleep appeared to represent the dangers of inaction, and the creep of ideological corruption into the latent mind. Ghosts, cadavers, fear, cold, and pain all characterized the tormented dreams of Sansón Flores's imagined audiences. His emphasis on the misery so overwhelmed the reader that the glimmers of action suggested at the end seemed a requisite latter-day concession that these poems ought, after all, to inspire reader action.

As with the "Lullaby," the general tone of Sansón Flores's collection of children's poems remained dogmatic, dark, and violent, rife with descriptions of vengeance that seemed removed from the nobler rhetoric of the educational officials. Furthermore, Sansón Flores's more militant politicization undermined the nationalism characteristic of Mexico's socialist education experiment, through his emphasis on international proletarian solidarity (reminding barefooted children that their country had done nothing to ameliorate their plight, for example). Literary characterizations of the Proletarian Child such as those proffered by Sansón Flores reflected the deceleration of the socialist movement in Mexico that marked the latter years of Cárdenas's administration, much like the institutionalization of the socialist education campaign stifled the more organic movements and nuanced implementations of early Revolutionary education reform.

Sansón Flores and the Spanish Civil War

Sansón Flores's political affiliation with Cárdenas facilitated the publication of *El niño proletario* in a serendipitous moment for both the poet and his *patria*. The Cárdenas administration had identified the Proletarian Child as an agent of Revolutionary change, and the publication of the verses penned by Sansón Flores helped to catalyze this newly retooled national symbol. But Sansón Flores benefitted perhaps more. Drawing on a tenuous, solicitous relationship with the president, the poet regularly addressed personal correspondence directly to Cárdenas in his office in Los Pinos over the course of his administration, submitting requests for financial subventions, medical expenses incurred from an unspecified surgery, employment in government positions, and even a nose job for his wife who he feared to be disfigured after an accident to her face. Evidence suggests that, despite the mounting demands upon Cárdenas as he opened the nation's coffers to the clamoring poor, Sansón Flores did receive a stream—if not steady or bountiful—of financial support from Cárdenas over the course of the *sexenio*.[70] The motives for maintaining this dependency remain unclear, but a clue comes from a handwritten note by Sansón Flores's wife, Aurora, to Luís Rodríguez, who served at the time as Cárdenas's private secretary, in 1936 (the same year as the publication of *El niño proletario*). In it, she acknowledges her husband's heavy drinking as the reason for which Cárdenas may have distanced himself from his long-time acquaintance, and pleads for clemency in his dark hour—she requests a restoration of the clientelist relationship that had prevailed in previous times, and recommends that Sansón Flores be granted a government position. After all, she implored, "he is good. He loves his people (*pueblo*) for whom he sings, and for whom he fights."[71] In short, a position of service would provide Sansón Flores with an ideological outlet, and would redeem him. Whether the contract for his children's book came before or after this spousal intervention is unclear, but Cárdenas's apparently favorable response did procure Sansón Flores a coveted office position in the thick of the most ideologically charged climate available to a Mexican diplomat at the time: the Mexican embassy in Spain, in the thick of the Spanish Civil War. Ironically for Sansón Flores, this fortuitous turn of events signaled not the acceleration of his career, but rather the denouement of his Revolutionary fervor.

Sansón Flores had revealed his internationalism in *El niño proletario*, and set his sights to the broader global mobilization of the proletariat. Following the curious correspondence with Cárdenas and his staff, Jesús Sansón Flores rode the red tide from Mexico to Spain in 1936 at the outbreak of its civil war, where he served (in his first and only publicly held office) as secretary to the Mexican ambassador for a little over a year. Mexico took a globally symbolic stance in defense of the Republican cause, as nearly the only country in the world to supply them with weapons, an act of solidarity from the left-leaning administration of Cárdenas. Perhaps expecting to be enveloped in a utopic milieu of sympathetic compatriots, Sansón Flores went to Spain with high expectations to see his revolutionary verses realized in the proletarian struggle. Yet his firsthand experiences in the politically polarized, bellicose Madre Patria embittered him. The Spanish Civil War corrupted his vision of childhood innocence conflated with political purity, embodied by the Proletarian Child.[72]

As a diplomatic presence in Spain, and in accordance with the Mexican Embassy's wartime policy, Sansón Flores oversaw the protection of human lives on both Republicans and Franquistas (fascist Francisco Franco supporters). His obligatory neutrality garnered criticism from some of Sansón Flores's more radical colleagues back in Mexico, and seemed to exacerbate the poet's own internal frustrations.[73] In 1938, he published a slim book of poems inspired by his experiences, *Bajo el Sol de España*, comprised of only nine short verses prefaced by a prolonged, defensive, caustic introductory essay. The collection suggested that firsthand experience with war had jaded him. In this volume, his tenacious grasp on the lexical iconography of class struggle seemed ossified; his words rang dutiful and dogmatic rather than idealistic and passionate. The decidedly adult-oriented publication featured gritty descriptions of wartime atrocities, and children no longer occupied center stage as the protagonists of the proletarian Revolution. As in *El niño proletario*, Sansón Flores returned to the device of the child as a signifier. But in this case, children assumed a symbolic role as victims, an emotional trigger targeting adults, and they appeared only in the final poem, aptly titled "Dead Children" ("Niños muertos").

The poet identified the dead children as child soldiers. In the face of Republican demise, was death the only alternative for these now-useless symbols of Revolutionary potential? These were not the vindicating youthful forces described in his previous collection; they were not even martyrs. They were the abandoned corpses of a hopeless struggle:

En la montaña, tendidos, con los ojitos abiertos, por el fascism abatidos quedaron los niños muertos.	In the mountain, stranded, with their little eyes open, beaten down by fascism lay the dead children.
. . .	. . .
—Ejércitos infantiles— —de sangre tierno regalo,— tal vez cayeron soñando estar también disparando desde Madrid, sus fusiles de hojadelata y de palo.	—Child armies— —the tender gift of blood,— perhaps they fell dreaming about also shooting from Madrid, with their rifles made of tin and of sticks.
¡En los escombros quedaron los niños ametrallados! Las estrellas los miraron con los puñitos cerrados.[74]	The gunned-down children remained in the ruins! The stars looked down upon them with their little fists clenched.

The final image—and the last line of the volume—of fists of solidarity frozen in rigor mortis, reflects Sansón Flores's own grim ideological resolve. Uncompromising even in death, these child soldiers nevertheless failed to upend the social order. As he had urged in his 1936 children's volume, children had taken up rifles and acted upon their class-based oppression. And to what end? Sansón Flores did not end his *Bajo el Sol de España* collection with images of the redemption that he had suggested, and very nearly guaranteed, in *El niño proletario*. He concluded with a stagnant image of death, one that suggested futile sacrifice. Along with the Republican children, the Revolutionary flame in Sansón Flores had died in Spain.

Meanwhile in Mexico, the trope of the Proletarian Child retained currency for a few more years. Fanaticism over the sheer symbolic power of this redemptive social type reached a near frenzy in 1937, when Cárdenas announced that Mexico would receive five hundred orphaned Republican children from the Spanish Civil War as a goodwill gesture. In the press releases, and during the florid official speeches that marked the arrival of the Spanish refugee children, the children's political position was assumed to be as fixed as their Spanish-accented Castilian (another misperception, since upon their arrival many of the children were discovered to speak only Basque).[75] Despite the fact that they were children (some as young as toddlers), the refugees that disembarked from the *Mexique* steam-liner were branded as Republican children, ascribing to them a certain political identity that they quickly learned to embrace as part of their new celebrity personas in the New World. Postcards of the Spanish children neatly dressed with their fists firmly raised in the air in solidarity with the Republican cause circulated throughout the country, and added an international dimension to the national narrative of the politicized child savior.

The arrival of the Spanish children breathed new life into the Cárdenas administration, briefly, garnering a sense of national pride in Mexico's ability to turn the tables and flaunt its political stability to its former colonizer by receiving refugees, an ironic twist that Cárdenas's public relations officials could not help but exploit in the occasional speech. The political success of the event hinged on the cultural power that the image of the Proletarian Child had garnered over the early ideological years of Cardenismo. The Spanish children's experiences in Mexico varied. It became a permanent home for some, who never returned to Spain. For others, Mexico represented a tortured purgatory, a mostly safe place but one in which they were occasionally trotted out to the public as a reminder of the government's beneficence. The Cárdenas administration and the national press burdened the young exiles with the weight of ideological purity, and positioned them as the newest wards of the Revolutionary Family. Cárdenas himself extended the metaphor by assuming the de facto role of *padrino*, or spiritual godfather, for all five hundred children, setting them up in the Escuela México-España in his home state of Michoacán (boarded along with a carefully vetted selection of "proletarian" Mexican children from neighboring villages), and inviting them to his nearby ranch for occasional pool parties and play sessions with Cárdenas's son, young Cuauhtémoc (at the time only four years old). For several months, the nation remained riveted to news reports that showed thriving blond Spanish children frolicking around Cárdenas's knees, their Spanish accents giving way to Mexican slang, and their intrinsic Republicanism melding with the Revolutionary nationalism of their Mexican peers at the Escuela.[76]

Yet with the passing of months, and years, the national appetite for a more radical, socialist version of Revolutionary nationalism abated. Across the Atlantic, the Spanish Civil War gave way to the Franco regime, and with the victory of the fascists, feelings of dejection set in among Spanish Republican exiles. At home, Cardenismo took a turn to the right, and then came to a halt with the conservative administration of Manuel Ávila Camacho. Socialist education vanished abruptly. Meanwhile, the Spanish children languished in Michoacán. The school fell into disrepair; the children became teenagers and many expressed resentment over their tokenism by rebelling, running away, or returning to Spain. And Jesús Sansón Flores, Revolutionary poet from Michoacán, returned to Mexico jaded from his experiences in Spain. Although he lived a long life, his poetry never regained its fervent ideological tenor, and never again did he address the nation's youth as the messianic solution to the Revolution's ills.

Conclusion

This brief episode of the middle years of the Cárdenas administration saw the confluence of various cultural, literary, and political forces—national and international—that elevated the Proletarian Child as a new social redeemer. At its core was the infusion of a new rhetoric of redemption into the public discourse—at all social and generational levels—from children's textbooks, to political cartoons, to international conferences, to official speeches. That language, captured pointedly in the poetry of Jesús Sansón Flores, marked the apex of Revolutionary fervor as embodied by the mythical, pure, Proletarian Child. Between 1935 and 1938, the Mexican government turned to socialist ideology and rhetoric to breathe new life into the Revolution, and relied on children in particular as both the symbols and the agents of this goal. Following the official line, Jesús Sansón Flores's poetry represented some of the most propagandistic of all of the socialist-tinged educational material being produced by his contemporaries, pedagogues and artists alike. His reliance on parallel structures appealed to the minds of children, with developmental tendencies to sort their world into binary categories. His verses swapped religious icons for secular ones, and replaced material rewards with moral ones. The publication of *El niño proletario*, however slim and insignificant, identified a literate child audience for the poet's message.

Official efforts to proletarianize the nation's youth did not last long, and the binary tensions of the Cold War ossified the momentum of the Revolutionary left. Yet from the children's perspective, the national attention they received from their participation in the orchestrated public events designed to capitalize on their cultural caché as proletarian children might have had a meaningful impact. Through the formal structure of the conference, child participants gained awareness of themselves as political beings. Consider this final image, a candid photograph from the Proletarian Children's Conference. Enrique Romero, a featured child delegate, assumed the stage at the opening ceremony. Children surrounding the stage raised their fists in solidarity, as he expounded on the need to take social action and to provide an international model. However orchestrated Enrique's speech might have been, however self-serving to educational officials who staged the event

Figure 6.4. El Maestro Rural, tomo VI, No. 7 (April 1935). Courtesy of Biblioteca Lerdo de Tejado.

to bask in international attention, the children in the audience experienced it from a different dimension. For a moment, they were involved in a political discussion. The children who could not attend the event but saw this photograph in their schoolteacher's copy of *El Maestro Rural* understood that the nation was interested in the concerns, demands, and abilities of the Proletarian Child. For a few short years that imagined reader, the Proletarian Child, was poised not merely to inherit the earth, but to redeem it.

Notes

"Numen" is a magical nutritive power inherent in a being, derived from ancient Roman philosophy.

All translations are the author's. The challenge of translating literary prose and poetry means that the content is sometimes conveyed at the considerable expense of the flow. The original text reads: "*Mi musa dará a mamar a los niños hambrientos. Mi Numen vacunará sus pechos con la linfa testicular de la protesta hirviente contra el Capitalismo. Porque en cada niño proletario hay un Mesías tomando el barro para hacerlo pájaros. Los pájaros del ideal futuro picoteando las jaulas del sistema burgués.*" Jesús Sansón Flores, *El niño proletario. Poemas clasistas* (México: Ediciones Ala Izquierda, 1936), 6.

1. *Michoacano* means resident of the state of Michoacán.

2. Among some of the most recent studies dedicated to placing children at the center of historical inquiry, see Susana Sosenski and Elena Jackson Albarrán, coords., *Nuevas miradas a la historia de la infancia en América Latina: Entre prácticas y representaciones* (México: Instituto de Investigaciones Históricas, Universidad Nacional Autónoma de México, 2012); Susana Sosenski, *Niños en acción: El trabajo infantil en la ciudad de México, 1920–1934* (México: El Colegio de México, Centro de Estudios Históricos, 2010); Nara Milanich, *Children of Fate: Childhood, Class, and the State in Chile, 1850–1930* (Durham, NC: Duke University Press, 2009); Bianca Premo, "How Latin America's History of Childhood Came of Age," *Journal of the History of Childhood and Youth* 1, no. 1 (Winter 2008): 63–76; Elena Jackson Albarrán, *Seen and Heard in Revolutionary Mexico: Children and Cultural Nationalism* (Lincoln: University of Nebraska Press, forthcoming 2014).

3. Lucía Martínez Moctezuma, "Retrato de una élite: autores de libros escolares en México (1890–1920)," in *Lecturas y lectores en la historia de México*, coord. Carmen Castañeda García, Luz Elena Galván Lafarga, and Lucía Martínez Moctezuma (México: CIESAS, 2004), 115–41.

4. Ibid., 130.

5. Enrique Florescano, "Notas sobre las relaciones entre memoria y nación en la historiografía mexicana," *Historia Mexicana* 53, no. 2, México e Hispanoamérica (October–December 2003): 391–416.

6. The *charro* and the *china poblana*, roughly a gallant Mexican cowboy and his braided, bejeweled partner, are an archetypal couple that are often figured as engaged in the regional folk dances such as the *jarabe tapatío*, sometimes inaccurately called

the Mexican Hat Dance. *Tehuanas* are women from the coastal region of Oaxaca with a distinctive, highly decorated dress, mythologized as the most beautiful of all Mexican women. *Toreros* are Mexican bullfighters, a Hispanophile trope adapted from the Spanish tradition.

7. Ricardo Pérez Montfort, "Los estereotipos nacionales y la educación posrevolucionaria en México (1920–1930)," *Avatares del nacionalismo cultural: Cinco ensayos* (México: Centro de Investigación y Docencia en Humanidades del Estado de Morelos/Centro de Investigaciones y Estudios Superiores en Antropología Social, 2000), 39.

8. Allison James and Adrian L. James, *Constructing Childhood: Theory, Policy, and Social Practice* (New York: Palgrave MacMillan, 2004), 14–15.

9. Elsewhere I examine more fully the development and implications for children of a "child-centered society" in Revolutionary Mexico, through cultural programs largely promoted by the SEP. See Albarrán, *Seen and Heard.*

10. Luz Elena Galván Lafarga, "Del ocio a la instrucción en *La Niñez Ilustrada.* Un periódico infantil del siglo XIX," *Estudios del Hombre*, no. 20 (2005): 214.

11. Carlos Martínez Assad, ed., *Los lunes rojos: La educación racionalista en México* (México: Secretaría de Educación Pública; Ediciones El Caballito, 1985), 11–14.

12. "ABC socialista para uso de los niños campesinos," *Los lunes rojos*, 101–18.

13. Ibid., 103.

14. José Ochoa Lobato, "No aceptamos los "Concursos Escolares," *Redención* (December 22, 1933), in *Los lunes rojos*, ed. Martínez Assad, 147–51.

15. Martínez Assad, *Los lunes rojos*, 16.

16. Engracia Loyo B., "En el aula y la parcela: vida escolar en el medio rural (1921–1940)," *Historia de la vida cotidiana en México*, tomo V, no. 1: *Siglo XX: Campo y ciudad*, coord. Aurelio de los Reyes (México: El Colegio de México, Fondo de Cultura Económica, 2006), 300.

17. Kimberley Reynolds, *Radical Children's Literature: Future Visions and Aesthetic Transformations in Juvenile Fiction* (New York: Palgrave MacMillan, 2007): 30–33.

18. Julia L. Mickenberg, *Learning from the Left: Children's Literature, the Cold War, and Radical Politics in the United States* (New York: Oxford University Press, 2006): 57.

19. John Dewey, cited in *Niños y libros: Publicaciones infantiles de la Secretaría de Educación Pública*, ed. Sarah Corona Berkin and Arnulfo Uriel de Santiago Gómez (México: Secretaría de Educación Pública, 1911), 21.

20. Mickenberg, *Learning from the Left*, 9.

21. *Niños y libros*, 24.

22. Patricia Hurtado Tomás, "Los libros de texto oficiales en las escuelas primarias durante la educación socialista en el Estado de México," in *Lecturas y lectores*, coord. Castañeda García, Galván Lafarga, and Martínez Moctezuma, 143–62.

23. Loyo B., "En el aula y la parcela," 302.

24. "White shirts" are a reference to the muslin garb associated with indigenous peasants, figured here as the protagonists of the Revolution. This is one of four verses. Archivo Histórico de la Secretaría de Educación Pública (AHSEP), Departamento Psicopedagogía e Higiene, exp. 5234, folleto 17, April 24, 1935.

25. Loyo B, "En el aula y la parcela"; Mary Kay Vaughan, *Cultural Politics in Revolution: Teachers, Peasants, and Schools in Mexico, 1930–1940* (Tucson: University of Arizona Press, 1997); and Mary Kay Vaughn, "The Educational Project of the Mexican

Revolution: The Response of Local Societies, 1934–1940," in *Molding the Hearts and Minds: Education, Communications, and Social Change in Latin America*, ed. John A. Britton (Wilmington, DE: SR Books, 1994), 105–27; Elsie Rockwell, *Hacer escuela, hacer estado: La educación posrevolucionaria vista desde Tlaxcala* (Zamora, Michoacán: El Colegio de Michoacán, Centro de Investigaciones y Estudios Superiores en Antropología Social, Centro de Investigación y de Estudios Avanzados del Instituto Politécnico Nacional, 2007).

26. Susanne Karin Eineigel, "Distinction, Culture, and Politics in Mexico City's Middle Class, 1890–1940" (PhD diss., University of Maryland, 2011), 103–5.

27. "La Escuela Socialista es escuela de la traición," *La Defensa del Hogar: Salvemos a la Patria Salvando a la Niñez*, no. 2 (March 22, 1936): 1.

28. "Todas las escuelas son para el Niño Proletario," *La Prensa* (January 16, 1935): 18.

29. *El Maestro Rural*, tomo VII, no. 2 (July 15, 1935): 11.

30. Sosenski, *Niños en acción*.

31. "Los niños proletarios," *El Universal*, June 9, 1934.

32. "La protección del niño proletario," *El Nacional*, July 11, 1935.

33. See Stephen Neufeld's chapter in this volume, "The Sly Mockeries of Military Men: Corridos and Poetry as Critical Voice for the Porfirian Army." See also Florescano, "Notes sobre las relaciones," 406–7; and Ricardo Pérez Montfort, "El estereotipo del indio en la expresión popular urbana, 1920–1940," in *Estampas de nacionalismo popular mexicano: diez ensayos sobre cultura popular y nacionalismo*, 2nd ed. (México: CIESAS/CIDHEM, 2003), 171–90.

34. Alexander Dawson, "From Models for the Nation to Model Citizens: *Indigenismo* and the 'Revindication' of the Mexican Indian," *Journal of Latin American Studies* 30, no. 2 (May 1998): 282–88.

35. Ibid., 296.

36. Ibid., 294–95.

37. Ibid., 284.

38. El Pípila was removed from the state-issued textbooks following their revision in 1992, but by then he already occupied an indelible position in the popular collective memory. See Luz Elena Galván Lafarga, "Arquetipos, mitos, y representaciones en libros de historia patria (1934–1939)," in *Lecturas y lectores*, coord. Castañeda García, Galván Lafarga, and Martínez Moctezuma, 168.

39. Timothy J. Henderson, *The Mexican Wars for Independence* (New York: Hill and Wang, 2009).

40. "Discurso Pronunciado por el Jefe del Departamento de Salubridad Pública Dr. Y Gral José Siurob, en la Asamblea previa de la 2ª Conferencia Antialcohólica Infantil dedicado a la Niñez Mexicana," AGN, LCR 553/11, August 30, 1940.

41. "También Habrá Congreso de 'Niños Proletarios,'" *Excelsior*, February 5, 1935.

42. "Interesantes asuntos tratados en el Congreso de Niños Proletarios," *El Universal*, October 16, 1935.

43. "El sentido clasista del niño proletario," *El Nacional*, March 7, 1935.

44. Elena Jackson Albarrán, "Hacer Patria en Revolutionary Mexico," in "Children of the Revolution: Constructing the Mexican Citizen, 1920–1940" (PhD diss., University of Arizona, 2008).

45. John Mraz, *Looking for Mexico: Modern Visual Culture and National Identity* (Durham, NC: Duke University Press, 2009), 85.

46. "El Congreso del Niño Proletario," *El Nacional*, February 14, 1935.

47. Elsewhere, I analyze the productive outcomes of this conference, if not necessarily for the child delegates (who most likely were performing according to a carefully crafted script), but for their peers who watched from a distance as children assumed the national stage and whose contributions were valorized by adults. The First Proletarian Conference of the Child *did*, therefore, have a positive effect—however intangible—on the way that children were incorporated into civic life in meaningful ways. See Albarrán, *Seen and Heard*.

48. "No fracasarán los niños," *El Nacional*, March 9, 1935.

49. This auspicious affiliation notwithstanding, one of his biographers maintains that he remained humble his entire life, and died in poverty in 1966. Raúl Arreola Cortés, ed., *Jesús Sansón Flores*, Cuadernos de Lectura Popular, Serie: La Honda del Espíritu (México: Secretaría de Educación Pública, Subsecretaría de Asuntos Culturales, 1968), 40.

50. Among those who received their formation at the Colegio San Nicolás were historian and journalist Jesús García Tapia and playwright Luis Octavio Madero. Arreola Cortés, *Jesús Sansón Flores*, 9.

51. Tomás Rico Cano, ed., *El poeta Jesús Sansón Flores: Antología* (Morelia: Comité Editorial del Gobierno de Michoacán, 1985): 10–11.

52. From *La voz del campo*, excerpted in Arreola Cortés, *Jesús Sansón Flores*, 19.

53. Arreola Cortés, *Jesús Sansón Flores*, 7–8.

54. Ibid., 20–21.

55. For a discussion of the signifying power of clothing in the Revolutionary era, see Adriana Acevedo Rodrigo, "Las apariencias importan: indumentaria e hygiene personal como marcas de civilización y ciudadanía en la educación para campesinos e indígenas, México, ca. 1921–1943," in *Ciudadanos inesperados: Espacios de formación de la ciudadanía ayer y hoy*, ed. Ariadna Acevedo Rodrigo y Paula López Caballero (México: El Colegio de México; Centro de Investigación y de Estudios Avanzados, Departamento de Investigaciones Educativas, 2012): 131–66.

56. Sansón Flores, *El niño proletario*, 8.

57. Ann Blum, *Domestic Economies: Family, Work, and Welfare in Mexico City, 1884–1943* (Lincoln: University of Nebraska Press, 2009), 179.

58. A good example of the use of a stylized accent in cinema can be found in the Golden Age feature film *María Candelaria* (Mexico 1943) starring the actress Dolores del Río.

59. Sansón Flores, *El niño proletario*, 11.

60. Ibid., 16–17.

61. Ibid., 23.

62. Sosenski, *Niños en acción*, 150–55.

63. Alberto del Castillo Troncoso, *Conceptos, imágenes y representaciones de la niñez en la Ciudad de México, 1880–1920* (México: El Colegio de México/Instituto Mora, 2006): 226–27. This is also discussed in Elena Jackson Albarrán, "Reseña," *Estudios de Historia Moderna y Contemporánea de México* 33 (Jan.–June 2007): 123–29.

64. Sansón Flores, *El niño proletario*, 12.

65. Ibid., 19–20.

66. Pérez Montfort, *Estampas de nacionalismo*, 185.

67. Sansón Flores, *El niño proletario*, 9.

68. Adolfo Ornelas Hernández, *El Niño Rural* (México: n.p., 1939): 50.
69. Sansón Flores, *El niño proletario*, 14–15.
70. A *sexenio* is a six-year presidential term.
71. Archivo General de la Nación, LCR Caja 1335, 710.1/1336, 1936.
72. Arreola Cortés, *Jesús Sansón Flores*, 22.
73. Rico Cano, *El poeta Jesús Sansón Flores*, 19–20.
74. Jesús Sansón Flores, "Niños Muertos," *Bajo el Sol de España* (México, D.F.: Sociedad de Amigos de España, 1938), 34.
75. Dolores Plá Brugat, *Los niños de Morelia* (México: Instituto Nacional de Antropología e Historia, 1985).
76. I develop this argument more fully in "Tata Cárdenas and the Niños Españoles: A Case Study in the Construction of Mexican National Identity," article manuscript in progress.

World War II propelled Mexico into a new period of growth and globalization. Eschewing the move toward a socialist left in favor of more capitalist growth and rapid urbanization, the leaders of the PRI (Institutional Party of the Revolution) pushed the country toward industrialization. The economic gains accumulated swiftly, coming to be known as the Mexican Miracle, which would last until the 1970s and often come at the expense of rural peoples, or on the back of petroleum speculations. During these decades the newly urban populace adjusted to city living in time-honored fashions—such as drinking—but also with novel media experiences such as watching movies in what became known as the Golden Age of Cinema, a period during which the national government subsidized the cost of movie tickets, allowing vast numbers of citizens to escape their quotidian realities, even if only for a few hours. The Golden Age represented a period of torrid production of films ranging from rural genres such as *rancheras* to urban comedies that produced national icons such as Cantinflas and Tin Tan. These movies, and the styles of drinking and masculinity they promoted, are the focus for Áurea Toxqui's chapter that connects tequila songs in film to how ordinary people would act in the growing cities.

"¡Ay Jalisco, no te rajes!"*	**"Oh Jalisco, don't back down!"**
Y me gusta escuchar los mariachis,	And I love to listen to mariachi music,
cantar con el alma sus lindas canciones,	to sing soulfully their nice songs,
oir como suenan esos guitarrones	to hear how their guitars sound,
y echar un tequila con los valentones.	and to have a tequila shot with the toughies.

* Manuel Esperón and Ernesto Cortázar, "¡Ay Jalisco, no te rajes!" in *Cancionero Popular Mexicano*, ed. Mario Kuri-Aldana and Vicente Mendoza (México: Fondo de Cultura Económica, 1987), I: 364.

¡Ay, Jalisco no te rajes!
me sale del alma gritar con calor,
abrir todo el pecho pa' echar este grito:

Oh Jalisco, don't back down!
from my soul a heated cry emerges,
let's cry from the top of the lungs:

¡Qué lindo es Jalisco, palabra de honor!

How beautiful is Jalisco, word of honor!

Pa' mujeres, Jalisco primero,
lo mismo en Los Altos que allá en La Cañada,
mujeres muy lindas, rechulas de cara,
así son las hembras en Guadalajara.

In regards of women, Jalisco is at the top,
likewise in Los Altos than in La Cañada,
beautiful women, with pretty faces
are the women in Guadalajara.

¡Ay Jalisco, Jalisco, Jalisco!
tus hombres son machos y son cumplidores,
valientes, ariscos y sostenedores,
no admiten rivales en cosas de amores.

Oh Jalisco, Jalisco, Jalisco!
your men are manly and reliable,
brave, fierce, and keepers of their word,
in matters of love, they don't accept any rivals.

Su orgullo es su traje de charro,
traer su pistola, pasear en el pinto,
y con su guitarra echar mucho tipo,
y a los que presumen quitarles el hipo.

Their pride is [wearing] their charro suit,
carrying their gun, riding the dappled horse,
and showing off with their guitar,
and taking the breath away from those who boast.

Discussion Questions

1. How are the men and women of Jalisco portrayed in this song?
2. What are the symbols that the song's author associates with the people of Jalisco?
3. What does this song tell us about the role of alcohol in Jalisco society?

CHAPTER SEVEN

"That Mariachi Band and That Tequila"

Modernity, Identity, and Cultural Politics in Alcohol Songs of the Mexican Golden Age Cinema

Áurea Toxqui

From the late 1930s to the 1950s, Mexican cinema experienced its greatest era, known as the Golden Age. Many factors made possible the development of a truly national cinema at the time. For experts focusing on economics and politics, World War II was a catalyst. For those highlighting cultural and social reasons, the people involved in the movie industry were responsible for this blossoming. However, for the common Mexican and Latin American aficionado, the music, songs, and performers were the key element of the films produced. Many melodramas and comedy movies used popular music to emphasize their drama and romance, such as in the emerging genre of *ranchera* films.[1] These movies weaved together romantic comedy, popular music, and rural settings. They became one of the most well-liked and enduring genres from this era. Lyrics and performances of many songs included in these kinds of movies have left an imprint on Mexicans of several generations and become classic references in popular culture.

Through the analysis of songs performed in a handful of ranchera movies of the Golden Age of Mexican Cinema, this chapter explores the role of alcohol in the nationalist discourse and cultural values of post-Revolutionary Mexico. Drawing from insights on gender roles, cultural politics, the impact of mass media, and popular culture, the analysis of these songs provide examples of the contradictions of the so-called Mexican Miracle, the period of growth and modernization experienced during the 1940s and 1950s. Since the 1920s, government officials and intellectuals sought to build a modern nation by educating the people, mostly the middle classes and those below them, through mass media. With the growth of the film industry, cinema became the best national educational media, which also fostered a national consciousness. Yet the results did not always match those the cultural producers expected.

This chapter argues that ranchera movies of the Golden Age praised tequila and distilled beverages, patriarchal values, and proscribed, yet often elastic, gender roles as part of an idyllic mestizo past and national identity promoted by post-Revolutionary governments. In so doing, these movies contributed to the acceptance of tequila and other Mexican distilled beverages as clean, modern, manly beverages in contrast to *pulque*, a fermented beverage of indigenous origins consumed among the urban masses. Tequila producers took advantage of this situation to promote their own merchandise as a truly cosmopolitan Mexican beverage. According to these entrepreneurs, although other imported spirits and beer were produced and distributed in a modern fashion as their product, they were foreign beverages. Even then, some consumers preferred those nondomestic drinks. Ranchera movies and their romantic portrayal of tequila also delivered unintended messages such as entrenching the association of drunkenness and quarreling with manliness. This was not the only paradox that this genre involved. Through the exploitation of the anachronistic national types of dashing *charros* and svelte beauties, ranchera movies gained Mexico a place in the global film market. In a time of modernization and industrialization, these films promoted highly gendered, conservative, and alcohol-imbibing national types rooted in an idyllic, but stereotypical and regional past. These paradoxes mirrored the contradictions that marked the governing regimes emerging after 1940. These governments sometimes adopted policies, in the name of the Revolution, that reversed the achievements of their predecessors as they reinstated centralization and fostered corruption, practices that the Revolution had fought to eradicate. While the country in general experienced industrialization and transformation, the poor got trapped in unemployment and poverty, and continued traditional practices and pastimes. Despite the promotion of tequila, champagne, cognac, and beer in the media, pulque remained as an element of social cohesion that provided one way that the working classes coped with the Mexican Miracle and its consequences in their lives.

The Golden Age Cinema, the Mexican Miracle, and the *Hispanista* Discourse

In the late 1930s a series of factors and individuals came together, favoring the emergence of a national cinema that transcended borders and decades. During World War II, Hollywood producers dedicated their efforts to making war propaganda films. Mexican filmmakers took advantage of this gap in the market and, responding to Mexican society's distance from the war, focused on producing nonmilitary commercial movies.[2] Transnational relations, and especially U.S.-Mexican collaboration during and after World War II, played a pivotal role in the rise of Mexico's cinematic industry. With the help of U.S. officials interested in keeping an ally through Spanish-language cinema, Mexican studios renovated and improved their quality, and also received from their allies a significant quantity of film stock.[3] After the war, Hollywood began its recovery, but Mexican movies continued enjoying the popularity they had earned among Latin Americans and Spanish-speakers in the United States, even if some citizens remained leery of U.S. interests and influence.

Golden Age cinema also benefitted from the work of exceptional individuals. Among them, there came a new generation of directors who had made themselves famous in Mexico or had returned during the Great Depression after working in Hollywood. These directors surrounded themselves with visual artists, photographers, sound engineers, musicians, and screenwriters, many of whom had studied abroad. Together, they enhanced some of the existing film genres and facilitated the emergence of new ones.[4] Their collaborative efforts contributed to the production of successful movies for Mexico and other markets. This could not have been possible without the work of talented and versatile actors who excelled in comedy or drama, musical or action, melodrama or horror. These actors delivered performances that remain classics today. Their dialogues, expressions, and songs have become not only part of Mexico's popular culture, but also a testament to the modernization and social changes the country was experiencing during those years.

From the 1940s through the 1960s, Mexico experienced significant growth as the result of Import Substitution Industrialization (ISI) policies. Protectionist quotas and tariffs, among other strong government supports in the 1950s, continued to build on the incipient industry that had emerged during World War II, which capitalized on the decreased flow of imports from the United States. The implementation of ISI policies and the development of commercial agriculture specializing in basic grains, luxury crops (such as avocados and tomatoes), as well as livestock feed, created a perception of a prosperous Mexico among politicians, industry owners, and large agricultural producers. The Gross Domestic Product expanded from 21.7 billion pesos to 74.3 billion pesos, experiencing an average annual increase of 6.4 percent.[5] Alongside the economic development came a baby boom, which resulted in Mexico having one of the most rapidly increasing populations in the world. By the 1960s, the country had managed to maintain a constant level of growth of 3.3 percent per year, per capita.

The politics and policies that led to this period of industrialization and economic progress represented a clear shift from previous post-Revolutionary regimes. Many groups understood this as a betrayal of the Revolution and its social agenda. The governments of the 1940s moved away from broad populism, socialist education, radical anticlericalism, and an *indigenista* (indigenous-based) discourse, toward a more conservative, capitalist, mestizo-oriented approach to politics.[6] In fact, in his inauguration, President Manuel Ávila Camacho (1940–1946) declared: "I am a believer," implying "I am a Catholic." His term and that of his successor, President Miguel Alemán (1946–1952), strengthened their alliance with the entrepreneurial groups in order to further industrialization.[7] They also emphasized an intense desire to promote social citizenship, in which all Mexicans, rural or urban, identified with a shared past and a sense of belonging. This, along with the formation of a highly masculine image of the nation-state, became some of the efforts of the one-party state to create the "Revolutionary Family."

The leaders of the Partido Nacional Revolucionario,[8] founded in 1929, focused on constructing this discourse of national belonging under a unifying and virile patriarchy presided over by the president and his party. To do so, they promoted a highly masculine image of the nation-state and national identity.[9] By the 1940s, they consolidated a sense of national unity through their increasing power and centralization, and by taking credit for the economic development the nation experienced. In this discourse of modernization, the nation required a mestizo past, heir of the Indians and the Spaniards, provided that the European side ultimately prevailed. Since the 1920s such an ideology had emerged as a result of an alliance between conservative landowning groups opposed to social and land reforms and Catholic peasants resentful of anticlerical government support for socialist education.[10] In the late 1930s, intellectuals and politicians found in the culture of Jalisco, particularly that of Los Altos (The Highlands), a region in the isolated northeast part of the state with a cool microclimate that reproduced agricultural conditions of Europe, the archetype of an ideal Mexican that the nation needed.

Mexican film directors, in an attempt to represent the elusive concept of *lo mexicano*, often made reference to a variety of racialized ideologies that sought to define the nation after the Revolution. Of these at times competing ideologies, *Hispanismo* emerged as a common genre in the works of movie makers. According to proponents of Hispanismo, the ideology favoring Spanish heritage over the indigenous and promoted by an alliance of landowners and Catholics, the Alteños (Los Altos people) embodied the "living, untainted repository of Spanish racial genes and cultural memes."[11] Alteños were taller and lighter in complexion than their fellow men from central and southern Mexico. They had attractive faces, almond-shaped large light brown eyes, and aesthetically pleasing corporal features in general. Alteños were able to preserve their European phenotype due to several factors. In the colonial period, the native groups in the region were almost eradicated as a consequence of their conquest during the Mixtón War (1540–1542) and subsequent epidemics.[12] The native depopulation continued when the discovery of rich mineral deposits in the area encouraged Spanish pioneers, among them convert Sephardic Jews, to migrate and work in the mines as well as in agriculture throughout the sixteenth century.[13] Culturally speaking, they were small-property owners who worked their own land, and as such, they had excellent horsemanship, wore boots, spurs, and suede leather outfits, and carried a knife most of the time.[14] They were also devoted Catholics, practiced endogamy, and ruled their lives by the values of Iberian culture, in which honor was based on family, purity of blood, and property.[15] It was common in the area to hear the following verse:

Vamos para Los Altos	Let's go to the Highlands
donde son buenos cristianos,	where people are good Christians,
y por no perder la sangre,	and to avoid losing their pure blood,
se casan primos hermanos.[16]	they married their first cousins.

In the 1920s and 1930s, Alteños supported movements in defense of the rights of the individual to private property and religious freedoms, and opposed the government's anticlerical and socialist policies. They participated in the Cristero Rebellion of 1926–1929, the creation of the right-wing Partido Acción Nacional in 1939, and the Sinarquista movement of the 1940s.[17] They embodied the traditional and religious individualists who had previously challenged the regime. But now in the eyes of Hispanismo proponents, Alteños became carriers of pure or uncorrupted essence, who proved able to preserve their ethnicity and cultural practices due to their steadfast refusal to racially mix with the neighboring indigenous populations. Therefore, Hispanismo followers created the myth of Alteño men and women as the ideal Mexican, almost criollo, free of backward influences in looks and attitudes, yet stalwart in traditional values.

According to Hispanismo, the Alteño culture provided a sense of an idyllic past, an allegedly shared mestizo identity, and a political stability rooted in tradition and patriarchy—all of these were pivotal values at the heart of the "Revolutionary Family." In the Alteño mythology, women embodied beauty and devotion, while men personified manliness and patriarchal values. The proponents perceived Alteñas as the most beautiful Mexican ladies, and recognized them for their piety and religious devotion. Several songs praising Los Altos and Jalisco in general made reference to them, such as "Esos Altos" ("Those Highlands") (1942):

¡Ay! Los Altos de Jalisco,
esa tierra, tierra linda,
puritito corazón,
tierra linda,
tierra de hombres,
toda mi alma, tierra mía
yo te doy en mi canción.
Las mujeres de mi tierra,
¡qué mujeres!,
Si por algo Dios dispuso,
que nacieran por aquí,
y les dio como permiso
ser bonitas como flores
pa'que de ellas escogiera
la más linda para mi.[18]

Oh! Those Highlands of Jalisco,
that land, beautiful land,
honest truth,
beautiful land,
land of men,
my homeland, my entire soul
I give you in my song.
The women of my homeland,
such beauties!,
It is not for nothing that God decided
they would be born here,
and allowed them
to be as pretty as the flowers
so I could choose from among them
the prettiest for me.

On their side, Alteño men in these songs were admired because of their manliness. They were daring and skilled men who rode horses and knew how to successfully manage a hacienda (large rural estate) or a rancho (small rural property). Their devotion to women, and their readiness to defend their property and their family, defined them. They were able to afford expensive charro suits, characterized by the elaborate silver embroidery work in the suit itself and in the wide-brimmed hat. An important component of their manhood lay in their sexual capacities, projected by the tightness of their pants, as well as the innuendo included in the reference to their reliability, their guns, and the fact that these men never back off. Their manliness also resided in their quick wit, gambling skills, mostly in cards and cockfights, their talent for mariachi music, their alcohol tolerance, particularly for tequila, as two popular ranchera songs—"¡Ay Jalisco, no te rajes!" ("Oh Jalisco, don't back down") (1941) and "Cocula" (1942)—praise:

Y me gusta escuchar los mariachis,	And I love to listen to the mariachis,
cantar con el alma sus lindas canciones,	to sing soulfully their nice songs,
oir como suenan esos guitarrones	to hear how their guitars sound
y echar un tequila con los valentones	and to have a tequila shot with the toughies
¡Ay, Jalisco no te rajes!	Oh Jalisco, don't back down!
me sale del alma gritar con calor,	From my soul a heated cry emerges,
abrir todo el pecho pa' echar este grito:	let's cry from the top of the lungs:
¡Qué lindo es Jalisco, palabra de honor!	How beautiful is Jalisco, word of honor!
Pa' mujeres, Jalisco primero,	As for women, Jalisco is at the top,
lo mismo en Los Altos que allá en La Cañada,	likewise in the Highlands or in the Valley,
mujeres muy lindas, rechulas de cara,	beautiful women, with pretty faces,
así son las hembras en Guadalajara.	are the women in Guadalajara.
¡Ay Jalisco, Jalisco, Jalisco!,	Oh Jalisco, Jalisco, Jalisco!,
tus hombres son machos y son cumplidores,	your men are manly and reliable,
valientes, ariscos y sostenedores,	brave, fierce, keepers of their word,
no admiten rivales en cosas de amores.	In matters of love, they don't accept any rivals.
Su orgullo es su traje de charro,	Their pride is [in wearing] their charro suit,
traer su pistola, pasear en el pinto,	carrying their gun, riding the dappled horse,

y con su guitarra echar mucho tipo,
y a los que presumen quitarles el hipo.[19]

and showing off with their guitar,
and taking the breath away from those who boast.

Although "Cocula" puts forward a similar theme, it also emphasizes a masculinity that encompasses different forms of violence that play a counterpart to sexual innuendo as well as the religious and musical sensibility praised in "¡Ay Jalisco no te rajes!" "Cocula," instead of praising women for their beauty, condemns them to punishment for their evil actions, such as breaking a man's heart:

De esta tierra de Cocula
que es el alma del mariachi
vengo yo con mi cantar,
voy camino a Aguascalientes
a la feria de San Marcos
a ver lo que puedo hallar.

From the land of Cocula
which is the soul of the mariachi music
I come with my song,
I'm on my way to Aguascalientes
to Saint Mark's fair
let's see what I can find.

Traigo un gallo muy jugado
para echarlo de tapado[20]
con algún apostador,
y también traigo pistola
por si alguno busca bola
y me tilda de hablador.

I bring with me an experienced rooster
to have a clean cockfight
with someone willing to place bets,
I also bring my gun
just in case someone wants to brawl
and calls me braggart.

De Cocula es el mariachi
de Tecalitlán los sones
de San Pedro su cantar
de Tequila su mezcal[21]
y los machos de Jalisco
afamados por entrones
para eso traen pantalones.

From Cocula comes the mariachi band
from Tecalitlán the music
from San Pedro its songs
from Tequila its mezcal
and from Jalisco its manly men
famous 'cause they dare
that's why they wear the pants.

Ando en busca de una ingrata
de una joven presumida
que se fue con mi querer.

I'm seeking an ungrateful,
arrogant young woman,
who ran away with my heart.

Traigo ganas de encontrarla	I want to find her
pa' enseñarle que de un hombre	to teach her the lesson that
no se burla una mujer.[22]	no woman can ever outsmart a man.

Both songs point out the basic elements of the Alteños' mythical reputation, which became the inspiration for several ranchera films. No matter the plot of the movie, romantic countryside comedies always included the same formula: mariachi music, nice songs, strong tequila, daring men, beautiful women, and spotless honor.

The romantic images of the *china*[23] and the charro, promoted as the national types since the nineteenth century, were already well inscribed in the common imaginary as Elena Albarrán mentions in chapter 6 of this anthology.[24] These types together with *tehuanas*, bullfighters, and musicians in charro suits had transcended borders and were already exploited commercially as the folkloric representation of lo mexicano (the Mexican character) since the Porfiriato.[25] By the mid-1930s, the Mexican film industry had attempted for two decades to overcome the success of foreign movies presenting Mexicans as singer charros, chinas with large mantillas, and men wearing wide-brim hats with tassels. Mexican filmmakers and intellectuals perceived this as a derogatory representation of the Mexican identity.[26] However, in 1936, intending to recover financially from some unsuccessful but highly artistic movies, Mexican filmmaker Fernando de Fuentes produced *Allá en el Rancho Grande* (*Out on the Great Ranch*) using those popular stereotypes and parodying a classic Spanish drama.[27] The movie got international attention, such as the award for best cinematography at the Venice Film Festival, and became a hit in the United States among Spanish-speaking and non-Spanish-speaking audiences. This achievement led other producers to follow de Fuentes's steps. In 1941, Joselito Rodríguez produced *¡Ay Jalisco, no te rajes!*, and the success of this movie consolidated this trend. Thus, filmmakers adopted the idyllic and anachronistic image of the pre-Revolutionary, landowning, dashing, and macho charro, and his svelte, pretty, submissive, and light-skinned female counterpart for their ranchera comedies.[28] In their search for profitable productions and international distribution, filmmakers adopted characters that would represent the nation in a masculine and dignified manner rather than the gullible and folksy singing charro in Hollywood movies.[29] Thus, Mexican cinema and its producers contributed to the formation of the post-Revolutionary national identity as well as its conservative, hypermasculine discourse and patriarchal ideology.[30]

The international popularization of ranchera movies and their Alteño characters was made possible by friendly U.S.-Mexican relations during World War II that provided the setting for Mexico's film industry to thrive. Mexican moviemakers took advantage of the newfound cooperation between both nations to develop films that were commercially successful inside and outside the country. The interplay between transnational forces and an idealized regional identity from Jalisco allowed for the development of a distinctly national character that embodied what cultural producers and government officials sought to promote as a metonym of the entire post-Revolutionary nation. Paradoxically, these characters were depicted living in a countryside that had not experienced the Revolution.[31] They both emerged as the icons representing national identity to both Mexican and foreign viewers of Golden Age cinema as well as the product of the intersection of global and local forces. These characters, considered archetypes of what is truly lo mexicano, as Seth Fein notes, had transnational origins that emerged as a result of strategic U.S. needs during World War II as well as the needs of the propaganda industry, which sought closer relations with Latin America.[32] Yet, as demonstrated, these transitional forces articulated themselves within a distinctly local identity that met the needs of Mexican cultural producers and government officials and that corresponded to a specific political and historical context of the Revolution's conservative turn.

The Ranchera Songs of the Golden Age and Their Interpreters

Since the early 1930s, filmmakers had discovered that the inclusion of popular music in their movies, whatever their genre, proved crucial to success in the theater. In fact, the addition of sound to films made possible the production of the first movies with genuinely Mexican characteristics. Interpretation, rhythm, and emphasis in the music altered the meanings of dialogues and scenes in a similar way that images included in printed songs and poems did. In contrast to corridos and poems, which were often anonymous, undated, and under- or unpublished, as several authors in this volume point out, ranchera songs were custom-made to serve as soundtracks. Directors and producers commissioned musicians to write songs praising Alteño and Jalisco culture, in order to guarantee the success of their ranchera movie. Among those composers stood out Manuel Esperón, Ernesto Cortázar, and Lorenzo Barcelata, who created numerous soundtracks for films of the Golden Age.[33] Esperón was the first composer who included mariachi music in a movie. He even taught mariachi musicians to read music in order to play in conjunction with an orchestra in his instrumental arrangements.[34] Together with Cortázar, Esperón composed the lyrics and music of many songs that became classics such as "Esos Altos," "Cocula," and "¡Ay Jalisco, no te rajes!" At times, those commissioned songs named the movies, for example, with *Allá en el Rancho Grande*, *¡Ay Jalisco, no te rajes!*, *El gavilán pollero*, *Así se quiere en Jalisco*, and *Me he de comer esa tuna*, to mention just a few.

Despite the fact that the songs analyzed in this chapter were commissioned to be in included in movies, they offer many insights into popular culture and its role in the formation of national identity. While filmmakers and composers evidently made a profit by exploiting the Alteño mythology, they contributed to spreading the idea of a shared past.[35] Even in small and remote villages, their films were shown, allowing people to participate in the building of an imagined community on a broader scale than ever before.[36] In this process, radio had already contributed by reaching almost every region of the country.[37] Although it is almost impossible to uncover how each member of the audience experienced the music and message of ranchera songs, the broad acceptance of the films and performers made evident the fact that the lyrics of these songs resonated with the values and beliefs of their audience. The constant playing of these songs in the radio and live performances, in the city as well as in the countryside, suggests that their lyrics crossed class boundaries and provided a unifying medium to identify Mexicans with a common past. Audiences did not share the same economic means, past, or regional tradition. They did not gather at the same time or same movie theater, concert hall, or radio, but these songs created moments of shared reflection about gender roles, regionalism, racial identity, family values, and national identity.

But the music and songs themselves could not ensure a commercial hit unless they also featured the performance of actors and actresses that visually fit the Alteño mythology. Thus, they cast only light-skinned, good-looking, slim actors and actresses for the leading roles in these movies.[38] Filmmakers found in Jorge Negrete, a major star of the Golden Age cinema, the perfect embodiment of Hispanismo ideals and Alteño masculinity because of his dashing and commanding presence, great singing voice, and horse-riding skills. He mostly performed roles of a daring, fair, and proper man, who defended the values of the patriarchal and idyllic rural society against the abuses of tyrants.[39] He got the nickname of "the Singing Cowboy" because of his interpretation of ranchera songs and his elegant donning of the charro attire. In 1941, Negrete interpreted "¡Ay Jalisco, no te rajes!" in the movie of the same name, in which he played the lead.[40] A year later, he had starred in *El peñón de las ánimas* (*The Rock of Souls*),

Figure 7.1. "Jorge Negrete singing in a cockfight pit," Mayo Brothers, ca. 1945. Courtesy of Archivo General de la Nación, Archivo Fotográfico de los Hermanos Mayo, Sección Alfabético Artistas.

in which he sang "Cocula."[41] Both songs soon became hits and were associated with the iconic culture of Jalisco state, particularly the region of Los Altos. This became evident when eighteen years later, in 1960, Luis Aguilar, another star of the Golden Age, played the role of Miguel, a brave and witty Jalisco man in the popular movie *De tal palo tal astilla* (*A Chip Off the Old Block*).[42] As testimony to his Jalisco heritage, he wore a charro suit, sang several songs making reference to the Alteño culture, including the two aforementioned songs, and drank heavily, particularly tequila.

Tequila and Lo Mexicano

Filmmakers, composers, and vaudeville sketch writers, among others, capitalized on the macho stereotype of Jalisco and Alteño men, which greatly attracted audiences with the censorship approval of the Catholic Church.[43] Songs such as "Tequila con limón" (Tequila and lime, 1944), commissioned to be included in movies, made evident this capitalization. The lyrics and their popularity in radio and popular theater, vastly exemplify different levels of intersections, such as mass media, popular culture, regional and national identities, popular religiosity, and the cultural politics of the post-Revolutionary state as well as the interest of Mexican entrepreneurs in competing in the global entertainment industry.[44] This song, interpreted by Jorge Negrete in the 1944 movie *Me he de comer esa tuna* (*I'll Have to Eat That Prickly Pear*), praises the virile traits of Alteños. The first stanza introduces Jalisco men as rancheros, who work the fields with machetes, and get blisters and cuts while plowing. As hard-working countryside men, they fulfill the expectations of their gender as breadwinners. These activities fit well with the idyllic mestizo past and identity that Hispanismo followers proposed:

Traigo música en el alma,
y un cantar aquí en el pecho;
un cantar que me desgarra
cuando lo hecho con amor;
lo aprendí por esos campos,
con heridas de barbecho;
con tajadas de machetes
y vibrar de guitarrón.

I have music in my soul
and a song here in my heart;
a song that leaves me shattered
when I release it with love;
I learned it in those fields,
with wounds made while plowing;
with cuts made with machetes
and the trembling of the guitar.

The next stanzas praise their popular religiosity, virility, and fierceness through different skills in their leisure time, such as in horse racing, horsemanship, bullfights, and cockfights.[45] Even if they lose a race or a match, they are ready to recover their money at the gambling table:

Lo aprendí por el palenque,
apostando a un gallo fino,
y me siento suficiente
pa' cantarlo por aquí.
Al orgullo de Jalisco,
lo nombraron mi padrino,
y no tiene mas ahijados,
porque ya me tiene a mi.

I learned it at the cockfight,
placing bets on a fine rooster,
and I feel I am good enough
to sing it around here.
Jalisco's pride
was appointed as my godparent,
and it has no other godchildren,
because it already has one in me.

A las patas de un caballo,
juego siempre mi dinero;

On the legs of a horse,
I place my bets;

y si algunas veces fallo,	and when I sometimes lose,
me desquito en un albur.	I even up the score by gambling.

The song also celebrates Alteño men's quick wit to face any challenge in life, such as uncovering cheaters while gambling, and knowing how to cheat as well. It also acclaims, as a trait of their race, their quarrelsome nature and readiness to shoot their guns or come to blows:

Sangre brava y colorada,	Brave and red,
retadora como filo de puñal,	challenging as a knife's blade,
es la sangre de mi raza,	is the blood of my race,
soñadora y cancionera,	it is a dreamer and singer,
sangre brava y peleonera,	brave and troublemaker
valentona y pendenciera	valiant and quarrelsome blood
como penca de nopal.	just like the cactus stalk.

This *machista* behavior is counteracted by the sensibility that also characterizes Alteño men:

Pa' gritar "¡viva Jalisco!"	Cry aloud "Long live Jalisco!"
Con el alma y corazón.	With the soul and heart.
Que bonito y que bonito	It is too nice, too nice
El llegar a un merendero	To arrive at the saloon
Y beber en un jarrito	And drink in a little clay jug
Un tequila con limón.[46]	A shot of tequila with lime.

Despite the fact that tequila is mentioned only at the end of the song, it is clear that it is the beverage of choice for brave men.

Tequila, mariachi music, and manly charros became a representative trilogy of the fluid concept of *mexicanidad*, the sense of Mexican identity. As such, they became included in the national pantheon of icons, which included a mix of symbols of American and European origins, just as Hispanismo followers envisioned. For post-Revolutionary Mexico, this pantheon included other widespread accepted virile representations such as cacti, machetes, guns, gambling, horse riding, cockfights, and Revolutionary armies.

Tequila's manly overtones represented one of many other characteristics that made Hispanismo followers see the beverage as a suitable replacement for pulque. The latter with its viscous consistency, foul smell, and its unhygienic and traditional method of production could not compare with tequila's clarity, strong but pleasant smell, and clean semi-industrial process.

Since pre-Hispanic times, the process of making pulque has remained the same.[47] It is obtained by fermenting the sap of the *maguey pulquero*, a member of the agave family. This species grows only in cold and arid highlands, reproduces through vegetative process, and requires little labor. The maguey takes between ten to twelve years to reach its maturity. At that time, *tlachiqueros* (men who harvest the maguey sap) make some incisions in the plant and remove the flower bud to facilitate the extraction of the liquid. Tlachiqueros collect the sap in a rudimentary and not very hygienic process that involves skills and strength. After harvesting several plants, they transport the sap to the *tinacal*, the dark room where pulque is produced. They leave the sap to ferment in large tanks. Due to the levels of sugar, bacilli, and bacteria contained in sap, it naturally ferments in less than twenty-four hours. To accelerate fermentation, producers mix fresh sap with pulque seasoned with some roots and barks. After two or three days, the product must be shipped to the consumer centers promptly before it spoils, because there is no natural procedure to stop fermentation. Like any other fermented beverage, within days, pulque acquires a viscous consistency, a rotten odor, and a peculiar taste. Nowadays it is shipped in wooden barrels or fiberglass containers, but in the 1940s it was shipped in pigskin sacks.

Although tequila is produced from another member of the agave family, the blue agave, which requires a similar process of planting, pruning, and harvesting as the maguey, the method of production, consistency, taste, alcohol content, and smell differ greatly. As any other distilled beverage made of the agave family, it is a mezcal, but receives its name from the region where most of it is produced, Tequila, Jalisco. The blue agave grows in semiarid and oxide-rich highlands.[48] After seven to ten years it reaches maturity. Then, a *jimador* (agave harvester) prunes the leaves leaving the trunk naked. This core is called *piña* because of its resemblance to a pineapple and it has a lot of natural sugars. The piña is left in the groves to allow the sugars to mature. After a while, it is removed and taken to the distillery to begin the production of tequila. Piñas are washed to remove impurities and steamed in stainless-steel autoclaves; however, in the artisanal method, they are baked in brick ovens. The cooked piñas are shredded mechanically or ground with a rustic *tahona* (a giant stone wheel pulled by a horse or an ox) to extract their juices. The juices are then put into huge vats and mixed with water and yeast to promote fermentation. This takes two to twelve days, depending on the method, industrial or artisanal. Once the fermented juice settles, it is distilled twice. After that it is bottled and labeled or aged for months or years. Distillation not only eliminates impurities, and any possible foul odor, but also increases the alcohol levels and gives a clear liquid consistency to the beverage. While pulque has an alcohol content of only between 3 and 6 percent, tequila can reach 38 to 40 percent. All these characteristics made tequila the perfect beverage to counter pulque as an icon of national identity.

Alcohol had an important place in the collaborative efforts of government and society in the construction of lo mexicano, since the nineteenth century. After the Revolution, rulers promoted a unifying national identity, intending to heal the divisions that the war caused. In the late 1920s and early 1930s, the indigenista ideology dominated these efforts by emphasizing the country's native past, while praising the folkloric aspects of indigenous peoples' aesthetics and traditions. Filmmakers, muralists, and poets, among others, celebrated pulque, *tepache* (made with pineapple skin), and *teshuino* (made with corn), as well as the drinking culture more generally, as authentic representations of mexicanidad.[49] Rulers had a different perspective, though. In their attempt to modernize and sober the population, politicians launched and supported antialcohol campaigns intending to eradicate drunkenness and the consumption of native beverages that contributed to the perceived backward conditions of indigenous groups.[50] Pulque became a special target because of the spread of its consumption throughout the Central Plateau and its reputation. Since the colonial period, the beverage had been associated with Indians, who were perceived as drunken, slothful, smelly, lazy, and dangerous individuals. Beyond that, during the years of Revolutionary warfare, the shortage on grain and raw sugar led producers of fermented beverages to resort to chemical substances that were highly unhealthy. Presidents Álvaro Obregón, Plutarco Elías Calles, and Lázaro Cárdenas (1920–1940) preferred that the national drink suggest the modern and clean nation they aspired to create. They thus opted to support beer to reflect their progressive, industrial, and sanitizing aspirations, despite its foreign origins.[51] Mexican breweries took advantage of these efforts and launched marketing campaigns intending to take over the lucrative alcohol market in the country. Beer producers blamed pulque for the population's degeneration and natives' weaknesses because of its unhygienic and stupefying qualities. Breweries capitalized on the widespread myth that *pulqueros* (pulque producers) fermented their product with unhealthy substances such as human feces. Sadly, pulqueros, in their intent to discredit each other's pulque, created misconceptions like these, which still affect the reputation of the beverage in the twenty-first century. Paradoxically, brewers, while praising their product, stressed its shared qualities such as its low alcohol content and its health benefits. They marketed beer as a "family friendly, rigorously hygienic and modern drink that promoted health as a diuretic, stimulated circulation of blood, cleansed the kidneys, and was ideal for lactating women."[52]

Tequila: A Cosmopolitan Beverage, a Countryside Icon

Tequila producers had made several attempts in promoting their product as a national spirit since the late nineteenth century, but they had to wait until the height of Hispanismo and its influence on the Golden Age, as well as the advent of the Mexican Miracle and its modernizing attitudes, to see their product vindicated. In the 1920s, tequila makers saw the Revolutionary policies as an opportunity to advance their product in the national market. Despite their efforts in emphasizing the modern, industrial, clean, and nonindigenous, yet truly and authentically Mexican, nature of their product, they did not succeed in uplifting tequila's reputation. Politicians and the middle and upper classes generally associated the beverage with the hordes of rough men who fought in the Revolution. Mariano Azuela, in his novel *Los de Abajo*, depicted Revolutionary armies as bunches of dirty, hot-blooded, anarchic, coarse, and ragged individuals who had a preference for tequila.[53] In consequence, the drink got the connotation of "a disgusting, lower class, violence-inducing beverage."[54] But by the 1940s, the government worked to cleanse and whiten the image of popular Revolutionary armies and heroes in order to include them in the national pantheon of icons. The dirty, ragged, short, dark-complected peasants that appeared in many pictures of revolutionary armies, now were depicted in murals and other visual manifestations as clean, lighter skinned, virile, and tall countrymen riding horses and wearing charro suits, who recovered their manhood fighting in the Revolution.[55] Thus, in conjunction with the help of Hispanismo discourse and the Golden Age, tequila producers saw their expectations coming true. ISI policies and economic growth required cultural narratives emphasizing modernity and industrialization. Tequila, with its clear consistency and technological manufacturing process, provided a suitable image for a national beverage in post-war Mexico. Despite being made of an indigenous plant, the agave, it was cleared and refined through distillation; a technique introduced by the Spaniards since the early colonial times. It was also modern enough to compete with other cosmopolitan drinks, and was achieving domestic and international popularity through mass media.

The Sauza family, makers of Tequila Sauza, played an important role in promoting the idea of their product as an example of the modern, non-Indian, post-Revolutionary Mexico. Particularly, Francisco Javier Sauza, third-generation owner, worked diligently to spread the idea that tequila was: "refined liquor equal to the best and most cultured spirits of the world."[56] He was confident that tequila's qualities would earn international respect for Mexicans and for Mexico as a modern nation. He used the mass media, mostly radio and then television, to promote these ideas and advertise his product. Sauza and his advertising agent, the Spaniard Eulalio Ferrer, used the popular images of an idyllic life, horse-riding charros, and light-skinned men and women to launch a series of successful national and international marketing campaigns. Still, tequila faced strong competition from beer, with its aura as a clean, modern, low-alcohol, and inexpensive drink, as well as the power of the breweries union and their efficient distribution strategies.[57] However, tequila had the advantage of a strong presence in ranchera movies, radio, and popular theater. Sauza's sponsored program *Noches Tapatías* (*Nights of Guadalajara*)[58] provides an example of the popularity of the Alteño mythology throughout the country as a consequence of the Golden Age cinema. *Noches Tapatías* began in 1952 as a radio program. In 1956, it became a popular weekly television show that remained on the air until 1980. Almost every ranchera music star appeared on the show at some point. Between segments there were Sauza advertisements promoting tequila as part of the national, but non-Indian, identity.[59] The broadcast of *Noches Tapatías* for many decades proved the success of the Hispanismo discourse, the Alteño mythology, and their influence in popular culture as part of the cultural, economic, and political policies of post-Revolutionary governments, particularly those of the Mexican Miracle.

The Mexican tourism industry also took advantage of the international image of tequila as part of "lo mexicano." Tourists were encouraged to enjoy the Mexican experience by visiting the Tenampa.[60] This was the most popular cantina and place to listen to mariachi music, drink tequila, and taste the mildly spicy Jalisco food, another example of its nonindigenous heritage, in Mexico City in the 1940s and 50s. In the early 1920s, Juan Hernández, a native of Cocula, Jalisco, opened in the Garibaldi Square a small restaurant offering food from his hometown.[61] Among the main dishes served there were birria (goat stew), pozole (chicken or pork and corn stew), and *tortas ahogadas*, literally translated as "drowned sandwiches" (pork in a spicy au jus served on a French baguette). People washed down their food with the specialty of the house, *ponche* (punch), a tequila concoction flavored either with *arrallán* (*Alibertia edulis*) or pomegranate. This drink was traditional in Jalisco and its neighboring state, Colima. Very soon, these cocktails became highly popular and the place became a saloon. To entertain customers, Hernández hired mariachi bands from his hometown. When he died, his widow Amalia Díaz Ochoa took charge of the establishment, which saw its heyday in the 1940s. Connoisseurs perceived these years as the Golden Decade of mariachi music in Garibaldi Square, the hub of mariachi bands. The Tenampa became a piece of Jalisco in Mexico City. The success of this place resided in bringing together local cuisine, drinks, and music in a way that would become iconic for many visitors looking for the "real Mexican experience."

Tequila also met the political requirements of the era. By the 1960s, a new political need emerged to reconcile northern Mexico with central Mexico, tying the industrial border with the rest of the nation. In this context, films such as *De tal palo tal astilla,* previously mentioned, proved invaluable. The film connects the ideals of two discourses on manliness and toughness: one proposed by the culture of northern Mexico influenced by the U.S.-Mexico border, and the other influenced by the culture of central Mexico represented by Jalisco. The directors portrayed northern Mexico as a wild land, where bandits did as they pleased and only the most courageous men might stop them. Gumaro was one of the main characters representing the northern man, who with his dirty tricks and toughness tries to keep other bandits at bay. The mayor, tired of Gumaro's erratic behavior, decides to hire a "brave man." So he goes to Jalisco, "land of the real macho men," to hire a new sheriff, seeking someone brave enough to face Gumaro and the other bandits of the region. The mayor hires Miguel, an Alteño. When Gumaro and Miguel meet for the first time, they engage in a drinking competition trying to prove their manliness by showing their high tolerance to alcohol. Both start drinking double and triple shots, and end up drinking entire bottles. While Gumaro drinks *sotol,* a distilled beverage distinctive of Chihuahua and Coahuila border states, Miguel is a tequila drinker. Neither of them gives up in the competition and ultimately they become great friends, bonding in mutual respect and alcohol. They join efforts and eradicate banditry in the region. With this resolution, the filmmakers delivered a message that fit political needs by highlighting unity across the nation predicated on shared drinking, and further strengthened a national discourse on an ideal masculinity.

Tequila and its portrayal in the media reflected not only the cultural politics and values of the Mexican Miracle, but also its contradictions. The national discourse of this period represented a fluid combination of modernity and tradition. It emphasized industrialization, hygiene, and urbanization, as well as a shared mestizo past, idyllic roots, and overemphasized gender roles. While urban working classes, influenced by this discourse and politics disseminated through media, adopted tequila as a sign of manliness and Mexican-ness, they also adopted other traits portrayed in ranchera movies and songs that were not necessarily what the government, commercial, and media elites expected. Moreover, while the government had promoted campaigns to curb alcohol consumption, especially of traditional libations, Golden Age films showed audiences that tequila consumption could be appropriate in specific contexts and for specific individuals.

Borrachos, Dolidos, Pero Machos: Drunk, Hurt, but Manly

Pedro Infante, another great star of the Golden Age cinema, gained popularity playing charro roles, but his characters depicted an Alteño who proves his manliness by womanizing, gambling, and drinking. In contrast to Negrete's rare drunkenness, Infante's portrayals of a heartbroken charro

Figure 7.2. "Pedro Infante in *El gavilán pollero,*" Gabriel Figueroa, 1950. Courtesy of Museo del Estanquillo, Colección Carlos Monsiváis.

who drowns his sorrows in alcohol have remained an iconic reference in popular culture (see figure 7.2). In these scenes, he sings and drinks, intending to cast the woman who broke his heart into oblivion. He gets drunk in the cantina surrounded by a mariachi band, other friends, or other women, but never in front of his love interest. Sometimes he becomes so inebriated that he starts crying. Even when this might be interpreted as weakness because it seemingly undermines his male pride in a macho culture, it at the same time represented the Alteño devotion to women. In ranchera movies, these actions portrayed an almost cathartic ritual in which the despairing man reveres the woman who betrayed or hurt him. In the 1950 film *El gavilán pollero* (*Chicken-Chaser Sparrow Hawk*), Infante plays José Inocencio Meléndez, a cunning gambler and womanizer, whose girlfriend, in revenge for his escapades, leaves him for his best friend.[62] José Inocencio, hurt, goes to the cantina. Despite his machista attitude and rogueries, he sings "Ella" (She) (1950):

Me cansé de rogarle, me cansé de decirle que yo sin ella de pena muero . . . Ya no quiso escucharme . . . si sus labios se abrieron fue pa' decirme . . . ya no te quiero.	I got tired of begging her, I got tired of telling her that without her I die of sorrow . . . She no longer wanted to listen . . . if she opened her lips it was only to tell me . . . I no longer love you.
Yo sentí que mi vida se perdía en un abismo profundo y negro como mi suerte . . . Quise hallar el olvido al "estilo Jalisco," pero aquellos mariachis y aquel tequila me hicieron llorar.	I felt that my life was falling in an abyss steep and dark as my luck . . . I wanted to cast [her] into oblivion in "Jalisco style," but that mariachi band and that tequila made me cry.
Me cansé de rogarle . . . con el llanto en los ojos alcé mi copa y brindé . . . por ella . . . No podía despreciarme, era el último brindis	I got tired of begging her . . . with tears in the eyes I raised my glass and drank a toast . . . to her . . . She couldn't despise me, it was the last toast

de un bohemio . . .	offered by a bohemian man . . .
por una reina.	to a queen.
Los mariachis callaron . . .	The mariachi band got quiet . . .
de mi mano, sin fuerza,	from my powerless hand,
cayó mi copa	my glass fell
sin darme cuenta . . .	without my noticing it . . .
Ella quiso quedarse	She wanted to stay
cuando vió mi tristeza,	when she noticed my grief,
pero ya estaba escrito	but it was already written
que aquella noche	that very night
perdiera su amor.[63]	I lost her love.

In a country where alcoholism is highly recurrent to a point of being a marker of the people's identity and a leading cause of death among men aged fifteen to twenty-four, this song, with a few others, has become an icon of betrayal, fate, and binge drinking.[64] Its lyrics make numerous references to the values and attitudes promoted by Hispanismo, including the manliness and courage associated with the Alteño mythology. Drinking tequila while listening to mariachi music not only made reference to Jalisco, but also to a manly way of handling loss. In this context, drunkenness, crying, and demonstrations of weakness represent signs of manhood because they are done in the context of making a toast "to a queen." Alcoholic inebriation, as well as the cantina setting, legitimized and condoned demonstrations of a sentimental masculinity. They take place in the celebration of a worthwhile woman. Moreover, the acknowledgment that he has lost the woman's love gives the last proof that while he is a virile man, he still knows when he is defeated. In return, as listeners likely expected, the woman responds accordingly to "proper" gender roles by showing mercy on the suffering man. Her depiction as a compassionate individual, willing to sacrifice herself for the sake of others, illustrates the femininity embedded in patriarchal values of the Alteño discourse. In this song, loss and abandonment are already written in the destiny of this man. The lyrics justifying a brokenhearted but manly drunkenness made José Alfredo Jiménez's "Ella," also known as "Me Cansé de Rogarle" ("I Got Tired of Begging Her"), one of the most famous songs within the mariachi repertoire and cantina culture. In fact, it became so popular upon its release that it was included in two more films in the following years.[65] Jiménez was also the author of other classic songs for those hoping to drown their love sorrows in alcohol. Among those songs was "Tu recuerdo y yo" ("Your Memory and Me"), which became a hit in 1952 and 1953 after being performed in three different films (*Ansiedad*, *Tal para cual*, and *Reportaje*). Infante, Negrete, and Luis Aguilar, the biggest stars of the ranchera genre, played the lead roles in those movies.

Many songs and scenes of the Golden Age cinema depicted the urban or rural cantina as the quintessential macho setting. In this space, men not only develop bonds of trust, do business, enjoy themselves drinking, chatting, and gambling with their peers, and carousing with women, but also drown their sorrows.[66] Protected from the broader public gaze, but more importantly from their beloved woman's sight, in the cantina, they can let their emotions out:

Estoy en el rincón de una cantina, oyendo una canción que yo pedí. Me están sirviendo ahorita mi tequila, ya va mi pensamiento rumbo a ti.	I'm in a cantina's corner, listening to my requested song. Right now, they are serving me a tequila shot, my thoughts are heading toward you.
Yo sé que tu recuerdo es mi desgracia, y vengo aquí nomas a recordar, qué amargas son las cosas que nos pasan, cuando hay una mujer que paga mal.	I know that your memory is my misfortune, I come here just to look back, how bitter things are, when a woman betrays you.
Quién no sabe en esta vida la traición tan conocida que nos deja un mal amor. Quién no llega a la cantina exigiendo su tequila exigiendo su canción.[67]	Who in this life doesn't know the well-known taste of betrayal that a bad love leaves. Who doesn't get to the cantina demanding his tequila shot demanding his song.

As the lyrics explicitly state, it is not about binge drinking or a visit to the cantina for the sake of it: men have valid reasons. Imbibing alcohol helps them to cope with fate and betrayal. The song "Acuérdate, acuérdate" ("Don't Forget, Don't Forget"), also included in *El gavilán pollero*, explicitly states so: "when a man drinks his alcohol, it is because he wants to forget about his loves. Full of sadness he goes to the cantina to get drunk."[68] The lyrics of "Siempre, siempre" ("Always, Always") complement this idea explaining that getting drunk facilitates catharsis; it is the only way to "dissipate the sorrows, honest to God:"[69]

Ustedes se reirán, pero el borracho sufre	You might laugh, but the drunk man suffers
y goza con el vino y las botellas.	and enjoys with wine and bottles.
Las canciones de borrachos	The drunks' songs
quizás los hagan reír, pero a fondo son	might make you laugh, but they are truly
las quejas del hombre y de su sufrir.	the sorrows of the man and his pain.

The lyrics justify the practice of binge drinking and drunkenness. Men resort to drinking until they drop during a *borrachera* (binge), as a special occasion.[70]

Filmmakers, influenced by the conservative ideology of their time and their intent to socialize the urban masses, did not justify drunkenness as an objective in itself, at least not for the main characters. Their educational agenda was clear, leaders and powerful men were good role models, while the underdogs and deviant were demonized and punished.[71] Several scenes of Golden Age movies depicted ranchero men drinking, but not necessarily getting drunk because true men can hold their alcohol. These men embodied the role models envisioned by Hispanismo: sober, proper, and virile. Instead of imbibing pulque or other indigenous-origin concoctions, they consumed tequila and other distilled beverages bottled in labeled containers. They did not drink beverages of dubious origins, and more importantly, avoided drinks manufactured without industrial and hygienic methods. Among the approved colorless spirits were mezcal and sotol. Their clarity contrasted to the sticky and viscous pulque, just as the Alteño hero contrasted with the common man.

Under this educational and moralizing agenda, drunkenness was socially scorned; the elite especially spurned public display of female intoxication because it transgressed the patriarchal values reinforced by the Alteño mythology, the Hispanista discourse, and the Revolutionary Family. Perhaps the most popular characterizations of female drunks of the Golden Age cinema appeared in "La Guayaba" ("The Guava") and "La Tostada" ("The Toast") in the 1947 film *Nosotros los Pobres* (*We the Poor*) and its 1948 sequel *Ustedes los Ricos* (*You the Rich*).[72] They were supporting characters portraying the female version of the helpless deviant in this urban melodrama. The scenes of these women drinking were short and discreet, consistent with the moralistic approach that the director of the movie, Ismael Rodríguez, preferred. In contrast, there existed only one full scene depicting a woman singing and drowning her sorrows in alcohol in ranchera movies of the Golden Age, and that came in an earlier film. Manolita Arreola performed "Borrachita de tequila" ("Little Woman Drunk on Tequila") also known as "La Tequilera" ("The Tequila Drinker") in the 1938 film *Juan Sin Miedo* (*Fearless Juan*). This scene showing Arreola drinking, singing, and praising tequila is perceived by the critics as one of the first referential scenes of the Golden Age cinema, which paradoxically later on praised female domesticity and propriety. Such a scene could be shown because the film was produced during Cárdenas's anticlerical regime, when women's rights saw at least a limited promotion. Even when Cárdenas's government did not differentiate from their predecessors in persuading women as wives and mothers, and guardians of the home, to organize antialcohol leagues in their communities to prevent male alcoholism, it sponsored social programs and reforms intending to improve female welfare and political participation.[73] By the 1940s, when the Hispanismo discourse became the predominant ideology, a scene of a drunken woman singing and praising tequila became impossible to screen.

The original title and the lyrics of the "Borrachita de tequila" showed a combination of traditional values, modern attitudes, and double standards, highly representative of Mexican society between the late 1930s and 1950s. The name of the song calls the tequila drinker "*borrachita*" (little drunk woman), rather than "*borracha*" (drunk woman), reinforcing deeply rooted values in Mexican culture. Mexicans used, and still use, diminutives to designate those who are different, such as "*el negrito*" (the little black guy), "*el gordito*" (the little chubby guy), "*el cojito*" (the little crippled guy). This kind of expression serves as a means of partial political correctness, if also including a negative connotation. The phrasing intends to show compassion and embracing of differences, but instantly implies some kind of discrimination and judgment. As the lyrics included below show, the woman's reproachable behavior resides in the fact that she drinks and speaks about tequila in the same way that men do. She drinks because she wants to alleviate her pain with tequila as a "real Mexican woman." With courage, she accepts love, betrayal, and her fate. Tequila has been her companion since her birth because, as the song states, she was baptized with it instead of water. Despite these descriptions of apparent empowerment, the last verse rejects any agency when she recognizes that she has lost the love of her life because of her drinking problem. In contrast to the celebration of male drunkenness and tequila consumption in songs and movies, female tequila use and inebriation not only challenged patriarchal values, but also had terrible and punishable consequences:

Borrachita de tequila	Drunken from tequila
llevo siempre el alma mía	I carry my soul always
Para ver si se mejora	Hoping to heal it
de esta cruel melancolía.	from this cruel melancholy.
Ay por ese querer,	Oh, it is because of that love,
pos que le he de hacer	what can I do?
Si el destino me lo dio	If fate gave it to me
para siempre padecer	to make me suffer forever
Como buena mexicana	As a real Mexican woman,
sufriré el dolor tranquila.	I'll quietly endure this pain.
Al fin y al cabo yo mañana	After all, tomorrow
tendré un trago de tequila.	I'll have a tequila again.
Ay por ese querer,	Oh, it is because of that love,
aunque me haya traicionado	even when it has betrayed me,
no lo puedo aborrecer.	I can't abhor it.
Me llaman la tequilera	They call me the tequila drinker
como si fuera de pila	as if it was my first name
porque a mi me bautizaron	because I was baptized
con un trago de tequila.	with a tequila shot.
Ya me voy mejor,	Better I should go,
pos que yo hago aquí?	'cause what I am doing here?
Dizque por la borrachera	Because of my drinking binge
dicen todos, lo perdí.[74]	everybody says, I lost him.

At the same time, the religious imagery of the song that described her baptism as a tequila shot undermined her as the moral guardian of the home. Both through her inebriation in the public realm and her seemingly weak religious devotion, *la borrachita* figure challenged social taboos that relegated women to the private sphere as the angel of the hearth.

In contrast, people generally accepted occasional male public drunkenness if there was a reason behind it. In almost all the scenes of this period showing leading male characters getting drunk, the choice resulted from having a sorrow to drown, an issue of lost love or profound grief. Brokenhearted, he needed to let out his emotions. Filled with intense feelings or passions, the man weeps in public. But this crying and drinking became permissible because the men nonetheless dealt with their feelings in a manly way. Macho culture and patriarchal values allowed men to do whatever they pleased and ignore others' opinions, provided they did not fall into overly effeminate patterns. As the song "Ando muy borracho" ("I'm So Drunk") (1952) states:

Ando mucho, pero mucho muy borracho	I am drunk, very, very drunk
Por un amor que me trae mal herido	Because of love sorrows
Ando mucho, pero mucho muy borracho	I am drunk, very, very drunk
Y qué, y qué me importa si me envicio	So what, so what if I am drunk.
Ay cuánto sufrimos los que mucho amamos	Oh, how much we suffer when we love too much
Primero reímos y después lloramos	First we laugh and then we cry
Qué me importa si hoy por mi puro gusto	I don't care if today for the sake of it
Yo río, pus muy mi risa. Si lloro, muy mi llanto	I laugh, it is my laugh. If I cry, it is my crying
Y si al mundo no le gusta	If people don't approve,
Que vaya mucho al diablo.[75]	They can go to hell.

Even comical urban characters followed this macho stereotype. One example of this machista attitude was the performance of the song "Oye vale" ("Hey Buddy") by two great comedic stars of the Golden Age, Tin Tan and Cantinflas, in two different movies: 1947's *El Niño Perdido* (*The Lost Kid*) and 1949's *El portero* (*The Doorman*), respectively.[76] In *El portero*, Cantinflas plays a witty and cunning doorman who is commissioned to hire a group of mariachi musicians to celebrate the birthday of one of the tenants in his building. He and his buddy, interpreted by his long-time stage partner Marcelo, go to the Tenampa, the aforementioned popular venue, to listen to mariachi music in the Mexican capital at the time. Cantinflas, rather than hiring the band, gets inebriated and sings:

Oye vale	Hey buddy
qué borracho ando esta noche	how drunk I am tonight
de sentimiento.	soulful drunk.
Tú no sabes	You don't know
tú no sabes que por maje	you don't know that I was fooled
me hicieron guaje.	because I'm stupid.

[. . .] Oye vale
acompáñame al Tenampa
donde se canta
achis miachis.
Que me toquen los mariachis
"Guadalajara."

No se te hace
que en verdad como mi tierra
no hay otra tierra
ahí se queda
de 'onde son los meros machos
y los borrachos [. . .].[77]

[. . .] Hey buddy
come with me to the Tenampa
where the music
is super duper.
Let the mariachis sing to me
"Guadalajara."

Don't you think
that truly, as my homeland
there is no other land
no matter what
where real macho men
and drunks come from [. . .].

Tin Tan's and Cantinflas's performances of this song provide testimony of the changing tastes and attitudes triggered by the Golden Age cinema. The lyrics touch on several stereotypes of the Alteño mythology. The comedians performed this song as if they were drunk, imitating and making fun of those characters who drown their sorrows in ranchera movies. Interestingly, Tin Tan's and Cantinflas's macho attitudes in these performances contrasted with their dance moves and attires, constantly criticized as signs of female leanings. The inclusion of a cantina song in an urban comic movie illustrates the increasing popularity of the Alteño mythology among cinemagoers, many of whom started adopting tequila as their beverage of choice. Among them were individuals working in masonry, carpentry work, and other such trades. Tequila thus became associated with the working classes. In contrast, the urban middle classes preferred to adopt more cosmopolitan beverages such as champagne, whiskey, or cognac.

These diverse preferences proved that the concept of lo mexicano did not go unchallenged or uncontested. Different groups accepted, resisted, or negotiated this fluid construct to their own benefit and taste. Urban middle classes were aware that the consumption of beverages such as champagne, cognac, scotch, and beer represented a practice that elevated social status if done properly. Post-Revolutionary rulers envisioned a nation of modern citizens who would consume alcoholic beverages that represented the embracing of modernity and technology, and symbolically provided a clear break with the past. While the upper classes had already been consuming European liquors and beer, the younger generations and middle classes now also began to consume more cosmopolitan beverages. These drinks, with their industrial methods of production, embodied the new modern identity that the Mexican government wanted to achieve, and provided an obvious alternative to tequila.[78]

Cinemagoers of the 1940s and 1950s became increasingly familiar with new technology, household appliances, industrial life, communications technologies, and other imported consumer goods in general. Canny filmmakers acknowledged this phenomenon and promoted this behavior by including characters who drank imported spirits. Soon the urban middle classes adopted these beverages, to the point that it became expected for them to appear in films of the Golden Age. Tin Tan, in his version of "Oye Vale," included an introduction that revealed the recent adoption of foreign beverages among urban residents:

Buenos días señores tengan sus mercedes	Good morning to all your graces
Muncha jaitancia en esta runión	Lots of boasting in this gathering
Y que sean muy felices toditos astedes	I wish happiness to all of you
Y que me perdonen esta versación.	And forgive me this verse.
Bajen botellas de champaña y coñaque	Bring down bottles of champagne and cognac
Y emborrachémonos	And let's get drunk
Hasta que nos caiganos	Until we drop
Y nos levántenos	And we get up
Y nos vuélvanos a cair.	And we drop again.

Tin Tan's version represented an example of the several sketches in which comedians made fun of social changes produced by the Mexican Miracle. He presented himself as an individual whose vocabulary reveals his humble and provincial origins. He mixed old and modern Spanish expressions, commonly associated with the way people spoke in the countryside. Among those words were *muncha jaitancia* instead of *mucha jactancia* (lots of boasting), *runión* rather than *reunión* (gathering), *astedes* for *ustedes* (you in plural), *caiganos* instead of *caigamos* (drop), and *cair* rather than *caer* (drop). His limited exposure to modern urban life and education made him mispronounce foreign words, in this case, the name of foreign beverages. Instead of properly pronouncing "champagne," he says "champaña" and instead of "cognac," he calls it "coñaque." Thus, in his sketch he was making fun of those individuals who had newly arrived to the city and their changes in taste and wannabe aspirations. They had limited incomes and skills, belonged to the upper end of the working classes, but presented themselves as middle class. They were a mix of regionalism and cosmopolitanism that resulted in pure pretention. The newcomers asserted their superior status based on the "evidence" of their lighter complexion, especially when compared to their darker-skinned neighbors. They also called attention to their honorable role in the Revolution, their choices of lifestyle, and emphasized the status of clerical jobs their family members performed. Some of them could not avoid imitating movie stars such as Negrete and Infante, and once in a while they drank tequila despite its plebeian origins.[79] In so doing, this group, along with other urban classes, emulated or internalized the types of behaviors that they saw depicted as normal on the big screen. They learned how to live in the city, and perhaps as importantly, how and what to drink there. As Carlos Monsiváis stated, the cinema was modernizing the spectators' tastes because they went to the movies not simply to dream and enjoy, but to become educated in city life.[80]

Pulque and *Los Olvidados* (The Forgotten Ones) of the Mexican Miracle

Despite the constant depiction of tequila and other beverages as the ideal in movies, pulque remained present in everyday life. In films, it represented the plight of marginal urban groups. The poor's attachment to pulque (and other fermented beverages) reflected their daily struggles and lack of progress. The Mexican Miracle had not only left behind and marginalized the lower classes, but they also now confronted the intrusions of modernity and industrialization in their daily practices. They continued to drink in *pulquerías* (pulque taverns) for the comfort of the familiar, even in a context where such an activity faced considerable stigma as backward or racially inferior. Filmmakers were aware of the challenges and living conditions of the poor, but they chose to depict a "festive and vindicating" poverty in their movies, rather than a grinding one.[81] In place of pity or outrage at injustice, the poor inspired a sort of grudging admiration for remaining stoic and finding entertainment and comfort among their own kind. Among the few exceptions to this trend was *Los Olvidados* (1950), one of the most highly acclaimed Mexican films both nationally and internationally.[82] The film depicts not only the material consequences of industrialization and modernity among the city's poor inhabitants, but also the social evils that emerge from all of them, such as parental abandonment, cruelty, resentment, and wickedness. *Los Olvidados* represented a strong critique of post-war Mexico's unequal distribution of wealth and social services. In contrast, the movie

Nosotros Los Pobres also tells a tale of the capital's underworld, but rather celebrated the dignity and good nature of the poor. Its depictions of noble poverty acknowledged pulque as the beverage of choice for those at the margins of the society.[83] The movie opens with a song introducing the characters and the first shot shows the sign of the pulquería "La Uno," which sold pulque from the Plains of Apan, considered by many as the best of its kind.

The marginalized poor in these pulquerías had reason to drink. The idyllic Mexico depicted in the ranchera movies, with manly yeomen riding horses, serenading women, and drinking tequila, contrasted with the real Mexico. In the cities, the country was experiencing urbanization and industrialization. Mexico City was even getting some cosmopolitan overtones, but the countryside remained mostly forgotten. Not every Mexican benefited from the Mexican Miracle and its prosperous cosmopolitan façade.[84] Prosperity brought increasing strains from migration to the city, an infrastructure that did not keep up with demographic growth. A dramatic contrast grew between the rich and the poor, the countryside and the city; and an increasing widespread corruption. Peasants left their villages in search of work in the cities. Once there, slums provided the only housing available. ISI policies had led to an increasingly uneven distribution of national income. While the middle class had grown around 15 percent in population, the wage gap between skilled and unskilled workers increased, creating proletarian and lumpenproletarian groups. The latter tried to survive despite job dislocation, social and racial discrimination, price increases, and hoarding. Considerable corruption started from the top with the president, and trickled down to the lowest rank of officials. Mexicans lived under a false premise of democracy in which every six years they elected a new president, but never could opt for a different party. Although Revolutionaries had fought against caciques, local and regional bosses, new ones had now emerged. Together with union leaders and deputies, these bosses had become the new face of local and regional power. Moreover, to keep profits high and costs down, the wages paid to workers needed to remain depressed. The courts or the army broke all strikes. Schools grew, but they had no books, and the teachers earned meager salaries. Highways connected centers of production to ports and the U.S.-Mexico border, while most remaining parts of the countryside lacked infrastructure. In summary, poverty, unequal distribution of wealth, discrimination, underdevelopment, and repression of freedoms were everyday realities.

Despite all of these contradictions and inequalities, the country remained stable and levels of violence stayed low. This relative peace came as a side effect that primarily resulted from the expanding economy and the state's achievements in centralizing power.[85] Once in a while, peasant and urban masses organized, along with unions, and raised their voice to challenge the grand narrative of the post-Revolutionary government. For some, these post-war regimes had betrayed the goals and promises of the Revolution.[86] The government masterfully applied a carrot-and-stick policy. They successfully suppressed political dissent, at times using covert or open violence to coerce citizens. At times, they responded to the needs of subjects, other times they co-opted complainants, while at others the regime proved flexible enough to let individuals dissent. The cultural politics of the government allowed citizens to vent, criticize, and complain through popular culture and mass media.[87] This functioned as an exhaust valve, and the discontent with the government never embodied a real threat to its power through the 1950s. But more importantly, drunkenness and brawling became the chief means through which urban masses coped with their problems according to the popular media of the time. This was not an exclusive practice of post-Revolutionary Mexico by any means. Since the colonial period, intoxication had not only strengthened camaraderie, but also led to frequent eruptions of violence. The excessive consumption of alcohol exacerbated jealousies, labor and domestic disputes, and local tensions, which ended in individual or communal confrontation, rebellion, and death.[88] By the end of the Mexican Miracle, things were not that different; urban masses used drink and songs as a temporary escape from the government, the rich, the hoarding merchants, and their employers.

Conclusion

Mexico's Golden Age witnessed the production of a plethora of films and songs that celebrated new values that both government officials and cultural producers used to define national identity at home and abroad. In particular, drinking songs played in films and aired on radio praised distilled and industrially produced libations, such as tequila, as fitting for the modern tastes that citizens needed to develop. Tequila producers took advantage to profit from the growing demand for their product, a demand at least partly spurred by its celebration in the drinking songs shown in films. The songs that extolled the virtues—and less often vices—of modern alcoholic beverages did so within a transnational context. This shaped a particular form of national identity based on proscribed gender roles that defined proper manliness and sentimental manhood as well as an idealized regional figure, the Alteño, who came to define the national character to audiences, both foreign and domestic. Yet for all the celebration of modern industrially produced beverages as a symbol of Mexico's economic miracle, popular classes and new arrivals to Mexico City from the countryside continued to imbibe traditional drinks such as pulque. The divide between the proper, modern alcohol choices of the upper- and middle-classes, on the one hand, and the so-called backward tastes of the poor, on the other, reflected the broader social divisions that arose from the rapid (yet often uneven) economic growth of the Mexican Miracle. The poor continued to drink traditional libations as a means to cope with everyday realities and to forge a sense of social cohesion in their new urban environment.

Notes

The author expresses her gratitude to Michael Matthews and Stephen Neufeld for their great comments and outstanding editing to this chapter, as well as to Víctor Macías-González (University of Wisconsin–La Crosse), Jeff Pilcher (University of Minnesota), Gretchen Pierce (Shippensburg University), and Elena Albarrán (Miami University) for their insightful comments. All translations are the author's and any mistake in this piece can be only attributed to her.

1. *Rumbera* movies embodied another important emerging genre during the Golden Age of Mexican cinema. These films combined dramatic or romantic urban narrative with dancing talent, taking place mostly in cabarets.

2. Joanne Hershfield and David R. Maciel, *Mexico's Cinema: A Century of Film and Filmmakers* (Wilmington, DE: Scholarly Resources Books, 1999), 35.

3. Ibid.; Seth Fein, "From Collaboration to Containment: Hollywood and the International Political Economy of Mexican Cinema after the Second World War," in *Mexico's Cinema*, Hershfield and Maciel, 126–27; Seth Fein, "Myths of Cultural Imperialism and Nationalism in Golden Age Mexican Cinema," in *Fragments of a Golden Age: The Politics of Culture in Mexico Since 1940*, ed. Gilbert Joseph, Anne Rubenstein, and Eric Zolov (Durham, NC: Duke University Press, 2001), 164–69.

4. Hershfield and Maciel, *Mexico's Cinema*, 35.

5. Peter H. Smith, "Mexico Since 1946: Dynamics of An Authoritarian Regime," in *Mexico Since Independence*, ed. Leslie Bethell (Cambridge: Cambridge University Press, 1991), 324.

6. Gilbert Joseph, Anne Rubenstein, and Eric Zolov, "Assembling the Fragments," in *Fragments of a Golden Age*, Joseph, Rubenstein, and Zolov, 3, 4, 7.

7. Stephen Niblo, *Mexico in the 1940s: Modernity, Politics, and Corruption* (Wilmington, DE: Scholarly Resources, 1999).

8. Renamed as Partido de la Revolución Mexicana (PRM) in 1938, and later on rebaptized as Partido Revolucionario Institucional (PRI) in 1946.

9. Sergio de la Mora, *Cinemachismo: Masculinities and Sexuality in Mexican Film* (Austin: University of Texas Press, 2006), 2–3.

10. Joanne Hershfield, "Race and Ethnicity in the Classical Cinema," in *Mexico's Cinema*, Hershfield and Maciel, 84, 89–90; José Orozco, "Esos Altos de Jalisco: Immigration and the Idea of Alteño Exceptionalism, 1926–1952" (PhD diss., Harvard

University, 1998); Nancy Leys Stepan, *The Hour of Eugenics: Race, Gender, and Nation in Latin America* (Ithaca, NY: Cornell University Press, 1991), 147–50.

11. José Orozco, "Tequila Sauza and the Redemption of Mexico's Vital Fluids, 1873–1970," in *Alcohol in Latin America: A Cultural and Social History*, ed. Gretchen Pierce and Áurea Toxqui (Tucson: University of Arizona Press, 2014), 201.

12. José Antonio Gutiérrez Gutiérrez, *Los Altos de Jalisco: Panorama histórico de una región y de su sociedad hasta 1821* (Mexico City: Conaculta, 1991), 119–45.

13. Cristina Palomar Verea, *El orden discursivo de género en Los Altos de Jalisco* (Guadalajara, Jalisco: Universidad de Guadalajara, 2005), 89–90.

14. Olga Nájera-Ramírez, "Engendering Nationalism: Identity, Discourse, and the Mexican Charro," *Anthropological Quarterly* 67 (1994): 1–14.

15. Gutiérrez Gutiérrez, *Los Altos de Jalisco*, 183–88; Palomar Verea, *El orden discursivo*, 103–6.

16. Gutiérrez Gutiérrez, *Los Altos de Jalisco*, 187.

17. Orozco, "Tequila Sauza," 201.

18. Manuel Esperón and Ernesto Cortázar, "Esos Altos," *Cancionero Popular Mexicano I*, ed. Mario Kuri-Aldana and Vicente Mendoza (México: Fondo de Cultura Económica, 1987), 118. Jorge Negrete performed this song in the film *El Peñón de las ánimas* (*The Rock of Souls*) in 1942.

19. Manuel Esperón González and Ernesto Cortázar, "¡Ay Jalisco, no te rajes!," *Cancionero Popular Mexicano* I: 364.

20. A rooster fighting in a "tapado" style means that its spurs are covered with fabric or leather to prevent the immediate injury of either bird. In this way, the cockfight can last longer until one rooster is hurt, tired, and unable to keep fighting.

21. "Mezcal" is the generic name for the distilled beverages made of any plant from the aloe family. Tequila is a mezcal produced in the region of the same name.

22. Manuel Esperón González and Ernesto Cortázar, "Cocula," *Cancionero Popular Mexicano* I: 277.

23. The china represented a stereotype representation of Mexican woman clad in a white blouse and skirt, often with embroidering, fringes, and colorful patterns, as well as a shawl.

24. The mestizo characteristics of the charro and the china made nineteenth-century politicians and intellectuals choose them as the embodiment of the nation. This was a common trend throughout the Americas in the 1800s. Ricardo Pérez Montfort, in his studies of popular culture and the formation of national identity, analyzes the emergence of horse-riding mestizo characters such as the Argentine gaucho, the Chilean *guaso* (cowboy), or the Colombian *llanero* (cowboy of the plains), among others, as national types. All of them were regional characters chosen as the ideal image to unify their nation and represent their culture. Ricardo Pérez Montfort, "Folklore e identidad. Reflexiones sobre una herencia nacionalista en América," in *Avatares del nacionalismo cultural: Cinco ensayos* (Mexico City: Centro de Investigación y Docencia en Humanidades del Estado de Morelos-Centro de Investigaciones y Estudios Superiores en Antropología Social, 2000), 15–34.

25. A discussion on the commercial exploitation of these characters as representative of "lo mexicano" outside Mexico during the Porfiriato can be found in Helen Delpar, *The Enormous Vogue of Things Mexican: Cultural Relations between the United States and Mexico, 1920–1935* (Tuscaloosa: University of Alabama Press, 1992);

Francisco Montellano, *C. B. Waite, Fotógrafo: Una mirada diversa sobre el México de principios del siglo* XX (Mexico City: Grijalbo-Conaculta, 1994); Ricardo Pérez Montfort, "Los estereotipos nacionales y la educación posrevolucionaria en México (1920–1930)," in *Avatares del nacionalismo cultural,* 35–68. Pérez Montfort argues that the sophistication and embellishment of the charro suit, while emphasizing its Mexican character that took place during the Porfiriato, encouraged Revolutionary governments in the 1920s and 1930s to adopt the charro and the china dancing the *jarabe tapatío* (a Jalisco dance) as national symbols. Ricardo Pérez Montfort, "Una región inventada desde el centro. La consolidación del cuadro estereotípico nacional," in *Estampas del nacionalismo popular mexicano: Diez ensayos sobre cultura popular y nacionalismo* (Mexico City: Centro de Investigaciones y Estudios Superiores en Antropología Social, 2003), 121–48.

26. Lisa Jarvinen, "Hollywood and Spanish-Speaking Audiences," in *The Wiley-Blackwell History of American Film,* ed. Cynthia Lucia, Roy Grundmann, and Art Simon (Chichester, West Sussex, UK: Wiley-Blackwell, 2012), II: 174–75.

27. Federico Dávalos Orozco, "The Birth of the Film Industry and the Emergence of the Sound," in *Mexico's Cinema,* ed. Hershfield and Maciel, 25–26, 32; Perla Ciuk, *Diccionario de directores del cine mexicano* (Mexico City: Conaculta, 2000); Carlos Monsiváis, "Notas sobre la cultura mexicana en el siglo XX," in *Historia general de México: Versión 2000,* ed. Centro de Estudios Históricos, El Colegio de México (Mexico City: El Colegio de México, 2005), 1051; Jorge Ayala Blanco, *La aventura del cine mexicano en la época de oro y después* (Mexico City: Grijalbo, 1993), 54–55; Palomar Verea, *El orden discursivo,* 66–70.

28. Filmmakers were aware of the anachronism of these characters. In fact, in 1956 Juan Bustillo Oro produced *Los Hijos de Rancho Grande* (*The Children of Rancho Grande*), sequel of *Allá en el Rancho Grande.* In this film, which combined ranchera and comedy genres, the characters make fun of the old-fashioned and extinct idyllic Alteño culture. But at the end of several unfortunate events, they recognize their preference for this idyllic tradition rather than the modern practices of their time. *Los Hijos de Rancho Grande,* film, directed by Juan Bustillo Oro (Mexico City: Tele Talia Films, S. A., 1956).

29. Ayala Blanco, *La aventura del cine mexicano,* 55. Monsiváis. "Notas sobre la cultura mexicana en el siglo XX," 1053–54.

30. De la Mora, *Cinemachismo,* 2–9, 83.

31. Ayala Blanco, *La aventura del cine mexicano,* 56–57.

32. Fein, "Myths of Cultural Imperialism," 160–61.

33. Pablo Dueñas, "La aparición del cine y la radio en el moldeamiento de la música popular," in . . . *y la música se volvió Mexicana,* ed. Instituto Nacional de Antropología e Historia (INAH) (México: CENIDIM, Instituto Nacional de Bellas Artes, INAH, Conaculta, 2010), 273–80.

34. Esperón was not innovating mariachi music; he was just following the steps of classical composers. José Pablo Moncayo, Blas Galindo, and Carlos Chávez, among others, in their attempt to create a real nationalistic Mexican music, introduced trumpets and clarinets into the mariachi band during Cárdenas's regime. These additions were highly welcomed beyond the classic halls, and radio and films contributed to their popularization. Ricardo Pérez Monfort, "Acercamientos al son mexicano: el son de mariachi, el son jarocho y el son huasteco," in *Avatares del nacionalismo cultural,* 128–32.

35. Contributions to the formation of Mexican national identity by artists and creators were not new by the mid-twentieth century, as William Beezley suggests in his discussion of nineteenth-century puppeteers and board-game makers. See William Beezley, *Mexican National Identity: Memory, Innuendo, and Popular Culture* (Tucson: University of Arizona Press, 2008), x, 26.

36. Benedict Anderson, *Imagined Communities: Reflections on the Origin and Spread of Nationalism* (New York: Verso, 2003), 41–46.

37. Joy Elizabeth Hayes, *Radio Nation: Communication, Popular Culture, and Nationalism in Mexico, 1920–1950* (Tucson: University of Arizona Press, 2000).

38. Hershfield, "Race and Ethnicity," 90–92; Carl J. Mora, *Mexican Cinema: Reflections of a Society, 1896–1988* (Berkeley: University of California Press, 1989).

39. Only in the movie *Me he de comer esa tuna* (*I Have to Bear It* or *I'll Have to Eat That Prickly Pear*, 1945) did Jorge Negrete deliver a scene in which his character got drunk. Otherwise, his characters drank tequila without reaching drunkenness. *Me he de comer esa tuna*, film, directed by Miguel Zacarías (Mexico City: Producciones Grovas, S.A., 1944).

40. *¡Ay Jalisco, no te rajes!*, film, directed by Joselito Rodríguez (Mexico City: Películas Rodríguez S.A. de C.V, 1941).

41. *El peñón de las ánimas*, film, directed by Miguel Zacarías (Mexico City: CLASA films, 1942).

42. *De tal palo tal astilla*, film, directed by Manuel M. Delgado (Mexico City: Filmadora Chapultepec, S.A., 1960)

43. Hershfield, "Race and Ethnicity," 90–92. De la Mora, *Cinemachismo*, 6–9, 76–77, 81–83, 98–104.

44. Anne Rubenstein. "Bodies, Cities, Cinema: Pedro Infante's Death as Political Spectacle," in *Fragments of a Golden Age*, ed. Joseph, Rubenstein, and Zolov, 200–210; Marco Velázquez and Mary Kay Vaughan, "*Mestizaje* and Musical Nationalism," in *The Eagle and the Virgin: Nation and Cultural Revolution in Mexico, 1920–1940*, ed. Mary Kay Vaughan and Stephen E. Lewis (Durham, NC: Duke University Press, 2006), 111–12.

45. Cockfighting as a practice with strong connotations of manhood is not unique to Mexicans or Latin Americans, as Clifford Geertz has demonstrated, it is also a common tradition in other regions of the world; Clifford Geertz, *The Interpretation of Cultures* (New York: Basic Books, 1973).

46. Negrete's version of "Tequila con limón," in the movie *Me he de comer esa tuna*; Manuel Esperón and Ernesto Cortázar, "Tequila con limón," *Cancionero Popular Mexicano*, I: 280.

47. Áurea Toxqui, "Pulque," in *Alcohol and Drugs in North America: A Historical Encyclopedia*, ed. David M. Fahey and Jon Miller (Santa Barbara, CA: ABC-Clio, 2013), 2: 575–80.

48. José Orozco, "Gabriel Espíndola Martínez: Tequila Master," in *The Human Tradition in Mexico*, ed. Jeffrey M. Pilcher (Wilmington, DE: Scholarly Resources, 2003), 227–28.

49. Hershfield, "Race and Ethnicity," 87–88; Julia Tuñón, "Between the Nation and Utopia: The Image of Mexico in the Films of Emilio 'Indio' Fernández," *Studies in Latin American Popular Culture* [serial online] 12 (1993): 159–75. Accessed December 15, 2012.

50. Gretchen Kristine Pierce, "Sobering the Revolution: Mexico's Anti-Alcohol Campaigns and the Process of State-Building, 1910–1940" (PhD diss., University of Arizona, 2008); Amie Wright, "'La Bebida Nacional': Pulque and Mexicanidad, 1920–1946," *Canadian Journal of History* 44 (2009): 1–24; Stephen E. Lewis, "The Nation, Education, and the 'Indian Problem' in Mexico, 1920–1940," in *The Eagle and the Virgin: Nation and Cultural Revolution in Mexico, 1920–1940*, ed. Mary Kay Vaughan and Stephen E. Lewis (Durham, NC: Duke University Press, 2006).

51. Pierce, "Sobering the Revolution," 145–46, 151–54, 162–67; Orozco, "Tequila Sauza," 195; Mario Ramírez Rancaño, *Ignacio Torres Adalid y la industria pulquera* (México City: Plaza y Valdés and Instituto de Investigaciones Sociales, Universidad Nacional Autónoma de Mexico, 2000); Áurea Toxqui, "Grupo Modelo," in *Alcohol and Drugs in North America: A Historical Encyclopedia*, ed. David M. Fahey and Jon Miller (Santa Barbara, CA: ABC-Clio), 1: 289–90.

52. Ramírez Rancaño, *Ignacio Torres Adalid*, quoted in Orozco, "Tequila Sauza," 195.

53. Tim Mitchell, *Intoxicated Identities: Alcohol's Power in Mexican History and Culture* (New York: Routledge, 2004), 109–10.

54. Orozco, "Tequila Sauza," 194. Orozco supports his point with an analysis of Mariano Azuela's novel *Los de abajo*.

55. De la Mora, *Cinemachismo*, 5.

56. Orozco, "Tequila Sauza," 199.

57. Graciela Márquez Colín and Gabriela Recio, "Politicians and Brewers in Mexico: Taxing Beer in the 1920s" (Paper presented at the 6th Biennial Meeting of the Alcohol and Drug History Society, Buffalo, NY, June 2011). Beer producers also took advantage of the mass media. In the film *Pablo and Carolina*, Pedro Infante, another Golden Age cinema star, played the role of a young man whose family owned the so-called brewery Carta de Oro (Golden Card) in Monterrey, Nuevo León. It was not a coincidence that the name of the brewery and the location were close to reality. In fact, the leading brewery, Cervecería Cuauhtémoc, had its headquarters in that city and produced the beer Carta Blanca (White Card).

58. "Tapatías" is the female demonym from Guadalajara, capital of Jalisco.

59. Orozco, "Tequila Sauza," 200–201.

60. Jeffrey M. Pilcher, "José Cuervo and the Gentrified Worm: Food, Drink, and the Touristic Consumption of Mexico," in *Holiday in Mexico: Critical Reflections on Tourism and Tourist Encounters*, ed. Dina Berger and Andrew Grant Wood (Durham, NC: Duke University Press, 2010), 221–40.

61. Marta Delfín Guillaumin, "Fiesta de Santa Cecilia, antecedentes históricos," *Plaza Garibaldi* (Mexico City: Subdirección de Difusión Cultural de la Delegación Cuauhtémoc, Noviembre, 1990), 6.

62. *El gavilán pollero*, film, directed by Rogelio A. González Jr. (Mexico City: Producciones Mier y Brooks, S. de R.L. y C.V., 1950).

63. José Alfredo Jiménez, "Ella" ("She"), *Cancionero Popular Mexicano*, I: 306.

64. Mitchell, *Intoxicated Identities*, 2–6.

65. Miguel Aceves Mejía and Luis Aguilar, two other big stars of the Golden Age and ranchera movies, also performed "Ella." The first one sings it in the movie *Por querer a una mujer* (*For Loving a Woman*, 1951); the latter in *Nadie muere dos veces* (*Nobody Dies Twice*, 1953).

66. De la Mora argues that in ranchera comedies of the Golden Age, cantinas and their cultural practices were central to the construction of Mexican masculinities because the male bonding taking place in these spaces coarticulated with expressions of male homosexuality, therefore challenging and redefining fixed notions of heterosexual masculinity. De la Mora, *Cinemachismo*, 70–71, 89–91.

67. José Alfredo Jiménez. "Tu recuerdo y yo," *Cancionero Popular Mexicano*, I: 285.

68. "Cuando un hombre toma sus licores, es que sus amores los quiere olvidar. Se dirige con gran sentimiento y hacia la cantina se va a emborrachar"; Unknown author, "Acuérdate, acuérdate." *Cancionero Popular Mexicano*, I: 389.

69. Pedro Infante's version of Rubén de Fuentes's and Rubén Méndez's "Siempre, siempre," also known as "Siempre que me emborracho" ("Every time I get drunk"), performed in the movie *Ahí viene Martín Corona*, film, directed by Miguel Zacarías (Mexico City: Producciones Zacarías, 1951).

70. Mitchell, *Intoxicated Identities*, 4.

71. John Mraz, "Tomorrow, Today, and Always: The Golden Age of Illustrated Magazines in Mexico, 1937–1960," in *Fragments of a Golden Age*, ed. Joseph, Rubenstein, and Zolov, 151.

72. *Nosotros Los Pobres*, film, directed by Ismael Rodríguez (Mexico City: Películas Rodríguez S.A. de C.V. y Cinematográfica Rodríguez S.A. de C.V., 1947). *Ustedes Los Ricos*, film, directed by Ismael Rodríguez (Mexico City: Producciones Rodríguez Hermanos, 1948).

73. Stephanie Mitchell and Patience A. Schell, eds., *The Women's Revolution in Mexico, 1910–1953* (Lanham, MD: Rowman and Littlefield Publishers Inc., 2006).

74. Alfredo D'Orsay, "Borrachita de tequila," *Cancionero Popular Mexicano*, I: 91.

75. Cuco Sánchez, "Ando muy borracho," *Cancionero Popular Mexicano*, I: 262; Pedro Infante performed this song in the movie *Ansiedad* (*Anxiety*, 1952–53); *Ansiedad*, film, directed by Miguel Zacarías (Mexico City: Producciones Zacarías, 1952).

76. *El niño perdido*, film, directed by Humberto Gómez Landero (Mexico City: AS Films, S.A., 1947); *El portero*, film, directed by Miguel M. Delgado (Mexico City: Posa Films, S.A., 1949).

77. Pepe Guízar. "Oye Vale," *Cancionero Popular Mexicano*, I: 305. Actually, Pedro Infante recorded this song in 1950, but it was never included in any of his movies.

78. Orozco, "Tequila Sauza," 186; Toxqui, "Grupo Modelo," 289.

79. Pilcher, "José Cuervo and the Gentrified Worm," 232–33.

80. Monsiváis, "Notas sobre la cultura mexicana," 1056–57.

81. Carlos Monsiváis, *Mexican Postcards*, ed. and trans. John Kraniauskas (London: Verso, 1997), 100.

82. *Los Olvidados*, film, directed by Luis Buñuel (Mexico City: Ultramar Films, 1950).

83. The musical *Música de Siempre* (*Music of All Times*) also provides recognition of the presence of pulque among Mexicans, but it does not show its consumption, nor praise it. The movie incorporates music and singers from different parts of the world. Among those artists were the Argentine Carlos Gardel performing a tango and Edith Piaf singing "La Vie en Rose" ("The life in pink") in Spanish. The director of the movie chose to represent Mexico with a ranchera song and used the setting of a pulquería as the backdrop. *Música de Siempre*, film, directed by Tito Davidson (Mexico City: Asociación Nacional de Actores y Alianza Cinematográfica, S.A., 1958)

84. John W. Sherman. "The Mexican 'Miracle' and Its Collapse," in *The Oxford History of Mexico*, ed. Michael C. Meyer and William H. Beezley (New York: Oxford University Press, 2000), 575–607; Smith, "Mexico Since 1946," 321–96.

85. Anne Rubenstein, *Bad Language, Naked Ladies, and Other Threats to the Nation* (Durham, NC: Duke University Press, 1998), 5.

86. Gilbert M. Joseph, Anne Rubenstein, and Eric Zolov, "Assembling the Fragments: Writing a Cultural History of Mexico Since 1940," in *Fragments of a Golden Age*, Joseph, Rubenstein, and Zolov, 4–8; Arthur Schmidt, "Making It Real Compared to What?: Re-conceptualizing Mexican History Since 1940," in *Fragments of a Golden Age*, ed. Joseph, Rubenstein, and Zolov, 44–51.

87. Rubenstein, *Bad Language*, 3–4; Joseph, Rubenstein, and Zolov, "Assembling the Fragments," 8–11; Schmidt, "Making It Real Compared to What?" 43–54; Thelma Camacho Morfín, "La Historieta, mirilla de la vida cotidiana en la Ciudad de México (1904–1940)," in *Historia de la Vida Cotidiana en Mexico: Siglo XX* (Mexico City: El Colegio de México-Fondo de Cultura Económica, 2005), 5: 49–81.

88. William B. Taylor, *Drinking, Homicide, and Rebellion in Colonial Mexican Villages* (Stanford, CA: Stanford University Press, 1979); Susan Deans-Smith, "The Working Poor and the Eighteenth-Century Colonial State," in *Rituals of Rule, Rituals of Resistance: Public Celebrations and Popular Culture in Mexico*, ed. William H. Beezley, Cheryl English Martin, and William E. French (Wilmington, DE: SR Books, 1994), 47–75; Michael C. Scardaville, "Alcohol Abuse and Tavern Reform in Late Colonial Mexico City," *Hispanic American Historical Review* 60, no. 4 (1980): 643–71; Steve J. Stern, *The Secret History of Gender: Women, Men, and Power in Late Colonial Mexico* (Chapel Hill: University of North Carolina Press, 1995); Juan Pedro Viqueira, *Propriety and Permissiveness in Bourbon Mexico* (Wilmington, DE: SR Books, 1999); Pamela Voekel, "Peeing on the Palace: Bodily Resistance to Bourbon Reforms in Mexico City," *Journal of Historical Sociology* 5, no. 2 (1992):183–208; Pablo Piccato, "'El Paso de Venus por el disco del Sol': Criminality and Alcoholism in the Late Porfiriato," *Mexican Studies/Estudios Mexicanos* 11, no. 2 (1995): 203–41; María Áurea Toxqui Garay, "'El Recreo de los Amigos': Mexico City's *Pulquerías* during the Liberal Republic (1856–1911)" (PhD diss., University of Arizona, 2008).

Many historians believe that the Revolution, at least for the growing middle class, ended with the massacre of student protesters in the Plaza of Tlatelolco in 1968. Coming at the end of the Mexican Miracle, this violence signaled a shift in legitimacy rapidly put into song and poem by citizens who felt betrayed by the broken promises of the PRI. Rising oppression and falling oil prices excluded all but the wealthiest from prosperity and security. By the 1980s, the nation faced a number of serious problems including massive debt, drastic devaluation, and systemic corruption on a staggering scale. In the midst of the "lost decade," catastrophe struck the nation when an earthquake in excess of eight on the Richter scale devastated Mexico City. In the aftermath of the tragedy, the government's response revealed ineptness in their efforts to deal with the catastrophic events. Grassroots and neighborhood organizations stepped in to deal with the crisis and help their fellow citizens where the government was unable—or, at worst, unwilling—to. In so doing, the capital's citizens demonstrated that a robust civil society existed and, out of the turmoil, a number of popular organizations emerged, advocating affordable housing, indemnification for the victims, and women's and indigenous rights. Amanda Ledwon investigates how the national government sought to commemorate that tragic event through reformulation of well-known and well-regarded poems from 1968, suitably altered to memorialize the earthquake and its aftermath. She examines how neighborhood organizations responded to these reworked cultural productions with their own visions of governance.

"Algo sobre la Muerte del mayor Sabines"*

Te enterramos ayer.
Ayer te enterramos.
Te echamos tierra ayer.

"Something on the Death of The Older Sabines"

We buried you yesterday.
Yesterday we buried you.
We shoveled dirt on you yesterday.

*Jaime Sabines, "Algo Sobre la Muerte del Mayor Sabines," *Ofrenda de Poesía Para Nuestra Ciudad y Nuestros Muertos*, Ciudad de México, Noviembre de 1985." Gallery 3 exp. 1, 11–01–00–00, c.3 MMH Archivo General de la Nación México D.F.

Quedaste en la tierra ayer.
Estás rodeado de tierra
desde ayer.
Arriba y abajo y a los lados
por tus pies y por tu cabeza
está la tierra desde ayer.
Te metimos en la tierra,
te tapamos con tierra ayer.

Perteneces a la tierra
desde ayer.
Ayer te enterramos
en la tierra, ayer.

Yesterday you stayed in the dirt.
You are surrounded by dirt
since yesterday.
Over and under and on both sides,
by your feet and by your head,
there is dirt since yesterday.
We put you in the earth,
we covered you yesterday with the
earth.

You belong to the earth
since yesterday.
Yesterday we buried you
in the earth, yesterday.

Discussion Questions

1. Why might this poem have been chosen to commemorate Mexico City's 1985 earthquake?
2. What types of symbolic imagery does the poet employ? Why might have he chosen these symbols?
3. How might the repeated invocation of "yesterday" speak to historical understandings of these events as part of popular memory?

CHAPTER EIGHT

Let Us Weep Among the Dust

Recycled Poems of 1968 and Operas of Earthquake

Amanda Ledwon

One of *los topos* (the human "moles") who dug through the collapsed buildings after the 1985 earthquake likened it to the aftermath of 1968 because of the similar echoes of devastation. Tlatelolco, the site of the student-led march, appeared again as a war zone, and although he "barely participated" in the student movement in 1968, that year Hector Méndez witnessed the birth of a new social conscience brought about by the massacre of the students at the Plaza de las Tres Culturas (Plaza of Three Cultures). That initially peaceful demonstration resulted in hundreds of students killed by the directive of the ruling party, the Partido Revolucionario Institucional (Institutional Party of the Revolution, PRI).

This chapter argues that after the 1985 earthquake, the PRI attempted to draw upon the social consciousness of 1968 through high-culture celebrations of poetry and music, and that this proved ineffective over the long run, never reaching the lower classes. Moreover, PRI officials' choice of poems reveals that their commemoration often relied on works that stressed death, disorder, and government-sponsored violence (for example, even harkening back to the human sacrifices of the Aztecs). In so doing, they undermined some of the message that they attempted to convey and drew readers' attention to their own failures as servants of the public good and as the protectors of the public trust. The Secretaría de Educación Pública (the Secretariat of Education, SEP), under writer Miguel González Avelar, organized various cultural events that targeted the city's elite as well as the ordinary public. For example, their Día de los Muertos (Day of the Dead) program—an event that took place in the wake of the catastrophic 1985 earthquake—included a pamphlet of poetry targeting the 1968 consciousness of the national narrative and the imaginative representation of that remembered moment, the *imaginaire*.

Serge Gruzinski's notion of the imaginaire lends itself to this study insofar as an image is never adapted solely at face value. He argued that the repetition of value-loaded visual descriptions provided a semantic shortcut for viewers and producers that could be reapplied strategically to explain or frame ongoing crises. Images evoke political meanings and take on new realities with each turn of historical events. Gruzinski noted that these images "have whatever 'reality' and content that an age, a culture, a group consents to give to them." [1] The PRI reactivated the imaginaire of 1968 by compiling and republishing celebrated poets important to the student movement in later years. These representations contain a fluidity that can overlap with the past or into the future, and the poetic images of 1968 and 1985 likewise offered rejuvenated memories in order to frame contemporary events.

This essay analyzes two previously unexamined cultural artifacts: a government poetry pamphlet and a commissioned opera, to examine the trajectory of the post-catastrophe imaginaire. I begin with the 1968 backdrop of an unsettled reactionary student population directly attacked by a political machine bent on silencing demonstrations. The essay continues with the imaginaire of 1985 and addresses the earthquake and responses from various neighborhoods and political organizations. The government brought the two sets of images and memories together with an "imaginaire of tradition" during traditional Día de los Muertos festivities. Through combining these imaginaires, the pamphlet of poetry published for the Día de los Muertos festivities repurposed the consciousness of the 1968 student movement, and celebrated the importance of popular solidarity. By discursively equating the student massacres with an earthquake, the PRI sought to make mourning seem natural, apolitical, and nationalist. The poems redefined the city itself as the chief victim of the disaster, rather than acknowledging individuals and their losses. This also worked to obscure the government's role in failing the people. Lastly, the PRI launched an operatic interpretation of the earthquake that reinforced praise for the people's movements that rose in response to the disaster. The operatic commemoration of the earthquake reenacted the solidarity of the bucket brigades in the streets that saved the lives of trapped individuals when emergency relief teams did not respond. After two annual performances this cantata has not resurfaced, and the government did little to recognize the continued importance of the people's solidarity movement. The 1985 PRI government leaders ignored their own failures in dealing with the crumbling city in the aftermath of the earthquake, much as they had previously avoided blame for the 1968 student massacre. Instead the SEP co-opted the people's poetry from 1968 to use in 1985, and briefly praised the people's actions through a commemorated performance of high culture.

The PRI transformed previously used images of Mexican culture, and if post facto representations of culture illuminated political moments, the symbolic images also reinforced patriotic sentimentality. [2] In fact, the PRI secretary general in 1972 noted (perhaps cynically) that: "only with popular power can the president and the PRI democratically and freely resolve the country's problems."[3] Through cultural examinations citizens remembered images and representations of the not-too-distant past with an idealized nostalgia. The PRI had manipulated images since their 1929 inception by taking the name of the "revolutionary party" and by recycling loaded rhetoric constructed with a specific image of national culture in mind. By using compositions from José Carlos Becerra, Efraín Huerta, José Emilio Pacheco, Octavio Paz, Xavier Villaurrutia, Rosario Castellanos, Miguel Guardia, Jaime Sabines, and Fray Ángel María Garibay, the party attempted to co-opt Mexican poets during the chaos ensuing after the 1985 earthquake. Through the poetry presented at the Día de los Muertos celebration, a reaffirmation of nostalgia reminded the audiences that normalcy would return and the country would move forward. At the same time, localized gatherings not affiliated with the government, and commemorative events hosted by independent barrios (neighborhoods) sought to fundraise and rebuild independently. This only increased the distance between government efforts and popular demands for reconstruction and property rights.

After the earthquake of 1985, the PRI severely undermined its relationship with Mexico City residents by disappointing them first with ineptitude in dealing with catastrophe and later by failing to adequately memorialize the dead. For example, the regime presented citizens with an offering of a memorial pamphlet of familiar poets that did little to assuage popular grief. The poems, written by a host of prominent national authors, often focused on themes of a crippled city and human suffering. For elite audiences the poems could have offered a vision of a resilient town and resilient citizenry that, in the past, had overcome crises in its own self-formation into a modern, developed capital. Yet the darker themes articulated in the works may have also served to emphasize the government's botching of the earthquake relief efforts as well as reawakening memories of that state-sponsored violence of 1968. This link would have been especially powerful, considering that many of the poets appearing in the government's pamphlet had, a generation earlier, harshly criticized the failures of government policymaking during the student protests. In this way, the poems put forward a contradictory message. On one side, they celebrated the people's resilience in the face of tragedy. Simultaneously though, the poets drew attention to how human suffering and the city's destruction resulted from a government that had promoted tremendous economic development at the expense of social justice and adequate living conditions.

The PRI sought reinforcement of their political legitimacy in the Día de los Muertos festivities.[4] As a modern celebration, the living celebrated the dead with a commemorative ritual more aesthetic than sacred. Traditionally, the living hoped that they would meet the dead at some mystical halfway point between life and death. From October 31 to November 2, images of death mixed with life: nighttime celebrations lit up graveyards and life was sweetened with sugared breads and candies. People commemorated their loved ones, and affirmed the presence of life in death, in a symbolic discourse where traditional sacred icons met modern electrical lights, and they offered tequila alongside pre-Hispanic tobacco. The space of cultural meanings that this constituted permitted the elite room to frame death as they saw fit. In this atmosphere the PRI issued contemporary poetry once used by the students of 1968 as propaganda for the masses of 1985. Mingling high culture and low culture, they took advantage of the opportunity to re-entrench the status quo as a product of their contrived imaginaire.

High and Low Imaginaires

Differing in style and grandeur from other statues on the Alameda Central, the large municipal park in downtown Mexico City, a modest plaque attempted to bridge the metaphorical distance between the politicians and the people. The engraving in the ground, *Septiembre 19 de 1985* (September 19, 1985), marks the date of the strongest recorded earthquake in Mexico City. This compromise stands in lieu of the traditional statues that decorate the Alameda. Instead a smaller park labeled on maps as Plaza de la Solidaridad (Solidarity Plaza) was granted to the people after petitions to Congress that requested a significant monument in honor of the camaraderie. It was at this location where the Hotel Regis crumbled to the ground, crushing many occupants, yet this was not necessarily the most devastated or significant disaster site. Next to the engraving in the concrete, a flagpole is held up by enormous bronzed hands coming out of the ground. When the petitioners from the barrios asked for a commemorative monument sponsored by the government, they were unaware that the almost immediate high-culture response enacted by SEP instead favored poets and cantatas.

In the aftermath of the earthquake the SEP, under Miguel González Avelar, took unprecedented measures to reactivate Mexican nationalism and collective identity. His personal memories as a twenty-six-year-old during the students' movement of 1968, at which time he had been in the PRI only six years, did not dissuade him from working for the state. A central figure in politics, in addition to being senator of Durango, González Avelar had a long résumé in government service as a director of the professors at UNAM, a reformer of the diplomatic corps at the Instituto Matías Romero, and a stint in public relations with the Foreign Relations Secretariat. More significantly to this study, he also published sophisticated works as an author and a poet, and enjoyed a long friendship with such intellectuals as Juan José Arreola, considered the premier short story writer in the genre of magical realism. His own complex writings, including works composed entirely in palindromes, suggest a highly developed intellect, and his political instincts nearly led him to the presidency as he joined the ranks of the six *presidenciables* chosen as the PRI shortlist for the 1988 election. Nothing in his biography therefore would indicate a man unable to recognize the contradictory messages in the poetry he directed the SEP to publish, or one unaware of the impact of dredging up old imaginaires for new purposes. Rather, the apparent failure to draw on more appropriate cultural messages reflects instead how the government counted on the fluidity of meanings in the imaginaire to show audiences both that the PRI was conscious of historical errors and nonetheless could manage the message through canny cultural production. The possibility that González Avelar subtly worked against his own party in this through his selections cannot be dismissed either, especially given his penchant for satirical wordplay. Yet on the surface, the campaign seemed a genuine experiment in reaching Mexicans with a clear message of national unity.

The SEP utilized the elements of indigenous heritage, traditions of celebration, gains of Independence, honor of the Revolution, and characteristics of perseverance to carry on what previous scholars defined as the project of Mexican identity or Mexican-ness. Thematic origins of identity stemmed from texts by cultural critics like Samuel Ramos, Octavio Paz, and more recently Carlos Fuentes, Elena Poniatowska, and Carlos Monsiváis.[5] After a little over a month had passed, the SEP presented *chilangos* (Mexico City residents) with poetry as an *ofrenda* (altar) for November 1, 1985.[6] The ofrenda of poetry as a part of Dia de los Muertos tradition acted in the same manner as the prayer card at a funeral service, yet it offered poetry to be read instead of prayer. One year later, on September 20, 1986, a commemorative recital offered poetry readings, testimonial accounts, and musical performances. In the chaotic time after the earthquake, commemorative events provided the elite a chance to communicate their chosen message to ordinary people. Yet such events only served to highlight the government's ineffective response. They publicly made known the growing divide between PRI officials—often self-identifying as the apostles of the Revolution and as the bearers of the vision of social justice—and the country's lower and working classes that had expected a more capable response to post-earthquake relief efforts. Instead, residents of the city's poorer sections received poetry and opera.

Previously, scholars examined high culture in the artistic spheres of classical music, opera, and other performances with limited audiences. It can be defined in opposition to popular culture, where the latter consists of daily practices and instilling the pleasure in everyday life, yet the two are not oppositional.[7] In fact what is popular can become a part of national identity as easily as elements of high culture. The response by the SEP possibly misread the possibilities of cultural transmission. They compiled a pamphlet of poetry distributed on the Día de los Muertos, and a spring performance of an opera-like cantata, intending to seem in touch and sensitive to the plight of the lower classes. In the chaotic atmosphere of 1985, they hoped to reconnect with the citizens of Mexico City. Nevertheless, in the earthquake victims' (*damnificados*) continued protests and demands it became clear that these highbrow measures failed in pacifying popular anger.

The Echoes of 1968

The year 1968 marked a turning point in Mexican history. Leading into that year, the PRI sought to perpetuate the cultural narrative of a resilient country that could sustain itself internally, supported by strong economic growth. The dream of the Mexican Revolution played out through the idea of the Mexican Revolutionary Family metaphor, one in which the state acted as an all-knowing father figure who paternalistically guided his family of citizens through the economic transitions of a developing nation.[8] The country had matured in the eyes of the international community. With 6 to 8 percent growth annually from the 1940s to the 1960s, national leaders set their sights on gaining the status of a "first world" nation, and after earning the right to host the Olympics in 1968, the potential to become a global leader seemed on the horizon.[9]

Scholars have also argued that a Cultural Olympiad, which accompanied the 1968 Olympics, further constructed the cultural hegemony of Mexico.[10] Conceived in 1966, the Cultural Olympiad sought to represent a matured modernity of the state. For every one of the twenty Olympic events, a cultural counterpart celebrated the arts. In an attempt to differentiate Mexico from its previous stereotypes of a developing nation and in order prove the readiness of the city, the organizers of the Cultural Olympiad staged performances and poetry contests to begin in January of 1968. Controversy surrounding the organization of the Olympics itself began from the winning bid. President Adolfo López Mateos (1958–1964) set winning the bid as a personal goal and once achieved, he became the head of the Mexican Organizing Committee (MOC).[11] After criticism for spending too much money, López Mateos stepped down due to "health concerns" and Pedro Ramírez Vásquez, the nation's prominent architect, resumed the duties of the MOC and representing Mexico as a continued cultural presence throughout the games.

While the student protests of 1968 now overshadow the Olympic year, the nation set the trend in becoming the first host country to integrate a cultural component to the games. International poetry contests and folkloric dance performances created an attractive atmosphere to the worldview.[12] In many symbolic gestures Mexico renewed images of tradition and modernization, even lighting the Olympic flame at the archaeological site of Teotihuacán on Columbus Day after retracing the route of Cortés.[13] With over 1,500 cultural events throughout Mexico City, the very youth that would soon protest in October "no doubt took advantage of the various publicly subsidized cultural performances being offered."[14] Octavio Paz, author and intellectual, who published the 1966 modern poetry compilation *Poesía en movimiento* (*Poetry on the Move*) represented his home country and spoke at some of these performances. One resulting factor of the Cultural Olympiad was that "the tools of the oppressors became the language of the protesters."[15]

Students challenged the government's vision and the PRI implemented a plan to silence student voices. Early in the summer, students protested against those in power who, in their eyes, had proven themselves manipulative and traitorous. Students of 1968 across the nation called on elements of the Cuban Revolution of 1953, the telephone workers' strike of 1958, the railroad workers' strike of 1959, and the medical students' strike of 1965, and they emulated international youth counterculture movements. They concluded that the government had failed to meet the ideals outlined in the Constitution of 1917.[16] They also questioned the priorities of the government in hosting the Olympic Games in a country where endemic poverty remained a terrible problem. Protesting since July of 1968, students of many colleges in the capital gathered together in one culminating march ten days prior to the opening ceremony of the Summer Olympics. In that march, the PRI sent soldiers to fire upon the student protesters and indiscriminately killed approximately 400 individuals.[17] This marked a turning point in the national narrative, and it created a sense of betrayal that undermined the PRI's claim to be the representative of the Revolution. Authors' and poets' works became vehicles for protesting the senseless massacre.

Certain writers already held a privileged position in the definition of Mexican identity both at home and abroad. Until October of 1968, poets and scholars often held governmental appointments and some represented the PRI internationally (and González Avelar continued his involvement with this later). Octavio Paz accepted many appointments in the diplomatic corps of the government prior to 1968. He joined the corps in 1945 and traveled to Paris, New York, New Delhi, Tokyo, and Geneva as a government representative. The influential *Labyrinth of Solitude*, originally published in 1950, earned him unofficial status as one of the fathers of national identity. He articulated archetypal aspects of what it meant to be Mexican. His discussion of the many masks of Mexicans addressed the differing attitudes toward life, death, and vulnerabilities for men and for women. Paz asserted that the Mexican is "a person who shuts himself away to protect himself: his face is a mask and so is his smile . . . he builds a wall of indifference and remoteness between reality and himself."[18] When differentiating between men and women, he noted the "macho" ideal of men who do not back down from a fight, who maintain a stoic front especially in war or politics. For their part, women maintained prudence and did not seek attention, rather they attracted it, unless they exhibited characteristics of *mala mujeres* (bad women) who acted aggressively. In his travels he further developed the narrative of the "many Mexicos."[19]

The 1966 volume titled *Poesía en movimiento* collected the leading Mexican poets from 1915 to 1966 and presented some defining yet controversial works that would shape the student movements. Collectively edited by Octavio Paz, Ali Chumacero, José Emilio Pacheco, and Homero Aridjis, this definitive collection of Mexican poetry resurfaced in a 2006 text titled *Cartas cruzadas* (*Crossed Correspondence*), which documented the conversations between Paz and his editor Arnaldo Orfila Reynal at Siglo XXI Press. [20] Paz and his editor discussed intricate details including whether to label the text an anthology, an idea that the writer refused. An anthology limited and measured boundaries for *mexicanidad* (Mexican-ness) and Paz wished for a more all-encompassing goal detailing the forward movement of poetry and society.[21] He decided to incorporate modern poetry and modern poets, thus creating a seemingly advanced nationalist narrative that would further the country's international status. *Poesía en movimiento* responded to an earlier edition of poetry that Paz felt did not reflect a modern nation. Antonio Castro Leal tried to gather *La Poesía mexicana moderna* (Modern Mexican Poetry) in 1953 but included many nineteenth-century poets who rhymed or had fixed metric patterns. Paz preferred to include a modern experimental aesthetic.[22] He and the editors of *Poesía en movimiento* remained adamant on maintaining the original language of the poetry. After the published translation appeared in the English language, they wrote to the *New York Review of Books* in protest, reiterating previous corrections they had made and where incorrect translations had undermined their original meanings. For example, the use of "Méjico" was redacted in the translation, which diminished the intended indigenous connection and deliberate evocation in the volume.[23] The 1968 narratives and their accompanying imaginaire included rhetoric of the Cultural Olympiad as constructed in 1966. The poetry included a forward-moving, modern imaginaire.

Poesía en movimiento was important not just as a marker of 1968 mexicanidad but was also central in building the 1985 ofrenda presented in memory of Mexico City's dead. The ofrenda duplicated the imaginaire from *Poesía en movimiento.* José Carlos Becerra, Efraín Huerta, José Emilio Pacheco, Octavio Paz, Xavier Villaurrutia, Rosario Castellanos, and Jaime Sabines contributed to both publications. Additions in the ofrenda included excerpts from Miguel Guardia's sonnets, "Poesía Indígena" ("Indigenous Poetry") translated by Fray Ángel María Garibay Kintana, and an unattributed poem titled "Visión de los Vencidos" ("Vision of the Vanquished"). The text of *Poesía* had defined the contours, poetically, of one cohesive image or imaginaire of the events of the student movement and the massacre. By republishing these poets of 1968 a generation later, the PRI took control over the framing of identity the verses had offered. They revived an imaginaire steeped in tragedy and loaded with nationalism. In the context of the 1985 Día de los Muertos, the poets' older productions on death and memory could now be turned to the party's advantage.[24]

The Devastation of 1985

Seventeen years after the 1968 student movement, the PRI remained in power. In the midst of an economic crisis with inflation rising, the gross domestic product falling, and unemployment increasing, the guarantees of the Revolution were falling short. At 7:19 in the morning on September 19, 1985, an earthquake measuring 8.1 on the Richter scale shook the surface of Mexico City and caused major high-rises to waver in the skyline. Observers often note that the Torre Latinoamericana, a forty-five-story building and major landmark in the city, could be seen swaying ominously on the horizon. In addition to exposing government unpreparedness in emergency response, the earthquake proved that endemic corruption had led to unenforced building codes and shoddy construction methods, further devastating the capital city. With 250 buildings collapsed on the first day, and injured people trapped in the wreckage, chilangos immediately mobilized. In contrast, government-sanctioned emergency response teams reacted ineffectively and late. The number of deceased is now estimated at between 10,000 and 40,000 individuals. Nonetheless, headlines on Thursday, September 20, initially proclaimed vaguely that thousands of victims remained affected, before the aftershock later that night.[25] A 7.5 aftershock left the capital city further in distress despite both official and citizen-initiated responses to the ongoing disaster.

Information remained less than trustworthy as the week continued. Headlines on Friday stated that another earthquake hit but without deadly consequences.[26] The *Excélsior* newspaper printed lists of the injured, indexed by hospitals, but not by alphabetical order, making it confusing for the public trying to find their relatives and friends. Many went in person to mass-casualty sites to seek their dead loved ones. *Excélsior* reported that 1,300 corpses had been removed from the rubble but published no names of the dead.[27] Later commentary on the earthquake criticized the process for identification of cadavers, as well as the immediacy with which they were removed and disposed, which resulted in continued doubts about the true numbers of the dead. One report stated that 2,000 were confirmed dead after the second day, but that close to 7,000 cadavers had been identified while 28,000 people were still missing.[28]

The connection between tragedy past and present soon became obvious. Renowned journalist and cultural critic Carlos Monsiváis wrote for *Proceso* magazine during the events of the earthquake. His on-the-scene interviews documented an unsettling situation for individuals across the city. On September 22 Monsiváis stated that the earthquake created "*Otra Noche de Tlatelolco*" or "Another Night in Tlatelolco" because many of that area's apartment buildings had been damaged and many residents died.[29] This seems a crucial point of connection. To observers at the time, little difference existed between the natural disaster around them and the massacre of 1968. Undeserved deaths and the failure of the government pervaded the moments, and the spaces, of the cityscape. In how people remembered Tlatelolco, as a part of something near to collective memory, the imaginaire remained closely associated with government failure and public tragedy. Little of significance marked a distinction between the dead of 1968 and 1985 from this perspective.

In the absence of government action, the people banded together with a newfound solidarity to react. The Nuevo Leon apartment building in the Tlatelolco complex was one of the approximately 250 buildings in the city that were destroyed after the earthquake. Residents of the building assembled to assist each other in forming bucket brigades to haul away the rubble and search for survivors. A positive sense of solidarity pervaded through the streets, not just of Tlatelolco, but throughout all the *colonias* (neighborhoods) in Mexico City.[30] The lower classes found strength in one another as they reached out in desperation.

The few positive stories to come out of the earthquake involved the solidarity between residents as strangers rescued someone else's loved ones from collapsed structures. The miracle babies gained notoriety after surviving the earthquake beneath the rubble of Juárez Hospital and General Hospital, two of the busiest hospitals for neonatal care in the city. Thirteen of these babies survived the earthquake and were uncovered up to fourteen days after the initial tremor. Identified only by the newborn hospital bracelets on their tiny wrists, each baby was close to a water source (e.g., a broken water pipe) and sheltered in a warmer area often protected by large posts or pillars. In addition, authorities noted that because newborns were not yet used to large spaces, the confined collapsed buildings did not have the same dramatic psychological effects suffered by adults trapped in similar situations.[31] The men who found the miracle babies became known as *Los Topos*, or The Moles, and received accolades as heroes for their good deeds. Their actions also became part of future action plans for natural disasters.[32]

While a spontaneous solidarity pulled the city together, official leaflets distributed en masse offered rhetoric that opposed popular actions. The leaflets expected citizens to "allow rescue workers to do their jobs, stay at home, your solidarity is valiant."[33] The government urged that the orderly response would come from their own agents. Yet Monsiváis also noted that "disorder prevails: different military groups, police, and doctors perform[ed] without coordination and agreement."[34] *Proceso's* October 7 headline stated: "After the Quake, Manipulation, Authoritarianism, Minimization: A Civil Society strikes against the powers that be and rejects submission."[35] The posted motto of the streets of Colonia Morelos read: "if your house is in danger of falling then settle in the streets, don't abandon the *colonia*." A chant throughout the colonia declared: "Peritaje rapido / Hechos no promesa / Vecinos dañados unidos" ("Bring experts fast / make no promises (signed) / Damaged Neighbors United"). The protesters demanded effective assistance from the government of President Miguel de la Madrid (1982–1988). They laid the blame for an unsatisfactory response on the office of the presidency and the PRI. At a meeting of the Congress of the Deputies, residents argued that their dead could speak better than city officials.[36]

Advisers to de la Madrid briefed him within minutes of the earthquake on the serious damage, resulting in the postponement of his trip to the coast of Michoacán. Propaganda-style pamphlets written in English suggest that he flew over the scene by helicopter and toured the most affected areas by bus. He also called a meeting of his cabinet and established two emergency commissions, one to deal with the earthquake in the Federal District and one for the rest of the nation.[37] Because 40 percent of the city was without electricity he also sent out the army and the city police under the guidance of Ramón Aguirre Velázquez, mayor of Mexico City. His efforts to maintain peace and to secure the property of citizens largely failed.[38]

These initial actions by President de la Madrid and Mayor Aguirre proved superficial at best, and at worst furthered a breach in the trust of citizens for his administration and the PRI party. Some unscrupulous army and police officials looted and pillaged the city, and many prevented citizens from helping to rescue trapped individuals. Citizens of the apartments at Tlatelolco could hear their neighbors shouting for help after being trapped in the rubble, but police would not allow them to get close or assist. Bizarrely, the president also denied or limited international assistance so that the country might appear more capable in dealing with the disaster in the eyes of the international community than they actually were.[39] When de la Madrid took office, he promised recovery from the 1982 debt crisis through liberalization of the economy. Scholars have maintained that he shunned international disaster aid in hopes that his own initial programs would salvage the economy and prove sufficient to save the city. Instead these actions stalled assistance and angered citizens.[40] An economy on the rebound and global leadership would have proven the viability of the PRI and the Revolution, but the earthquake halted any achievements under the de la Madrid term.

The regime instead attempted to protect its image as the world looked on, anticipating the International Association of the Federation of Football (FIFA) World Cup Championships to be held in Mexico City in 1986. De la Madrid called FIFA President João Havelange almost immediately after the quake to reassure him that the stadium was not damaged and that the games would still go on.[41] Aware of de la Madrid's priorities, a political cartoon in the September 23 edition of *Excélsior* portrayed FIFA President Havelange as a vampire with pointed teeth and wearing a black cape saying: "We are not interested in the dead nor the injured, only the stadiums for the World Cup."[42] While the political cartoon criticized the value placed on FIFA, the front page of the sports section on September 21 held a picture of the stadium half the size of the page with a large banner heading proclaiming: "Los Estadios Sin Daños" ("The Stadiums are not Damaged").[43] This did little to remedy the troubles facing earthquake survivors.

Official messages from government organizations posted in public spaces gave much-needed "*Recomendaciones a la Población*" ("Recommendations to the Population"). One broadside described proper precautions to take after an earthquake, covering everything from sanitizing water to volunteering—the latter being an action the posters discouraged.[44] Auxiliary health organizations set up under the president's emergency directive arranged for distribution of potable water, dissemination of information on where to take cadavers, and assistance programs. The Secretaría de Salud (SdS, Secretary of Health) also set up interim housing for up to ninety days. Because of the devastating effects of the earthquake and a lack of preparedness by government officials, the ninety-day housing proved too limited. Some chilangos lived in tents in public places for years because of the lack of effective assistance programs.[45] One year prior to the earthquake, the government closed the Prevention of Disasters and Management of Risk Office as a result of austerity measures implemented to combat a troubled economy. That office initially set up and planned for all responses to natural disasters such as major earthquakes. With this closure, the government had no plan or agency in place to deal with a major earthquake.[46]

Issues of home ownership complicated relief efforts. Without the Prevention of Disasters and Management of Risk Office, problems multiplied for the city's residents who did not own their homes formally. Previous to the earthquake, residents of the Tlatelolco apartment complex initiated negotiations to become owners of their apartments. In the earthquake the fifteen-story building of Nuevo Leon, within the Tlatelolco complex, collapsed and the middle-class citizens residing there had little recourse to initiate reconstruction. Residents expected that since they had purchased their homes, they could hire independent technicians to repair damages and be responsible for maintenance. As negotiations dragged on, residents became more concerned that buildings would remain in disrepair. After the earthquake, residents demanded a say in the rebuilding efforts. The earthquake caused incipient protest groups to transform into fully active oppositional factions. The damnificados (earthquake victims) of Tlatelolco marched in protest, and they were not alone.

More organizations formed and joined in the press for government action. The Unión Popular de Inquilinos de la Colonia Morelos (Popular Union of Colonia Morelos Tenants) presented a long list of demands for rebuilding materials to Congress. They first organized using flyers depicting an imploded house from the neighborhood. Another organization called Barrios en Lucha (Neighborhoods in Struggle) posted flyers in neighborhoods and called for a meeting of los damnificados. Their posters prominently displayed the image of revolutionary Pancho Villa, suggesting that the damnificados, not the PRI, genuinely acted in the spirit of the Revolution as protectors of the lower classes. Demands from the Barrios en Lucha on one particular flyer included: economic compensation; the right to

Figure 8.1. "Barrio en lucha" poster. Anonymous artist, ca. 1985.

live a dignified life in the area they lived in prior to the earthquake without unjustified relocation; assistance with sufficient rental opportunities (money and location); employment through government assistance; the right to be secure in their own homes. As one of the more active associations, Barrios en Lucha organized a march on October 26, 1985. Thousands showed up in support, marching from the Angel of Independence to Los Pinos to show President de la Madrid the unity of los damnificados.[47]

On October 26, 1985, 40,000 individuals joined in protest to march against the PRI. Collectively, the Coordinadora Única de Damnificados (CUD, Unified Coordinating Committee of Earthquake Refugees) represented the displaced peoples of the city.[48] They marched to Los Pinos (the president's residence) and members from the PRI negotiated with the people. The PRI announced that they would relocate the displaced peoples from Tlatelolco and move them to "equivalent housing as far as seventy miles away." Guillermo Carrillo Arena, head of the federal Environmental Agency, belittled the CUD in an attempt to squash the movement. However, after several of the buildings he approved collapsed, de la Madrid fired him from his post. After a new team from the PRI continued to negotiate with the CUD, the people's movement thrived.

"The 19th of September Seamstresses Union" had also marched with Tlatelolco residents in October. They sought to draw attention to concerns regarding the women's deplorable treatment during the earthquake, and to demands that employers pay out any outstanding wages owed to deceased workers' families. On the morning of September 19, tens of thousands of seamstresses worked while locked in cramped factories guarded by strict foremen. With no escape routes and with foremen blocking doors, 1,600 workers perished. At least 800 garment shops caved in. Reports by women who escaped documented that the army and the police used heavy equipment to haul away the sewing machines and processing tools rather than assist the trapped victims. Of the seamstresses that survived, between 40,000 and 70,000 were left jobless.[49] The families of the seamstresses who perished received no restitution from the industry owners and did not receive the wages due to the women. As the story gained media attention the union strengthened. Ultimately, the Ministry of Labor granted independent union status to the seamstresses and they won 90 percent of their severance claims.

Nonetheless, direct pressure by the PRI prevented the organization's ability to flourish democratically, and struck some old nerves. When the time came for leadership elections, the PRI-affiliated Labor Federation Unions bullied the women into voting for their chosen people. The women said it was if they were fighting a "three headed monster of bosses, the government, and official unions." The seamstresses opposed the PRI's understood practice of organizing unions. Traditionally the PRI put agreeable leaders in positions of power independent of elections. This imposition reminded the seamstresses of the 1968 movement and the charro-style union management of earlier times, and for many students of that movement, now in their forties, it rekindled past disappointments. They also connected the PRI's initial responses to the October march on Los Pinos with their past experiences of oppression and dismissal. Noting that the party line still had not changed since the student massacre in the Plaza at Tlatelolco, more grassroots organizations protested the party in power.[50]

A Tradition of Death

As unrest and turmoil played out yet again in the streets of Mexico City, old traditions continued in city life. The tradition of All Saints Day, also called Día de los Muertos, memorialized the annual celebration of life and death each November 1 and 2. The festival that followed the earthquakes held special significance because many residents of Mexico City remained missing and unaccounted for, presumed to be dead. Traditions from the holiday included elements from the precolonial to the modern day, and utilized both public and private spaces, as residents built altars dedicated to the dead. It should be noted that although the traditional term for Día de los Muertos altars is ofrenda, the pamphlet of poetry discussed in this chapter, titled *Ofrenda de Poesía Para Nuestra Ciudad y Nuestros Muertos* (*Offering of Poetry for Our City and Our Dead*), does not accompany a physical altar. Decorated skulls inspired by Aztecs and crosses of Roman-Catholic origin adorned memorials in the home and at gravesites. Altars in the home contained photographs of the deceased and gifts to welcome them in case of their return. For adults, gifts included tobacco and alcohol, while for children, gifts included new toys and candy. Other offerings included elaborate breads, decorative paper cutouts, and candied decorated *calaveras* (skulls). Known for celebrating the tradition in a more secular manner, the capital city took a more aesthetic, artistic, and intellectual stance than did much of the country. Satirical poems written on large broadsides, also called calaveras, hung throughout the city and poked fun at custom and politics.[51] Altars in the city adorned nonreligious institutions such as museums, restaurants, and community centers. In an effort to tap into the traditions and to establish a secular presence in the public sphere of Día de los Muertos, the SEP published an offering of its own, in the form of recycled poetry for the city and for the dead.

In *Death and the Idea of Mexico*, Claudio Lomnitz argues that in 1985 a political renaissance in using the Día de los Muertos emerged. A cartoon in *La Jornada* magazine illustrated a calavera painting with the slogan “2 de Noviembre no se olvida” (“November 2 is not forgotten”) on a wall of a graveyard, playing on the popular slogan which first appeared after the 1968 student massacre.[52] The political possibilities to shape the image of the disaster, on a holiday meant to commemorate the dead, appealed to the government as a means to allay blame for their own mishandling of the situation.

For González Avelar’s SEP, the time seemed opportune to use the message of poets and poems in a way that supported the PRI and the nationalist narrative. Considering that Octavio Paz recognized death as a part of national character, this subject translated a culturally significant message.[53] The SEP intended to remind Mexicans of a cohesive national identity utilizing a Day of the Dead ofrenda of Mexican poetry that echoed across time periods. The Day of the Dead folklore permitted the living and the dead to meet at the threshold that usually separated them, and so the past and present could also come together in rhetoric.[54] The moment of the imaginaire of

1985 festivities embedded cultural productions in customary practices. Tradition blurred politics in the context of the emotional chaos faced by people still seeking the missing and dead victims of the earthquake.

The Government's Ofrenda and Reintroduced Poets

The poetry of the ofrenda resonated with the Día de los Muertos theme by incorporating death in every piece, and tying the holiday to contemporary imaginaires. With recognizable names, faces, and legends surrounding them, poets of the ofrenda spanned history from Nahuatl poetry of the sixteenth century to the 1983 poem of José Emilio Pacheco, "Crónica Mexicáyotl." The poems included in the ofrenda were not written to commemorate the earthquake or Día de los Muertos; rather these poets were writing about various other moments, some personal, as in Jaime Sabines's poem on the death of his father, and some historical, as with the anonymous voice of the vanquished. González Avelar selected poets in this compilation who resonated with the population and because these poems reminded the students of 1968 that at one point, in the not too distant past, they had been the focus of the nation. The losses of September 19 would be redeemed, as had (in theory) those of October, sixteen years previously.

In the first four selections, the subject of the city acted as an organic living entity injured and facing death. By focusing on the city as the chief victim of the quake, the compilation coincidentally robs the human victims of their tragedy and agency; there are no dead in this grieving. José Carlos Becerra's "Épica" presents the city as injured despite progress:

Me duele esta ciudad	I grieve for this city
me duele esta ciudad cuyo progreso se me	I grieve this city whose progress is
viene encima como un	coming upon me
muerto invencible,	like an invincible death,
como las espaldas de la eternidad dormida	as the backs of eternity sleeping
sobre cada una de mis	on each of my
preguntas.[55]	questions.

"Invincible deaths" or undefeatable deaths kept propelling the forward progress of the city and embodied the ethic of resilience within mexicanidad. The poem, originally published in 1967, made mention of pyramids, a reference responding to the creation of the mass transit subway system known as the Metro in Mexico City:

En estas palabras hay un poco de polvo egipcio	In these words there is a little dust of Egypt
hay unas cuantas vendas, hay un olor de	there are a few bandages, there is a smell of
pirámides adormecidas en	pyramids asleep
el algodón del pasado,	in the cotton of the past,
y hay también esa nostalgia que nos invade en	and there is also nostalgia that creeps upon us
ciertas tardes,	on certain things
cuando la lluvia se entrada en nuestro corazón	when the rain gets tangled up in our hearts as
como los cabellos húmedos y largos	the wet, long hair
de una mujer desconocida.	of an unknown woman.

During construction of the Pino Suárez station of the Metro, workers unearthed an Aztec pyramid still on display today.[56] The pyramid at Pino Suárez, though distinctly Mexican, resembled the Egyptian pyramids. The "cotton of the past" referred to the death shrouds of the ancient dead—the oldest victims of the city. Just as classical Egyptian mummies wrapped in cotton preserved the past of Egypt, the people of Mexico City sought to preserve their dead with the Pino Suárez pyramid. Along with the resilience of the citizens and the preserved past, the legend of La Llorona (the weeping woman) as the "unknown woman" wept for the city. Paz described her as the long-suffering Mexican mother. Legend stated that La Llorona wandered the streets late at night, weeping and searching for her lost loved ones. In addition, a preconquest legend attributed this same status to the goddess Cihuacóatl.[57] With the 1985 republication of this poem, the anonymous bereaved of the earthquake became the nameless subjects keening for the city's hurts, just as La Llorona cried for her own suffering. Yet again, the city and its pain remained the prime subject.

Efraín Huerta, in 1944's "Declaración de Amor" ("Declaration of Love"), proclaimed his love for the city as a mother figure.[58] He portrayed the city personified, and it walked as a shadow much like the La Llorona character of Becerra's poem:

Ciudad que lloras, mía,	My City that cries,
maternal, dolorosa,	maternal, sorrowful,

bella como camelia
y triste como lágrima,
mírame con tus ojos
de tezontle y granito,
caminar por tus calles
como sombra o neblina.

beautiful as camellia
and sad as a tear,
look at me with your eyes
of volcanic rock and granite,
to walk your streets
as a shadow or fog.

Lloyd Mallan argued that for each proclamation of death and darkness in Huerta's poetry there is an opposing force, which mentions life and light in his lyrical style.[59] He notes also that poets of this period leaned toward this lyrical tradition, and Huerta's poem illustrated the light and life through the heart of dawn and flowing blood. Darkness loomed because of the men who hate the city but in the next lines he spoke of laughing children and loving men:

Porque yo creo que el corazón
del alba
en un millón de flores,
el correr de la sangre
o tu cuerpo, ciudad, sin huesos
ni miseria.

Los hombres que te odian no
comprenden
cómo eres pura, amplia,
rojiza, cariñosa, ciudad mía;
cómo te entregas, lenta,
a los niños que ríen,
a los hombres que aman claras
hembras
de sonrisa despierta y fresco
pensamiento, . . .

Because I believe that the heart
of dawn
in a million flowers,
the flow of blood
or your body, city, without bones
or misery.

Men who hate you do not
understand
how you are pure, ample,
red, tender, my city;
how you give of yourself, slowly,
to the laughing children,
to the men who love bright
women
of an open smile and fresh
thought, . . .

The poem was written during the great urbanization of the city and referred also to a sexualized femininity in the metropolis character. Yet because the city blossomed again in these verses, the poem also proclaimed the promise of reconstruction for the damnificados in 1985.

Huerta and Becerra both lived through and supported the railroad workers' strike of 1959. They wrote with inspiration from the conflict and supported other popular protests like the 1968 student movement. As a result they gained the reciprocal support of the student protesters who viewed these intellectuals as intermediaries between the students of the university and the PRI. The 1968 student movement also found inspiration from other external influences such as rock and roll and the beat generation to voice a counterculture against the official PRI rhetoric.[60] Huerta and Becerra gave the students a homegrown contemporary example. Another national poet picked up on this lyrical style and at times emulated it, José Emilio Pacheco.[61]

Pacheco's lyrics proclaimed his love for the city as faith and light but contrasted it with horror and darkness. In "La noche nuestra interminable" ("Our Endless Night"), Pacheco highlighted the function of the poet as historian, stating that generations have relied on his pages of poetry, and that the pages will outlast the disasters of the city:

Mis paginitas, ángel de mi guarda, fe	My little pages, my guardian angel, the faith
de las niñeras antiquísimas,	of the ancient nannies,
no pueden, no hacen peso en la balanza	cannot weigh down the scale
contra el horror tan denso de este. mundo	against the horror of this world so dense.
Cuántos desastres ya he sobrevivido,	How many disasters have I already survived,
cuántos amigos muertos, cuánto dolor	how many dead friends, how much pain
en las noches profundas de la tortura.[62]	in the dark nights of torture.

As applied to 1985, these words fit prominently within the themes of the city succumbing to natural disaster. The events of 1968 and 1985 reaffirmed the relationship that many citizens had with death. After 1968, those who rejected the official story of the student massacre gained the support of intellectuals and poets alike. In this context, officials' decisions to publicize a poet who had been sympathetic of the student movement and critical of the government's use of violence would only serve to remind readers of its past inequities. Thus PRI officials skirted a difficult line as they sought to promote poetry that emphasized national unity and perseverance yet were forced to rely on cultural producers whose past works often stressed state-sponsored violence (a theme that could have been linked to the government's inept response as another form of state-sponsored violence). In an attempt to situate themselves as the guide that would navigate the city's denizens through traumatic events of 1985, officials drew upon the country's most celebrated poets, even though these had often been those most critical of the PRI after the 1968 student massacre.

Pacheco also wrote poetry commenting on the massacre of students of 1968 in the poem "Manuscrito de Tlatelolco" ("Manuscript of Tlatelolco"). He juxtaposed Nahuatl poetry translated by Fray Ángel María Garibay Kintana to "reactivate historical texts and underscore their modernity."[63] Ironically, this approach quite closely resembled that of the PRI's intent in republishing Pacheco as part of their new construction of the 1985 imaginaire. The poet's use of the story of the slaughter of indigenous people validated its historical merit and presented a new context for understanding the student massacre of 1968. Mary Docter asserted that this gave a double temporal perspective. The double presentation of poetry first by Garibay, and then rewritten by Pacheco, allowed the reader to compare the bloody past with current anguish and shifted the time frame between two historical moments. The 1985 ofrenda likewise attempted to reactivate historical poems and underscore their modernity, perhaps offering a triple temporality to this tale. Moreover, Pacheco's emphasis on the conquest and colonial subjugation of indigenous peoples would surely resonate as a reminder of modern-day forms of state repressions and the people's subjugation. Perhaps most notably, the colonial violence or negligence echoed in the state's handling of the 1968 protests, and again in 1985.

An edited version of "Crepúsculos de la ciudad" ("Twilights of the City") contained six sonnets in total but the ofrenda only published the first one.[64] Octavio Paz documented the imagery of a city entrenched in human suffering, with a setting sun illuminating a crumbling city. Paz's ultimate vision of the city remained bleak:

Devora el sol final restos ya inciertos;	The sun devours the final remains, now uncertain;
el cielo roto, hendido, es una fosa;	the broken sky, split, is a grave;
la luz se atarda en la pared ruinosa;	the light lingers on the ruinous wall;
polvo y salitre soplan sus desiertos.	dust and saltpeter blow on their deserts.

So many elements of desolation and destruction remained after the earthquake, and imagery from "Crepúsculos" reminded readers of this aftermath. Paz set his sights on the hopelessness of the future and in this poem, the city failed to recover. The affected citizens of the earthquake who formed protest groups for their specific barrios felt that their hearts remained locally bound. Few of them relocated and they chose to demonstrate instead, even though the government relief agencies preferred that they move to alternate temporary housing. That powerful connection to their place was echoed in Paz's poetry:

Todo lo que me nombra o que me evoca	All that names me or that evokes me
yace, ciudad, en ti, signo vacío	lies, city, in you, an empty sign
en tu pecho de piedra sepultado.	buried in your chest of stone.

In *Labyrinth of Solitude* Paz noted that for each change that the people adapted to over time, some element forced a break in the relationship to the past, thus resulting in a new mask. To refuse the acquisition of so many masks, he claimed that his country needed to sever the connection with her past.[65] He restated this point later in the work noting that a foundation of violence resulted in repeated violence so that the brutality of October 2, 1968, stemmed from the original Aztec brutality in the country's early history. Akin to other poets in the ofrenda, Paz protested the government after the 1968 massacre of students. As a result of the PRI's severe repression, Paz resigned from the post of ambassador to India. His artistic politics differed from this strong political response. He claimed "that poetry 'claimed no party' and should be 'tainted by no party'" although ironically his poetry had perhaps more political weight than that of any of his contemporaries.[66]

Pacheco acknowledged Paz's concept of many masks and personalized the phenomenon of death in the poem "Crónica Mexicayotl" ("Mexicaytol Chronicle").[67] He asserted the idea that the Nahuatl-speaking people laid claim to the land of Mexicayotl, the legendary Aztec empire, yet that land remained worthless and in ruins. Pacheco further clarified that while death and destruction hit the country, it was not the first time. While the Mexicayotl land died, the Aztec Empire and its people also died:

En otro giro de la procesión	In another twist of the procession
o de la tribu errante que somos,	or wandering tribe that we are,
henos aquí sin nada como principio	behold us here with nothing to start with
sapos y lagartijas nuestro alimento.	toads and lizards our food.
Sal nuestra vida, polvo nuestra casa.	Salt our life, our house dust.
Añicos y agujeros en la red,	Shards and holes in the net,
nuestra herencia de ruinas.	our inheritance of ruins.

Por fin tenemos
que hacerlo todo a partir
de esta nada que por fin somos.

We finally have
to do everything starting
from this nothingness that at last
we are.

"Crónica Mexicáyotl" reminded readers that another civilization occupied the area that modern Mexico rested on. Specifically in the area of Tlatelolco the PRI reintegrated an indigenous heritage by attempting to change the name of the area to Plaza de las Tres Culturas in honor of the three cultures that met at its historic junction. Underlying the Plaza de las Tres Culturas, Nahuatl archaeological ruins remained, still partially exposed. On another side of the plaza sat the seventeenth-century church of Templo de Santiago, and upon the completion of apartment-style housing in 1966, high rise edifices abutted another side of the plaza. Octavio Paz noted that despite the PRI's attempts to change the name, citizens still called the area by the historical Tlatelolco.[68] The "Crónica" also demonstrates that poetry could act as a mediator between the government's attempts to define city space and the popular understandings and memories of those same areas.

The popular imaginaire did not preclude a profound sense of the tragic past. "Visión de los Vencidos / Cantares acerca de la Conquista" ("Vision of the Vanquished / Songs about the Conquest") depicted a history of what it was like for the early ancestors of the *patria* (homeland).[69] The vanquished became so due to their military defeat at Tlatelolco. The ancient indigenous actors relied on a sparsely populated family network, which guaranteed no safety or food:

Y era nuestra herencia una red
de agujeros.

And our inheritance was a fishing
net full of holes.

Con los escudos fue su resguardo,

With the shields we lost our
security,

Pero ni con escudos puede ser
sostenida su
Soledad . . .

But not even with shields can you
sustain
Your loneliness . . .

Llorad, amigos mios,
Tened entendido que con estos
hechos
Hemos perdido la nación mexicatl
¡El agua se ha acedado, se acedó
la comida!

Weep, my friends,
Know that with these acts
We have lost the Mexica nation.
The water has bittered, the food
bittered!

Esto es lo que ha hecho el dador de la vida en Tlatelolco . . .	This is what the Giver of Life has done in Tlatelolco . . .

For the victims of the 1968 student massacre and the 1985 earthquake, this elegy to the vanquished resonated in the repeated fate of Tlatelolco. Here then, this poem fostered a symbolic historical link between the city's past destruction at the hands of conquistadors and that of the PRI as demonstrated by its poor city planning (made obvious by the earthquake) and its reliance on social violence (made obvious by its violent reaction to student protest). As such, it would be difficult for readers to miss how the events of 1968 and 1985 were part of a broader national historical memory that stressed loss and devastation at the hands of their leaders, both past and present. Perhaps González Avelar intended this connection as part of his own protest, but in any case, the audience made their own interpretations as they dealt with sorrows.

Images of death pervaded much of the poetry in the offering. In Xavier Villaurrutia's "Nocturno Muerto" ("Nocturne of Death"), images established the state of solitude, which Octavio Paz admired:

¿Quién medirá el espacio, quién me dirá el momento en que se funda el hielo de mi cuerpo y consuma el corazón inmóvil como la llama fría?	Who will measure the space, who will tell me the moment when the ice of my body melts and consumes the still heart, like a cold flame?
La tierra hecha impalpable silencioso silencio, la soledad opaca y la sombra ceniza caerán sobre mis ojos y afrentarán mi frente.[70]	The earth is made impalpable silence made silent, the solitude opaque and the ash shadow all will fall over my eyes and will cover my forehead.

Villaurrutia's connection with death created common ground to connect him to the alienation that Paz discussed in *Labyrinth of Solitude*, stating: "The Mexican is always remote, from the word and from other people, and also from himself."[71] Villaurrutia commonly wrote poems about death and "Nocturno Muerto," written in 1938, created a vision of dying alone similar to many victims of the earthquake. After the earth and buildings fell, if the neighborhoods remained silenced, then their victims died. The poem memorialized the dead of 1985 but also effectively celebrated Día de los Muertos.

Rosario Castellanos also wrote about the loneliness surrounding death. In "Amanecer" ("Dawn") she conversely presented death as dawn or an awakening.[72] "Amanecer" reminded Mexicans that during Día de Los Muertos death and life were not contradictory conditions.[73] In the cosmic sense she pleaded for life to connect to death, for she wanted no more sobbing or sadness, much as the idea of solitude found in Paz's and Villaurrutia's mexicanidad:

¿Qué se hace a la hora de morir? ¿Se vuelve la cara a la pared?	What happens at the moment of death? Do you just turn your face to the wall?
¿Se agarra por los hombros al que está cerca y oye?	Do you just grab the nearest person by the shoulders and listen?
¿Se echa uno a correr, como el que tiene las ropas incendiadas, para alcanzar el fin?	Or do you start to run, like a person who has his clothes on fire, to die faster?
¿Cuál es el rito de esta ceremonia?	What is the death ritual now?
¿Quién vela la agonía? ¿Quién estira la sábana?	Who is keeping watch as it dies? Who smoothes out the shroud?
¿Quién aparta el espejo sin empañar?	Who takes away the mirror without fog?
Porque a esta hora ya no hay madre y deudos.	At this hour there is no mother, there are no relatives.
Ya no hay sollozo. Nada, más que un silencio atroz.	There is no sobbing. Nothing, just a terrible silence.
Todos son una faz atenta, incrédula	They are all a part of that, unbelieving,
de hombre de la otra orilla.	staring at the man's face on the other shore.
Porque lo que sucede no es verdad.	Because what's happening is not true.

Noting that "no mothers" mourn the dead, Castellanos did not make reference to La Llorona; instead, she evoked the "man on the other side," the Dios de Muertos (god of the dead) who greeted the deceased at dawn.

In retrospect of 1968, Rosario Castellanos also wrote a poem titled "Memorial de Tlatelolco" ("Memorial of Tlatelolco"), in which she presented the side of the slain students.[74] The account followed the shootings during the night, and the darkness that obstructed the truth. She highlighted the dawn that followed as that which illuminated the minds of those who had not participated in the protest, yet had in that morning realized that their trust in the PRI vanished.[75]

Castellanos, the lone female poet in the compilation, supported women's fight for equal treatment under the law. In 1970 she wrote an editorial piece in *Excélsior* about a strike in the United States where women united in solidarity with men on behalf of domestic workers.[76] She attempted to set an example for women to participate equally in society. Castellanos, as a feminist of the era, supported the new wave of protest built in the tradition of the students of 1968. Elena Poniatowska noted that women's support during the cleanup of the earthquakes promoted high degrees of solidarity and had effectively forced some search parties to look for the injured in collapsed buildings.[77] Still connecting to implied memories of the 1968 events, other poems contributed to the new imaginaire but avoided the directly political in their attempt to deal with highly intimate issues regarding death.

A deep personal mourning marks Jaime Sabines Gutiérrez's poem "Algo Sobre la Muerte del Mayor Sabines" ("Something on the Death of the Elder Sabines"), written in the process of his father's illness and death.[78] This poem stressed the permanence of death, unlike those of other poets who countered death with elements of life. He repeated symbols like the earth, dirt, and land signifying the moment of burial and an end. The earth covered the father's feet, his head, and on all sides, as if embracing him. Sabines's poem attempted to soothe those with dead loved ones, reminding them that loved ones remain buried with the patria:

Te enterramos ayer.	We buried you yesterday.
Ayer te enterramos.	Yesterday we buried you.
Te echamos tierra ayer.	We shoveled dirt on you yesterday.
Quedaste en la tierra ayer.	Yesterday you stayed in the dirt.
Estás rodeado de tierra	You are surrounded by dirt
desde ayer.	since yesterday.
Arriba y abajo y a los lados	Over and under and on both sides
por tus pies y por tu cabeza	by your feet and by your head
está la tierra desde ayer.	there is dirt since yesterday.
Te metimos en la tierra,	We set you in the dirt,
te tapamos con tierra ayer.	yesterday we covered you with the earth.
Perteneces a la tierra	You belong to the earth

desde ayer.	since yesterday.
Ayer te enterramos	Yesterday we buried you
en la tierra, ayer.	in the earth, yesterday.

That Jaime Sabines's poetry influenced the citizens of the capital was in evidence at one of his last poetry readings in 1996. Overflow crowds stood outside the Palacio de Bellas Artes (the renowned performance auditorium) to hear his voice over loudspeakers, and the crowds recited the poems with him.[79] José Emilio Pacheco commented that his poems contained "everything for everybody." Sabines differed from other poets insofar as he included simple language and everyday settings, and instead of elaborate meter or metaphor, he sought to resonate on a more basic level. He also wrote on the 1968 student movement in a poem called "Tlatelolco 68." In that poem he acknowledged both the official story and the reality, and stated that morbid memory remained with the witnesses and would not be washed away as easily as the bloodied streets. It is surprising that González Avelar would include a poet with so negative a vision in SEP's official program for the dead. It seems that the poet's popularity played some part in this, but also it may be that including a critical perspective reflected a deeper strategy. Co-opting the poet into a new imaginaire set prior criticism into a new context, one where protest would be crass and disrespectful of the earthquake's victims, and with the stress now on solidarity, old disagreements might be left behind.

Additionally, some of the verses balanced this controversial approach with elements more positive and optimistic. Miguel Guardia focused on three major themes through his poetry: love, death, and solitude.[80] In "Juntaremos las Bocas" ("We Join Mouths"), the three themes resonated. Love is a kiss, a hug, and a melting of hearts:[81]

Juntaremos las bocas	We will join our mouths
lentamente . . .	slowly . . .
. . . Serás en tu caricia	. . . You will be mine in your
ciegamente . . .	caress . . .
. . . . .para fundir tu corazón y	. . . to melt and join your heart
el mío . . .	and mine . . .

Yet, in between these lines that described a loving relationship, elements contrary to love defined the poet's stance. A setting sun, a silence, and gloomy love reiterated the mexicanidad of solitude as found in the other poems and in Paz's *Labyrinth of Solitude*:

. . . Mientras afuera se depinta el día . . .	. . . While outside the day is fading . . .
. . . Nada diremos. Muda y quietamente . . .	. . . We will say nothing. Silently and quietly . . .
. . . En este amor atávico y sombrío . . .	. . . In this atavistic and gloomy love . . .
. . . Nuestras eternas soledades, Muerte. . . .	. . . Our eternal solitudes, O Death. . . . .

Guardia closed the poem with solitude because an eternal love tied individuals and "solitudes" together. This poem reminded those with lost individuals from the earthquake that people we loved remain in eternal memory.

Similarly, Jaime Sabines described death as "soft and sweet as a bed with woman" as he made love to death in the final moments. He described death as "a bitch" that represents Mexico as La Chingada, the mother that is constantly abused as Octavio Paz noted in his chapter on the sons of La Malinche:

Es blanda y dulce como una cama con mujer	It is soft and sweet as a bed with woman
Lloremos.	Let us weep.
Cantemos: la muerte, la muerte, la muerte,	Let us sing: death, death, death,
hija de puta, viene.	The bitch, comes.
La tengo aquí, me sube, me agarra	I have her here, she pulls me up, she grabs
por dentro.[82]	my gut.

Ultimately Sabines admitted to knowing the tragic nature of death. If he is the last one invited then he will do his best to dance:

Que el mundo sepa que sabemos ser trágicos.	Let the world know that we know how to be tragic.
Lloremos por el polvo	Let us weep among the dust
y por la muerte de la rosa en las manos	and for the death of a rose in my hands
Yo, el último, os invite . . .	I, the last, I invite you . . .
que va a bailar la danza que bailemos!	who will dance the dance that we dance!

Tranca la tranca,
con la musiquilla del concierto
¡qué fácil es bailar remuerto!

Bar by bar,
to the ditty of the concert
How easy it is to dance doubly
dead!

Sabines spoke of "we" and "us" in the poem, demonstrating the bonds that tie all Mexicans together. It also represented the solidarity movements after the quake of 1985. Poniatowska documented that even gang members assisted when grandmothers attempted to pull rubble off trapped individuals. The powerful bonds of lower-class sentimentality and companionship, especially in the absence of concerted government assistance, represent one of the more profound aspects of this disaster. Whatever his true purposes, González Avelar's choice of commemorative poetry connected the disaster victims discursively in the shared experiences of death and tragedy, but did little good in bringing about a nationalist sentiment of trust in the Revolutionary regime.

"Poesía Indígena" ("Indigenous Poetry") as translated from Nahuatl by Fray Ángel María Garibay came last in the ofrenda, and posited an alternative standpoint in contrast to the finality of death.[83] The indigenous concept of death cycled rather than ended, and modern intellectuals incorporated this cyclical element in poetry and fiction. As discussed earlier, Pacheco utilized indigenous poetry to connect precolonial indigenous slaughters to the massacre of students in 1968. Carlos Fuentes likewise wrote modern fiction using this cyclical concept. His epic *Terra Nostra* put the reader on edge, while turning the text into a spiral so that the reader might experience the cyclical concept of the indigenous people's calendar.[84] The poetry included in the ofrenda reiterated the concept of the cycle of life. In this case, the poem emphasized repeating cycles of violence and devastation as central to the Mexican experience. In "Anhelo de Inmortalidad" ("Longing for Immortality"), the indigenous voice of the poet mentions that he does not want to die and at the same that time he goes to where there is no death:

¡Ojalá nunca muera, ojalá nunca
perezca yo!
Allá donde no hay muerte, allá
donde se
Triunfa, allá voy yo:
¡Ojalá nunca muera, ojalá nunca
perezca yo![85]

May I never die, may I never
perish!
There where there is no death,
wherever it
prevails, there I go:
May I never die, may I never
perish!

The ofrenda presented a collection of poetry to summarize the mexicanidad of the people in the moments following the 1985 earthquake. Death, love, solitude, and resilience resonated with the literate public who familiarized themselves with poets like José Emilio Pacheco, Octavio Paz, Rosario Castellanos, Jaime Sabines, as well as indigenous poets. The more renowned poets had previously commented on the ineptitude or criminality of the PRI after the 1968 student massacre. Some of these poets understood the compromises required of politicians, and when approached had declined the responsibility of entering politics themselves. With this ofrenda the PRI utilized the potentially political moment of Día de los Muertos and interjected a reminder of themes from the national narrative, themes that they wished to continue. Yet the choice of poets also served to remind readers of state violence and state indifference (here, an alternative form of violence leveled against the people through inaction). They thus undermined government attempts to mold the historical narrative in which the victims of 1985 were commemorated.

An Operatic Memory of Solidarity

As an addendum to the poetic reframing of the disaster, the SEP also called for an artistic rendition that would cater to the cultured classes of the city. A commissioned opera-like performance documented the 1985 earthquake and its aftermath through theater and song. As a genre, the *loa* brought the historical and the religious into a modern context. The program booklet for this operatic performance notes the importance of the loa as a traditional religious music prevalent in colonial times and extending back to Spain's Golden Age. The loa was a short allegorical piece performed to praise or to commemorate an important event. Examples of Golden Age loas came from writers such as Sor Juana Inés de la Cruz and Pedro Calderón de la Barca. Sor Juana's "The loa for the auto sacramental of The Divine Narcissus" played out a dialogue between America, the Occident, Religion, and Zeal. Her allegorical loa twisted Church doctrine in support of indigenous gods. While some historians define loa merely as a "psalm," a more accurate delineation would also include that the loa acts as a dedication to a commemorated people. Music does not necessarily accompany a loa.[86]

Early operatic performances housed intellectuals and politicians, with few non-elites participating. The elite sought to model Europe's refined style and valued opera as a modernizing element to the culture of Mexico City. Two early operas written by Melesio Morales (1866) and Aniceto Ortega

(1871) demonstrated ambiguities in *mestizaje* and the role of Mexican heritage in the country's future. Former President Benito Juárez (1861–1872) and his successors established many "civilizing" efforts, which included "Europeanizing" Mexico. One operatic scholar on Mexico City cites that the "audience reinforced the prevalent beliefs on race, gender, and nation in the opera scene because its tastes helped to determine which works and which singers succeeded on the stages Mexico City."[87] The historical record therefore reflects a pattern of using opera to work out social conflicts.

The 1985 reenactment consisted of a scenic cantata, the "Lamentaciones" ("Lamentations"), composed by Federico Ibarra Groth, a Mexican-born graduate of UNAM. The trilogy with which the cantata was ultimately performed fell under the broader scope of *Loa para la Ciudad que Espera* or *Loa for which the City Waits*.[88] This high-culture opera-style performance appealed to a specific elite audience, one mostly removed from the damnificados in the public squares. It also drew on the finest of elite musical talents from the nation.

With an award-winning composer, author, and conductor, all Mexican, the PRI commissioned a particular and prideful celebration of survival. The biographical sketch of the composer, Federico Ibarra Groth, included praise for an award-winning curriculum of compositions in varied musical genres and degrees earned from around the world. José Ramón Enríquez Alcázar, the author of the opera, was also a journalist for the newspapers *Excélsior, Uno Mas Uno, El Universal*, and the magazine *Proceso*. Known for his poetry, plays, and essays, he too won national awards. The conductor of the opera, Armando Zayas, claimed assistant directorships at UNAM's department of music, the Orquesta Sinfónica Nacional, La Compañía de Danza Mexicana, and La Orquesta Conservatorio.[89]

The compositions consisted of a trio of cantatas with the final one culminating in the destruction from the earthquake. First performed to a large audience at the Auditorio Nacional as a part of a commemorative recital on the one-year anniversary of the earthquake, the third cantata, "El Derrumbe" ("The Breakdown"), reenacted the events of the previous September.[90] Religious undertones filled the lyrics of "El Derrumbe" and both the composer Federico Ibarra Groth and author José Ramón Enríquez Alcazaron energized the overarching title *Lamentaciones: Loa para la Ciudad que Espera* (*Lamentations: Loa for the City that Waits*) with religious rhetoric. Described in the libretto (program booklet) to the larger piece, the loa rekindled an old Spanish liturgical work, yet for the modern Mexico of 1985 it did not address the old Spanish religious themes such as *misterios de la fe* (mysteries of faith).[91]

The author selected the title of the musical piece to reflect religion. In choosing *Lamentaciones* (*Lamentations*) as the title, and not *Lamentos* (wailing) for example, images of the Old Testament compare the city with the plight of the ancient Hebrew people during the catastrophe of their exile into Babylon. In the opening lyrics, the main character, La Muerte (Death) stated:

El fulgor de mis ojos y la luna	The glow of my eyes and the moon
son tres lagos de azufre . . .	are the three lakes of sulfur . . .
Yo la deidad antigua que renace y lenta,	Reborn as an ancient deity, I slowly
se despereza en los rincones	creep in the corners
para el nuevo holocausto.	preparing for the new holocaust.

Death evoked the lakes of fire as portrayed during the apocalypse. Also, the use of the word "holocaust" manipulated the political potential of the moment, utilizing a word associated with the extermination of the European Jews during World War II. Literally translated as "burnt offering," the word "holocaust" provided a spiritual context for the Mexican people to find meaning in this event that killed so many.

Six months later a smaller venue housed the performance of the three cantatas of the *Lamentaciones* at the Pinacoteca Virreinal de San Diego (The Viceregal Art Gallery of Saint Diego) suggesting that the numbers of the audience decreased from the commemorative event.[92] Located close to where the Hotel Regis stood prior to the earthquake, the Pinacoteca reminded the visitors of the tragedy that killed so many one and a half years prior. Architecturally the site occupied a former convent and, like the loa, reminded concertgoers of the country's past religious ties. The second performance of "El Derrumbe" reaffirmed a similar purpose to the poetry of the ofrenda presented on Día de los Muertos in Mexico City. The traditionally religious loa contained biblical rhetoric, yet made no overt call on the Catholic faith. Rather, for the PRI the cantatas remained rooted in secular mexicanidad.

Artwork accompanying the libretto supported the resurgence of a mexicanidad that remembered the historic roots of conquest and indigenous heritage. Images from the Florentine Codex depicted a captured indigenous prisoner of war. The winners of the battle carried him, tied to a chair and noose around his neck, to an unknown fate. Another sequence depicted an indigenous leader torturing his victim with spikes set in his back. The last image accompanying "El Derrumbe"'s text depicted a battle fought with steel swords and shields where one soldier fights wearing a Spanish colonial cloak, while the other soldier shows an almost naked muscular flesh. Biblical terminology accompanied images from the Florentine Codex to frame a performance in a former convent close to the site of a hotel fallen from the earthquake. The elite audience of that performance at the smaller venue gained a perspective celebratory of national character. This came in part from the resilience of the Mexican people and in part rose through the SEP's combined efforts in reconnecting the importance of mexicanidad to the pivotal year of 1985.

The composer of the 1985 loa attempted to reinvigorate it by stripping it of religious meaning. Groth described this piece as a scenic cantata involving actors, singers, chorus, and instrumental music. In addition to the earthquake's "Lamentations," the loa presented the thematic and temporal topics: Mexico's "Ancient Mexicans," "After the Spanish," and finally "Modern Mexico." The writer and composer both attempted to remind the audience that despite tragic beginnings the city transformed itself and adapted. Similar to the poetry in the ofrenda, the city is the actor in the loa and the subject of its appraisals. Yet within that city, many people remained in need.

The desperation of the populace further connected operas and the earthquake. Famed tenor Plácido Domingo assisted in the bucket brigades in the days following September 19.[93] He traveled from Chicago to search for relatives who lived in Nuevo León building of Tlatelolco. In searching for his aunt, uncle, and cousins, he gained notoriety through the moment of solidarity. At first he wanted no special treatment because of his fame. However, after realizing that little help came from the government, Domingo used the media attention to his advantage. The relationship between the damnificados and the government was so broken that Domingo attempted to assist and asked for international help on live television so that the families of Tlatelolco could receive much-needed assistance and equipment. While working with those affected by the earthquake, Domingo planned a series of concerts that he would perform to raise money for the homeless and injured. Because of these efforts to help the people of Mexico City he received the award of the "Aztec Eagle" and is still referred to as a "hero of the 1985 earthquakes."[94] His story, nonetheless, highlights even further the plight of the damnificados as they remained at the mercy of an incompetent and often unresponsive regime.

Conclusion

The PRI government saw the potential to tap into the existing imaginaires through verse and music. People could be reached, messages communicated, and events mourned, in the sets of images and ideas that popular poetry conveyed. The PRI nonetheless had a difficult time controlling what sorts of longer genealogies of meaning they touched upon when they attempted to recycle politically charged poets from a generation earlier. Popular enthusiasm, for instance in the reception to Sabines's poems, rose from a certain resonance with the beauty of simple language, and with historical experiences that still held power over imaginations. The PRI and González Avelar could not divorce their choice of commemorative poetry from artists who had been critical of them in the past, simply because these writers had built the imaginaire, and become inextricable from what was at the heart of Mexican verse.

In combining government-sponsored commemorative events with demands from the most affected by this earthquake, two responses are evident. The government released a cultural plan aimed at recycling a narrative from a vindicated 1968 student movement. By co-opting a formerly controversial narrative, the SEP under González Avelar manipulated and translated how the nation would take in the imaginaire. Pushing this nationalist narrative on the people did not succeed and the lower classes persisted in their protests and accusations. For them the reality of simply sustaining themselves with the basics of shelter, food, and water proved near impossible. The poems worked against the regime's attempts to ascribe a new imaginaire in so dire a political and environmental context. PRI officials' attempts to use the nation's most celebrated poets as a catalyst for national unity and solidarity after the 1985 earthquake were undermined by the fact that those literary icons had been critical in their analyses of past government actions and inactions. What remained from each of these responses continues as the new imaginaire, the remembered moment from 1968 and 1985 that transected time and is revisited every September 19 at the now traditional wreath-laying in honor of the victims of the earthquake at the Plaza de la Solidaridad.

Solidarity proved to be an important outcome of the people's immediate reaction to the earthquake. The government did not grant an International Solidarity Day (although a Day of Remembrance exists). In addition, requests were made to build a monument to the victims of the earthquake. Instead, at the site of the Hotel Regis, the most infamous of the collapsed buildings, a park now exists. The dead received no memorial.

Notes

1. For a discussion on the *imaginaire* and imagination see Serge Gruzinski, "Introduction," in *Images at War: Mexico from Columbus to Blade Runner (1492–2019)* (Durham, NC: Duke University Press, 2001), 1–6.

2. Regarding recycling official stories see Gilbert M. Joseph, Anne Rubenstein, and Eric Zolov, "Assembling the Fragments: Writing a Cultural History of Mexico since 1940," in *Fragments of a Golden Age: The Politics of Culture in Mexico Since 1940*, ed. Gilbert M. Joseph, Anne Rubenstein, and Eric Zolov (Durham, NC: Duke University Press, 2001), 3–22; Elaine Carey, "Introduction," in *Plaza of the Sacrifices: Gender, Power, and Terror in 1968 Mexico* (Albuquerque: University of New Mexico Press, 2005), 1–9; Gruzinski, *Images at War*, 4.

3. Claire Brewster, "Aftermath of 1968," in *Responding to Crisis in Contemporary Mexico: The Political Writings of Paz, Fuentes, Monsiváis and Poniatowska* (Tucson: University of Arizona Press, 2005), 83.

4. Ibid., 150.

5. Samuel Ramos, *Profile of Man and Culture in Mexico* (Austin: University of Texas Press, 1962); Octavio Paz, *The Labyrinth of Solitude: Life and Thought in Mexico* (New York: Grove, 1961); Brewster, *Responding to Crisis in Contemporary Mexico.*

6. *Ofrenda de Poesía Para Nuestra Ciudad y Nuestros Muertos, Ciudad de México, Noviembre de 1985.* Gallery 3 exp. 1, 11–01–00–00, c.3 MMH Archivo General de la Nación México D.F.

7. For a discussion of popular culture and high culture, see William H. Beezley and Linda A. Curcio-Nagy, "Introduction," in *Latin American Popular Culture: An Introduction*, ed. William H. Beezley and Linda A. Curcio-Nagy (Wilmington, DE: SR Books, 2004), xi–xxi.

8. The "Mexican Revolutionary Family" metaphor comes from Joseph, Rubenstein, and Zolov, "Assembling the Fragments," in *Fragments of a Golden Age*, ed. Joseph, Rubenstein, and Zolov, 3–22.

9. On earning the Olympics, see Eric Zolov, "Discovering a Land Mysterious and Obvious: The Re-narrativizing of Post-Revolutionary Mexico," in *Fragments of a Golden Age*, ed. Joseph, Rubenstein, and Zolov, 234–72.

10. Eric Zolov, "Showcasing the 'Land of Tomorrow': Mexico and the 1968 Olympics," *The Americas* 61, no. 2 (2004): 159–88; Ariel Rodriguez Kuri, "Hácia México 68: Pedro Ramirez Vásquez y el proyecto olímpico," *Secuencia* 56 (May–August 2003): 37–73.

11. Joseph, Rubenstein, and Zolov, "Assembling the Fragments."

12. Frank Riley. "Of Poets and Pole Vaulters," *Saturday Review* 9 (March 1968): 58–60.

13. Zolov, "Showcasing the 'Land of Tomorrow,'" 177.

14. Ibid., 183.

15. Ibid., 188.

16. Carey, *Plaza of Sacrifices*, 11–32.

17. Elena Poniatowska, *La Noche de Tlatelolco* (México D.F.: Ediciones Era, 1994).

18. Paz, *Labyrinth of Solitude*, 33.

19. Paz, *Labyrinth of Solitude*, 193–94, 284–385; On "Many Mexicos," see Lesley Byrd Simpson, *Many Mexicos* (Berkeley: University of California Press, 1966).

20. Evodio Escalante, "Octavio Paz y los Cuarenta años de Poesía en Movimiento," *La Jornada Semanal* (Augusto 27, 2006); Adolfo Castañón, "Poesía en Movimiento O de la antología consideraba como una obra de arte," *Revista de la Universidad de México* (2006): 16–21.

21. Octavio Paz, "Aviso," in *Poesía en Movimiento* (México: Siglo Ventiuno Press, 1966), 3–10.

22. Deborah Cohn. "The Mexican Intelligentsia, 1950–1968: Cosmopolitanism, National Identity and the State," *Mexican Studies* 21, no. 1 (2005): 141–82.

23. Octavio Paz, Ali Chumacero, José Emilio Pacheco, and Homero Aridjis, "Unfortunate Inaccuracy," *New York Review of Books* (May 20, 1971).

24. Claudio Lomnitz-Adler, *Death and the Idea of Mexico* (New York: Zone Books, 2005), 436.

25. "La Ciudad de México, Zona de Desastre; Miles de Víctimas," *Excélsior* (México D.F.: September 20, 1985), 1A.

26. "Otro Sismo de 6.5 grados, pero sin Consecuencias Graves," *Excélsior* (Mexico D.F.: September 21, 1985), 1A.

27. "Han Sacado Ya 1,300 Cadáveres," *Excélsior* (México D.F.: Septiembre 21, 1985), 18A.

28. Diane E. Davis, "Reverberations: Mexico City's 1985 Earthquake and the Transformation of the Capital," in *The Resilient City: How Modern Cities Recover from Disaster*, ed. Lawrence J. Vale and Thomas J. Campanella (Oxford: Oxford University Press, 2005), 255–80.

29. For "Otra Noche de Tlatelolco" see Carlos Monsiváis, "La Solidaridad de la población en Realidad Fue Toma de Poder," *Proceso* (México, Septiembre 22, 1985), 6–11.

30. Elena Poniatowska, *Nada Nadie: Las Voces del Temblor* (México City: Biblioteca Era, 1988); specific examples are on pages 206–11 and 310–12.

31. George Russell, "Mexico Miracles Amid the Ruins," *Time* (June 24, 2001).

32. Agencia, "Los Topos de Tlatelolco: A 20 años de los sismos, Los Topos de Tlatelolco han trascendido fronteras; son una organización capaz de enfrentar cualquier situación de desastre," *esmas.com*, Septiembre 2005, accessed on September 21, 2011, http://www.esmas.com/noticierostelevisa/terremoto/475628.html.

33. "Ciudadano," cited in Louise Walker, "Economic Fault Lines and Middle Class Fears: Tlatelolco, Mexico City, 1985," in *Aftershocks: Earthquakes and Popular Politics in Latin America*, ed. Jürgen Buchenau and Lyman L. Johnson (Albuquerque: University of New Mexico Press 2009), 184–221.

34. Monsiváis, "La Solidaridad," 6–11.

35. Carlos Monsiváis, "Tras el sismo, manipulación, autoritarismo, minimización, Los Poderes contratacan ante una sociedad civil que rechaza la sumisión," *Proceso* (Octubre 7, 1985).

36. Monsiváis, "La Solidaridad," 6–11.

37. Presidencia de la República, Dirección General de Comunicación Social, *The Mexico City Earthquake September 19, 1985* (Mexico, 1985).

38. Carlos Velasco Molina, "Estricto Patrullaje Militar Para Garantizar paz: Aguirre," *Excélsior* 20 (Septiembre 1985): 1a, 22a.

39. Walker, "Economic Fault Lines and Middle Class Fears," 184–221.

40. See, for example, Davis, "Reverberations," 255–80.

41. Walker, "Economic Fault Lines and Middle Class Fears," 190–91.

42. "Negociante," *Excélsior* (Septiembre 23, 1985).

43. "Los Estadios Sin Danos," *Excélsior* (Septiembre 21, 1985).

44. Mexico, *Recomendaciones a la Población: La Comisión Intersecretarial para auxilio de la Zona Metropolitana a través del Sector Salud y el D.D.F., recomiendan e informan a la población del área metropolitana lo siguiente*, 1985; Mexico, *A La Población*, 1985; Mexico, *Al Público en General*, 1985; Mexico, *Al Personal de la Secretaría de Salud*, 1985.

45. On efforts, see Rebecca Solnit, *A Paradise Built in Hell: The Extraordinary Communities that Arise in Disaster* (New York: Viking, 2009), 135–80.

46. Walker, "Economic Fault Lines and Middle Class Fears," 184–221.

47. *"Exigimos Informes Veraces del Fondo De Reconstruccion y el Destino de los Donativos Internacionales!"* 1985. Gallery 3 exp 3. 11–01–00–00, c.5 MMH Archivo General de la Nación México D.F. *"Barrios en Lucha: Organizate y Exige"* 1985. Gallery 3 exp 3. 11–01–00–00, c.5 MMH Archivo General de la Nación México D.F.

48. Julia Preston and Samuel Dillon, "Earthquake 1985," in *Opening Mexico: The Making of a Democracy* (New York: Farrar, Straus and Giroux, 2004), 95–116.

49. Phoebe McKinney, "Women and Labor Fighting to Survive: Mexico's 19th of September Union," Multinational Monitor, accessed September 21, 2012, http://www.multinationalmonitor.org/hyper/issues/1989/09/mckinney.html; Solnit, *Paradise Built in Hell*, 135–50; Elena Poniatowska, Personal Interview, July 28, 2000.

50. Preston and Dillon, "Earthquake 1985," 95–116.

51. Jean Moss, *Day of the Dead: A Pictorial Archive of Día de los Muertos* (Mineola, NY: Dover Publications, 2010), 3–6.

52. Lomnitz-Adler, *Death and the Idea of Mexico*, 457.

53. Octavio Paz, "Day of the Dead," in *Labyrinth of Solitude* (New York: Grove Press, 1961), 57–58.

54. Sue Vice, *Introducing Bakhtin* (Manchester: Manchester University Press, 1997), 191.

55. Jose Carlos Becerra, "Épica," *Ofrenda de Poesía*. 1985.

56. William Veeder, "El Metro: A History of A Monument in Motion," paper presented at the 126th American Historical Association (January 6, 2012).

57. Octavio Paz, "The Sons of La Malinche," in *Labyrinth of Solitude* (New York: Grove Press, 1961), 75.

58. Efraín Huerta, "Declaración de Amor," *Ofrenda de Poesía*, 1985.

59. Poets under thirty had a new lyricism; see Lloyd Mallan and Efraín Huerta, "The New Mexican Poetry: Paz and Huerta," *Prairie Schooner* 17 (1943): 63–70.

60. Eric Zolov, *Refried Elvis: The Rise of the Mexican Counterculture* (Berkeley: University of California Press, 1999), especially 93–131.

61. Ricardo Aguilar Melantzán, "Efraín Huerta and the New School of Mexican Poets," *Latin American Literary Review* 11 (1983): 41–55.

62. José Emilio Pacheco, "La noche nuestra interminable," *Ofrenda de Poesía*, 1985.

63. Mary Docter, "José Emilio Pacheco: A Poetics of Reciprocity," *Hispanic Review* 70 (2002): 373–92.

64. Octavio Paz, "Crepúsculos de la ciudad," *Ofrenda de Poesía*, 1985.

65. Diana Sorenson, "Tlatelolco 1968: Paz and Poniatowska: on Law and Violence," *Mexican Studies Magazine* 18 (2002): 297–321.

66. A contrast of Efraín Huerta and Octavio Paz resulted in this claim by Ricardo Aguilar Melantzán, "Efrain Huerta and the New School of Mexican Poets," *Latin American Literary Review* 11 (1983): 41–55.

67. José Emilio Pacheco, "Crónica Mexicayotl," *Ofrenda de Poesía*, 1985.

68. Paz, *Labyrinth of Solitude*.

69. Anonymous, "Visión de los Vencidos," *Ofrenda de Poesía*, 1985.

70. José Quiroga, *Understanding Octavio Paz* (Columbia: University of South Carolina Press, 1999), 76; Xavier Villaurrutia's "Nocturno Muerto," *Ofrenda de Poesía*, 1985.

71. Paz, *Labyrinth of Solitude*, 29.

72. Rosario Castellanos, "Amenecer," *Ofrenda de Poesía*, 1985.

73. Quiroga, *Understanding Octavio Paz*, 76.

74. Sandra Messinger Cypess, *Uncivil Wars: Elena Garro, Octavio Paz and the Battle for Cultural Memory* (Austin: University of Texas Press, 2012), 123–25.

75. Secretaría de Prensa y Propaganda, "El Movimiento del 68," *Cuadernos de educación Sindical* 26, http://www.stunam.org.mx/8prensa/cuadernillos/cuadern026.htm.

76. Carey, *Plaza of Sacrifices*, 178–79.

77. Poniatowska, *Nada Nadie*.

78. Jaime Sabines, "Algo Sobre la Muerte del Mayor Sabines," *Ofrenda de Poesía*, 1985; Varios, *La poesía en el corazón del hombre: Jaime Sabines en sus sesenta años* (México: UNAM, 1987), 10–12.

79. Julia Preston, "Jaime Sabines Gutiérrez, Popular Mexican Poet, Dies at 72," *New York Times*, March 22, 1999, http://www.nytimes.com/1999/03/22/arts/jaime-sabines-gutierrez-popular-mexican-poet-dies-at-72.html; Varios, *La poesía en el corazón del hombre*, 182–83.

80. Eladio Cortes, *Dictionary of Mexican Literature* (Westport, CT: Greenwood Press, 1992), 306.

81. Miguel Guardia, "Juntaremos las Bocas," *Ofrenda de Poesía*, 1985.

82. Octavio Paz, "Sons of La Malinche," in *Labyrinth of Solitude*, 65.

83. Fray Ángel María Garibay, trans., "Poesía Indígena," *Ofrenda de Poesía*, 1985.

84. Carlos Fuentes, *Terra Nostra* (New York: Farrar, Straus and Giroux, 1976).

85. Garibay, "Poesía Indígena."

86. Kieth Gregor, "Loa," *The Oxford Encyclopedia of Theatre and Performance*, ed. Dennis Kennedy (Oxford: Oxford University Press 2005); *Diccionario de la lengua Española* (Madrid: Real Academia Española, 2001); Diana Taylor, "The Loa for the Auto Sacramental of the Divine Narcissus," in *Stages of Conflict: A Critical Anthology of Latin American Theater and Performance*, ed. Diana Taylor and Sarah J. Townsend (Ann Arbor: University of Michigan Press, 2008), 81–85.

87. Anna Agranoff Ochs, "Opera in Contention: Social Conflict in Late Nineteenth-Century Mexico City" (PhD diss., University of North Carolina at Chapel Hill, 2011), 9.

88. Frederick Ibarra Groth and José Ramón Enríquez, *Loa para la Ciudad que Espera*, 1985. Gallery 3 exp. 2, 11–01–00–00, c. 4 MMH Archivo General de la Nación México D.F.

89. *Loa para la ciudad que espera*. Miercoles 25 de Marzo 21 hrs, Sabado 28 de Marzo 13 hrs. Gallery 3 exp. 1, 11–01–00–00, c. 9 MMH Archivo General de la Nación México D.F.

90. *In Memoriam 19 de Septiembre,* Sabado, 20/18:00 hrs 1986. Gallery 3 exp. 1, 11–01–00–00, c.4 MMH Archivo General de la Nación México D.F.

91. Jose Ramon Enriquez, "Noticia Introductoria," *Lamentaciones: Loa Para la Ciudad Que Espera,* Gallery 3 exp. 2, 11–01–00–00, c.4 MMH Archivo General de la Nación México D.F.

92. Ibid.

93. Emilio Diaz Cervantes, *Brigada Plácido Domingo* (Moneterrey, Mexico: Editorial Castillo, 1995); Roberto Ponce, "Los buenos, los malos y las feas cifras y realidades del terremoto según un libro de un Brigadista de Placido Domingo," *Proceso* (17 Septiembre 1995), 12.

94. Manuel Robles, "Se Impuso la Decisión Popular y Plácido Domingo recibió el Águila Azteca," *Proceso* (13 Septiembre 1986); Roberto Ponce, "Hechizó Plácido Domingo el Auditorio Nacional," *Proceso* (21 Junio 2012).

Conclusion

History does not repeat, but sometimes it rhymes.

—MARK TWAIN

Lyrics have given voice to the Mexican experience even since the earliest eras of the conquest and colony. In 1604, Bernardo de Balbuena's voluminous poetic work *Grandeza mexicana* told the Empire of the land's riches and wealth. New Spain represented a utopian potential:

México hermosura peregrina, y altísimos ingenios de gran vuelo, por fuerza de astros o virtud divina;	Beautiful pilgrim Mexico, towering with geniuses in flight, by the strength of stars or divine virtue;
al fin, si es la beldad parte del cielo, México puede ser cielo del mundo, pues cría la mahor que goza el suelo,	finally if beauty is part of heaven, Mexico could be the world's heaven, for it breeds greatness in its soil,
¡Oh ciudad rica, pueblo sin segundo, más lleno de tesoros y bellezas que de peces y arena el mar profundo![1]	Oh rich city, town second to none, more full of treasures and beauties than the deep sea has fish or sand!

For centuries scholars took this work more or less at face value. Here, they asserted, was lyrical proof of colonial optimism, pride, and potential.

Contemporaries knew better. Close interpretations of the political and social context of the time now offer us a different reading from the tradition of Balbuena as lauding greatness. The tract, it seems, reflected a deep and humorous satire of the disorder plaguing the politics of the capital.[2] Balbuena dedicated his work in its first edition to a notorious troublemaker, the Archbishop Francisco de Manso Zuñega y Sola, and the sonnets thus spoke in double entendre to a distinct lack of order and good governance. Far from dismissing the work, this is precisely what should lend it weight for historians seeking to learn about the roots of Mexican identity. Lyrical expression, powerful and contextual, gives us a lens for seeing historical changes sometimes easy to miss in broader political narratives.

Calling out leadership and making subtle attacks on too-comfortable elites, writers of verse showed that their works represented far more than empty vessels of language. Poets and songwriters worked inexorably to erode the bastions of hegemonic power. They eroded it with often nearly imperceptible challenges. Their words conjured images and sculpted memories among the broader populace. Ordinary masses had thereby a discursive set of beliefs, symbols, and visions that, simply by existing, challenged the narrower official narratives of the powerful. In these cultural productions they offered a counterhegemonic option for understanding society and events that they filled with popular aspirations and repetitions of favorite historical memories. At the same time, this was a slippery sort of collective memory. Highly contingent on place, performance, and audience, verses often expressed highly subject-specific meanings. In other words, the interpretive nature of the genre made it highly personal, and matters of import to contemporaries may not always make sense to us now. They saw and heard verse from their perspective, not ours. As such, as with the *Grandeza mexicana*, we should remember that any analyses of the lyrical past should be approached with humility and the awareness of deeper layers where oral and written verse has shaped the national counternarrative of history.

The place of Mexican music and poetry, as our chapters illustrate, reveal that the notion of *lo mexicano* shifted according to people's subjectivities. Gender, class, race, religion, and location reshaped both the meaning and articulation of verse. Popular groups, policymakers, and cultural producers—both elite and common—understood the power of verse in articulating their own visions of truth, identity, and memory. Music and poetry were and are ubiquitous mediums that infuse and surround Mexicans' lives. Yet scholars have tended to ignore those venues as epiphenomena to supposedly more important economic and political structures. Indeed some scholars have trivialized the value of examining cultural productions. Alan Knight and Stephen Haber have been two vociferous challengers to the so-called new cultural history. Alan Knight suggests that *all* history is cultural history and thus the label is meaningless. For Knight, defining culture as a system of signs and codes that produce meaning is too vague, making every historical study, in one way or another, cultural history.[3] Likewise, Haber challenges historians' attempts to examine people's subjectivities and the ways that people interpreted concepts such as the nation or their own identities. He tells readers that while anthropologists might be able to interview their subjects as a means to verify meaning, historians have no such opportunity.[4]

Implicit in both critiques is that scholars should give up such attempts to explore subjectivities and delve into the somehow more concrete genres of social, economic, and political approaches (as if those realms of investigation do not pose similar quandaries regarding the interpretation of documentary evidence). Whether studying the economic impact of railways on a country or the role played by peasants in revolution, ignoring the terms in which these events were understood by the less-literate people who were affected or who participated leaves a significant historical void. The chapters in this volume reject the defeatism inherent in Knight and Haber's position. Instead they take up the (admittedly ambiguous and messy) challenge to explore how people imagined and understood the complex historical developments that played out in their lives. Haber's contention that due to its "subjectivist epistemology" cultural history is "fundamentally flawed in its ability to advance knowledge" represents too narrow a view.[5] We contend that tackling topics related to people's subjectivities provides new insights that, while perhaps interpretive and hermeneutic, nevertheless offer new understandings of the possible ways that people experienced and came to grips with the multiple realities that shaped their lives. Exploring economic underdevelopment or understanding the roles of *jefe políticos* in the Revolution are clearly important avenues of investigation that advance our knowledge about Mexico. Yet as Claudio Lomnitz deftly notes, such studies often ignore the *terms* in which these developments take place.[6] Indeed, attempting to survey how people engaged and understood such historical developments represents an ontological necessity in the formation and advancement of knowledge. At times, we are forced to "imagine" the diverse ways that people comprehended the complexity of economic, political, and social developments that reshaped their experiences, yet we cannot imagine whatever we like.

Instead, as John Lewis Gaddis maintains, we must employ our experience, expertise, and intuition to do so, a process that involves heavy contextualization.[7] These essays show that people interpreted broader issues of economic and political change through verse. Studies might tell us about the battles that militaries fought, the impact of the railway on the economy, or that Catholic rebels opposed the secularizing policies of the state. Yet they do little in helping advance our understanding of why men enrolled in the military and what that meant to them, or about how ordinary people viewed the arrival of the locomotive, or how Catholic rebels characterized the government that they took up arms against. Moreover, approaches that ignore the cultural venues where people expressed their outlooks fail to provide insights of the actors (aside from the elite) that drove history. This volume, humbly and recognizing the difficulties and pitfalls inherent in such an endeavor, has sought to provide these insights.

Beyond that, an exploration of the songs and poems recited and heard provides an understanding of the shifting social imaginary. While it is difficult to determine how people received the lyrics that entered their lives, the essays here make known that the topics and issues that verses addressed found audiences with whom those subjects resonated. Music and poetry could introduce ordinary people to topics and political agendas that they did not previously consider. At the same time, an analysis of music and poetry, at the very least, shows that socially and economically marginalized groups used verse to question and air their understandings of historical events and, in so doing, sought political incorporation and a more meaningful political voice. Elite groups and policymakers understood the power of verse and, as several chapters disclose, attempted to use such venues to shape the political values and consumption preferences of common people, often with mixed results.

This volume has sought to provide a view of how ordinary people expressed their worldviews and understanding of the human condition. The lyrics examined offer glimpses into the quotidian experience that elite and common people expressed through verse. It has shown that both groups used music and poetry to push their own agendas and influence those who listened. Elite groups attempted to shape the consumer choices of individuals while politicians hoped to promote a positive opinion of officials. Simultaneously, popular sectors used these cultural venues to shape listeners' views about the government, war, gender, and religion, among a host of other pressing matters. Beyond that, the interpretive nature of poetry and music—that is, the multiple meanings that readers and listeners could take away from or impute upon words—presents a complex task to scholars interested in such analysis. Yet herein lies the value of such studies. The ambivalent and ambiguous meanings of verse have been contextualized by the authors of this volume to provide a multiplicity of possible meanings and interpretations. The chapters presented have sought to make people from the margins of society the focus of the story, while simultaneously examining powerbrokers' use of verse and top-down attempts to inculcate particular values or instill positive views of the state. In so doing, they hope to elucidate that the boundaries between high and low culture, and upper and lower class, blurred. We can "imagine" that wealthy members of society also enjoyed the lyrics of popular corridos or political critiques penned in penny presses and that, at the same time, the poor savored erudite poetry or were moved by lyrics of opera.

Analysis of verse tells us about societal changes and class issues. The selections of this volume reveal several findings about the value of music and poetry as serious sources for historical investigation as well as about the broader role of music and poetry in Mexican society. Examining the role of verse shows the tensions within society between different social groups both in times of war and peace. As French shows, even in times of incredible devastation and horrors, love poems and intimate expressions continued, as if in a world all their own. Individuals also penned lyrics that poked fun at the pretensions of the elite and mocked political rivals. Military men used verse as a means to vent their frustrations with higher-ranking members of their army units. Likewise, *cristero* rebels used song to undermine the masculinity of their military opponents and, in so doing, reshaped their own Catholic identities along gendered lines. Chapters by Conway and Matthews also demonstrate that individuals used music and poetry as a means to participate in broader national discussions from which they were excluded. Women used verse to tackle topics related to war and its social impact. Ordinary people wrote, sang, and listened to songs that questioned the era's most pressing policymaking decisions. In this way marginalized groups found everyday ways to engage broader national debates while not directly challenging government officials, a practice that could endanger their lives or well-being. In these forums an alternative sense of memory and politics comes to light.

Significant conceptions of shifting gender relations also fill lyrical expression. As the chapters by Conway, Neufeld, Andes, and Toxqui show, an exploration of music and poetry reveals the centrality of gendered understandings in the discussion of a myriad of seemingly unrelated topics. The interactions and relations between men and women illustrated negotiations of power in daily life. Women penned verses that emphasized their femininity and marginalization within politics as a means to put forward public opinions without challenging prevailing gender norms. Military men of the Porfiriato and Mexican Revolution articulated their understandings of manhood as they mocked their superiors and enemies. Men likewise made public a sentimental masculinity that allowed them to transcend social norms that privileged machismo, when they penned love poems or drunkenly sang songs of heartbreak at cantinas. As French shows, the intimate exchanges of lovers also speak to social relations and gendered expectations at the intersections of oral and written literacies. Furthermore, these chapters show that gendered performances shifted according to context, at times challenging, and at times consolidating gendered ideologies. Verse writers confronted unspoken rules and norms that governed behaviors of men and women, including stereotypes of the domestic and the virile, and made a monolithic sense of patriarchy instable.

Actors representing the regime or the wealthy classes sought to engineer the broader populace through the propagandistic potentials of the lyrical. The use of music and poetry by politicians and educators highlights that elite groups understood the power of verse in shaping people's hearts and minds. Jackson Albarrán discloses how members of the Revolutionary administration of Cárdenas used poetry to expose the shortcomings of Revolutionary social reforms and reminded audiences of the promises of social justice yet to be fulfilled. Toxqui highlights how media moguls and corporate leaders saw music as an influential medium in shaping people's consumption choices, promoting modern tastes such as industrially produced alcohol. Yet, as the authors of this volume recognize, how people interpreted those attempts remains ambiguous. In moments of national crisis, such as the 1985 earthquake in Mexico City analyzed by Ledwon, government officials used poetry in their attempts to ease social divisions made worse by administrative ineptness. Despite the rise of new media innovations, or in conjunction with them, and with the rise of a consumer society, poetry remained as powerful a medium as it had been in previous centuries.

Comprehending changes in national identity likewise runs through our chapters. Mexicans used verse to proclaim their own understandings of the nation, especially in relation to historical memory. Female writers during the U.S.-Mexican War conjured up the memories of national heroes when invoking men to defend their nation from its northern invaders. During the Porfiriato, memories of past U.S. aggression surely shaped the virulent anti-Americanism that was so regularly cited in songs about railways. Military men hailed the memories of the military victories in their poetry and, in so doing, stressed their views of what constituted a virile, masculine nation. The religious rebels of the Cristiada likewise invoked the memory of the country's Catholic past as an essential aspect of the national identity, an identity jeopardized and undermined by a secularizing state. During the Cárdenas years, Jesús Flores Sansón used the recent memory of the military phase of the Revolution to publicize the incompleteness of social reforms enshrined in the Constitution of 1917. In this way, he constructed the Revolution itself as a marker of national identity that depended on youth participation to persevere. The well-being of the nation's children became a patriotic concern, particularly as they represented the carriers of socialist ideals in the embodiment of the Niño Proletario. The memory of past tragedies and injustices carried enormous weight as the nation struggled on a trajectory of fulfilling Revolutionary aspirations, and as the government sought to capitalize on the power of verse as a means to obtain consensus.

New technology brought lyrical expression to the people in ever more orchestrated and increasingly managed ways. The rise of mass media like radio or television or films, widely available since the 1930s and bolstered by the Mexican Miracle, changed the ways that music and poems reached the masses. Lyrics came to people in new spaces, the kitchen radio, for instance, or on the big screen. Songs of the Golden Age performed on radio and in films often portrayed essentialized notions that stressed alcohol consumption as central to the Mexican character. Moreover, as Toxqui shows, film producers and the government portrayed regional identities and a historical memory of an idealized mestizo past to hawk industrially produced libations. The new masculine archetype would be a sentimental tequila drinker. Likewise the PRI government, in its commemoration of the 1985 earthquake, carelessly invoked painful memories of the 1968 student massacre as it searched for poems and poets to memorialize the devastation. Setting aside their own blame for past incompetence, they hoped to frame the tragedies as something suffered primarily by the city itself, personified in poems, rather than give recognition to the common classes. In both cases, attempts to manipulate popular sentiments through government-managed media often missed the mark. The people sought, and found, more authentic interpretations of their condition outside of official mass media.

Efforts to shape public ideals from these message-loaded propagandistic venues at times fell short—the ordinary people had their own spaces and conceptions of how things worked. Verse in various forms reflected an internalized sense of historical memory and shared experiences. Satirical excess, erudite references, and melodramatic performances added to the authenticity attributed to popular works. Style and context mattered in the deliberate invocations of *patria*, gender, intimacy, and nationalism. As in the contrast between *ranchera* and bolero, or between rock and corridos, writers added the weight of traditions and embellished their imagery with nostalgic themes. The easy touchstone of repeated tropes or stylistic flourishes allowed instant association with other works of the same genres, and created a sense of authentic *mexicanidad* for listeners. This lent strength to claims that ranchera music, for instance, demonstrated the "real Mexico" with its romantic melodrama, its manly *charros*, and its rural themes. Other genres instead highlighted urbanity and modernity, a counterpoint to an authenticity thought by some as mired in backwardness. Ambivalent senses of nation inspired competing definitions and tastes. This evolving framework where people made claims to representing the essence of their country proved difficult for elites to dominate with top-down messages filtered for political gains. The regime largely failed to promote an authentic identity, as they could not reliably define it for the masses. Moreover, we can also "imagine" that these cultural productions likewise blurred the boundaries that divided the categories of the rural/traditional and the urban/modern. Surely country folk watched films that celebrated urban life and the delights of new technologies. They listened to boleros that highlighted the moral ambiguity that characterized modern life. City residents, perhaps nostalgically, went to the movies to see productions that focused on rural life and that used ranchera music to enchant audiences. An examination of music and poetry allows us to consider and engage such possibilities, offering a more dynamic understanding of social relations and social divides.

In sum, the essays in this volume show that music and poetry were central to the formation of elastic and amorphous identities that changed according to time, place, and context. Indeed, the interpretive nature of this research shows that multiple meanings existed for different social groups as they produced and consumed cultural works. Attempting to grasp the myriad of possible meanings allows us to situate ourselves within the mindset of people made alien by time and space. In so doing, we begin to give voice to groups that have been too often ignored by scholars, a historical void often attributed to a lack of written sources. This volume represents an initial foray into an exploration of music and poetry and their role in Mexico. By no means exhaustive, the volume raises many questions and exposes many blind spots in our historiography. A number of topics recommend themselves. For examples, an examination of the role of music and poetry during the Wars of Independence, the use of verse by indigenous groups, the commemoration of religious icons in lyrics, or the popularity of the *narcocorridos* all represent topics to which we hope scholars turn their attention. An examination of how and why certain musical and poetic genres resonated with audiences more than others also represents a possible new topic for scholarly attention. Ultimately, a comprehensive sense of the meanings and uses of verse through Mexican history could only enhance our understanding of the experiences that shaped its peoples.

Music and poetry demonstrate something much more integral to identities than mere political or economic understandings. People listened to verses, and repeated them, because lyrical play appealed as fun. Social gatherings, often with drinks, certainly with friends, improved with verse whether read from texts or sung from heart. As historians we should remember that the beauty and sublimity of poems and songs made life better. The politics of the everyday embedded into a deliberate and necessary leisure, and reveal a Mexico inverted. Humor, betrayal, love, fear, war, and hope lay at the heart of expressions that defined public sentiment in intimate ways. That they did so, in a context of joy and companionship, reflects how Mexicans sought to express who they were, and what they made of the changing world around them, in verse.

> Ya con ésta me despido,
> antes de que yo me vaya,
> ya les canté a mis amigos
> los raíces de nuestra historia.[8]

Notes

1. Bernardo de Balbuena, *Grandeza Mexicana* (México: Emprenda Diego López Doualos, 1604).
2. Bob Ferry, "It Wasn't All That Grand: Politics, Crisis and the Probable Motivation for Bernardo de Balbuena's La Grandeza Méxicana, 1604," Conference paper, Rocky Mountain Conference for Latin American Studies, Santa Fe, NM, April 5, 2013.
3. Alan Knight, "Popular Culture and the Revolutionary State: Perspectives on Mexican Historiography," *Latin American Research Review* 37, no. 2 (2002): 139–40.
4. Stephen Haber, "Anything Goes: Mexico's 'New' Cultural History," *Hispanic American Historical Review* 79, no. 2 (1999): 320–21.
5. Ibid., 312.
6. Claudio Lomnitz, "Final Reflections: What was Mexico's Cultural Revolution?," in *The Eagle and the Virgin: Nation and Cultural Revolution in Mexico, 1910–1940*, ed. Mary Kay Vaughn and Stephen E. Lewis (Durham, NC: Duke University Press, 2006), 340.
7. John Lewis Gaddis, *The Landscape of History: How Historians Map the Past* (Oxford: Oxford University Press, 2004), 3–5, 14–15, 108–9.
8. [Now with this I say goodbye, / until I go away, / I already sang to my friends / the roots of our history.]; this is a standard final stanza for corridos, recompiled and translated by author.

Contributors

Elena Jackson Albarrán is assistant professor of history and Latin American, Latino/a, and Caribbean studies at Miami University. Her research interests on child agency and representation in twentieth-century Mexico are reflected in her book *Seen and Heard in Mexico: Children and Revolutionary Cultural Nationalism* (University of Nebraska, 2014), and in an anthology coedited with Susana Sosenski, *Nuevas miradas a la historia de la infancia en América Latina: Entre prácticas y representaciones* (UNAM, 2012). Her publications have also appeared in *A Companion to Mexican History and Culture, Studies in Latin American Popular Culture, The Americas*, and *Relaciones*. Her current work is on child art and transnational politics in the interwar period.

Stephen J. C. Andes received his doctorate at Oxford University and is assistant professor in the history of Latin America at Louisiana State University. The Mexico Section of the Latin American Studies Association awarded him the best dissertation prize in 2010–2011. His first book, *The Vatican and Catholic Activism in Mexico and Chile: The Politics of Transnational Catholicism, 1920–1940* (Oxford University Press, 2014), is a study of Vatican policy toward Catholic activism in Latin America between the two world wars. Andes's work has appeared in *The Americas* journal and online in popular blogs such as *Religion Dispatches*.

Christopher Conway is an associate professor of Spanish at University of Texas, Arlington, and his area of research is nineteenth-century Latin

American literature, a field in which he has published several book chapters: "Ni salvajes ni sietemesinos: la restauración de la masculinidad en Nuestra América," in *Perfiles del Heroísmo en La Literatura Hispánica de Entresiglos XIX-XX*, ed. Luis Álvarez Castro and Denise DuPont (Valladolid, Spain, 2013) and "Tecnologías de la mirada: Ignacio Manuel Altamirano, la novela nacional y el realismo literario," *Decimonónica* 10, no. 1 (2013). He has also edited *The U.S.-Mexican War: A Binational Reader* with Hackett Publishing in 2010 and is currently finishing work on his monograph, *A Cultural History of Nineteenth-Century Latin America*, for Vanderbilt University Press.

William French is an associate professor of history at the University of British Columbia. He is the past director of the Latin American Studies Program at that institution and codirector of the Oaxaca Summer Institute. He is the author of *Peaceful and Working People: Manners, Morals, and Class Formation in Northern Mexico* (Albuquerque: University of New Mexico Press, 1996), and coeditor with William H. Beezley and Cheryl E. Martin, *Rituals of Rule, Rituals of Resistance: Public Celebrations and Popular Culture in Mexico* (Wilmington, DE: Scholarly Resources, 1994). He also coedited with Katherine E. Bliss, *Gender, Sexuality and Power in Modern Latin America* (Boulder, CO: Rowman and Littlefield, 2006). He has published articles in the *Hispanic American Historical Review* and the *Canadian Journal of Latin American and Caribbean Studies*, and contributed to the *Oxford History of Mexico*. He is currently completing a book on love letters, diaries, and courtship in nineteenth- and twentieth-century Mexico.

Amanda Ledwon is a PhD candidate at the University of Texas at Dallas, where she is specializing in the history of modern Mexico. Her most recent work focused on comics and collective memory, while her broader research is based on grassroots movements, government response, and popular culture surrounding the 1985 Mexico City earthquake. In addition to her studies, she is an adjunct professor at Collin College in McKinney, Texas.

Michael Matthews is an associate professor in the Department of History and Geography at Elon University in North Carolina. He earned his master's degree at Simon Fraser University and his PhD at the University of Arizona. His recent essay "*De Viaje*: Elite Views of Modernity and the Porfirian Railway Boom" was published in *Mexican Studies/Estudios Mexicanos* (Winter 2010). His book, published by the University of Nebraska Press

(Fall 2014), is titled *The Civilizing Machine: A Cultural History of Mexican Railroads*.

Stephen Neufeld is an assistant professor in the History Department of California State University at Fullerton. Originally from Calgary, he earned his master's degree at UBC in Vancouver, and his PhD from the University of Arizona, with the assistance of a doctoral fellowship from SSHRC (Canada). His publications include "Performing the Masculine Nation," in *Negotiating Identities in Modern Latin America* (University of Calgary Press, 2007), and "Behaving Badly in Mexico City: Discipline and Identity in the Presidential Guards, 1900–1911," in *Forced Marches: Soldiers and Military Caciques in Modern Mexico* (University of Arizona Press, 2012), which explore issues of identity, gender, and the military in modern Mexico.

Áurea Toxqui is an assistant professor of history at Bradley University, Illinois, and she studies popular culture to understand processes of identity and state-building formation, power, and resistance in Mexico. She focuses particularly in the analysis of tavern culture, social interaction, gender roles, drunkenness, and crime in response to urbanization and industrialization during the nineteenth and twentieth centuries. Her published work includes "Taverns and Their Influence in the Suburban Culture of Late-Nineteenth-Century Mexico City," in *The Growth of Non-Western Cities: Primary and Secondary Urban Networking, c. 900–1900*, ed. Kenneth R. Hall (Rowman and Littlefield, 2011), and "Pulque," "Fruit Liquors," "Cerveceria Cuauhtemoc-Moctezuma," and "Grupo Modelo," in *Alcohol and Drugs in North America: A Historical Encyclopedia*, ed. David Fahey and Jon Miller (ABC-Clio Encyclopedia, 2012). She is coeditor of *Alcohol in Latin America: A Social and Cultural History* (University of Arizona Press, 2014).

Index

Academia de Letrán, 10
Acevedo, Aurelio, 195–96
Acordada, 85–86
agraristas, 181, 197–98, 210n1
Aguilar, Luis, 268
El águila y la serpiente, 209
Aguirre Velázquez, Ramón, 308–9
Ahearn, Laura, 150
Alacoque, Marguerite-Marie, 190
Alameda Central, 301
El Album Mexicano, 44–45
Alemán, Miguel, 260
Allá en el Rancho Grande (film), 13, 265, 291n28
Altamirano, Ignacio Manuel, 10, 63
Alvarez, Victor Salvador, 62
Annum sacrum, 190
Ansiedad (film), 279
Aridjis, Homero, 305
Arreola, Juan José, 301
Arreola, Manolita, 281
Arroyo, José Adolfo, 191–92
Atl, Dr. (Gerardo Murillo), 229
Atzimba (opera), 13
El Automóvil, 125
Averill, Charles, 35
Ávila Camacho, Manuel, 216, 248, 260
Avitia Hernández, Antonio, 182, 186–87
¡Ay Jalisco, no te rajes! (film), 265
Azuela, Mariano, 273

Badillo, Josefa Heraclia, 46–49
Balbuena, Bernardo de, 6, 337
banditry, 94
Bantjes, Adrian, 204
Barandal, 14
Barcelata, Lorenzo, 266
Barrios en Lucha, 310–11
Las batallas en el desierto (novel), viii
beatas, 182
Becerra, José Carlos, 299, 306, 314, 316
Beezley, William, 8, 139n4
Belize, 82
Bella Unión Hotel, 36
Bernal, Antonio Arias, 236
Best Maugard, Adolfo, 229
Bhabha, Homi, 83
Blancarte, Roberto, 205
boleros, 13, 164, 344
Bonilla, Helia Emma, 125
Brading, David, 6
Bravo, Ignacio, 82–84
Bulnes, Francisco, 140n21
Buntline, Ned, 35
Butler, Matthew, 23, 188

Caifanes, 14
El Calavera, 48
Calderón de la Barca, Pedro, 327
Calderón, Fernando, 41–42, 44
Calderón, Guadalupe, 41–42, 43–44
Calles, Plutarco Elías, 144, 191–92, 194–95, 200, 208, 212–13n43, 221, 272
Campo, Gustavo, 10
Campos, Francisco, 193–95, 206, 208
Cananea strike, 136
canción, 8, 28n23
Cancionero folklórico de México, 147–48, 150, 153
cancioneros, 7, 186
Cantinflas (Mario Moreno Reyes), 255, 283–84
Cárdenas, Cuauhtémoc, 248
Cárdenas, Lázaro, 13, 23, 206, 216, 218–19, 223, 227, 234, 245, 247–48, 272
Carpio, Manuel, 36
Carranza, Venustiano, 144
Carrillo Arena, Guillermo, 311
Carrillo Puerto, Felipe, 205, 222
Cartas cruzadas, 305
Castellanos, Rosario, 299, 306, 322–23, 327
Castillo Troncoso, Alberto del, 240
Castro Leal, Antonio, 305
Catholic Church, 179, 269
Catholicism, 261
El caudillo (film), 197
Centro de Estudios Linguísticos y Literarios, 147
Cervantes, Miguel de, vii
Chak Mul, 14
Chapultepec, 70, 73–75
charros, 13, 220, 221, 250n6, 258, 262, 265, 270, 274, 276–77, 290n24, 344
Chávez, Carlos, 12
Chávez, Francisco M., 206
china poblana, 220, 221, 250n6, 265, 290n23, 290n24
Christian, William, 192
Christ the King (cult of), 190–91, 192–93, 200, 208
"El Chuchumbé," 6
Chumacero, Ali, 305
Church-state relations, 184–85, 207–8
cinema: diffusion of music by, 13; drinking as theme in, 276–86; Golden Age of, 13, 255, 257–58, 266–68, 273, 276, 279–86, 288, 343; industry, 259, 265–66; *rancheras*, 255, 257–58, 279; songs about drinking in, 277–280, 281–82, 283–86. *See also* media
Clausell, Joaquín, 97
Cold War, 249
Colección de cartas amorosas, 125
Congresos de Instrucción Pública, 220
Constitutionalists, 144
Constitution of 1857, 55, 110
Constitution of 1917, 144, 179, 183, 193, 206–7, 216, 304, 343; article 3 of, 183, 222, 223; article 5 of, 183; article 24 of, 183; article 27 of, 183–84; article 130 of, 184
Conventionists, 144
Coordinadora Única de Damnificados, 311
coplas, 6, 9, 10, 27n12, 119, 145–48, 149–50, 153–55; acrostic, 158–59; body as theme of, 162–64, 167; courtship and, 160–61, 170–71; death as theme of, 171–73; as love letter, 155–56; orality/literacy debate and, 157–58, 166; as proof of love, 166–67; time and, 154; trust as theme of, 168–69; violence as theme of, 171. *See also* love letters
corridos, vii, 5, 6, 7, 9, 58, 61–62, 110–12, 137, 145, 183, 185; anti-Americanism in, 90–91, 114–15, 117–18, 126–28, 133, 137–38; anticlericalism in, 204–6; challenges to government in, 66–67, 99, 110, 131–32; Cristero Rebellion and, 183–84, 185–88, 206–8; depictions of women in, 93, 115, 199; execution as topic of, 84–91; Indians as topic of, 76–77, 82–84; masculinity and, 18, 91, 183–84, 194–95, 198; Mexican Revolution as topic of, 12; nationalism as theme in, 120–21; Plutarco Elías Calles as topic of,

191–92, 194–95; railroad as topic of, 112–18; railroad accidents as topic of, 118–29, 132–35; social function of, 8; as source of popular views, 11, 118; themes in, 11, 13; U.S.-Mexican War as topic of, 38
corruption, 16–17
Cortázar, Ernesto, 266–67
Cortes, Hernán, 71, 80–81
creole consciousness, 6
Cristero Rebellion/Cristiada, 18, 23, 179, 181, 183–85, 187, 196–97, 202, 209–10, 210n9, 223; masculinity and, 194, 198–99, 200–202, 204, 209, 341, 342; La Segunda, 184, 187
Cruz, Sor Juana Inés de la Cruz, 7, 8, 327; poetry of, 7
Cuauhtémoc, 71, 75, 80–81, 242
Cuban Revolution, 304
Cultural Olympiad, 303–4, 305
cumbia norteña, 15
Curtis, Newton, 35

Dabove, Juan Pablo, 65
damnificados, 310–11
danzón, 14
David (periodical), 196
de Certeau, Michel, 151
décimas, 5, 156, 159, 161
de la Madrid, Miguel, 308–9, 311
de la Rosa P., J. J., 231–33
De tal palo tal astilla (film), 268, 275
Dewey, John, 224
El Diablito Rojo, 130–31
Día de los Muertos, 298–99, 300, 302, 312–13, 321–22, 327
Díaz, Maria Elena, 140n9
Díaz, Porfirio, 10, 55, 58, 92, 108, 109–10
Díaz Ochoa, Amalia, 275
Docter, Mary, 318
Domingo, Plácido, 330
Domínguez-Ruvalcaba, Héctor, 189, 200, 209
Don Cucufate, 130
Don Quijote (novel), vii
Dowling, Lee, 7

Earle, Rebecca, 69
earthquake (1985), 25, 296, 297, 306–12, 321, 327, 331, 342, 343; government response to, 309–12
education: Congreso Pedagógico and, 222; Escuela Racionalista and, 222–23; Porfirian, 221; secularization of, 222; "socialist," 222–24, 226, 248
Enríquez Alcázar, José Ramón, 328
Escandón, Antonio, 134
Escuela México-España, 248
Escutia, Juan, 73
Esperón, Manuel, 266–67
Esposito, Matthew, 63
estupro, 166, 169
Excélsior, 307, 309, 323

Fallaw, Ben, 204–6
famous 41, 189
fandangos, 6, 9–10
Fein, Seth, 266
Ferdinand Maximilian (Maximilian I), 55, 81
Fermin (children's book), 224
Florentine Codex, 329–30
Flores, Felipe, 187
Folkloric Society of Mexico, 155
folk religion, 90
Foucault, Michel, 16
Fox, Vicente, 15
Frazer, Chris, 11, 16, 61, 65, 84
Franco, Francisco, 246
French Intervention, 9, 66
Frenk Alatorre, Margit, 147–48, 149–50, 161
Frías, Heriberto, 63, 96–97
Fuentes, Carlos, 326
Fuentes, Fernando de, 265
fueros, 55, 68

Gaddis, John Lewis, 339
García, Adriana, 14
García, Jesús, 121–22
García Cubas, Antonio, 36
García Téllez, Ignacio, 227, 230
García Torres, Vicente, 40
Garibaldi Square, 274–75

Garibay, Fray Ángel María, 299, 306, 318, 326
Garrido Canabal, Tomás, 222; education policies of, 222–23
El gavilán pollero (film), 277, 279
gender, 18, 188–89, 208–9, 341–42; femininity, 18, 39, 43, 49, 93, 188, 199–200, 209, 278, 316, 341; masculinity, 14, 18, 21, 23, 35, 45, 58, 63, 84, 91, 93–94, 95, 98, 161, 170, 173–74, 182–83, 188–90, 193–95, 198–200, 201, 204, 209, 264, 267, 275, 278, 294n66, 341–42; in poetry narratives, 36–39, 44–46
Gil Blas Cómico, 12
"La golondrina," 11
Gondra, Isidro Rafael, 40
González, Aurelio, 147
González, Luis, 62
González Avelar, Miguel, 298, 301–2, 304, 313, 314, 321, 324
González González, Natividad, 199
Gorostieta, Enrique, 202
Gramsci, Antonio, 16
Grandeza mexicana (poem), 6, 337–38
Great Depression, 259
Gretton, Thomas, 128–29, 141n33
Gruzinski, Serge, 298
Guadalajara, 116
Guardia, Miguel, 299, 306, 324–25
Guatemala, 73, 94
Guatimozín (opera), 9
Guzmán, Martín Luis, 209

Haber, Stephen, 338–39
Haitian Revolution, 75
Havelange, João, 309
Hernández, Adolfo Ornelas, 242
Hernández, Juan, 274–75
Hidalgo, Father Miguel, 81, 229
Los Hijos del Quito Patio, 14
Hines, Lewis, 224
Hispanismo, 261–62, 267, 269–70, 273–74, 278, 280–81. See also *lo mexicano*; *mexicanidad*; national identity; race
hombres de bien, 42
honor, 22, 42, 67–68, 79, 85, 88, 95, 115, 154–55, 168–70, 172, 174, 189, 261
Huerta, Efraín, 299, 306, 315–16
Huerta, Victoriano, 74, 144, 191
The Hunted Chief: Or the Female Ranchero (novel), 35

Ibarra Groth, Federico, 328, 330
Import Substitution Industrialization (ISI), 259–60, 273, 287
indigenistas, 228–29
Infante, Pedro, 276–77, 286, 293n57
Interoceanic Railway, 121

Jalisco, 13, 25, 200, 266, 274, 278; Alteño mythology, 262, 267, 278, 280, 284; Alteños, 261–65, 266, 268; Los Altos, 202–3, 260–61, 288; songs about, 262–64, 269–70
jarabe, 8, 9, 12, 28n23, 250–51n6, 291n25
Jesuits, 190
Jiménez, José Alfredo, 278–79
La Jornada, 313
Juan Sin Miedo (film), 281
Juárez, Benito, 9, 44, 55, 229–30, 328
Juventud, 234

Kirkpatrick, Susan, 40
Knight, Alan, 338–39
Kuntz Ficker, Sandra, 142n49

Labyrinth of Solitude, 304–5, 319, 321, 324
Lake Texcoco, 132
Lange, Dorothea, 224
Lara, Agustín, 13
Lares, Ismael, 194–95
Leo XIII (Pope), 190
Letechipía de González, Josefa, 41–42, 44–45
leva (forced conscription), 85, 97
ley fuga, 105n89
Limantour, José Yves, 62, 134–35
La Llorona, 315
loa, 327–28; to commemorate 1985 earthquake, 328–30
lo mexicano, 261, 265, 272, 274, 284, 290n25, 338

Lomnitz, Claudio, 313, 339
López Mateos, Adolfo, 303
López Velarde, Ramón, 220
Los de abajo (novel), 273
love letters, 153–54, 174–75; promise of marriage in, 165–66, 175
Loyo B., Engracia, 226
Luchichi, Ignacio, 70–71

Madero, Francisco, 144
El Maestro Rural, 225, 227, 230, 250
Maldita Vecindad, 14
La Malinche, 325
Mallan, Lloyd, 316
"Las mañanitas," 11
mariachi, 9, 13, 270, 291n34
Marianism, 6
Massacre 68, 14
Mayas, 76, 82, 94
Mckee Irwin, Robert, 189
media: broadsheets, 8, 10, 61, 110, 119, 124–25, 127–29, 137; cinema, 13, 255, 257–58, 286, 343; newspapers, 84–85; penny press, 12, 111, 121, 125, 127, 129, 132; radio, 196, 269, 274, 343; songbooks, 119–20, 125, 129; television, 13, 274, 330, 343; textbooks, 220, 224–25; women's magazines, 10, 12 , 39, 40
Me he de comer esa tuna (film), 269
Memorias de Pancho Villa, 209
Mendoza, Ezequiel, 192
Mendoza, Vicente, 11, 111, 115, 119, 124, 185
metro, 315
Mexican Central Railroad, 116, 126, 127, 142n49
mexicanidad, 3, 19, 58, 60, 69–70, 73, 98, 99, 270, 272, 302, 305, 324, 329. See also *lo mexicano*; national identity
Mexican Miracle, 255, 257–58, 273, 274, 275–76, 285, 287–88, 296
Mexican Railway, 133–34
Mexican Revolution, 12, 16, 108, 144, 159, 197, 209, 216, 219
Mexico City, 36
México Gráfico, 122
México Militar, 95
Meyer, Jean, 184, 186, 193
mezcal, 271, 280
Michel, Concha, 204–5
Mickenberg, Julia, 224
military, 58–60; daily life of, 85–86
military bands, 8–9
miracle babies, 307–8
Mixtón War, 261
Modotti, Tina, 231
Monsiváis, Carlos, 7, 154, 286, 307–8
Morales, Melesio, 327
Mora, Trinidad, 193–94, 196, 208
Moreno Rivas, Yolanda, 6, 9
Morrow, Dwight, 184
Mraz, John, 231
El Mundo Ilustrado, 122
El Museo Mexicano, 44

Napoleon III, 55
narcocorridos, 15, 344
national anthem, 9
National Conservatory, 9, 10
national identity, 13, 19, 60, 69–70, 73, 98, 99, 115, 136, 189, 200, 220, 258, 265; mestizo, 25, 260, 269, 275, 290n24; music and, 8; outside of Mexico, 13. See also *Hispanismo*; *lo mexicano*; *mexicanidad*
National Institute of Anthropology and History, 186
National Philharmonic Society, 9
National Railways of Mexico, 134
Navarrete, Heriberto, 201–4, 209
Negrete, Jorge, 267–68, 269, 286
Nervo, Amado, 12
Nezahualcoyotl, 6, 10, 71, 242
"The 19th of September Seamstresses Union," 311–12
El niño perdido (film), 283
El niño proletario: Poemas clasistas, 236, 242, 244–47, 249
"Niño Proletario" (Proletarian Child), 23–24, 216, 219, 221, 222–23, 227–29, 231–34, 236–38, 241–44, 245, 343; First Conference of the, 233, 242; as topic of poetry, 236–43; symbolically linked to Indians, 229, 237

Niños Héroes, 71, 73–74, 230
Noches Tapatías, 274
Nosotros los pobres (film), 280, 287
Nunó, Jaime, 9

Obregón, Álvaro, 144, 158–59, 179, 223, 272
obsequios (gifts), 20, 58, 64, 91, 99
Olivera de Bonfil, Alicia, 184, 186
Los olvidados (film), 286–87
Olympic Games (1968), 303–4
Ong, Walter, 150
opera, 9, 302–3; Mexican themes in, 10
orality/literacy debate, 149–53, 161–62, 173; *copla* and, 157–58, 166
Orfeón Popular, 9
Orfila Reynal, Arnaldo, 305
Ortega, Aniceto, 9, 327–28
Otero, Mariano, 34

Pacheco, José Emilio, vii–viii, 299, 305, 306, 314, 317–18, 319–20, 324, 326–27
Pacheco, Lidio, 182, 196
Padres de Familia, 227
Palacio de Bellas Artes, 25, 324
"La Paloma," 11
Pan-American Child Conference, 230–31
Panorama de las Señoritas Mejicanas, 40
Paredes, Américo, 185
Partido Acción Nacional (PAN), 261
Partido Nacional Revolucionario (PNR), 234, 260
Partido Revolucionario Institucional (PRI), 14, 255, 296, 298–301, 303–4, 309, 311–12, 317, 319, 327, 329, 331, 343
Payno, Manuel, 63
Paz, Octavio, vii, 8, 14, 25, 299, 304–6, 318–19, 321, 324–25, 327
Pedroza, Aristeo, 202–3
El peñón de las animas (film), 267–68
Pershing expedition, 74
Pimas, 77
Pius XI (Pope), 191
Plaza de la Solidaridad, 301, 331
Poesía en movimiento, 304, 305–6
poetry, 6–8, 58, 62, 300; Carmen Romero Rubio as topic of, 92–94; challenges to government in, 130; death as theme in, 314–17, 319–20, 321–27; depictions of violated women in, 35–36; Mannerist-Baroque, 7; masculinity as theme of, 45–46; Mexico City as topic of, 318–19; by military men, 58–60, 64–65, 70, 78–82; modernist, 11–12; national history as topic of, 81–82; Neoclassical; 7, 11; by nineteenth-century women, 34, 39–40, 43; Romantic, 10, 11, 42; science as topic of, 78–80; targeted to child audience, 236–243; Tlatelolco as topic of, 321–22; U.S.-Mexican War as topic of, 44–46, 46–49, 70–74; war as topic of, 94–98; working-class children as topic of, 236–37, 246
Poniatowska, Elena, 323, 326
Popocatépetl, 79
Porfiriato, 9, 11–13,
El Portero (film), 283
Posada, José Guadalupe, 10, 119, 122–25, 127, 134
positivism, 79
prendas, 161, 164–65
Prevention of Disasters and Management of Risk Office, 310
Prieto, Guillermo, 35, 63, 73
Proceso, 307–8
pulque, 270–71, 272, 280, 286–87, 294n83; *pulquerías*, 286; production of, 271
pulqueros, 272

Quas primas, 191
Quintana Roo, Andres, 10
Quintanar, Pedro, 181, 195–98

race, 59, 60, 69, 76, 99, 156, 220–21, 229, 236, 270. See also *Hispanismo*; *lo mexicano*; *mexicanidad*; national identity
railroads, 108, 109–10; indemnification of accident victims, 121, 127, 131; U.S. ownership of, 134–35

Rama, Angel, 151–52
Ramírez, Valentín Avila, 196–98
Ramírez Vásquez, Pedro, 303
Ramírez, Victoriano ("El Catorce"), 200–204, 208–9
rancheras (film genre), 255, 257–58, 266, 287; songs of, 266, 277–78, 344. *See also* cinema; media
ranchero (music genre), 15
rapto, 154, 165–66, 169
Regional Confederation of Mexican Workers (CROM), 222
Reportaje (film), 279
El Republicano, 41, 43–44, 46
The Republic (Plato), 48
Restored Republic, 9, 55
La Revista Azul, 12
La Revista Militar, 93
La Revista Moderna, 12
"Revolutionary Family," 248, 260, 262, 280, 303
Revolutionary Labor Confederation of Michoacán (CRMDT), 234
Revolution of Ayutla, 55
El rey poeta (opera), 10
Reyes, Bernardo, 62
Reyes, Juan José de los (Niño Pípila), 229, 252n38
Río Blanco strike, 136
Rivera, Diego, 224, 226, 243–44
Rivera, José María, 9–10
rock music, 14–15, 316
Rockwell, Elsie, 226
Rodríguez, Ismael, 281
Rodríguez, Joselito, 265
Rodríguez, Luís, 245
romance (ballad), 7
Romero Rubio, Manuel, 92
Romero Rubio de Díaz, Carmen, 91–92; as topic of poetry, 92–94
rumbera (film genre), 289n1
rurales, 86
Russian Revolution, 223

Sabines, Jaime, 299, 306, 314, 323–27
Sacred Heart of Jesus, 190–91, 208
Sáenz, Moisés, 229
Salas, J. Encarnación "Chon," 197
Salud García, María de la, 41
Sansón Flores, Jesús, 216, 218–19, 221, 234–44, 244–48, 342
Santa Anna, Antonio López de, 9, 31
Santa Teresa, 76–77
Santiago Silva, José de, 186
Sauza, Francisco Javier, 274
Scott, James C., 16, 60, 61, 83, 112, 135, 140n8
Scott, Winfield, 72
Secretary of Public Education (SEP), 224–27, 230, 243–44, 298, 301–3, 313, 324, 327, 331
The Secret Service Ship; or, The Fall of San Juan d'Ulloa (novel), 35
La Semana de las Señoritas Mejicanas, 40–41, 44
Semanario de las Señoritas Mejicanas, 39
El Sembrador, 225
Shrine of Sacromonte, 119
Sierra, Justo, 220
Sigüenza y Góngora, Carlos de, 6
Simiente, 225
Simmons, Merle, 9, 11, 143n66, 185
Siqueiros, David Alfaro, 226
Siurob, José, 230
SIZE, 14
"Sobre las olas," 11
soldaderas, 87–88
sones, vii, 6, 8, 9, 27n12
Sosenski, Susana, 227
sotol, 275, 280
Spanish Civil War, 219, 245–48; refugee children of, 247–48
student movement (1968), 296, 297–98, 299, 304, 306, 316–17, 324, 331; student massacre, 25, 296, 297–98, 299, 304, 306, 317, 321, 326, 343

Talamantes, Epigmenio, 197
Taller, 14
Tal para cual (film), 279
Taylor, Zachary, 72–73
Temamatla (railroad accident), 119–20, 131
Tenorio-Trillo, Mauricio, 136

tequila, 258, 270, 273–76, 280–82, 284–86; production of, 271–72
tequileros, 15
Terán, Luis, 66
Terdiman, Richard, 112, 122, 137
Terra Nostra (novel), 326
Thompson, E.P., 4–5
Thompson, Guy, 9
Los Tigres del Norte, 15
Tin Tan (Germán Valdés), 255, 283–84, 285
Tlatelolco (Plaza de las Tres Culturas), 296, 307, 310–11, 320–21, 322, 330
Tomochic, 76–77, 96–97
tourism, 274–75
Treaty of Guadalupe Hidalgo, 31

Unión Popular de Inquilinos de la Colonia Morelos, 310
El Universal, 228
Urquizo, Francisco Luis, 63
U.S. literature: depiction of Mexican men in, 35; Manifest Destiny and, 35; masculinity and, 35; U.S.-Mexican War and, 35
U.S.-Mexican War, 10, 33–34, 342; in U.S. literature, 35; U.S. occupation of Mexico during, 36; as topic of corridos, 38; as topic of poetry, 44, 70–74
Ustedes los ricos (film), 280

Valdés, Mario, 202–3
Valentín de la Sierra (film), 197
Valenzuela, Jesús, 12
Vanegas Arroyo, Antonio, 10–11, 119, 122–25, 127, 129
Vasconcelos, José, 12, 220, 229
Vaughn, Mary Kay, 10, 13, 226
Vázquez Valle, Irene, 186
Vázquez Vela, Gonzalo, 227
Velázquez Andrade, Manuel, 224
Velázquez, Marco, 13
Venice Film Festival, 265
Vigueras, Maximiliano, 187
Villa, Francisco "Pancho," 12, 74, 144, 189, 195, 242, 310
Villaurrutia, Xavier, 299, 306, 321
Las Violetas de Anáhuac, 12
Virgin of Guadalupe, 6, 76, 92, 192–93, 205, 206–7
The Volunteer or, The Maid of Monterey (novel), 35

Wald, Elijah, 15
Wars of Independence, 39, 344
women: depiction in corridos, 93, 115, 199; poetry by, 34, 39–40, 43; songs about, 264–65. *See also* gender
World Cup (1986), 309
World War II, 255, 259, 266

Yaqui, 76–77, 94
Yucatán, 82

Zapata, Emiliano, 12, 144, 189, 239, 242
Zavala, Juan, 114
Zayas, Armando, 328
zócalos, 9
Zolov, Eric, 14